DRAWING THE CURTAIN

Drawing the Curtain

Cervantes's Theatrical Revelations

EDITED BY ESTHER FERNÁNDEZ AND
ADRIENNE L. MARTÍN

UNIVERSITY OF TORONTO PRESS
Toronto Buffalo London

© University of Toronto Press 2022
Toronto Buffalo London
utorontopress.com
Printed in the U.S.A.

ISBN 978-1-4875-0877-7 (cloth)   ISBN 978-1-4875-3893-4 (EPUB)
                                  ISBN 978-1-4875-3892-7 (PDF)

Toronto Iberic

Library and Archives Canada Cataloguing in Publication

Title: Drawing the curtain : Cervantes's theatrical revelations / edited by
    Esther Fernández and Adrienne L. Martín.
Names: Fernández, Esther, 1975–, editor. | Martín, Adrienne L., editor.
Series: Toronto Iberic; 78.
Description: Series statement: Toronto Iberic; 78 | Includes bibliographical
    references and index.
Identifiers: Canadiana (print) 20220267006 | Canadiana (ebook) 20220267057 |
    ISBN 9781487508777 (cloth) | ISBN 9781487538934 (EPUB) |
    ISBN 9781487538927 (PDF)
Subjects: LCSH: Cervantes Saavedra, Miguel de, 1547–1616 – Criticism
    and interpretation. | LCSH: Revelation in literature. |
    LCSH: Theater in literature.
Classification: LCC PQ6351 .D73 2022 | DDC 863/.3 – dc23

We wish to acknowledge the land on which the University of Toronto Press
operates. This land is the traditional territory of the Wendat, the Anishnaabeg,
the Haudenosaunee, the Métis, and the Mississaugas of the Credit First
Nation.

University of Toronto Press acknowledges the financial support of the
Government of Canada, the Canada Council for the Arts, and the Ontario Arts
Council, an agency of the Government of Ontario, for its publishing activities.

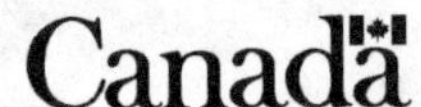

Contents

List of Illustrations   vii

Acknowledgments   ix

Introduction: The Poetics of the Imagined Stage   3
ESTHER FERNÁNDEZ AND ADRIENNE L. MARTÍN

Part One: Alternate Theatricalities in Cervantes's Drama

1   Cervantes and the Simple Stage   17
BRUCE R. BURNINGHAM

2   Queer *cambalaches* in *El rufián dichoso*   42
JOHN SLATER

3   Of Players and Wagers: The Theatricality of Gambling for
Salvation in *El rufián dichoso*   72
SONIA VELÁZQUEZ

4   Writing to Rescue from Oblivion: The Phantasms of Captivity in
El trato de Argel   99
JULIA DOMÍNGUEZ

5   Captivating Music, Memory, and Emotions in *Los baños
de Argel*   126
SHERRY VELASCO

6   In the Name of Love: Cervantes's Play on Captivity in *La gran
sultana*   150
ANA LAGUNA

7 Revolving Sets: Spatial Revelations in the *entremeses*   177
ESTHER FERNÁNDEZ AND ADRIENNE L. MARTÍN

Part Two: Acts of Disclosure in Cervantes's Prose

8 *Coups de théâtre* in the *Novelas ejemplares*   201
B.W. IFE

9 Captive Audiences: Performing Captivity in Cervantes's Prose Narrative   221
CATHERINE INFANTE

10 Painting into Theatre: "The Suicide of Lucretia" as a *tableau vivant* in *El curioso impertinente*   243
MERCEDES ALCALÁ GALÁN

11 "Muchas y muy verdaderas señales": The Theatrics of Truth and Sincerity of Fiction in *La Galatea*   277
PAUL MICHAEL JOHNSON

12 Eavesdropping or Spying? Secret Places and Spaces in *Don Quixote*   306
EDUARDO OLID GUERRERO

13 *Don Quixote* and the Performance of Aging Masculinities in Early Modern Spain   331
JOSÉ R. CARTAGENA CALDERÓN

List of Contributors   355

Index   357

Illustrations

6.1　Konstantin Kapıdağlı, *Ottoman Sultan Selim III*, 1789　152
10.1　Titian, *Venus and Mars*, c. 1530　254
10.2　Tintoretto, *Susanna and the Elders*, c. 1555　256
10.3　Lucas Cranach the Elder, *The Suicide of Lucretia*, c. 1525　264
10.4　Lorenzo Lotto, *Portrait of a Woman Inspired by Lucretia*, c. 1537　265
10.5　Titian, *Tarquin and Lucretia*, 1571　266

Acknowledgments

We would like to thank our authors, whose enthusiasm and professionalism have sustained this project since its initiation. Our profound admiration for Cervantes and avid engagement with early modern Spanish theatre are shared passions that have united us along this path. All our colleagues have approached the theme of Cervantine theatricality according to their own particular theoretical interests and expertise to create a whole that is greater than the sum of its parts.

Our immense gratitude goes to Suzanne Rancourt of the University of Toronto Press, whose initial encouragement and ongoing guidance have made the publication process so gratifying. We also wish to thank Simon Coll for his scrupulous and timely copy-editing.

We are grateful to Rice University for a Scholarly and Creative Works Subvention, and to its School of Humanities for its generous financial support for the publication of this volume.

DRAWING THE CURTAIN

Introduction: The Poetics of the Imagined Stage

ESTHER FERNÁNDEZ AND ADRIENNE L. MARTÍN

Let us begin by invoking the bare stage, a notion with which Peter Brook conceptualized the theatrical event in his classic *The Empty Space* (1968). According to Brook, it was enough for one person to walk through an empty space while another watched for an act of theatre to be engaged.[1] Although Cervantes's early theatrical works apparently enjoyed some degree of commercial success, at least if we are to believe the history he fashions in the preface to his *Ocho comedias y ocho entremeses nuevos, nunca representados* (1615), those from his so-called second period – the ones published in that volume – never reached the public stage.[2] In recent years a good deal of scholarly ink has been spilled debating the reasons behind his lack of commercial success in the late 1580s and beyond. Was his art simply out of fashion by the time he returned to Spain after a twelve-year absence, including five years of captivity in Algiers? Were his plays too "writerly" as opposed to performative (when compared, for example, to Lope de Vega's), thus too demanding – if not impossible – to stage successfully? Too wanting in performative stagecraft?[3] A theatre of ideas rather than characters?[4] Or was it that he lacked the necessary first-hand knowledge in negotiating the spatial and artistic constraints imposed upon a by then less technically unencumbered professional theatre?

At first blush, we might be tempted to think that these creative impediments decouple the Cervantine voice from the stage outright; but no, these alleged handicaps may in fact bespeak Brook's conceptualization. Cervantes's unfamiliarity (and seeming struggle) with the realities of staging conventions in the final decades of the sixteenth century might help to account for at least one of his oeuvre's characteristic assets: the overwhelming presence in it of metatheatricality. In much of his prose we glimpse a frustrated dramatist grappling with an undertaking that does not value his artistic sense. In fact, the ongoing – even obsessive – concern with theatricality that we perceive most expressly in his prose works may be best understood as a sustained exploratory study of the possibilities of dramatic writing written not for the stage but for an audience of readers. Cervantes could imagine a wide range of fictional scenarios open to unlimited experimental theatricality precisely because he created (by necessity) within a dramatic mind space unconstrained by staging conventions. Hence Cervantes's theatre is conceived not on the stage, but on the theoretical plane of the page. The freedom that an imagined blank page – another empty space – provides the writer allows him to fully flesh out visionary ideas with the potential to radically spill into, inundate, and appropriate conventions from sundry other genres. *Drawing the Curtain: Cervantes's Theatrical Revelations* examines precisely how he experiments with and manipulates theatricality in and beyond his theatre to create performative spaces where limitless ideas can be rehearsed before an audience.

As is well known, this quintessential quality of the novelist's prose has been commonly acknowledged within Cervantism since Alonso Fernández de Avellaneda criticized it in the prologue to his spurious 1614 sequel to *Don Quixote*. There the still unidentified author insults Cervantes and his novels, saying that he should cease and desist from writing and "Conténtese con su *Galatea* y comedias en prosa; que eso son las más de sus novelas" (Let him be satisfied with his *Galatea* and comedies in prose, which is what most of his novels are).[5] What to Avellaneda is a defect is in fact one of the principal and generally celebrated features, especially in recent years, of Cervantes's entire oeuvre: its inherent dramaticality. And as many of the authors in this collection will attest, this theatricality is often constructed upon the concept of revelation. By "revelation," in its broadest sense, we refer back to its original meaning of epiphany (from the Greek *epiphainein*, "to show forth"), which in turn lies at the heart of several Greek terms for "mirror" that evolved into the notion of poetry as a mirror of beautiful actions or the act of contemplating something with acuity.[6] Among such ideas, theatre – and literature in general – as a mirror upon which we gaze and that reflects our world back onto us is commonplace in early modern times.[7] The notion sets the stage for dramatic anagnorisis, understood to be the process whereby something unexpected or previously hidden from the readers, from the characters, or from both, is revealed and discovered. The act of revelation suggests that something has been intentionally concealed, and thus its disclosure and the recognition of hidden truths produce moments of high drama.

At both the literal and the metaphorical level Cervantes's dramatic craftsmanship employs various techniques of disclosure, combined with other theatrical gestures, to place before the readers the topics and cultural concerns that guide his prose and dramatic works. One such dramatic technique is spectacle, which he often employs in surprising – even shocking – ways to engage the reader. We see this, for example, when in his novella *La fuerza de la sangre* doña Estefanía places young Leocadia on spectacular display to her rapist son Rodolfo in order to extract from him a marriage commitment and the restitution of Leocadia's lost honour.[8] Another example of dramatic spectacle occurs in *Don Quixote* (1605–15) when the Morisca Ana Félix, posing as a Moorish ship's captain, is revealed to be a woman and a Christian, while her lover languishes in a Moorish harem in female disguise.[9] The revelation galvanizes the spectators within the novel as well as the readers, who as external observers acknowledge Cervantes's mastery of disguise as a player of hidden identities that he wields skilfully and to great dramatic effect. A final example of Cervantes's employment of dramatic revelation is when Escarramán unexpectedly bursts onto the scene during Trampagos's wedding celebration in the *entremés El rufián viudo, Trampagos*. The entrance of a popular character firmly established in contemporary poetry (in Francisco de Quevedo's two acclaimed *jácaras*) represents a literal and spectacular (he still sports the chains of captivity) leap from the page onto the stage, to the delight of characters and audience alike.

The essays in this compilation further demonstrate from a series of diverse perspectives precisely how and to what effect Cervantes exploits theatricality. They show how he uses the impact of revelation and disclosure to create dynamic dramatic moments that compel his readers to engage with themes that are central to his life and works such as love, freedom, truth, confinement, and otherness. Our authors clarify how these complex and profound topics are filtered and realized through dramaticality, whether on the stage or on the page, whether by channelling Baroque painting into narrative *tableaux vivants*, for example, or by employing the art of memory to evoke the ghosts of past lived experiences and to repair the emotional pain of personal trauma. How, in other words, Cervantes orchestrates the stratagems of dramatic art and illusion to achieve the desired effects at the aesthetic and social levels.

By probing the dramatic essence of his theatre and narrative fiction, this collection addresses how one of Cervantes's great strengths as a writer is precisely this shift of theatricality from theatre to narrative. Classic monographs on his theatre do exist, of course, such as Joaquín Casalduero's *Sentido y forma del teatro de Cervantes* (1966), Jean Canavaggio's *Cervantès dramaturge. Un théâtre à naître* (1977), and Stanislav

Zimic's *El teatro de Cervantes* (1992). The most recent analysis of Cervantes's theatrical production is the brief study *El teatro de Miguel de Cervantes* (2016) by Ignacio García Aguilar, Luis Gómez Canseco, and Adrián J. Sáez. Previous compilations focus solely on Cervantes's drama, such as Héctor Brioso Santos's edited volume *Cervantes y el mundo del teatro* (2007); *Vida y escritura en el teatro de Cervantes* (2016), edited by María Heredia Mantis and Luis Gómez Canseco; and the conference proceedings *Cervantes, Shakespeare y la Edad de Oro de la Escena* (2018), edited by Jorge Braga Riera, Javier J. González Martínez, and Miguel Sanz Jiménez.

The one book that addresses narrative theatricality specifically is Eduardo Olid Guerrero's *Del teatro a la novela: El ritual del disfraz en las* Novelas ejemplares *de Cervantes* (2016), which focuses predominantly on the inner workings of disguise (in the broad sense) in the *Exemplary Novels*. Francisco Sánchez's *Lectura y representación: Análisis cultural de las* Novelas ejemplares *de Cervantes* (1993) also centres on theatricality in the same works. Other scholars have examined the dramatic nature of *Don Quixote* in journal articles. But until our compilation, no book-length study has been available in English of either Cervantes's theatre or the notion of theatricality in his dramatic and prose works.

Although the genre is not addressed in this volume, we should not overlook the fact that Cervantes's poetry can also display a generous measure of theatricality. To mention one example, the sonnet conversation between Babieca (el Cid's fiery stallion) and Rocinante (Don Quixote's aged mount), which appears among the introductory poems to Part One of *Don Quixote*, highlights Cervantes's mastery of satirical dialogue. Where but on an imagined stage could two equids engage in such a pithy critique of their masters? Moreover, Cervantes's mock epic *Viaje del Parnaso* (1614) was staged spectacularly and to considerable popular success in 2005–7 by Spain's National Classical Theatre Company (Compañía Nacional de Teatro Clásico; CNTC), directed by Eduardo Vasco. *Viaje del Parnaso* is not only Cervantes's most substantial poem, but also the one that incorporates the greatest number of theatrical elements, from dialogue to metatheatricality and, in the case of the CNTC's dramatized version, the utilization of puppets.[10] We hope that a future study will address the theatrical essence of Cervantes's poetry.

Thus, *Drawing the Curtain* provides a novel approach to a distinguishing characteristic of Cervantes's oeuvre, as well as an innovative lens to illuminate the themes that preoccupied him on the personal and intellectual level, among them the nature and significance of theatricality, of artifice, and of "masks." These pages discuss, for example, how he uses masks to draw his audience of readers into the performance of captivity and liberation in prose fiction. In other instances, Cervantes draws open the curtain that conceals specific hidden spaces – such as the harem – from public view, placing them onto the public stage. Other instances of eavesdropping and revelation uncover private soliloquies that reveal characters' true feelings and intrigues.

As many of the studies curated for this volume suggest, Cervantes's theatre and theatricality also respond to some of the personal and socio-cultural concerns of his time. The performative acts he presents and represents throughout his works are in some cases introspective and quasi-autobiographical in that they function as a means for the author to come to terms with himself and his own particular preoccupations by examining the larger world around him.

The first part of this volume, "Alternate Theatricalities in Cervantes's Drama," focuses on the different ways in which the master dislocates his dramatic works from the actual staging and its conceptual dimensions far beyond commercial expectations. Although this critical approach is not new to Cervantes studies, the essays that compose this section of the volume revisit the subject from critically innovative angles that provide renewed insights into a type of dramaturgy that could never leave the page.

Bruce R. Burningham uses performance space as a starting point to scrutinize how Cervantes negotiates what Hollis Huston has called the *simple stage*: the circle that the street artist opens in a crowd in order to perform. He adds a third dimension to Hollis's architecture – the jongleuresque sphere that is created by the performance itself – to engage critically with Cervantes's failure to incorporate this very basic and improvised stage into his *comedia* scripts. Burningham suggests that this may have cost Cervantes success as a commercial playwright – as compared, say, to Lope de Vega – but at the same time it freed his dramatic writing from all formulaic expectations, which in turn allowed him to discover a new art of writing for the stage that moved far beyond the assumptions and demands of his time.

The two pieces that follow focus on *El rufián dichoso* as a dramatic experiment with respect to hagiographic drama. As John Slater points out in his essay, this is a play with an identity crisis, more dare than show, a *comedia de santos* with only a light dose of saintliness. Its visual exuberance – to which a "cast of thousands" contributes – implies a the-atricality built around the performance of multiple identities achieved through gender-bending and narrative fluidity. As a counterpoint, Sonia Velázquez's study turns to gambling as one of the unrepresent-able qualities that reside at the very heart of the plot to explore what the theme contributes to a hagiographic play. In early modernity, biblical and legal writings as well as artistic reiterations conceived the gambler as an agent blind to spiritual matters. However, Velázquez interprets wagers as performances that engage with the uncertainty of the world. In this light, Cervantes imposes neither pious dogma nor social morality upon religious drama; instead, he contemplates on the resilience of the human condition. Once again, the author boldly morphs an established genre into something else that speaks more directly to his personal and artistic values.

The next three essays reflect on the theme of captivity as viewed from the stage. Julia Domínguez opens the triad with an analysis that takes *El trato de Argel* as its starting point. She draws on the art of memory to show how Cervantes lays bare his personal trauma of experiencing captivity through dramatic representation. *El trato de Argel* legitimizes the significance of singular acts of memory specific to the individual as a rich and inevitable source of creativity. Through a fictional dramatic portrayal that draws on the writer's personal memories of captivity, Domínguez details how he engages a representational memorial technique that contributes to shaping the audience's collective memory.

Sherry Velasco's essay delves further into the theme of captivity, considering the role of remembrance but focusing this time on the emotional effects produced by sad music in *Los baños de Argel*. In addition to the role of music as entertainment, Cervantes resorts to classical and early modern theories on the power of music and lyrics to move the listener, as well as the connections between memory, nostalgia, emotions, music, and casting (especially the impact of the female voice) for understanding how sad music might be a productive vehicle for alleviating the pain of traumatic experiences. Ana Laguna also addresses the theatrical aspects of captivity by scrutinizing the representation of desire in *La gran sultana*. She interprets the harem as a porous microcosm heavily punctuated by the political and racial frictions stirring the early modern Mediterranean world. From this perspective, the supposedly hermetic confines of a private space end up functioning as sites of personal and collective negotiation, where intersectional distinctions between gender, race, and faith appear as blurry and fleeting as desire itself.

Esther Fernández and Adrienne Martín round out the first part of the volume by focusing on Cervantes's proposal of spatiality in the *entremeses*, often considered his most accomplished, or even his most "Cervantine" theatrical works. The authors explore four specific scenarios or spheres – the domestic, the urban street, the supernatural, and the invisible backstage – to reveal how his theatre engages critically with the surrounding social reality. With their diversity of voice and character, combined with a plot structure and substance that exceed the generally simple comic incidents that characterize the genre, Cervantes's works challenge the parameters of the standard *entremés*.

The essays grouped in this first part demonstrate Cervantes's savoir faire when it comes to utilizing theatricality on the page, which is also a theoretical space where the author can erect an imagined stage to deepen, alter, and experiment with theatrical norms and hackneyed concepts, granting each a new ideological dimension. It is not surprising that such conceptual revisionism could have made it difficult for Cervantes's plays to find a commercial home; they were likely too risky for the public and a pastime heavily policed by conventional artistic norms and political authorities. And this is to say nothing of the inherent technical challenges they presented, such as unwieldy or excessive numbers of actors.[11] Nonetheless, it is illuminating to examine the dramatic experiments that he drafted on the page to gain a better understanding of the Cervantine poetics that often transcend the material capacities of the late sixteenth- and early seventeenth-century stage.

The reflexions that close the first part of *Drawing the Curtain* lead to the second part of this volume, "Acts of Disclosure in Cervantes's Prose," centred on the non-dramatic works that also served Cervantes as a *safe stage* upon which to rehearse his conception of theatricality in an even more radical way than in his dramatic productions. The essays in this section focus more specifically on the mechanisms of the act of revealing, a highly performative gesture that is never gratuitous and intrinsically dependent on the audience's response. The latent theatricality of Cervantine prose stressed in these studies reveals further the personal and social concerns that the author secludes between the lines. Drawing the curtain on these texts – both literally and figuratively – uncovers several Cervantine scenarios that remain to be conceptually investigated.

B.W. Ife introduces this second part by examining how recurrent *coups de théâtre* serve to represent critical moments in which the dramatic and novelistic nourish each other in the *Exemplary Novels* and how the constraints of live theatre are surmounted in prose fiction. While a marked concern with the concept of truth runs through all of Cervantes's fiction, these strategies of concealment and disclosure are not as revealing as they may appear initially. Ife thus evaluates why these *coups de théâtre* may be theatrical in nature but also may incite disbelief or even outrage.

Turning to the theme of captivity, Catherine Infante examines the performance of captivity and liberation in the episodes dedicated to Captain Ruy Pérez de Viedma and Maese Pedro's puppet show in *Don*

Quixote, along with the tale of the false captives in *Persiles y Sigismunda* (1617). Unlike in Cervantes's captivity plays, in these theatrical narratives readers are invited to witness how the fictional spectators react to the events retold and to assess the impact of audience response to these metatheatrical performances. In this way, Cervantes unpacks and exposes individual anxieties concerning bondage and freedom that deserve closer scrutiny.

Another type of vicarious performance in Cervantes's prose are the so-called *tableaux vivants* or dramatized paintings – pictorial quotes – whose theatricality depends on the presence of onlookers within the text who observe and react to the scenes that pass from canvas to life. Mercedes Alcalá Galán analyses one such *tableau vivant* in detail: "The Suicide of Lucretia" as rendered by Camila's sham suicide attempt in the interpolated story *El curioso impertinente* (The Tale of Impertinent Curiosity) in *Don Quixote* 1.34. As she convincingly argues, this evocation of an image that synthesizes a story pertaining to the common cultural heritage serves to incorporate the pictorial culture of his time and to enrich the novel's plot.

Examining the concept of truth is also at the heart of Paul Michael Johnson's essay, as he investigates how theatricality functions with respect to the display of love in *La Galatea* (1585). Although he discusses numerous theatrical aspects in relation to Cervantes's pastoral novel, the performance of gestures raises particular questions of reliability and, as Johnson demonstrates, makes us revisit the genre's connection to truth.

Within the framework of theatricality and artifice explored in this volume, Eduardo Olid Guerrero provides a nuanced study of espionage strategies deployed by several characters in *Don Quixote*, especially within the domestic and diplomatic spheres. In the multiple scenarios featured in his masterpiece, Cervantes models a wide array of scenes where participants overhear private conversations in everyday life spaces and other scenarios that emulate political intrigues that took place in the court and private domains of the wealthy and powerful during this period. Examining these scenes through the principles of theatricality, Olid Guerrero reveals the mechanics of spying to be one of the most delicate and most powerful political practices of the time.

The ultimate revelation with which we close this section and the volume is a personal one for Cervantes: the meaning of old age that is invoked numerous times in his later works. If Catherine Infante addresses how Cervantes used his prose to give life to his traumatic experience as a captive in his younger years, José R. Cartagena Calderón's innovative study examines the representation of aging masculinities in *Don Quixote* set against the backdrop of other social, cultural, and medical discourses on aging in early modern Spain.

As all these studies show, theatricality for Cervantes takes several radically different forms; nevertheless, such practice progressively acquires profound personal and social relevance in his oeuvre. On the many levels examined by our contributors, it is as if he vicariously experienced and expiated some of his frustrations, traumas, fears, and ideas through theatricality. The inherent metatheatricality of many of the scenes he devises obliges Cervantes to put himself in the shoes of others and compels us – spectators morphed into idle readers – to approach the author's personal and social concerns in a more immersive way.

The essays that constitute *Drawing the Curtain* scrutinize this seminal writer's diverse literary productions mainly within the expansive multidisciplinary paradigm of cultural studies. In this way they accommodate a wide array of contemporary theoretical issues and approaches from performance, perception, historical memory, and truth, to personal trauma, queer studies, age studies, and masculinities, while grappling with the question of Cervantes's supposed failings as a dramatist who was poorly understood and little appreciated during his own time. These novel approaches reflect the expertise of the individual authors and the most current scholarship being written on Cervantes today. By drawing the curtain on his poetics of the imagined stage, our authors reveal the intellectual depth, ideological density, and theatrical quintessence of his oeuvre.

NOTES

1 Brook, *Empty Space*, 9.

2 All Cervantes's extant theatrical works are included in Sevilla Arroyo and Rey Hazas's edition of his *Teatro completo*.

3 Bruce R. Burningham discusses these issues in his essay in this collection.

4 See Friedman's *Unifying Concept* regarding this notion.

5 Fernández de Avellaneda, *El ingenioso Don Quijote*, 53. All translations herein are our own.

6 Stafford and Terpak provide the history of the concept of revelation in *Devices of Wonder*, 24.

7 Hence in his critique of contemporary theatre, the Priest in *Don Quijote* will refer back to Cicero in affirming that drama should be "espejo de la vida humana, ejemplo de las costumbres y imagen de la verdad" (a mirror

of human life, an example of customs and image of truth; Cervantes, *Don Quijote*, 1.48).
  8 Cervantes, *Novelas ejemplares*, 319–20.
  9 Cervantes, *Don Quijote*, 2.63.
10 On the poem's theatrical texture and this production in particular, see Fernández, *"Viaje del Parnaso."*
11 See John Slater's discussion in this volume of the challenges presented by the numerous characters in *El rufián dichoso.*

REFERENCES

Braga Riera, Jorge, Javier J. González Martínez, and Miguel Sanz Jiménez, eds. *Cervantes, Shakespeare y la Edad de Oro de la Escena*. Madrid: Fundación Universitaria Española, 2018.

Brioso Santos, Héctor, ed. *Cervantes y el mundo del teatro*. Kassel: Reichenberger, 2007.

Brook, Peter. *The Empty Space*. New York: Touchstone, 1996.

Burningham, Bruce R. *Radical Theatricality: Jongleuresque Performance on the Early Spanish Stage*. West Lafayette, IN: Purdue University Press, 2007.

Canavaggio, Jean. *Cervantès dramaturgue. Un théâtre à naître*. Paris: Presses Universitaires de France, 1977.

Casalduero, Joaquín. *Sentido y forma del teatro de Cervantes*. Madrid: Gredos, 1966.

Cervantes, Miguel de. *Don Quijote de la Mancha*. Edited by Francisco Rico. 2 vols. Barcelona: Instituto Cervantes / Crítica, 1998.

Cervantes, Miguel de. *Novelas ejemplares*. Edited by Jorge García López. Barcelona: Crítica, 2001.

Cervantes, Miguel de. *Teatro completo*. Edited by Florencio Sevilla Arroyo and Antonio Rey Hazas. Barcelona: Planeta, 1987.

Fernández, Esther. *"Viaje del Parnaso*: Una odisea de títeres en escena." *Cervantes* 31, no. 2 (2011): 85–103. https://doi.org/10.1353/cer.2011.0019.

Fernández de Avellaneda, Alonso. *El ingenioso Don Quijote de la Mancha, que contiene su tercera salida y es la quinta parte de sus aventuras*. Edited by Fernando García Salinero. Madrid: Castalia, 1972.

Friedman, Edward H. *The Unifying Concept: Approaches to the Structure of Cervantes's Comedias*. York, SC: Spanish Literature Publications, 1981.

García Aguilar, Ignacio, Luis Gómez Canseco, and Adrián J. Sáez. *El teatro de Miguel de Cervantes*. Madrid: Visor Libros, 2016.

Heredia Mantis, María, and Luis Gómez Canseco, eds. *Vida y escritura en el teatro de Cervantes*. Valladolid-Olmedo: Universidad de Valladolid / Ayuntamiento de Olmedo, 2016.

Olid Guerrero, Eduardo. *Del teatro a la novela: El ritual del disfraz en las* Novelas ejemplares *de Cervantes*. Alcalá de Henares: Universidad de Alcalá, 2016.

Sánchez, Francisco J. *Lectura y representación: Análisis cultural de las* Novelas ejemplares *de Cervantes*. New York: Peter Lang, 1993.

Stafford, Barbara Maria, and Frances Terpak. *Devices of Wonder: From the World in a Box to Images on a Screen*. Los Angeles: Getty Research Institute, 2001.

Zimic, Stanislav. *El teatro de Cervantes*. Madrid: Castalia, 1992.

PART ONE

Alternate Theatricalities in Cervantes's Drama

1 Cervantes and the Simple Stage

BRUCE R. BURNINGHAM

Cervantes's theatre is an enigma, if not an afterthought. Given the centrality of *Don Quixote* within Spanish culture, this is not surprising. In fact, were it not for *Don Quixote*, we probably would not spend much time thinking about Cervantes's theatre. Even today, one is much more likely to encounter dramatizations of *Don Quixote* or of the *Coloquio de los perros* than performances of any of his plays. And given the relatively few texts in Cervantes's extant dramatic corpus (compared to the hundreds of plays left behind by other early modern Spanish playwrights), were we to remove *Don Quixote* from the equation (that is, had Cervantes never published his masterpiece), today he would likely be listed only among the period's minor dramatists. Still, *Don Quixote* is a brute fact that cannot be ignored, and hence we feel obligated to try to account for Cervantes's theatre, and in particular, for why he was not a more successful dramatist.

Of course, it is nearly impossible *not* to compare Cervantes's theatre to that of Lope de Vega, which is why, as Jonathan Thacker has noted, "readers of the past two centuries have tended to deem [Cervantes's] plays failures."[1] This is in part because Lope is – for better or worse – the "gold standard" by which all other early modern Spanish dramatists are measured ("es de Lope") and partly because, within the literary ambit in which Cervantes and Lope circulated, the two writers inevitably lived out their professional lives in competition with each other. In his well-known prologue to his *Ocho comedias y ocho entremeses nunca representados*, Cervantes speaks of the theatrical success he experienced during what critics have called his "first period" as a dramatist (between 1580 and 1587), but then says he gave it all up.[2] Indeed, while Thacker calculates that "Cervantes probably wrote 20 or 30 plays for the stage in the 1580s," the fact that almost all of these plays are now lost casts at least some doubt on Cervantes's claims of prior success.[3]

Several critics have theorized about what caused Cervantes to abandon the field to Lope, but regardless of the reasons, when Cervantes later made a second attempt at the theatre, as he notes with more than just a tinge of regret, he no longer found birds in last year's nests: "[V]olví a componer algunas comedias, pero … no hallé autor que me las pidiese" (I returned to writing a few plays, but … I never found an actor-manager who wanted them).[4]

Again, numerous scholars have tried to account for why Cervantes was not more successful during this "second period" as a dramatist, especially given his fame as the author of *Don Quixote*. Space does not allow me to gloss the vast majority of this prior criticism, much of it related to arguments having to do with Cervantes's supposed penchant – Jill Syverson-Stork's well-known book to the contrary[5] – for producing texts that are more "literary" than "theatrical" in nature. Nevertheless, my purpose here is to provide my own "take" on why I think Cervantes ultimately could not compete with Lope de Vega. And the key to my analysis is precisely the extent to which Cervantes rather problematically inscribes performance space into his full-length *comedia* texts. As I have argued elsewhere, primarily in *Radical Theatricality: Jongleuresque Performance on the Early Spanish Stage*, one of the crucial components of Lope's success in inventing and perfecting the *comedia nueva* is that he built his many literary innovations on top of a jongleuresque performance tradition that he inherited from the Middle Ages.[6] Put another way, Lope succeeded where Cervantes did not precisely because he inscribed this jongleuresque tradition into his plays and thus created scripts that appealed to the performers' sense of their own craft. In contrast, my contention here will be that Cervantes's inability to find theatrical impresarios willing to produce his plays was, in many ways, a function of their often rather weak jongleuresque qualities (despite all the other brilliant things that may be going on in Cervantes's scripts).

Before I make my case, however, a quick overview of my notion of the "jongleuresque" is perhaps in order. Readers who know my work will recall that my use of this term refers to an entire mode of popular performance that ranges from minstrelsy to circuses, from vaudeville to street theatre, from magicians to mountebanks. It is a performance tradition intimately tied to what Hollis Huston has called the "simple stage," which he defines as "the circle that the street performer opens in a crowd," a space paradoxically constituted by the very performance it is said to contain.[7] But, while I have focused in previous publications mainly on the reciprocal "contract" that occurs between performer and spectator within the "circle" that Huston argues is the essence of all theatre, in this essay I am more interested in Huston's sense of performance space itself and in the performative poetics that plays out within this space. For Huston, it is this simple stage that lies at the heart of even the most complex performances:

> The suspension of theatrical space is discovered on the simple stage, the stage that appears around the street performer, a stage that depends not on apparatus and technicians, but on the player herself and her ability to charm. That stage, the measure of a contract between actor and spectator, exists only for those moments when people stop what they are doing to watch a show. The behaviors that preserve that stage are the skills of smart performance.[8]

Indeed, for Huston, space and smart performance cannot be disconnected from each other due to the corporeal presence of the actor:

> An actor carries the theater with her, unpacks it at will. His problem is to act on space to produce an illusion called the stage. The stage is an apparition, a self-conscious space in which appears the illusion of time. The stage is the actor's instrument. You may say the actor's instrument is her body, but does the pianist play his fingers? the trumpeter her lips?[9]

Of course, for any theatrical *mise en scène*, there necessarily exist three overlapping and interrelated spaces, of which the simple stage is only one. The first of these spaces is the "fictive space" of the imaginary world created by the literary text itself. This first level of space, which exists independently of the other two, is available in its most basic form to readers who simply pick up the written text and experience it – through "the mind's eye," as Christopher Collins notes – just as they would if reading a novel: "The unbounded protean narrator ... invites us to imagine he is now one character now another, now in one place and now hundreds of miles removed."[10] The second of these spaces is the "physical space" of the stage on which the performance takes place, whether this be a thrust stage like Shakespeare's original Globe, the kind of black box theatre so typical of off-off-off-Broadway, or the kind of high-tech, formal proscenium arch of theatres like the Teatro Real in Madrid. Playwrights who write their plays (and practitioners who produce live theatre) with a particular physical stage in mind will necessarily adapt their depiction of the work's fictive space to fit the affordances and limitations provided by the anticipated physical stage. And the third space, what I will hereafter call a "jongleuresque sphere" (to add a third dimension to Huston's circular simple stage), is the space created by the performance itself. It is within this jongleuresque sphere that the most active components of the performance exist: the blocking, the gestures, the vocal inflections of the performers, the relative proximity of the actors to each other, not to mention their physical and emotional relationships to each other as well as to the members of the audience.

Significantly, as we will see, while this jongleuresque sphere is certainly related to both the fictive space and the physical space mentioned above, this third space also exists independently of the other two. It is precisely this independence that allows actors to perform a play with or without costumes and props, with or without physical sets, with or without a recognizable stage beyond the simple circle that the performance itself creates. It is this independence that allows theatre companies to take their shows on the road, "picking up" their performances and moving them to whatever physical stages they may find themselves playing on. In this regard, then, this jongleuresque sphere is the most malleable and portable of the three. However, while this third space overwhelmingly belongs to the contingent performers and their spectators, who collectively determine its exact shape and scope, successful playwrights will, nevertheless, build a preliminary version of this jongleuresque sphere into their scripts. In other words, even someone who experiences a dramatic text through purely silent reading can sense this jongleuresque sphere as it moves through the play from moment to moment and from beat to beat. As I said earlier, it is this third, jongleuresque space that Lope so successfully builds into his plays; furthermore, it is this third, jongleuresque space that I think Cervantes finds himself struggling with, at least in his full-length *comedias*, particularly the earliest ones.

While each of the first two spaces previously mentioned corresponds in some way to one of two categories of academic research on theatrical space (which I would define as "fictive-hermeneutical" and "physical-archaeological," respectively),[11] the space of the jongleuresque sphere, with its own specific performative poetics, is the least studied by academic researchers (even though it is very well understood by practitioners, who have learned it experientially over the course of their training and careers). This is not to say, however, that this third category of space is completely ignored in the academic study of theatrical space: inklings of this jongleuresque sphere appear obliquely in such recent studies as Vicente Pérez de León's 2008 examination of Cervantes's *entremeses*, in which he talks about "la proyección del espacio dramático imaginario del actor/personaje en el escenario" (the projection of the imaginary dramatic space of the actor/character onstage);[12] Jesús Maestro's *La escena imaginaria: Poética del teatro de Miguel de Cervantes*, where he insists that

Cervantes's theatre contains the very germ of "las cualidades esenciales que la poética del teatro moderno ha identificado en las principales formas y categorías dramáticas de la Edad Contemporánea" (the essential qualities that the poetics of modern theatre has identified in the principal dramatic forms and categories of the Modern Age);[13] and in Amy Tigner's 2012 "The Spanish Actress's Art: Improvisation, Transvestism, and Disruption in Tirso's *El vergonzoso en palacio*," where she argues that a particular scene of cross-dressing not only permits "both actress and character physical freedoms, [but] also invites impromptu speech precisely because it calls on such a wide range of skills."[14] However, because this free-floating jongleuresque performance space has simply not been studied to the same extent as the other two, Huston's monographic analysis of the simple stage is particularly important, which is why it is worth citing two more passages from *The Actor's Instrument* before proceeding to my own analysis of the way performance space is inscribed in Cervantes's dramatic texts. In the first instance, Huston argues for the centrality of the performer over all else:

> [It] has always been actors who animate theatrical space. There have been, are, and will be, performers' theaters; among them are many of the icons of our history, the sources of holy texts. Such theaters govern themselves through conventions or operating procedures. Those conventions, which a director might see as confinement, comprise a code of liberty for the actor, permitting play to the performer's reading of text and audience, to her charm, and to his professional skill of rescuing something from nothing.[15]

In the second instance, Huston elaborates a true "poetics of the simple stage" (with a nod towards the Italian *commedia dell'arte*, to which this present essay will eventually turn):

> The zanno's knowledge was smart practice rather than studied doctrine, a knowledge *how* rather than *that*. When Arlequino stepped within the circle, his smart feet, his cunning buttocks, would know what to do. Stage and house had not been pulled apart, and he did not have to choose between playing and seeing the play. He needed no direction and knew how to act.[16]

Which brings us back to Cervantes's dramatic corpus. With regard to his earliest *comedias* of the 1580s, a close reading of Cervantes's construction of performance space in *El trato de Argel* and *Numancia* demonstrates that the jongleuresque sphere of Huston's simple stage is largely absent, and what little jongleuresque space does exist within these plays is quite flat. For instance, the first two acts of *El trato de Argel* exist as almost pure exposition – what Edward Friedman calls a juxtaposition of "static conventions with the narrative elements"[17] – and lack any real "dramatic" conflict beyond the background noise of the cultural clash between Christianity and Islam. In terms of *Numancia*, as the play toggles back and forth between its imagined Roman and Numantian fictive spaces, and as it unfolds within the confines of the *corral* stage that Cervantes clearly envisioned when he wrote it, the characters who move about these spaces are themselves quite flat. Ostensibly, there is dialogue in these early plays. But what Cervantes really constructs is a series of alternating speeches – again, what Friedman calls a "controlled balance between concrete and abstract reality"[18] – declaimed by the various characters, who do not, by and large, actually engage in conversation. Likewise, there is very little movement suggested by this dialogue. Indeed, many of the characters in *Numancia* are purely allegorical in nature: España, El Duero, Enfermedad, Hambre, Guerra, La Fama (Spain, the Duero River, Sickness, Hunger, War, Fame), and so on. As such, they function primarily as ideas rather than characters, and therefore do very little to expand the rather flat performance space within which they are inscribed into the kind of three-dimensional jongleuresque sphere that good theatre both requires and creates.

Of course, some might object here that these types of allegorical characters are simply part of the literary and theatrical conventions of the day, and that it is therefore unfair to criticize Cervantes for tapping into these conventions. To these objections I would simply say, "You are right" – *except* that such conventions involving rhetorical devices like allegory are much more a part of the high-cultural literary tradition than they are part of the popular jongleuresque performance tradition. As a result, these allegorical figures would find themselves much more at home within the ritual space of liturgical drama, of *autos sacramentales*, or even of the courtly banquet and masque traditions than they would within the theatrical spaces of the commercial *corrales* of Madrid, where Cervantes's plays would have had to compete with those of Lope de Vega and others for a much-coveted "slot" in what was ultimately a limited season of plays. I will mention here that it is not inconsequential that Cervantes's theatre does not really avail itself of that most jongleuresque of all elements: the *gracioso*. Indeed, if we may take as a kind of touchstone Sor Juana Inés de la Cruz's complete *Festejo de Los empeños de una casa* (which, ironically, was not written for the commercial stage but which clearly understands its underlying performative poetics), the proper place for allegory is in the *loa* and the *sainete*, not in the main body of the *comedia* itself, where Sor Juana's *gracioso* Castaño not only plays such a central role, but really steals the show.[19]

That said, the other two spaces discussed above (again, the fictive-hermeneutical and the physical-archaeological) are well represented in *Numancia*. In terms of the first type of space (i.e., the imaginative space of the fiction created by the play), there are basically two distinct spaces in *Numancia*: the space among the Romans and the space among the Numantians. Additionally, the play essentially toggles back and forth between these two spaces as they eventually come together in the final act, when the Roman siege of Numancia is complete. The script itself is not very explicit with regard to the nature of these two fictive spaces, other than to suggest that the space associated with the Romans is the exterior camp that exists outside the Numantian city walls, while the space associated with the Numantians is located within those same walls. Indeed, act 1 is entirely given over to the Roman space, act 2 is entirely given over to the Numantian space, while acts 3 and 4 alternate between these two spaces until the distance between them has collapsed entirely, as the Romans enter the city only to find no Numantians left alive to conquer.

In terms of the second type of space (i.e., the physical space of the theatre for which *Numancia* is written), Cervantes has included a number of very specific stage directions indicating that he was clearly thinking of some kind of typical early modern Spanish *corral*. For instance, in act 2 the *acotación* reads: "Hágase ruido debajo del tablado con un barril lleno de piedras, y dispárese un cohete volador" (Noise is made under the stage with a barrel full of stones and a rocket is fired).[20] Such specificity not only instructs the company on how to produce the "special effects" that Cervantes describes, but also provides theatre historians with a reasonably good picture of the actual state of the scenic technology that made such special effects possible. (Indeed, the Teatro Cervantes in Alcalá de Henares displays just such a barrel full of stones as part of its public exhibit of early modern scenic technology.) A few lines later, when the *acotaciones* of *Numancia* indicate that a Demonio (Devil) should arise from the "huecos del tablado" (hollow space under the stage),[21] Cervantes again gives us an indication of the kind of physical affordances – in this case, a trap door – he assumes will be in place for the performance.

Where these two types of spaces come together in *Numancia* – and where they actually enter into a bit of conflict – is in act 3. In the very first scene of this act we find the following two *acotaciones*: "Aquí ha de sonar una trompeta desde el muro de Numancia" (Here a trumpet sounds from the wall of Numancia) and "Pónese Coravino encima de la muralla con bandera blanca puesta en una lanza" (Coravino places himself on top of the wall with a white flag tied to a spear).[22] Now, within the purely imaginative space of the fiction, it is easy to visualize the grand gestures evoked by both these descriptions. However, within the confines of the physical stage Cervantes seems to be writing for, the rather narrow "tablado" that he evokes in his *acotaciones* offers neither wing space on the sides from which to move large set pieces on- and offstage, nor fly space above from which to lower flats. Thus, whatever ultimate shape this *muralla* would have taken, its physical reality would have been a long way from the imagined reality posited by the script. Additionally, much of the "substance" of this *muralla* would have had to be created within the jongleuresque sphere of the performance space itself by the way in which the actors treated the *muralla*, giving weight and heft and gravitas to a set piece (whatever it may have been) that really had none. In other words, it is within this third type of space that the vast distance separating the imagined stone "wall" of the "real" Numantia from the wooden stage "wall" of the *corral* set would have had to be reduced by the work of the performers themselves, in much the same way that the horses of *Henry V* were given life by Shakespeare's actors. Says Shakespeare's very jongleuresque Chorus in the play's prologue: "Think, when we talk of horses, that you see them."[23]

This brings us to the *Ocho comedias* of Cervantes's later dramatic period. A close reading of these eight plays with an eye to questions of performance space demonstrates the extent to which Cervantes has certainly matured beyond the "flatness" of his earlier attempts. These later *comedias* contain many more jongleuresque elements than either *El trato de Argel* or *Numancia*. They include singing and dancing. They contain jongleuresque narration in the form of *romances* that tell, rather than try to show, complex action that would not have been easily representable on the delimited *corral* stages of the day. They include a great deal more genuine dialogue between characters (although there are still quite a number of allegorical figures throughout the corpus). They even include striking moments of psychological depth where characters genuinely speak *to* each other instead of *at* each other. In many ways, we can see in these plays Cervantes's own artistic growth as a dramatist, especially as one reads through the *Ocho comedias* in the order in which they appear in the published text. Nevertheless, these eight later *comedias* continue to exhibit many of the same problems found in *El trato de Argel* and *Numancia*. Indeed, Thacker even argues that "there is evidence that Cervantes ... rapidly reworked some of his earlier plays, transforming them on the page into three acts" as an obvious attempt to curry favour with the impresarios of the day, who would never "stage a play that involved a change from the winning three-act norm."[24] Needless to say, however, such tweaking of the formal elements in these earlier *comedias* would actually do very little to improve the inscription of their rather weak jongleuresque spheres, given that there is almost no relationship between what happens on Huston's simple stage during performance and the literary divisions that are found in the script.

Thus, a close reading of these later *comedias* also reveals the extent to which Cervantes seems to continue to struggle with the creation of a meaningful jongleuresque sphere in these plays. The first act of *Los baños de Argel*, for example, consists almost entirely of a series of quick vignettes that flash by almost like a slide show (and therefore remain quite "flat"), while the third act of *El rufián dichoso* descends into an amorphous metaphysical space only tenuously connected to the "real world." Indeed, the performance space of these later eight plays is particularly "slippery" and ambiguous in a number of crucial ways. For instance, at a most basic discursive level, Cervantes cannot seem to decide which verbs to use in his *acotaciones* to describe the entrances and exits of his characters. He shifts endlessly and inconsistently – both across plays and within plays – between the verbs "entrar" and "salir" (with occasional bouts of "ir" and "volver" thrown in for good measure). At times, "entrar" means that an actor actually enters the stage, while at other times, it means just the opposite: that an actor exits the stage (by "entering" the offstage area). Likewise, "salir" at times means that an actor comes out onto the stage from the offstage area, while at other times it means that an actor actually leaves the stage.

By way of comparison, Lope seems to consistently use "salir" to mean that an actor comes out onto the stage and "irse" to mean that an actor exits the playing area. Likewise, other playwrights of the period also seem to generally follow this same pattern. A random perusal of several plays by Luis de Belmonte Bermúdez, Calderón de la Barca, Ana Caro, Guillén de Castro, Sor Juana Inés de la Cruz, Agustín Moreto, Francisco de Rojas Zorrilla, Juan Ruiz de Alarcón, Luis Vélez de Guevara, and María de Zayas shows a general – and largely consistent – tendency to employ "salir" for entrances and "irse" for exits, especially within any particular play.[25] Of course, given the sheer number of *comedias* written between 1580 and 1695, there are bound to be some inconsistencies here and there (and even stylistic idiosyncrasies) among the thousands upon thousands of stage directions penned by playwrights who were hurriedly working to supply scripts to the *autores de comedias* of Madrid and elsewhere. My point here is not that Cervantes is the only playwright to exhibit such inconsistencies in his stage directions; rather, it is that he seems to be *more* inconsistent than others, even within a given play. Thus, while Cervantes's lexical ambiguity may seem irrelevant or unimportant at first glance, it is indicative, I think, of his general carelessness when it comes to specifying who is onstage at any particular moment.

Indeed, Florencio Sevilla Arroyo's edition of Cervantes's *Teatro completo* often includes footnotes indicating that Cervantes's initial list of characters for each *jornada* actually leaves out characters who will eventually appear onstage. For example, at the beginning of *La casa de los celos*, Sevilla Arroyo's very first footnote regarding the cast of characters stipulates: "Habría que añadir: Dos Salvajes, La Sospecha, un Ángel y un Paje" (It should be added: Two Savages, Suspicion, an Angel, and a Page), thus naming five personages not accounted for by the playwright.[26] Likewise, later in the same play, when the stage directions indicate "Éntrase Roldán" ("Exit Roldán," with "entrar" here meaning that Roldán leaves the stage), Sevilla Arroyo includes another footnote: "A juzgar por lo que sigue, también abandona la escena Reinaldos" (Judging by what follows, Reinaldos also exits the scene).[27] So it goes for so many of Cervantes's later *comedias*: it is often hard to tell exactly who is onstage and who is offstage at any given moment. I think Cervantes's inability to stick with a consistent vocabulary for marking the entrances and exits of his characters is less a writerly idiosyncrasy than it is a telling symptom of his rather imperfect sense of performance space.

In this same regard, then, it is often difficult to ascertain not just the *exact*, but even the *general* location of the fictive spaces inhabited by Cervantes's characters. His stage directions, for instance, almost never include clear Lopean descriptions like "Vista exterior de la casa de los Tellos" (Exterior view of the house of the Tello family) in *Valor, fortuna y lealtad*,[28] or "Sala en casa del Comendador" (A room in the Comendador's house) in *Peribáñez*.[29] But by the same token, nor do Cervantes's plays inscribe the kind of performative stagecraft found in the very first scene of Calderón's *La vida es sueño*, where Rosaura's opening lines include her advice to Clarín: "Quédate en este monte" (Stay here in this mountain), thus clearly indicating that both here and throughout the scene this setting is not only an exterior one, but is also located in a rocky geography.[30] One is hard-pressed to find anything like this in Cervantes's *Ocho comedias*. Indeed, one often has to read several pages into a scene before finally being able to figure out where the action takes place (and occasionally it is never made entirely clear).

Of course, as David Amelang argues in a recent study, Cervantes's stage directions are "unlike the typical *acotaciones* of most plays in this period," in that they are "longer and more fleshed out – more narrative, one could say – than the brief and uninteresting directions that were the norm in the *comedias* of the time."[31] Amelang is right here, and he clearly leans towards the Cervantes-as-literary-playwright side of the well-known debate (as do I, for that matter, if it is not already apparent), but this is precisely why Cervantes's plays tend to lack the kind of jongleuresque elements found in Lope's scripts, where the *acotaciones* remain (again, per Amelang) "within conventional expectations" and "limit themselves to providing information needed to understand and/or stage the play."[32] In other words, precisely because Cervantes's dramatic texts can contain a surfeit of information unrelated to the actual craft of theatre (the essence of which, as Huston insists, is the simple stage above all), they often have very little room left over for the jongleuresque sphere occupied by the performers.

But this brings us, ironically, to the question of the physical stage inscribed within Cervantes's dramatic texts and to the problem of what I am calling "no cabe" (it doesn't fit), a term I recently borrowed from Vicente Palacios, a Spanish scenic designer whose efforts in helping reconstruct original performances of early modern plays often include reminding his fellow team members that this or that idea is unworkable given the physical parameters of the original early modern stages: "Esto no cabe" (This doesn't fit), he would say.[33] For example, in rereading *La casa de los celos* with an eye specifically to the entrances and exits of the various characters, I became aware by the end of the very first scene of act 1 that there had to be an inordinate number of actors onstage by that time. When I counted heads, I realized that Cervantes had, in fact, incorporated a total of twelve characters all standing within the confines of a *corral* stage that, as Elizabeth Petersen has noted, would have measured only about "28 feet wide by 23 feet deep."[34] When I happened to mention this fact to Vicente Palacios during a casual conversation at the 2019 AITENSO conference in Madrid, his eyes widened and he started to laugh, realizing just how difficult it would be to develop any kind of meaningful interactive relationships between so many characters inhabiting so limited a performance space all at the same time.

Of course, it is certainly true that in the final scene of *Fuenteovejuna*, Lope also has twelve characters onstage at the same time. But in this case, Lope is bringing together his principal cast members for the grand finale (as happens in nearly all Spanish *comedias* of the period), whereas Cervantes is already amassing a large number of actors onto the stage during his opening scene. But even where other playwrights – for reasons having to do with what may be happening within the fictive space of the play itself – will occasionally place a dozen or more characters together onstage at the same time, such a conglomeration always runs the risk of overcrowding the early modern Iberian performance space.[35] For example, during the 2019 Almagro Festival, I happened to see a couple of productions in the *corral de comedias* that had clearly been conceived – and blocked – for the much larger performance spaces of twenty-first-century theatrical venues, and which had been brought to Almagro only secondarily following an initial run elsewhere. It was interesting to note that, while at least one of these companies seemed to adjust its jongleuresque sphere once inside the *corral*, using the house and other common areas to expand its performance space as needed, another company pressed forwards with what appeared to be its original blocking using just the "official" – and much smaller – playing area of the *corral* stage itself, and thus left its many actors often standing uncomfortably close together in a kind of awkward shoulder-to-shoulder chorus line.

Returning to *La casa de los celos*, in the final scene of act 1, Cervantes also calls for the following *tramoya*: "Vase retirando Roldán hacia atrás, y sube por la montaña como por fuerza de oculta virtud" (Roldán retreats backwards and goes up the mountain as if by force of hidden virtue).[36] In act 2, he later calls for the entrance of some kind of pageant wagon: "Parece a este instante el carro [de] fuego, de los leones de la montaña, y en él la diosa Venus" (At this moment, the fiery chariot of the mountain lions appears, and in it the goddess Venus).[37] In both cases, the complexity of what is being described raises questions about how these elements of spectacle would have been successfully accomplished on an early modern *corral* stage. Furthermore, act 1 of *El gallardo español* includes the following *acotación*: "Entra Alimuzel, a caballo, con una lanza y adarga" (Alimuzel enters on horseback with a spear and shield).[38] As with the numerous "mountains" scaled by one or another character in *La casa de los celos*, or even as with the grandiose "wall" depicted in *Numancia*, this evoked "horse" brings the fictive space and the physical space into at least some level of conflict. From the fictive side, it is quite moving to visualize the majestic arrival of Alimuzel on horseback. From the physical side, however, a number of logistical questions naturally arise (at least if we want to contemplate the possibility that this is a real horse). How, exactly, would this horse enter the stage? How would it "fit" within the physical setting of what would be a rather narrow *corral*, especially in relation to the other actors currently present, who are already (and necessarily) foreshortening the space between themselves in an effort to make the physical stage appear conceptually larger than it really is?

As with the issue of large numbers of cast members all onstage at the same time, the presence of live animals on the early modern *corral* stage is not an impossibility. Spectacles involving live animals – including, of course, the tradition of *tauromaquia* – have a long history in Iberia from at least the time of the Roman gladiatorial contests and running up through what John Beusterien has recently called the display of "trans-oceanic animals" in early modern Spain.[39] Moreover, the presence of live animals within (or at least alongside) various jongleuresque performance genres ranges from the simplicity of Maese Pedro's "mono adivino" as part of his itinerant puppet show in *Don Quixote* to what Michael Peterson has called the "animal apparatus" of complex modern circuses (like the Las Vegas *Siegfried & Roy* show).[40] Still, most of the performance spaces for such animal spectacles are either designed or carved out to accommodate the specific complications that come with the inherent unpredictability of non-human animal performers.[41] Nevertheless, as Adrienne Martín has recently noted, "There were no obstacles to prevent a small horse from entering through the main door of the Corral del Príncipe or the Corral de la Cruz [and then proceeding] to the central courtyard where the spectacles were held."[42] Likewise, Peterson discusses the presence of a live horse onstage in an 1823 English theatrical adaptation of Lord Byron's *Mazeppa*, where a "sequence of ramps allowed the horse to appear to cover ground without scene change or treadmill and added a very real sense of danger to the performance."[43] Yet, while this sequence of ramps no doubt added a "wow-factor" to the performance of *Mazeppa*, at some point, as Peterson shrewdly notes, live animals onstage contribute "nothing to performance but expense and inconvenience."[44] Thus, as Martín herself points out, it is also quite possible that early modern Spanish directors responded to the call for live animals onstage by simply disregarding the stage directions.[45] Instead, for example, they may have opted to make do with some kind of prop or hobby horse in place of the real thing.[46] Nevertheless, such a solution carries with it its own particular "costs," because the use of a hobby horse for a serious moment (such as the arrival of Alimuzel on horseback in *El gallardo español*) always runs the risk of converting the scene into something unintentionally comedic.

As an aside, and again by way of comparison, I will note that Cervantes seems to have learned a thing or two about the limits of performance as his career progressed. For instance, at the end of act 2 of *La casa de los celos* the text again evokes horses, but this time in a way that is radically different from the horse posited in *El gallardo español*. Here, one character asks, "Los caballos, ¿dónde están?" (Where are the horses?), to which another answers, "Aquí junto" (Nearby), thus indicating that they are located just offstage somewhere beyond the visual field of the spectators.[47] By keeping these horses safely outside the jongleuresque sphere of the performance, Cervantes eliminates both the need to worry about bringing live animals into the physical confines of the *corral* and the risk of undermining the theatrical moment with the sudden introduction of a less than convincing prop horse. This is not to mention the elephant that it is literally *not in the room*: that is, the pachyderm that plays such an important role in *La Gran Sultana*, but which Cervantes wisely mentions but never shows. Now, in raising these issues, I do not mean to suggest that a resourceful theatre company could not solve these problems. As Huston argues, talented performers can easily compensate for the deficiencies of this or that dramatic text (and they often do) because this is the essence of their craft. Nevertheless, having to resolve these kinds of issues simply adds one more (arguably, unnecessary) job to an already long list of tasks required to bring a play from page to stage. Which brings us, finally, to Cervantes's *entremeses*, where Huston's simple stage is on display with a flourish.

Cervantes's *entremeses* are, in many ways, the antithesis of his *comedias*. They are relatively short, comic, to the point, and mostly written in prose instead of verse, and they usually end with the various characters singing and dancing their way offstage. As a result, these relatively short interludes are *brimming* with jongleuresque three-dimensionality. Indeed, like so many of Lope de Vega's successful *comedias*, Cervantes's *entremeses* are "still very much grounded on [a] performative poetics that had thrived throughout much of the Iberian Middle Ages" and are "imbued with all the acrobatic energy of medieval fools, clowns, and buffoons."[48] This is due in no small measure to their well-documented connection to the Italian *commedia dell'arte*,[49] which, as I argue in *Radical Theatricality*, represents the early modern culmination of the pre-modern, pan-European jongleuresque performance tradition.[50] In fact, Cervantes's own description of Lope de Rueda's earlier performances highlights not just a literary connection between Rueda's *pasos* and the Italian *commedia* scenarios, but also a *performative* connection insofar as Rueda may have witnessed first-hand – if not participated in – the *commedia* performances offered by Michele Luigi Mutio's touring company when it came to Rueda's home town of Seville in 1538.[51] Moreover, during Cervantes's own travels in Italy between 1569 and 1575, it is quite likely that he would have seen at least some live *commedia* performances at one time or another, and thus internalized their jongleuresque poetics even further.

Thus, many of Cervantes's *entremeses* – particularly *El viejo celoso* and *La cueva de Salamanca* – exhibit clear traces of what Diana Taylor has called both the "archive" and the "repertoire" in their borrowing of *commedia dell'arte* stock characters, which are ultimately constructed in the

Italian scenarios not through language – since the scenarios are merely bare-bones scaffolding designed for improvisational performance – but through the skill set of the actors who routinely portrayed these stock characters: "The repertoire ... enacts embodied memory: performances, gestures, orality, movement, dance, singing – in short, all those acts usually thought of as ephemeral, nonreproducible knowledge."[52] Or, again, as I argue in *Radical Theatricality*, because Cervantes's *entremeses* were built around "the talents of men and women who had honed their craft within the jongleuresque tradition," these plays "inherited by synecdoche a plethora of traditional themes ... and modes of acting brought into the *corrales* by the actors themselves."[53] In other words, Cervantes's *entremeses* "work" onstage, in ways that his *comedias* generally do not, precisely because, by modelling them on the *commedia dell'arte*, he wrote them with the "smart practice" of performers in mind, even if he may not have been fully aware of this at the time.[54]

This is not the place, of course, to engage in an exhaustive examination of each of Cervantes's eight *entremeses* and their various connections to the *commedia dell'arte*. But I do want to highlight two interrelated moments from a production of Cervantes's *entremeses* staged by the Mexico City–based company EFE Tres Teatro, an adaptation titled *El Merolico: Entremeses cervantinos bululuados* that pays homage to "los grandes artistas del Bululú como lo fuera Lope de Rueda" (the great Bululú artists like Lope de Rueda) and that exemplifies the radically jongleuresque nature of Huston's simple stage. As EFE Tres Teatro's press packet explains, "Un merolico es un vendedor al estilo de los adivinos o barberos medievales" (A *merolico* is a mountebank in the style of medieval fortune tellers and barbers), while a Bululú comprises a theatre "company" of one, "un único comediante que representa obras, él solo, mudando la voz según la condición de los personajes que intepretaba" (a single actor who performed plays, by himself, changing his voice according to the characters he performed).[55]

Featuring Fernando Villa in a brilliant solo performance, *El Merolico* creates a frame narrative in the form of a "medicine show" whose itinerant mountebank grounds the production in the performative poetics of a jongleuresque tradition of street performance that goes back to the Middle Ages. Villa's *merolico* character greets his public (as if simply happening upon them in some public square) and then proceeds to offer them his wares, which turn out to be Bululú performances of *El viejo celoso*, *El retablo de las maravillas*, and *La cueva de Salamanca*. As Villa performs all the necessary characters for these three *entremeses*, he uses an inventive set of staging and costume devices to "flesh out" Cervantes's comic world within the confines of Huston's simple stage. For

El viejo celoso, Villa utilizes a single handkerchief and an accompanying set of gestures, vocalizations, and attitudes to embody all the characters, both male and female. For *El retablo de las maravillas*, Villa utilizes a set of hats (which sit idle, in full view of the audience, on a set of short, perpendicular sticks when not in use), again with an accompanying set of gestures, vocalizations, and attitudes to bring all the characters to life. For *La cueva de Salamanca*, Villa dons an ingenious frock coat that is constructed to incorporate a whole set of costume elements, including things like monocles, collars, hoods, and scarves, to represent each of characters portrayed. Needless to say, such a Bululú performance epitomizes Huston's simple stage on which "an articulate performer unpacks illusory space with his act," folding up the show once it is over "as if the event called performance had never happened."[56]

But I want to emphasize two particular elements of this adaptation. The first moment occurs at one point during Villa's performance, when one of the characters "enters" the scene and moves downstage left, crossing in front of Villa, who remains in the guise of one of the other characters. I placed the word *enters* in quotation marks above because we see this character's "entrance" only through the gaze of Villa in the physical person of an already established character, who "watches" as the new character enters the scene and moves downstage. In this way, Villa's performance itself creates the "absent" character who crosses in front of him by converting this invisible character into a presence that the audience can now "see" as well. Or, in the words of Huston, Villa "fills that space by keeping it empty, possessing it."[57] The second example is not just a moment, but an entire string of moments that constitute the entire performance segment of *La cueva de Salamanca*. I mentioned above that for this segment of *El Merolico*, Villa wears a special frock coat containing all the costume elements necessary to portray all of Cervantes's characters. But the other significant conceit built into this *Cueva de Salamanca* segment is a deliberate choice to limit the performance space to as small a theatrical geography as possible. For one particular performance of *El Merolico* that I happened to see, Villa's simple stage consisted of nothing more than a focused spot of light that was no bigger than one square metre.[58] Thus, for this segment of *El Merolico*, the fictive space of *La cueva de Salamana*, which encompasses both exterior and (multiple) interior scenes, is brought into existence by a performer who does not, himself, physically step beyond the confines of a very small simple stage. In other words, as evidence of the very strong jongleuresque sphere that Cervantes has inscribed within the script of *La cueva de Salamanca*, I offer the fact that his several characters move through an abundantly detailed fictive world not in spite of, but precisely because of the very tight jongleuresque sphere that Villa creates within his performance. Indeed, this particular segment of *El Merolico* provides a distinct counterexample to Palacios's notion of "no cabe": given a well-developed jongleuresque sphere already built into the script, no component of a play's theatricality is too big to fit into the most delimited of simple stages.

Now, it might be objected that what I am really analysing here is the work of a very talented contemporary performer and not (necessarily) the work of one particular early modern playwright. To a certain extent such an objection is well taken, and I have to admit that I have seen some really bad productions of Cervantes's *entremeses*, despite what I think are these texts' very strong jongleuresque elements. At the same time, however, when we recall Cervantes's eyewitness description of Lope de Rueda's own itinerant and simple theatre, there is little in *El Merolico* that would have been out of place in the Spain of the mid 1500s, especially in terms of the performative poetics of Huston's simple stage. Villa and EFE Tres Teatro merely capitalize on those jongleuresque elements that were (and are) always already a part of Cervantes's *entremeses*. If I may proffer an analogy borrowed from science, contemporary physics now tells us that "empty space" is really not empty. This is true, on the one hand, because quantum particles continually pop into and out of existence even in a vacuum and, on the other hand, because the very structure of space-time itself (i.e., its multiple dimensions, however many) is part and parcel of the "empty" vacuum it defines. The same is true, I would argue, of playscripts that encompass a well-rounded jongleuresque sphere that exists alongside the fictive-hermeneutical and physical-archaeological spaces that these plays may also contain. Unlike the majority of his full-length *comedias*, Cervantes's *entremeses* – which are both built on and flow from a jongleuresque tradition that culminated in the *commedia dell'arte* – articulate a performative poetics that is both multidimensional and clearly centred on Huston's simple stage.

I mentioned at the beginning of this essay that, even today, we are more likely to encounter dramatizations of *Don Quixote* than we are performances of any of Cervantes's plays. I will point out here, at the end, that even within the context of Cervantes's dramatic works themselves, we are still far more likely to see contemporary performances of the *entremeses* than we are of any of his full-length *comedias*. The reason for this, as I hope to have demonstrated here, is increasingly obvious. Contemporary actors and directors, like their early modern counterparts before them, can see a performative potential in Cervantes's *entremeses* that they just don't see in his *comedias* – and this performative potential has a great deal to do with the inscription (or lack thereof) of Huston's simple stage in these playscripts. In short, while Cervantes may be heavily invested in the imaginative space of his fictions, and while he is clearly aware of the physical space he is writing for, he seems to struggle with the jongleuresque sphere that he literally needs to sell to any theatre company interested in producing his plays. Without a keener sense of this jongleuresque sphere built into his texts, the professional actors of his day could not easily see themselves in the script, and thus simply moved on to other plays and other playwrights.

NOTES

1 Thacker, "Véote, y no te conozco," 206.
2 Cervantes, *Teatro completo*, 269–70.
3 Thacker, *Companion*, 20.
4 Cervantes, *Teatro completo*, 271. All translations, unless otherwise indicated, are my own.
5 See Syverson-Stork, *Theatrical Aspects of the Novel*.
6 Burningham, *Radical Theatricality*, 132–66, 215–20.
7 Huston, *Actor's Instrument*, 1.
8 Huston, 11.
9 Huston, 49.
10 Collins, *Poetics of the Mind's Eye*, 5.
11 The "fictive-hermeneutical" category corresponds to those academic studies that generally examine either the representation of space within dramatic texts (see Castillo, "Espacios de ambigüedad"; and Domínguez, "Los escenarios de la memoria") or the way in which the contingent performance spaces of real-world performances impact the meaning of specific theatrical productions (see Feinberg, "*Don Juan Tenorio*"; and Lech, "Metatheatre"). For other "fictive-hermeneutical" studies not necessarily related to Hispanism, see also Condon, "Setting the Stage for Revenge"; Connor, "Retranslating Strindberg"; Fitzpatrick, "Staging *The Merchant of Venice*"; Gotman, "Dancing-Place"; and Hopkins, "Mapping the Placeless Place." The "physical-archaeological" category corresponds to those academic studies that examine a kind of "archaeology of space." This category is in many ways an extension of theatre history, and is the most traditional and best known of the two. Within Hispanism (and particularly within the world of *comedia* studies), Cervantes himself was perhaps one of the first to engage in this kind of archaeological excavation of the early Spanish stage in his prologue to *Ocho comedias*, where he famously describes the rudimentary – and ambulatory – scenic

architecture employed by Lope de Rueda during the mid 1500s (Cervantes, *Teatro completo*, 267–8). See also Allen, *Reconstruction*; Cull, "Hablan poco y dicen mucho"; Greer, "Playing the Palace"; Rodríguez Cuadros, "Art of the Actor"; Ruano de la Haza, "The World as a Stage"; and Thacker, *Companion*, 123–42. The appeal of such archaeological studies, of course, lies in their helping us visualize just how an original (but now lost) ephemeral performance of a dramatic work might actually have looked by "placing" this visualization within the confines of the physical space in which it (might have) occurred. For other such archaeological studies (not necessarily related to Hispanism), see also George, "Adrià Gual"; Petersen, "Designed for an Experience"; and Tiner, "Performance Spaces".
12 Pérez de León, "Aproximación," 4.
13 Maestro, *La escena imaginaria*, 18.
14 Tigner, "The Spanish Actress's Art," 180.
15 Huston, *Actor's Instrument*, 12.
16 Huston, 78; original emphasis.
17 Friedman, *Unifying Concept*, 62.
18 Friedman, 47.
19 Juana Inés de la Cruz, *Obras completas*, 627–704.
20 Cervantes, *Teatro completo*, 210.
21 Cervantes, 212.
22 Cervantes, 221.
23 Shakespeare, *Henry V*, 1.1.27.
24 Thacker, "Lope de Vega," 42.
25 This assumes, of course, that literary editors have not simply "cleaned up" these stage directions while preparing the texts for publication.
26 Cervantes, *Teatro completo*, 383n1.
27 Cervantes, 412n62.
28 Vega, *Obras escogidas*, 445.
29 Vega, 773.
30 Calderón de la Barca, *La vida es sueño*, 75.
31 Amelang, "From Directions to Descriptions," 18.
32 Amelang, 13.
33 Palacios, "Mesa redonda."
34 Petersen, "Designed for an Experience," 172.
35 While it is fairly easy to ascertain the number of characters included in the *dramatis personae* of a particular play, I know of no detailed study – especially across multiple plays and multiple playwrights – of the number of characters presumed to be onstage together at any given time.
36 Cervantes, *Teatro completo*, 410.
37 Cervantes, 431.
38 Cervantes, 282.

39 Beusterien, *Transoceanic Animals*, 3. On *tauromaquia*, see also Amorós, "Tauromaquia."
40 Peterson, "Animal Apparatus," 33.
41 On the presence of live cats onstage, see Grant, "Pleasant Tragicomedy." On the general presence of non-human animals onstage, see Grant, Ramos Gay, and Alonso Recarte, "Live Animals on the Stage."
42 Adrienne L. Martín, "Onstage/Backstage," 131. See also Ruano de la Haza, *La puesta en escena*, 271–4.
43 Peterson, "Animal Apparatus," 38. A 2018 production of Lope de Vega's *Fuenteovejuna*, performed in the Plaza Lope de Vega in the town of Fuente Obejuna, included a rider arriving on horseback, an entrance that worked well precisely because of the outdoor location of the performance. See Ángel Luis Martín, *Fuenteovejuna*.
44 "The perception of animals is not (at first) textual; animals are not 'read' in performance unless considerable effort is made to *reduce* them to signs. In performance, the disturbing presence of an animal could perhaps be framed, repeated, distanced, abstracted – ideally, silhouetted – until it became one sign among many. But of course no theatre person in their right mind would do such a thing. Reduced to a sign, an animal contributes nothing to performance but expense and inconvenience" (Peterson, 43; original emphasis).
45 Adrienne L. Martín, "Onstage/Backstage," 130.
46 On the history of the European theatrical hobby horse and its ties to the Islamic world through Al-Andalus, see Harris, "From Iraq to the English Morris."
47 Cervantes, *Teatro completo*, 445.
48 Burningham, *Radical Theatricality*, 214.
49 On the connection between Cervantes's *entremeses* and the *commedia dell'arte*, see Algaba Granero, "Entremés y *commedia dell'arte*"; Maestro, "La '*commedia dell'arte*' y el entremés cervantino"; and Rotta, "*Commedia dell'arte* in the Theater of Cervantes." On the influence of the *commedia dell'arte* on *Don Quixote*, see also Roca Mussons, "*Don Quixote* y 'El capitano'"; and Vélez-Sainz, "El *Recueil Fossard*." On the connection between the *commedia dell'arte* and early modern Spanish theatre in general, see D'Antuono ("Bandello," "Calderonian Honor," "The 'Comedia' in Italy," "El gracioso de Lope de Vega," "Evolution," "Lope de Vega y la commedia dell'arte," "Pantalone Hispanicized," "Tirso de Molina and Italy"); Lewis-Smith, "*La casa de los celos* y la *commedia dell'arte*"; O'Neill, "Improvisation in *La entretenida*"; and Sito Alba, "The *Commedia dell'arte*."
50 Burningham, *Radical Theatricality*, 217.
51 Shergold, "Ganassa," 359n3.
52 Taylor, *Archive and the Repertoire*, 20.

53 Burningham, *Radical Theatricality*, 165–6.
54 Huston, *Actor's Instrument*, 78. It is true, of course, that Cervantes's
    entremeses were also published under the rubric of plays that were "nunca
    representados" (Cervantes, *Teatro completo*, 263). My own theory about
    why they too had difficulty finding a home onstage, despite their much
    stronger jongleuresque qualities, is simply that they are often too long
    and too complex to really serve the intended purpose of an *entremés* (i.e.,
    as short pieces designed to be featured between the acts of full-length
    comedias). Cervantes's *entremeses* suffer from the same tendency toward
    "surfeit" (although, in a different way) that I see in his *comedias*. In short,
    his *entremeses* are much more like modern one-act plays than "interludes,"
    and thus perhaps failed to interest those *autores de comedias* who might
    actually have been shopping precisely for the kind of *entremeses* written so
    successfully by Luis Quiñones de Benavente and others.
55 This quote about Lope de Rueda comes from a press release packet sent to
    me by Fernando Villa on 10 November 2017.
56 Huston, *Actor's Instrument*, 76.
57 Huston, 76.
58 While I have seen multiple performances of *El Merolico* in both the United
    States and Spain, the specific performance I refer to here occurred at the
    Chamizal National Memorial in El Paso, Texas, on 14 April 2018 (dir.
    Fernando Villa and Fernando Memije, prod. EFE Tres Teatro).

REFERENCES

Algaba Granero, Aroa. "Entremés y *commedia dell'arte*: *El viejo celoso* a través
    de la máscara. La versión de Veneziainscena." *Anagnórisis: Revista de
    Investigación Teatral*, no. 15 (2017): 44–67.
Allen, John J. *The Reconstruction of a Spanish Golden Age Playhouse: El Corral del
    Príncipe, 1583–1744*. Gainsville: University of Florida Press, 1983.
Amelang, David J. "From Directions to Descriptions: Reading the Theatrical
    Nebentext in Ben Jonson's *Workes* as an Authorial Outlet." *Sederi*, no. 27
    (2017): 7–26. https://doi.org/10.34136/sederi.2017.1.
Amorós, Andrés. "Tauromaquia." In *Historia de los espectáculos en España*,
    edited by Andrés Amorós and José María Díez Borque, 507–17. Madrid:
    Castalia, 1999.
Beusterien, John. *Transoceanic Animals as Spectacle in Early Modern Spain*.
    Amsterdam: Amsterdam University Press, 2020.
Burningham, Bruce R. *Radical Theatricality: Jongleuresque Performance on the
    Early Spanish Stage*. West Lafayette, IN: Purdue University Press, 2007.
Calderón de la Barca, Pedro. *La vida es sueño*. Edited by Ciriaco Morón.
    Madrid: Cátedra, 1987.

Castillo, Moisés R. "Espacios de ambigüedad en el teatro cervantino: *La conquista de Jerusalén* y los dramas de cautiverio." *Cervantes* 32, no. 2 (2012): 123–42. https://doi.org/10.1353/cer.2012.0018.

Cervantes, Miguel de. *Teatro completo.* Edited by Florencio Sevilla Arroyo. Barcelona: Penguin, 2016.

Collins, Christopher. *The Poetics of the Mind's Eye: Literature and the Psychology of Imagination.* Philadelphia: University of Pennsylvania Press, 1991.

Condon, James J. "Setting the Stage for Revenge: Space, Performance, and Power in Early Modern Revenge Tragedy." *Medieval and Renaissance Drama in England: An Annual Gathering of Research, Criticism and Reviews,* no. 25 (2012): 62–82.

Connor, Rachel. "Retranslating Strindberg: Adaptation, (Re)location and Site-Related Performance." *Journal of Adaptation in Film and Performance* 11, no. 1 (2018): 71–83. https://doi.org/10.1386/jafp.11.1.71_1.

Cull, John T. "'Hablan poco y dicen mucho': The Function of Discovery Scenes in the Drama of Tirso de Molina." *Modern Language Review* 91, no. 3 (1996): 619–34. https://doi.org/10.2307/3734089.

D'Antuono, Nancy L. "Bandello, Lope de Vega, and an Unedited *Commedia dell'arte* Scenario: *Il castico della disonesta moglie.*" In *LA CHISPA '83: Selected Proceedings,* edited by Gilbert Paolini, 79–87. New Orleans: Tulane University, 1983.

D'Antuono, Nancy L. "Calderonian Honor and the *Commedia dell'arte: Il medico di suo honore.*" In *Texto y Espectáculo: Selected Proceedings of the Symposium on Spanish Golden Age Theater,* edited by Barbara Mujica, 127–36. Lanham, MD: University Press of America, 1989.

D'Antuono, Nancy L. "The 'Comedia' in Italy: Lope's *La discreta enamorada* and Its *'commedia dell'arte'* Counterpart." In *LA CHISPA '81: Selected Proceedings, February 26–28, 1981,* edited by Gilbert Paolini, 69–81. New Orleans: Tulane University, 1981.

D'Antuono, Nancy L. "The Evolution of *Il cavaliere perseguitato*: Literary Interdependence in Bandello, Lope de Vega and the *commedia dell'arte.*" *Bulletin of the Comediantes* 44, no. 1 (1992): 103–12. https://doi.org/10.1353/boc.1992.0029.

D'Antuono, Nancy L. "El gracioso de Lope de Vega: Máscara desenmascarada." In *Studies in Honor of Gilberto Paolini,* edited by Mercedes Vidal Tibbits and Claire J. Paolini, 81–95. Homenajes 12. Newark, DE: Cuesta, 1996.

D'Antuono, Nancy L. "Lope de Vega y la *commedia dell'arte*: Temas y figuras." In *Lope de Vega y los orígenes del teatro español,* edited by Manuel Criado de Val, 217–28. Madrid: Edi-6, 1981.

D'Antuono, Nancy L. "Pantalone Hispanicized: The Comic Father Figure in Lope de Vega's *La francesilla.*" In *Italo-Hispanic Literary Relations,* edited by

J. Helí Hernández, 41–55. Scripta Humanistica 49. Potomac, MD: Scripta Humanistica, 1989.

D'Antuono, Nancy L. "Tirso de Molina and Italy: *La celosa de sí misma* and Its Italian Counterpart." *RLA: Romance Languages Annual* 10, no. 2 (1998): 525–8.

Delgado, Maria M., and David T. Gies, eds. *A History of Theatre in Spain.* Cambridge: Cambridge University Press, 2012.

Domínguez, Julia. "Los escenarios de la memoria: Psicodrama en *El trato de argel* de Cervantes." *Bulletin of the Comediantes* 61, no. 1 (2009): 1–23. https://doi.org/10.1353/boc.0.0010.

Feinberg, Matthew I. "*Don Juan Tenorio* in the Campo de Cebada: Restaging Urban Space after 15-M." *Journal of Spanish Cultural Studies* 15, nos. 1–2 (2014): 143–59. https://doi.org/10.1080/14636204.2014.931673.

Fitzpatrick, Lisa. "Staging *The Merchant of Venice* in Cork: The Concretization of a Shakespearean Play for a New Society." *Modern Drama* 50, no. 2 (2007): 168–83. https://doi.org/10.3138/md.50.2.168.

Friedman, Edward H. *The Unifying Concept: Approaches to the Structure of Cervantes'* Comedias. York, SC: Spanish Literature Publications, 1981.

George, David. "Adrià Gual as Illustrator, Stage and Costume Designer." *Journal of Iberian and Latin American Studies* 20, no. 3 (2014): 273–89. https://doi.org/10.1080/14701847.2014.1008261.

Gotman, Kélina. "The Dancing-Place: Towards a Geocultural and Geohistorical Theory of Performance Space." *Choreographic Practices* 3, no. 1 (2012): 7–23. https://doi.org/10.1386/chor.3.1.7_1.

Grant, Teresa. "'A Pleasant Tragicomedy, the Cat Being Scap't'? William Sampson's *The Vow Breaker* (1636) and the Instability of Genre." *Studies in Theatre and Performance* 38, no. 2 (2018): 113–29. https://doi.org/10.1080/14682761.2018.1451947.

Grant, Teresa, Ignacio Ramos Gay, and Claudia Alonso Recarte. "Introduction: Real Animals on the Stage." *Studies in Theatre and Performance* 38, no. 2 (2018): 103–12. https://doi.org/10.1080/14682761.2018.1451941.

Greer, Margaret R. "Playing the Palace: Space, Place and Performance in Early Modern Spain." In Delgado and Gies, *A History of Theatre in Spain,* 79–102.

Harris, Max. "From Iraq to the English Morris: The Early History of the Skirted Hobbyhorse." *Medieval English Theatre,* no. 25 (2003): 71–83.

Hopkins, D.J. "Mapping the Placeless Place: Pedestrian Performance in the Urban Spaces of Los Angeles." *Modern Drama* 46, no. 2 (2003): 261–84. https://doi.org/10.3138/md.46.2.261.

Huston, Hollis. *The Actor's Instrument: Body, Theory, Stage.* Ann Arbor: University of Michigan Press, 1992.

Juana Inés de la Cruz. *Obras completas.* Edited by Francisco Monterde. Mexico City: Porrúa, 1989.

Lech, Kasia. "Metatheatre and the Importance of Estrella in Calderón's *La vida es sueño* and Its Contemporary Productions." *Bulletin of the Comediantes* 66, no. 2 (2014): 175–93. https://doi.org/10.1353/boc.2014.0036.

Lewis-Smith, Paul. *"La casa de los celos* y la *commedia dell'arte."* *Theatralia: Revista de poética del teatro*, no. 5 (2003): 375–83.

Maestro, Jesús G. "La *'commedia dell'arte'* y el entremés cervantino: Sobre el diálogo dramático." *El extramundi y los papeles de Iria Flavia* 4, no. 14 (1998): 15–43.

Maestro, Jesús G. *La escena imaginaria: Poética del teatro de Miguel de Cervantes.* Madrid: Iberoamericana, 2000.

Martín, Adrienne L. "Onstage/Backstage: Animals in the Golden Age *Comedia.*" In *A Companion to Early Modern Hispanic Theater*, edited by Hilaire Kallendorf, 127–44. Renaissance Society of America 2. Leiden: Brill, 2014.

Martín, Ángel Luis, dir. *Fuenteovejuna.* Plaza Lope de Vega, Fuente Obejuna, 2018. https://www.youtube.com/watch?v=9lUCl2vCqJc.

O'Neill, John. "Improvisation in *La entretenida*: Tracing the Influence of Plautus and the *Commedia dell'arte* on Cervantes." *Cervantes* 36, no. 1 (2016): 11–37. https://doi.org/10.1353/cer.2016.0002.

Palacios, Vicente. "Mesa redonda: Escenografía y puesta en escena." Round table presented at the XIX Congreso de la Asociación Internacional de Teatro Español y Novohispano de los Siglos de Oro, Universidad Complutense, Madrid, 15 October 2019.

Pérez de León, Vicente. "Una aproximación teórica al equilibrio y espacio dramático en el entremés cervantino, con su posible incidencia en el canon del teatro breve de los Siglos de Oro." *Bulletin of Hispanic Studies* 85, no. 1 (2008): 1–14. https://doi.org/10.3828/bhs.85.1.1.

Petersen, Elizabeth M. "Designed for an Experience: The Natural Architecture of *Corrales.*" *Comedia Performance* 7, no. 1 (2010): 170–99. https://doi.org/10.5325/comeperf.7.1.0170.

Peterson, Michael. "The Animal Apparatus: From a Theory of Animal Acting to an Ethics of Animal Acts." *TDR/The Drama Review: The Journal of Performance Studies* 51, no.1 (2007): 33–48. https://doi.org/10.1162/dram.2007.51.1.33.

Roca Mussons, María A. *"Don Quijote* e 'Il capitano.'" *Theatralia: Revista de poética del teatro*, no. 5 (2003): 415–29.

Rodríguez Cuadros, Evangelina. "The Art of the Actor, 1565–1833: From Moral Suspicion to Social Institution." In Delgado and Gies, *A History of Theatre in Spain*, 103–19.

Rotta, John Bernard. "The *Commedia dell'arte* in the Theater of Cervantes." *Dissertation Abstracts International, Section A: The Humanities and Social Sciences*, no. 37 (1976): 1598A.

Ruano de la Haza, José María. *La puesta en escena en los teatros comerciales del Siglo de Oro*. Madrid: Castalia, 2000.

Ruano de la Haza, José María. "The World as a Stage: Politics, Imperialism and Spain's Seventeenth-Century Theatre." In Delgado and Gies, *A History of Theatre in Spain*, 57–78.

Sevilla Arroyo, Florencio. "Introducción." In Cervantes, *Teatro completo*, 9–93.

Shakespeare, William. *Henry V*. In *The Riverside Shakespeare*. Edited by G. Blakemore Evans and J.J.M. Tobin. 2nd ed. Boston: Houghton Mifflin, 1997.

Shergold, N.D. "Ganassa and the '*Commedia dell'arte*' in Sixteenth-Century Spain." *Modern Language Review* 51, no. 3 (1956): 359–68. https://doi .org/10.2307/3718388.

Sito Alba, Manuel. "The *Commedia dell'arte*: Key to the Source of *Don Quijote*." *Theatre Annual: A Journal of Theatre and Performance of the Americas*, no. 37 (1982): 1–13.

Syverson-Stork, Jill. *Theatrical Aspects of the Novel: A Study of* Don Quixote. Valencia: Albatros Hispanófila, 1986.

Taylor, Diana. *The Archive and the Repertoire: Performing Cultural Memory in the Americas*. Durham, NC: Duke University Press, 2003.

Thacker, Jonathan. *A Companion to Golden Age Theatre*. Woodbridge: Tamesis, 2007.

Thacker, Jonathan. "Lope de Vega, Calderón de La Barca and Tirso de Molina: Spain's Golden Age Drama and Its Legacy." In Delgado and Gies, *A History of Theatre in Spain*, 36–56.

Thacker, Jonathan. "'Véote, y no te conozco': The Unrecognizable Form of Cervantes's *El rufián dichoso*." *Hispanic Research Journal* 10, no. 3 (2009): 206– 26. https://doi.org/10.1179/174582009X433176.

Tigner, Amy L. "The Spanish Actress's Art: Improvisation, Transvestism, and Disruption in Tirso's *El vergonzoso en palacio*." *Early Theatre: A Journal Associated with the Records of Early English Drama* 15, no. 1 (2012): 167–90. https://doi.org/10.12745/et.15.1.902.

Tiner, Elza C. "Performance Spaces in Thomas Chaundler's *Liber apologeticus*." *Early Theatre: A Journal Associated with the Records of Early English Drama* 18, no. 1 (2015): 33–49. https://doi.org/10.12745/et.18.1.1170.

Vega, Lope de. *Obras escogidas*. Vol. 1. Edited by Federico Carlos Sainz de Robles. Madrid: Aguilar, 1990.

Vélez-Sainz, Julio. "El *Recueil Fossard*, la compañía de los Gelosi y la génesis de *Don Quijote*." *Cervantes* 20, no. 2 (2000): 31–52.

2 Queer *cambalaches* in *El rufián dichoso*

JOHN SLATER

Cervantes's *El rufián dichoso* is a confounding thing. The play – about a would-be hoodlum, Cristóbal de Lugo, who becomes the saintly friar Cristóbal de la Cruz – spans years and continents. It features an allegorical interlude at the beginning of the second act – on the nature of the *comedia* – that would seem to render any *entremés* superfluous. The stage directions are not stage directions at all, but rather winking asseverations of the historical veracity of the play's action. (And stage direction is missing when we need it most.)[1] *El rufián dichoso*, or *Fortunate Ruffian*, has a whopping forty-one characters packed into a lean 2,800 verses; it feels brisk and overstuffed at the same time. In terms of its genre, it lies somewhere between an opulent pageant and a closet drama.[2] It is nearly a hagiographic play, a *comedia de santos*, but goes light on saintliness; Melveena McKendrick said that Cristóbal de Lugo's conversion lacks "any psychological plausibility."[3] In his introduction to the *Ocho comedias y ocho entremeses nuevos, nunca representados* (1615), Cervantes – claiming to have imagined that his praises as a playwright were still sung ("pensando que aún duraban los siglos donde corrían [sus] alabanzas") – is crestfallen to find that no one wants to stage his plays.[4] Those were crocodile tears. *El rufián dichoso* reads more like a dare than a show.

The dare partly consists in imagining what the play would look like if it were staged as written. The play's editors have often been so

This chapter forms part of the research project "Desde los márgenes: Cultura, experiencia y subjetividad en la Modernidad: Género, política y saberes (siglos XVII-XIX)" (PGC2018–097445-A-C22), under the auspices of Spain's Ministerio de Ciencia, Innovación y Universidades. I am grateful to Sonia Velázquez and Paula Plastić for their helpful suggestions at various stages.

unwilling to do this – intransigently refusing to imagine the spectacle conjured by the playtext's words – that, as Thacker documents, editors have either suppressed or explained away its peculiarities.[5] In these editors' defence, Cervantes wrote an unworkable play, its challenges so insurmountable that *El rufián dichoso* has never been staged with all its characters.[6] Sometimes, the exuberant theatricality of *El rufián dichoso* cries out for the bodies of actors, and at other times, Cervantes makes staging the play seem so unfeasible, so unlikely, that feels daringly bad. Its queerness resists us.

Lying somewhere between playtext and closet drama, the apparent identity crisis of *El rufián dichoso* – its uncertain genre – is at the heart of how and what the play means. Its generic ambiguity suggests the extent to which the play is about problems of representation. These problems of representation have to do with drama and historiography – the overlapping domains of representation implied in any *comedia de santos* – and the ways in which Cervantes uses drama and historiography as arenas in which sexuality and identity are first taxonomized and then queered.

Queerness in *El rufián dichoso* consists of drag, same-sex attraction, the rejection of normative categorization (temporal and geographic), and cross-gendered ventriloquism, as well as the uncoupling of actorly identity from dramatic role in order to construct hybridized identities. It may seem terminologically anachronistic to speak of Cervantes's foregrounding of queerness but, in the spirit of Jones and Leahy's recent meditation on the historically responsible uses of ahistoricism, and drawing on the work of Barbara Fuchs, Diana de Armas Wilson, Sherry Velasco, Jonathan Thacker, and others, this chapter takes *El rufián dichoso* seriously as written.

One thing this chapter takes seriously is Cervantes's statement that the play and its abundance of characters can be staged with only two female actors (in addition to male actors). This means that when more than two female characters appear onstage at once, some of those characters must be played by male actors. Cross-dressing is a practical necessity, most notably when Cruz is tempted by lascivious nymphs, a scene that places Cruz's companion, Antonio, in the position of witness to or historian of Cruz's spiritual trials. As we shall see, Antonio's presence as witness signals another form of cross-dressing: linguistic transvestism. The words of female characters in act 1 are recast and echoed in the voices of conspicuously cross-dressed characters in acts 2 and 3. The cross-gendered repetition of lines from one act to another and the reappearance of male actors in female roles, a process of casting and recasting, makes promiscuous dissemination a defining feature of *El rufián dichoso*.

As a show, the work of recasting lines and roles thematizes queering. Doubles accumulate with increasing insistence across the space of *El rufián dichoso*'s three acts: Antonia and Antonio; the "bienaventurada pecadora" (blessed sinner) and the "rufián dichoso" (fortunate ruffian); prayers interrupted by a desiring woman and prayers interrupted – with the very same words – by cross-dressed nymphs; finally, histories told by cross-dressed souls that are echoed by Antonio, Cruz's lifelong companion. Throughout these recastings, Cervantes's play represents how discursive "propriety" simultaneously attempts to overwrite queering and impose order (without success).

El rufián dichoso is also queer as text. Cervantes demands that we consider the play a text, and not only a show, by making its ironic and involved stage directions integral to its interpretation. It is a play that never fully commits to leaving the page. Cervantes also calls attention to the play's textuality by repeatedly claiming that *El rufián dichoso* faithfully reproduces its hagiographic sources. What the play's textual antecedents cannot explain, however, are the multiple vectors of desire, the uncertain permutations of identity, and the ways in which a law of antonomasia, by which words are severed from their origins, prevails.

Antonomasia's severing is at work in the nominally Mexican setting of acts 2 and 3. Mexico is a toponym that seems to have floated free of geography: *El rufián dichoso* does not represent daily realities of Mexican life. At the same time, the word "México" in this play has to do with the extension of imperial power in precisely the way Nebrija feared it might: it is where the relationship between propriety and property is troubled. Cervantes's skewing of the relationship between propriety and property invokes and playfully distorts the politics of possession.[7] Words in Cervantes's play, no matter how proper, seem never quite to belong to one character; their promiscuousness – emblematized by a paean to Venus – suggests a permeable and iterated self. Refracting the world of normative desire through a queer dialogue of old and new, *El rufián dichoso* represents the problem of possession from an anamorphic perspective.

De Armas Wilson, Fuchs, and Velasco, among others, have demonstrated that the production of meaning in Cervantes's texts is intimately related to the construction of gender. Other interpretations of Cervantes's drama have set aside queerness in order to focus on a differently gendered set of issues: Cervantes's possible rebuke of Lope's *comedia nueva*. However, reading Cervantes's plays as simply a Parthian shot from he who found no "pájaros en los nidos de antaño" (birds in the nests of yesteryear), or as a form of symbolic violence between male rivals, obscures the complexities of the sexual politics at work in

El rufián dichoso.[8] In short, seeing this play as a tool with which to rebuff a rival can distort the intimacy of same-sex relationships in *El rufián dichoso* and risks missing altogether what a ruffian's *dicha* (blessedness or good fortune) might be in the space of this play.

El rufián dichoso is both a dare and a show. Good fortune, the ruffian's *dicha*, is never just one thing in a play that is defined by hybridity and resistance to categorization. Taking *El rufián dichoso* seriously both as a work of drama – in which a limited company of actors plays more than three dozen characters – and as a readerly work – neither entirely closet drama nor playtext – makes perceptible that identity, sexuality, and gender operate as unrelated variables that become contingent only in the constructedness of history.

Cruz and *comedia* between Worlds

At the opening of act 1, Lugo is a glamorous if ersatz rufián; as Zimic and Henry explain, Lugo is not a true pícaro although he acts like one.[9] Taking holy orders, Lugo becomes Cruz – a surname that chiasmically invokes the character's double life – and travels to Mexico with his sidekick Lagartija (who reluctantly abandons the underworld of Seville – or *hampa sevillana* – to become fray Antonio). Cruz dies having lived holy life worthy of canonization. Thacker stresses that the historical personage upon which Cruz was based was never actually canonized, making this not quite a *comedia de santos*.[10] Neither entirely a ruffian nor officially a saint, Núñez Rivera calls Lugo/Cruz's life "baciyélmica," both fish and fowl, while Friedman draws attention to Lugo/Cruz's "range of identities, each enacted self-consciously."[11] Much of the plot – e.g. Cruz's ordination and transatlantic journey – takes place offstage or between the acts, while what happens onstage is frequently episodic and vaguely allegorical, as if the action onstage were always looking beyond itself. These tics in the play's construction have led critics – Canavaggio, Close, Rosa Rivero, Thacker, Zimic – to debate the play's dramatic unity.[12] Thacker helpfully explains that Cervantes's interest is form rather than unity, using accretion and a "chronological building up of the elements" to create a commentary on dramatic action; Rosa Rivero says categorically that the play manifests a total lack of unity of action.[13]

Zugasti definitively demonstrated that *El rufián dichoso* echoes its hagiographic sources more insistently than critics had perceived: the play depicts events that hew close to Juan de Marieta's *Historia ecclesiástica* (1596). Cervantes's play is both about history – closely following historical source texts – and about historiography: characters often pause to summarize (generally unreliably) what the audience has just seen. In one such instance of retelling highlighted by Núñez Rivera, Lugo recounts his past exploits in a passage laden with rhymes that are alternately forced (*rufo/pantufo*) or queasily perfect (*pasatiempo/tiempo*):

> … procurar que ningún rufo
> se entone do yo estuviere,
> y que estime, sea quien fuere,
> la suela de mi pantufo. [*sic*]
> Estas y otras cosas tales
> hago por mi pasatiempo,
> demás que rezo algún tiempo
> los salmos penitenciales.

> (… making sure that no pimp shoots his mouth off if I'm around and that he pays me respect, whoever he is, down to the sole of my shoe. That's the stuff I do for fun, and then sometimes I pray a penitential psalm.)[14]

This is unsubtle, conspicuous rhyming in a passage restating the plot of a play that mirrors a hagiographic antecedent. Taken together, rhyming, restating, and mirroring – sound, structure, and source – create a layered strategy that foregrounds reiteration.

One of the key layers of this iterative strategy is the interaction between the acotaciones (stage directions) and what transpires onstage. For example, the play's first stage directions, its very first words, draw attention to the word "gancho":

> *Salen LUGO, envainando una daga de* ganchos, *y el LOBILLO y* GANCHOSO, *rufianes. LUGO viene como estudiante, con una media sotana, un broquel en la cinta y una daga de* ganchos, *que no ha de traer espada* [emphasis mine].

> (Lugo enters, sheathing a curved dagger, with Lobillo and Ganchoso. Lugo is dressed as a student, with a short gown, a buckler at his waist and a curved dagger rather than a sword.)

From "ganchos" to "Ganchoso" to "ganchos" (again), the repetition is so notable that Lugo's first line sounds like a response to the author of the stage direction: "No se repita" (Don't repeat).[15] Readers have the sense that Lugo, in Pirandellesque fashion, rebukes the playwright as much as he addresses Lobillo.[16] From the outset, pounding polyptoton – "ganchos," "Ganchoso," "ganchos" – and metatheatrical commentary about repetition – "No se repita" – are motifs in *El rufián dichoso*.

Repetition is theorized by allegorical "ninfas" or nymphs who appear at the beginning of act 2 (and, Maria Grazia Profeti subtly suggests, drone on a little long).[17] The nymphs enter, the stage directions indicate, "cada una con su tarjeta en el brazo: en la una viene escrito 'Curiosidad,' en la otra, 'Comedia'" (each with a card on the arm: on one is written *Curiosidad* [Curiosity] and on the other *Comedia*).[18] Their identities are established definitively with these cards or "tarjetas." Despite this, the first lines the characters speak seem painfully lumpish:

CURIOSIDAD: Comedia.

COMEDIA: Curiosidad ...

At first blush, it appears that Cervantes neither attempts any subtlety nor asks the audience to discern the characters' identities (identities that Curiosidad and Comedia are literally wearing on their sleeves).

One way of understanding this is to envision the scene as very stiff: perhaps instead of permitting identity to unfold through action, Cervantes wants to draw our attention to the overlapping systems of identification that Aurelio González calls "double theatrical textuality": what readers read in the stage directions, what spectators read on the cards of costumed bodies, and the lines that are spoken by the characters.[19] In the introduction to their edition of the play, Jenaro Talens and Nicholas Spadaccini suggest that Cervantes writes for a more discerning audience than did Lope. But Comedia and Curiosidad's ham-handed introductions would make even the unwashed *vulgo* ask, Why is Cervantes treating us like idiots?

One answer, to paraphrase Peter Schjeldahl, is that even Cervantes had Monday mornings. Another, following A.A. Parker's defence of Calderón's worst writing, is that if the writing is bad, it is bad on purpose: if he "*wanted* to write in 'good taste' he probably also *wanted* to write in 'bad taste.'"[20] A third answer is that Cervantes is up to something that has little to do with the commercial theatre of the early seventeenth century.

Many have noted that there is very little Mexican about Cruz's Mexico. Childers surmises that Cervantes sets much of the action of acts 2 and 3 in Cruz's convent in order to avoid depicting daily life; Henry, quite daringly, argues that Cruz's Mexico is akin to Pablos's Indies in the *Buscón*: a longed-for paradise of transformation to which the character, stuck in a picaresque purgatory, never arrives: "Relocation to Mexico may not connote any possibility of reform."[21] The uncertain reality of Cruz's Mexico invites the audience to reflect on what we see *instead* of a journey from one world to another: Curiosidad and Comedia's dialogue.

As Thacker explains, the placement of Curiosidad and Comedia's scene is odd: it is at the beginning of act 2 but, because act 1 is so much longer than the subsequent two acts, almost exactly halfway through the play.[22] Both eccentric and in the middle, their dialogue serves as a bridge between worlds, Thacker says, and between forms of betweenness (from not-quite-ruffian to not-quite-saint in a place not-quite-identifiable as Mexico).[23]

Another problem of identification, Thacker explains, arises because the audience has probably seen the actors playing Comedia and Curiosidad play different roles in act 1. He suggests that it may be logical to cast the actress who had played the prostitute Antonia in act 1 in the role of Comedia in act 2. Curiosidad, meanwhile, is probably played by a male actor; as a result, the audience may genuinely have trouble seeing beyond Antonia's reappearance and Curiosidad's transvestism so as to discern the scene's allegorical nature.[24]

Curiosidad and Comedia, as a pair, represent related transformations: if the audience has trouble recognizing Curiosidad because of her gender, Curiosidad, explains Thacker, struggles to identify Comedia because of her genre.[25] They are both dressed "bizarramente" (extravagantly), but Comedia is dressed in the new style and Curiosidad in the old ("antiguos trajes"), at the very moment that Lugo is becoming Cruz and travelling to New Spain.[26] The dialogue between Curiosidad and Comedia takes place in a liminal space between old and new, Seville and Mexico, Lugo and Cruz; what is allegorized is the no man's land between uncertain gender and confusing genre.

Throughout *El rufián dichoso*, the fact that actors constantly take on new and newly gendered roles makes it as difficult for the audience to recognize the characters as it is for Curiosidad to recognize Comedia. The audience's problem of perception, in this scene, is solved by the "tarjetas," the cards actors carry in order to be legible as allegorical characters. More broadly, palimpsestic characterization, roles reassigned and overwritten, read and performed carves out a hybrid space where, to borrow Fuchs's terms, "narrated transvestism" meets "staged transvestism."[27]

Comedia and Curiosidad's scene functions as a lens of queer refraction. What we see on the other side of their scene, the place Cervantes calls Mexico, is the spot where the desires of Seville return reconfigured and regendered. To understand how Mexico becomes a locus of reconfiguration, where what is old becomes new, it will be helpful to return to act 1, to the beginning of Lugo's journey towards Mexico, and the nature of the genre to which Cervantes nods: the *comedia de santos*.

Historiography, Hagiography, and Queerness

The *comedia nueva* delights in recounting histories and in populating its stage with historical personages. Perhaps no subgenre of the *comedia* engages with historical narratives more concertedly than the *comedia de santos*, biographical plays about the path to sainthood. Nevertheless, the relationship of hagiography to the *comedia de santos* is complicated. As *the* canonical genre of historiography, hagiography exists as an argument for canonization, the point at which what would otherwise be fable is ratified as truth. Hagiography is the narrative miracle by which the fabulous becomes factual.

The *comedia de santos,* on the other hand, is frequently the most visually stunning of all the *comedia*'s commercial subgenres: characters take flight to Paradise, fall to Hell, demons appear, boils and bubas disappear, the lame rise up, enemies of the faith are brought low. The subtext of the *comedia de santos* is that visual excess is good for the box office.

The narrative stuffing of almost all hagiography is the basic idea that what exists on earth persists after death. Visual excess generally meets persistence after death in the third act of a *comedia de santos*. Lope de Vega's *San Isidro Labrador*, for example, stages the persistence of sanctity in the body of the departed saint; in a sense we watch the cadaver become a miracle-working relic in which a residue of the saint's holiness and power lingers. Saintly, narrative continuity from life to death is most certainly not what Cervantes is after.[28]

Act 1 of *El rufián dichoso* recalls Diana de Armas Wilson's summary of male intimacy in "El curioso impertinente": "Two men trafficking in the body of a woman without her leave."[29] A "dama," just after professing her desire for Lugo, watches him discreetly inform her husband of the danger to his honour; "¿Qué es lo que tratan los dos? / ¿Si es de mí?" ("What are those two men talking about," she wonders, "What if it's me?").[30] It is.[31]

Once in Mexico, the traffic is not in women's bodies, but rather in women's roles. The final words of the play, stage directions, suggest that all of the female roles in this play can be played by only two women ("todas las figuras de mujer de esta comedia las pueden hacer solas dos mujeres").[32] As Barbara Fuchs notes, normally the "end of the play brings the end of the ambiguity," but the end of the ambiguity in *El rufián dichoso* is not the clarity we Queer expecting.[33] What is clarified is that, with only two women actors, some female characters were to have been played by men, be they ninfas, Almas, or damas.

If act 1 is characterized by ruffians' strutting and posturing and the prostituting of women's bodies, in acts 2 and 3, Cervantes creates an extravagantly homosocial space, in which men's pleasure and emotional fulfilment are represented through the recasting of women's voices and dress. "Cambalaches," or swaps, and traffic are constant, but the "archetypes of exchange" that de Armas Wilson marvellously elucidates in the case of the "Curioso impertinente" allow the self to persist beyond gender in *El rufián dichoso*.

The homosocial spaces of the final two acts are defined by Cruz and his companion Antonio (the reconstructed Lagartija). Antonio provides the hagiographic point of view and is the only witness to Cruz's temptations and triumphs. Cruz implores his friend to recount the story faithfully: "Amigo fray Antonio, di a los padres / mi vida, de quien fuiste buen testigo" (My friend, friar Antonio, tell the priests of my life, you who have been its faithful witness).[34] The name "Antonio," as substitute for "Lagartija," denotes a character who uneasily separates himself from the world of the hampa to which he belongs, just as antonomasia, to paraphrase Quintilian, is the separation of an epithet from the word to which it belongs. If Lugo/Cruz's traffic in the body of a woman without her knowledge recalls the context of Lotario and Anselmo, "o como se llamaban por antonomasia, los dos amigos," Antonio harks to that of la infanta Antonomasia – the world of the ducal palace in the second part of *Don Quijote* – in a play of separation, swaps, and similitudes.[35]

Antonio's star turn as hagiographic witness reaches its apogee in act 2, when he witnesses Cruz being tempted by nymphs and then watches as Cruz painstakingly negotiates the salvation of an unrepenting woman. At the opening of act 3, what Antonio had seen in act 2 becomes a historical account recounted by others that bears almost no relation to Antonio's experience. In other words, the retelling of Cristóbal de la Cruz's life within the play distorts the events we watch Antonio witness. The effect, for the audience, is to see in real time the work of history as trope, through history's narrative separation from the events to which it refers. In addition to Cruz's exchange of one form of life for another – ruffian for friar – the name changes – Lugo to Cruz, Lagartija to Antonio – and the shift from Seville to Mexico, the traffic in narratives that overwrite and alter the past takes the place of plot.

The events from act 2 that become history at the outset of act 3 begin with the assurance in a stage direction that "Todo esto es verdad de la historia" (All of this is historical truth).[36] Comedia and Curiosidad's allegorical scene at the beginning of act 2 prepared us for the contingency of history and theatre: "Ya represento mil cosas / no en relación, como de antes, / sino en hecho" ("I now represent a thousand things," says Comedia, "not through the spoken word, as I used to, but through action").[37] The action or "hecho" represented in act 2 concerns Ana de Treviño, a woman on her deathbed who obstinately refuses to confess her sins or prepare for the afterlife.

A physician examines Treviño and finds her body to be perfectly legible; he reads "esta verdad a la clara" (this truth clearly): she will fall to death's knife ("cuchillo").[38] The physician is particularly concerned with discursive propriety, his own as well as Ana's; he insists that his professional duties oblige him to speak of her coming death – "Mi oficio me obliga a decillo," "[M]i oficio me obliga" – and to advise her to stop joking around and confess. Neither the physician's cajoling – "quédense aparte las burlas" (leave aside your joking) – nor warning – "Hablando se ha de quedar muerta" (if you keep talking, you will die) – make her straighten up. Orthodoxy and recalcitrance are perfectly juxtaposed in the physician and his patient: a history truthfully written in the stage directions, a collection of symptoms correctly read by a physician, a professional obligation to speak fulfilled, and a patient's inappropriate flippancy scolded. Decorum prevails.

The play leaves Treviño at this critical moment and cuts to Cruz kneeling in prayer, about to be accosted by lascivious nymphs, or more accurately, six men "vestidos como ninfas lascivamente" (lasciviously as nymphs).[39] The nymphs – "prostitutes of the *hampa*," Thacker clarifies – tempt Cruz by singing to him of the sensual pleasures of his former life. They sing, "No hay cosa que sea gustosa / sin Venus blanda amorosa" (There is nothing pleasing without tender, loving Venus). This inverts the aching, unquenched desire that Antonia had expressed for Lugo in act 1:

No me lleva a mí tras él
Venus blanda y amorosa,
sino su aguda ganchosa
y su acerado broquel.

(It is not Venus, tender and loving, that has me hooked, but his sharp curved dagger and his steel buckler.)[40]

Antonia speaks these words to Lugo's patron, the Inquisitor Tello de Sandoval, in a scene that mirrors the scene of nymphs and Cruz. Just as the nymphs interrupt Cruz at prayer, Antonia, in act 1, speaks her "Venus blanda y amorosa," interrupting the Inquisitor as he prays, "Domine, ad adiuvandum me festina" (Make haste, O God, to deliver me).[41] The bridge between Antonia's "Venus blanda y amorosa" spoken to the Inquisitor in act 1, and the nymphs' "Venus blanda amorosa" sung to Cruz in act 2, is the dialogue between Comedia and Curiosidad. Cross-dressing the tongue, to borrow Elizabeth Harvey's phrase, Antonia's words come back in the voices of the male nymphs.[42]

Whether or not Tello the Inquisitor is tempted by Antonia, Lugo/Cruz clearly is not in act 1. Antonia calls him "un leño" (a blockhead), attributing his inattentiveness to inexperience, and later calls him a man in name only ("¿Hombre? / … no tiene más el nombre").[43] As a man *in name only*, he becomes a visual figure for the emptiness of the epithet: he is, as de Armas Wilson might have it, "troped by antonomasia."[44] The curved dagger, which symbolizes Lugo for Antonia, is what he wears, the stage directions say, in lieu of a sword ("no ha de traer espada"). Women are never a serious temptation for Lugo. For his part, when Lugo/Cruz sees Antonia, he exclaims, "*Demonio*.... ¿Por qué me persigues?" (*Devil*, why do you hound me?).[45] The nymphs, when they reprise Antonia's "tender Venus," are accompanied by "*demonios* vestidos a lo antiguo" (*devils* dressed in the old style).[46] There is a devilry that haunts Cruz, but it is not feminine.

The singing and dancing of the nymphs produces a moment that is both a conspicuously metatheatrical masque and, the stage direction insists with unmistakable irony, historically accurate: "Todo esto desta máscara y visión fue verdad que así lo cuenta la historia del santo" (This entire masque and vision were true and are recounted just so in the history of the saint).[47] A second stage direction, even more pointed in its irony, insists on the simultaneous theatricality and veracity of the scene: "Todo esto fue así, que no es visión supuesta, apócrifa ni mentirosa" (All of this happened just this way, and this is not an invented, nor apocryphal, nor fabricated vision).[48]

This exaggeration and artifice – men playing nymphs and devils, dressed lasciviously and in the old style, in a vision that is both masque and history – parallels the scene between Comedia – dressed in the modern style – and Curiosidad – dressed in the old. It also shares aesthetic terrain with Sontag's memorable explanation of camp as sensibility, and the spectacle of the Condesa Trifaldi and her *dueñas barbudas*, identified by both Fuchs and Velasco as campy.[49] It is certainly possible to love this scene and doubt that the demon/nymphs' draggy, old-timey, singing burlesque communicates to the audience a powerfully eroticized visualization of Cruz's inner temptation. The stage direction, protesting too much – "no es visión supuesta, apócrifa ni mentirosa" – guarantees our incredulity.

Whether one reads this scene as straight or camp, as hagiography or burlesque, it is difficult to make sense of the role of historiography given the surplus of visual signification. On the one hand, Cruz's resistance to temptation is one of the key acts of holiness we see him perform and is thus crucial to the hagiographic narrative. On the other, Antonio alone witnesses the nymphs' sensual song and dance. Cruz never opens his eyes.[50] Antonio, then, is the only source for this history, and a very problematic source for two reasons.

First, Cruz claims not to believe him – "Debía de estar durmiendo y / soñaba" (You must have been asleep and dreaming) – and Antonio claims not to believe his own eyes: "[H]e visto lo que aún no creo" (I just saw what I still can't believe).[51] Second, Antonio watches and listens while Antonia's expression of overwhelming attraction from act 1 – "Venus blanda y amorosa" – is adapted by men dressed lasciviously as nymphs; this so complicates the vectors of desire that Cruz's spiritual triumph – the quiddity of the hagiography – hardly seems to matter.

Thacker argues that the ninfas are a "complex abstraction of Lugo/ Cruz's inner temptations." That very plausible psychological explanation does not quite explain the dramatic extravagance, why Cruz's temptation echoes Antonia in the presence of Antonio, or why neither Cruz nor Antonio will aver to what happened. Although the characters dare not speak of it, the play as closet drama – the stage directions to which only readers are privvy – makes clear that the masque constitutes a lesson in history making. It was not invented, not apocryphal, and not fabricated. Antonio calls it, hedging, "la no fantástica danza" (the not fantastical dance).[52] The nymphs' musical number – in all its fey, theatrical glory – is the point at which we see the fantasticity of theatre meet the fabulousness of history.

Taken together, the nymphs' musical number and the scene in which Ana de Treviño rejects her physician's enjoinders make clear the discursive stakes: there exists a world of discursive propriety characterized by legibility, reliability, and duty, on the one hand, and on the other, the realm of fabulous history in which Antonio is our unreliable guide.[53]

Cristóbal de la Cruz and Ana de Treviño meet so soon after the masque that Cruz has to implore Antonio, "esas danzas no imagine" (stop imagining those dances) during the encounter.[54] Treviño is on her deathbed, insisting to a cleric, the Clérigo, that her sins are such that God's forgiveness would be illogical. The Clérigo genuinely seems to believe that the way to save Treviño's soul is to recite the Vulgate ad nauseum, warning her that he has an inexhaustible store of Latin quotations – "[O]tras muchas [alabanzas]" – and threatening never to stop reciting them: "[I]n aeternum cantabo."[55] He is a pedant, cut from the same cloth as her physician; Treviño calls the Clérigo a "moledor" or "grinder."[56] Mercifully, Cruz steps in, at first continuing the Clérigo's tiresome Latin quotations, prattling in *redondillas*, and calling Treviño a fool ("insipiens"), before raising the metrical stakes by shifting to stately *octavas reales*. When Treviño follows suit, trading *octavas reales* blow for blow, Cruz retreats to *redondillas*. Again, she pursues him into *redondillas*, parrying. Getting nowhere, Cruz – in what Childers calls a "momentary flash of inspiration" – decides to strike a deal.[57] He proposes a swap, a "cambalache." Cruz will assume the "grave cargo" or terrible cost of her sins and give her the carryforward of his severe religious observance:

> Pon tú el arrepentimiento
> de tu parte, y verás luego
> cómo en tus obras me entrego
> y tú en aquellas que cuento.

> (For your part, you put up the repentance and then you will see how I give myself over to good works on your behalf and you will get the benefit of those past good works I was telling you about.)[58]

All she must do is confess.

Treviño is sceptical. She wants "fiadores," guarantors who back the deal ("aseguren el concierto"), and witnesses.[59] "¿A quién me dais?," she asks flatly, somewhere between "Whom do you offer me?" and "Who you got?"[60] For guarantors, Cruz, antes up Jesus Christ of Nazareth and his blessed mother, the Virgin Mary; the witnesses will be all the saints in heaven. Treviño asks that the contract be read aloud in act 2's final *redondillas*; sensing the upper hand, Cruz switches to strangely dissonant blank hendecasyllables. He will trade all his good works ("todas las buenas obras"), all his spiritual capital, and "en contracambio" (in exchange) he will assume her debts or sins, the only catch being that she confess ("ponga la confesión").[61] This is a blood oath, sealed with the blood Christ shed.[62]

Once Treviño supplies her "Sí, acepto" (I accept), it almost feels as though she had negotiated poorly. Treviño asks for immediate confession but the Clérigo is too busy praising God to answer while Antonio speaks only of Cruz. Treviño, eager to close the deal, demands, "Padre, no me dilate este remedio" (Father, do not delay my cure).[63] Instead of answering, Cruz issues instructions to Antonio about properly marking the spiritual conquest over a new penitent ("esta nueva penitente").[64] Blockheaded men are so busy trafficking in a woman's soul that they cannot hear her asking to close the deal.

When Cruz finally invites Treviño to go somewhere to confess – his "Vamos do estemos solos" (Let's find someplace where we can be alone) makes one think that Cruz has a plan for everything but this – she mutters an exasperated, "En buen hora" (Finally).[65] Cruz believes he has notched the win, but Treviño has bargained hard and saved her soul. She even earns an epithet – "bienaventurada pecadora" or "blessed sinner" – that neatly recalls Cruz's: *El rufián dichoso*.

Act 3 begins with a Ciudadano and a silent Prior taking the stage to recount what we just saw in act 2. It is a historiographical meditation on the limits of representation that parallels Comedia and Curiosidad's theoretical reflections on the *comedia* at the beginning of act 2. The Ciudadano marvels at the ineffability of Treviño's salvation: he cannot "referilla / con aquellas razones que merece" (transmit the story with the details that it deserves).[66] This comes as a surprise to the audience; the entire encounter between Cruz and Treviño was carefully negotiated orally and in contractual language. In the Ciudadano's version in act 3, Treviño's reaction to Cruz's proposed exchange was immediate and overwhelming: "[A]lzó al momento un piadoso grito / al cielo y confesión pidió llorando" (She lifted at that very moment a pious cry to heaven and she tearfully asked for confession).[67] Treviño's actual words upon hearing of the proposed exchange in act 2 were: "¿Cómo puede hacer eso?," "¿Dónde están los fiadores …? ¿A quién me dais?," "… los testigos, ¿quién serán?" "El contrato referid" ("How can you do that?," "Where are the guarantors?," "Whom will you give me?," "Who will the witnesses be?," "Recite me back the contract").[68] It is possible that the tears the Ciudadano speaks of were shed offstage, but as Núñez Rivera argues, almost no time passes between the acts.[69] What is more, "voz humilde y corazón contrito" noticeably fails to describe the Treviño the audience knows.

This historicizing irritates Luzifer, and what rankles him most is that Cruz's "alta, famosa y verdadera historia" will be told.[70] Which version might he mean? The Ciudadano's decorous version embodies authorized history, steering well clear of what Antonio witnessed. The Ciudadano's tale is "verdadera historia" in the early modern sense: a subgenre of patently improbable accounts that masqueraded as history.[71] Mary Malcolm Gaylord referred to the preposterous "historias verdaderas" as the "great linguistic cross-dresser of the day."[72] The twist in *El rufián dichoso* is that what is improbable about the Ciudadano's "verdadera historia" is the strained propriety of the obviously inaccurate history. Neither Treviño's deal making – interrupted by the ninfas' lascivious dance – nor the doubled mirror images of the "bienaventurada pecadora" and "rufián dichoso," Antonia and Antonio, have a place in the Ciudadano's hagiography. The Prior who silently accompanies the Ciudadano seems to function as the rubric of officialdom.

As was the case with the singing nymphs – a lavish spectacle that we see but which Cruz refuses to – we are left to wonder what the purpose of the scene between Cruz and Treviño was if it is so quickly to be overwritten by the Ciudadano's competing account. Once again, Antonio is our only onstage, ocular witness to what the stage directions claim is historical fact.[73] We, the reading audience, watched Antonio see what he saw and we read what we read. The Ciudadano's version of history cannot undo that. His duplication of accounts causes us to reflect on Treviño's stunning triumph. Hers is a story that cannot be made to fit a hagiography. She may at first blush seem to be just another stained sheep or *ovejuela almagrada*, but she remained a canny negotiator until the end, outlasting the Clérigo, duelling with Cruz, and finally convincing him to perform a miracle on her behalf. This is certainly how Luzifer sees it; for Luzifer, Cruz is simply a "cambiador, que en usuras trata" ("trader" or a "swapper" who "deals in usury") and Treviño is a public woman who snatches ("arrebata") her salvation.[74] The deal, according to Lucifer himself, is not on the up and up.

Thanks to Zugasti, we know that the swap – Cruz's accrued holiness for Treviño's lifetime of iniquity – was, in fact, part of the source hagiography. In Marieta's biography of Cruz, as in the play, Treviño's sins transform him into a leprous, disfigured monster. The Prior calls Cruz's sores a "borrado sobrescrito," which Childers analyses as a "palimpsest" that records the repeated rewritings of history.[75] This "sobrescrito," both sign and overwriting, are the physical reminder of the words that could not be erased: Cruz's deal with Treviño. The "sobrescrito" also recalls the fabulous history that the Ciudadano attempted to erase or "borrar."[76] Cruz's body, like Treviño's, is supposed to be classifiable as the artefact of a salvific trajectory; men of authority find in Treviño's moribund body and Cruz's monstrous body the legible signs of straight history. The historicizing Ciudadano reads in Cruz's life a story of fortitude: "[L]eo / la paciencia de Job" (I read the patience of Job).[77] Cervantes's readers may hear the "borra que nos cubre": the *dueñas doloridas'* beards.[78]

Queer *cambalaches*

Job was a chit in a cosmic deal; Satan dared God to try Job by taking away Job's riches and afflicting him with boils from the sole of his foot unto the crown of his head. Reading Cruz's sores or "llagas" in light of Job's boils, the Ciudadano concludes that Cruz's suffering is edifying. Very differently, the demonic forces that muster in act 3 – Saquiel, Visiel, and Lucifer himself, who presumably struck the deal to test Job – feel cheated. Saquiel exclaims in disgust, "¡Y que tuviese Dios por bueno y justo / tal cambalache!" (How can God have thought this switcharoo was just and good!).[79] Visiel calls it "mohatra," or corrupt double-dealing.[80] Whether "cambalache" or "mohatra," the devils have an obvious theological point: we cannot atone for one another in this life. Treviño and Cruz's swap is more *Freaky Friday* than soteriology.

There is no theological tradition within the Roman Catholic Church by which human beings who are not the Son of Man can ransom one another from damnation, or trade places in the ledger book of sin. Cruz places salvation in a bourse where good works and sin are fungible instruments to be traded. Saquiel and Visiel know that human beings do not get to play Jesus Christ for each other.[81] But that is not precisely Saquiel's complaint. Instead, he says that an eternity in Hell, on the one hand, and living out one's final years as a leper, on the other, are not commensurate forms of suffering:

Que no es equivalente aquesta lepra
que padece este fraile, a los tormentos
que pasará doña Ana en la otra vida.

(That leprosy that the friar is suffering is not equivalent to the torments doña Ana would have suffered in the next life.)

Saquiel here follows Aquinas, who said that the trade in obviously mis-valued objects is sinful fraud that destroys justice itself.[82]

As a story of Christian charity, Cruz and Treviño's switcharoo or "cambalache" is theologically suspect but historically accurate. Zugasti makes clear that the episode, minus the cross-dressing, is taken from the pages of Marieta's contemporaneous hagiography.[83] The Ciudadano's version of history elides altogether Cruz's role as trader, hustler, and swapper – *cambiador*, *mojatrero*, and *cambalachero* – and skips over the ninfas' campy routine. (Saquiel, Visiel, and Luzifer render the events more convincingly.) Thus, *El rufián dichoso* entails at least three versions of Cruz's life. The first is Marieta's history and other possible historio-graphic antecedents. The second is what the audience sees as a queer staging of Cruz's history, adducing to Marieta's biography sensuous scenes of gender ambiguity in the performance of the ninfas and later, as we shall see, the Almas. This is Cruz's life seen from Antonio's inti-mate perspective, refracted through the lens of Comedia and Curiosi-dad. The third comprises the instances of historicizing within the play, as when the Ciudadano recasts Cruz's life as straight history.

Cruz dies offstage.[84] His final thirteen years are recounted in two scenes that again draw us back to the ducal palace of *Don Quijote*. Cruz's final years are initially recounted by three "Almas," or souls, dressed in white taffeta tunics and white veils ("tunicelas de tafetán blanco" with "velos sobre los rostros").[85] The debates over the gender of the *dueñas doloridas* recounted by Velasco are once again neatly resolved in *El rufián dichoso*: at least one of these veils covers a beard. That is, with three Almas onstage and only two women to play female parts, at least one of the Almas is a male actor.

It is not just the veiled beard that alludes to the world of the ducal palace, however. The Almas' white taffeta tunics ("tunicelas de tafetán blanco") echo Altisidora's "tunicela de tafetán blanco" when Altisidora was, in Don Quijote's opinion, returned from death to life ("opinión de don Quijote, vuelta de muerte a vida").[86] The Almas' scene occupies a point between the transcendence of the souls' eternal hallelujahs and the decidedly terrestrial erotics of Altisidora's visit to Don Quijote's room, analysed by Gallego Zarzosa. Between transcendence and eroticism, uncertainty reigns. At one point, it seems as though the Almas will ascend to Heaven with Cruz – "al alma devota suya / bien será la acompañemos" – but they then decide to join the earthly throng of mourners led by Antonio:

> … mezclémonos agora
> entre su acompañamiento,
> escuchando el sentimiento
> de este su amigo que llora.

> (… let's mingle now among those who accompany the body, listening to the sadness of his crying friend.)[87]

What they hear from Antonio, "este su amigo," is their own words. The story the Almas had told of Cruz's final years – "Trece años ha que ha vivido / llagado" (Thirteen years he has lived with these sores) – is echoed by a stricken Antonio: "Trece años ha que lidias / por ser caritativo" (Thirteen years you have struggled because you were so charitable).[88]

As was the case in the ninfas' scene – in which Antonio witnessed the recasting of Antonia's words – there is here a cross-gendered linguistic directive by which lines are reassigned across performative contexts. While the Almas tell their story of the "thirteen years," tripping along in *redondillas*, Antonio drops into sombre unrhymed *liras* to announce the final switch or "cambalache": Cruz's body, now free from sores, has become a collection of relics.

To be sure, the ducal palace of the second part of *Don Quijote* and the New Spain of *El rufián dichoso* reflect conventionalized practices of gender ambiguity. In January of 1616, as José Manuel Lucía Megías documents, the processions honouring the Immaculate Conception featured not only the famous Don Quixote, Rocinante, and Sancho, but also a young boy playing the part of the Virgen Mary and dressed in a tunic of white taffeta ("tunicela de tafetán blanco").[89] I do not contend that the "hermoso niño" who played the role of María would have been interpreted as an instance of cross-dressing. It is obvious, however, that the beautiful young boy as holy mother embodied multiple forms of ambiguity, including at the level of grammatical gender: "[M]uchos dudaron, según iba hermoso y quieto, si era viva [*sic*] o de bulto" (Many doubted because he was so beautiful and still, whether he was alive or a statue). Like Altisidora, who for Don Quijote existed in a state between animate and inanimate – "vuelta de muerte a vida" – the similarly dressed "hermoso niño" was either alive ("viva") or a statue ("de bulto"). The *dueñas doloridas*, the ninfas and Almas of *El rufián dichoso*, the niño hermoso – who like Altisidora and the Almas wears a "tunicela de tafetán blanco" – all perform gendered hybridity.

Dichas and Decoherence

On the page and in the universe, quantum mechanics says, a single entity may occupy two spaces: Sancho's *rucio*, like all matter, may be anywhere and anywhere else simultaneously. But telling an actor to be two places at once is not a helpful direction. *El rufián dichoso* has forty-one characters. This is a conservative count and depends, for example, on all the "Ciudadanos" or citizens being the same from one scene to the next (which does not entirely make dramatic sense). The superabundance of characters and the peculiar *acotación* indicating that "todas las figuras de mujer de esta comedia las pueden hacer solas dos mujeres" have led to considerable speculation about the practicality of staging this play. Vern Williamsen believed that *El rufián dichoso* was "nearly unproduceable as theater." Thacker calls the stage directions "novelesque," suggesting that some experience of the play beyond dramatic representation is implied by the play's text. José Padilla adapted *El rufián dichoso* for nine actors – three of them women – playing twenty-eight characters. Padilla cut the ninfas and the Almas.

In general, what Padilla had to cut (or shave) and what editors have fixed (or misgendered) trace very neatly the play's queerness. The problems of *El rufián dichoso*'s representability, noticed by so many, suggest that it is concerned with problems of representation. It is only through visualizing the nearly impossible staging of the play that its seemingly disparate elements – ninfas and Almas, Antonia and Antonio and Ángel, and the play's general exuberance – become aesthetically integrated.

If there were to be only two women actors, and most companies would be hard-pressed to roster more than ten male actors, a reasonable number of possible actors for *El rufián dichoso* might be twelve. It would also make sense to avoid having actors play different roles in consecutive scenes. Furthermore, the demands of the roles of Lugo/Cruz and Lagartija/Antonio probably mean that the actors playing those leading roles could not play others. We might then imagine one possible distribution of the roles this way:

Actor 1: Lugo
Actor 2: Lagartija
Actor 3: Lobillo/ciego/Ángel/Ninfa 4/clérigo/Alma 1
Actor 4: Ganchoso/uno/Peralta/Ninfa 3/Visiel
Actor 5: Corchete 1/Músico/Gilberto/criado/Ciudadano 1
Actor 6: Corchete 2/Músico/Criado/Ciudadano
Actor 7: Alguacil/Pastelero/Médico/Ninfa 1/Saquiel
Actor 8: Dama/ Curiosidad /Ninfa 1/Alma 2
Actor 9: Antonia/Comedia/Ana/Alma 3
Actor 10: Marido/Padre/Prior
Actor 11: Tello/Ninfa 6/Fraile
Actor 12: Ninfa 5/Lucifer/Virrey

To pull this off would be as much an act of athleticism as acting. There would be sprinting backstage, panting onstage, and the audience would unquestionably recognize actors in different roles from one scene to the next. The predominant spectacle of the play would be the quick shedding and adoption of roles. If a single actor played the role of Cruz and no other, the "cambiador" himself would become a point of visual stability, not an example of picaresque transformation. The shedding, the swirl, and the sweat would destabilize what character *means* onstage, stripping it of fixed value and making it about the repeated detaching of a role from the actor's body to which it has been assigned. It would be a visual figure of antonomasia.

The paucity of women actors, a constraint on casting seemingly arbitrarily introduced by Cervantes, makes the social machine of the theatre – the assemblage of play text, troupe, and space – represent the world in a very particular way. Male actors are spread thin and women's bodies are made scarce. One way to think about this, following Irigaray, is that through this manufacture of scarcity – by artificially creating a shortage of women's bodies – *El rufián dichoso* creates a visual fetish of sociocultural endogamy.[90] Another way to think about this is that Cervantes uses the *cambalache* to interrogate decorum: pairing unlikes, and calling attention to the production of unlikes, pieces that very nearly fit.

Anthony Cascardi has ruminated on the technical differences between "a closet drama and a theatrical representation" and the ways in which space alters "language in inestimable ways."[91] *El rufián dichoso* navigates conceptual and linguistic terrain between the two, neither entirely a readerly closet drama nor a theatrical representation, neither unhistorical nor simply hagiographic. It is in this between space, this "borrado sobrescrito," of rewriting and overwriting, that the play's performances of identity, its cross-gendered repetitions, its multiple forms of transvestism, its complicated vectors of desire, its visual excess, its wild, panting, extravagant theatricality, in short its queerness becomes suffused through the entire play.

Conclusion

What kind of *mundo* is this *teatro*? It is, as Enrique Santos's tango would have it, a queer "cambalache," a second-hand store and a swap meet where square dealing and corruption, New World and underworld, the hustler and the saint, "un gran profesor" and "un burro" ("a great professor" and "an ass"), are one and the same:

> ¡[D]a lo mismo que sea cura,
> colchonero, rey de bastos,
> caradura o polizón!

> (It doesn't matter if you're a priest, a bum, or a heavy, shamelessly a scoundrel, or you keep it on the sly.)[92]

It is a world in which stability and identity seem to melt before our eyes, coming into their fluidity.

Even when a scene ends, even when Lugo becomes Cruz, what is past is not over. Echoes and actors return in new guises. It is this persistence beyond the scene or beyond a life that *El rufián dichoso* shares with hagiography. Cruz inhabits time in a way that resists chrononormativity. And what is true of time holds for space. What the play calls Mexico is invaded by the ghosts of Lugo's Seville, creating a sense that the setting unfolds as more than one place, a hybrid. The bodies of actors become loci of erasure – one role overwrites another – as well as indices of persistence across time: the ghosts of Seville are hauntologically present in the hybridized space of Mexico.[93]

The play's first *acotación* repeatedly drew attention to the hooks and snags called "ganchos." The gancho is a marker of assumed identity (as in Ganchoso's name) and a modifier (in "daga de ganchos" it specifies a type: a curved dagger). As a stub, the "gancho" is evidence of a missing branch and the missing fruits by which the tree might be known. It indicates the taxon of no kind, or of too many kinds, inimical to the fixities of official history. As the repetition of "ganchosa" reminds us, *El rufián dichoso* creates a textual spectacle of narrative metatheatricality in which the self is a "gancho," both hook and stub, upon which one hangs an identity for as long as the scene lasts.

NOTES

1 It is not clear, for example, how many "Ciudadanos" are on stage at the beginning of act 3. One Ciudadano takes the stage to open the act (2179). Two more Ciudadanos, numbered Ciudadano 1 and Ciudadano 2, enter forty-five verses later. The first, unnumbered Ciudadano does not exit, but never speaks again. Is he Ciudadano 1?
2 Williamsen and Abraham, "Vern's Miscellaneous Notes."
3 Thacker, "Véote," 207; and McKendrick, "Writings," 147. See also Varas, "*El rufián dichoso*," 17.
4 Cervantes, *El rufián dichoso*, 101.
5 Thacker, "Véote," 214.
6 See Sonia Velázquez's chapter in this volume.
7 Mary Gaylord explains that "literary propriety" is a matter of "literary property" in Lope's oeuvre (Gaylord Randel, "Proper Language," 231–2).
8 The idea that Cervantes's plays sometimes feel stiff or on the nose because he was reaching back to a purer, more elemental theatre that predated the *comedia nueva* is related to the contention that much of Cervantes's theatre is about his distaste for the dramatic universe that Lope wrought. As Childers explains, by the end of the twentieth century, critics largely held that Cervantes's theatre was a response to and a rejection of Lope's ("Ese tan borrado sobrescrito"). However, to understand Cervantes's drama as an artefact or epiphenomenon of rivalry between two men is to hamstring our interpretation of Cervantes's plays, just as reading *Don Quijote* as a response to Rodríguez de Montalvo would impoverish our understanding of *Don Quijote*. I owe a tremendous debt to the scholars who have illuminated the differences between Cervantes's theatre and that of Lope. But to those who lament that an obtuse *vulgo* never properly rewarded Cervantes's dramatic greatness – the sour grapes school of theatre history – or complain that Lope was merely an exponent of absolutist ideologies whose

theatrical triumphs were an index of his unscrupulousness, Belardo's response might well have been "¿Pensará vuestra merced ahora que es poco trabajo hacer una comedia?" (Does your worship still think it is an easy thing to write a play?).

9 Zimic, "La caridad," 87. Henry says that Lugo "desperately" desires acceptance and so plays the role of ruffian ("Cervantine Theater," 105).

10 Thacker, "Véote," 207.

11 Núñez Rivera, *El rufián dichoso*," 122; and Friedman, "Self-Fashion Show," 41. Sancho Panza coins the term "baciyelmo" (1.44) to refer to an object that is both a barber's basin and Don Quixote's helmet. Fuchs connects the baciyelmo to *Don Quijote*'s transvestisms more broadly (*Passing for Spain*, 27).

12 Debates about the dramatic unity of *El rufián dichoso* have sometimes turned bitter, as when Casalduero dismissed Schevill and Bonilla's ideas about *El rufián dichoso* as vulgar, superficial, mistaken, confusing, mediocre, and indicative of a lack of literary training (*Sentido y forma*, 104). The most helpful summaries of critical approaches to *El rufián dichoso* are Henry's ("Cervantine Theater") and Thacker's ("Véote").

13 Thacker, "Véote," 213; and Rosa Rivero, "La acción," 236.

14 Cervantes, *El rufián dichoso*, 810–17. Cervantes has long been considered a bad versifier and a good poet; see Domínguez Caparrós, *Métrica de Cervantes*, 15–17.

15 Cervantes, *El rufián dichoso*, 2.

16 On the Pirandellesque in Cervantes's drama, see Arboleda, *Teoría y formas*, 91.

17 Profeti, "Cervantes," 558.

18 Cervantes, *El rufián dichoso*, 177.

19 González, "Espacio," 902.

20 Parker, *Allegorical Drama*, 175; emphasis in original. As Julio Baena explains, Cervantists have long made a related argument: that what appear to be errors, inconsistencies, and contradictions in fact constitute a semiotic system. Thomas A. Lathrop contends that Cervantes's intentional errors in spelling and emplotment transport readers to the world of chivalric romances ("Contradiction"). Dian Fox winningly maintains that these inconsistencies are so remarkable that readers have the sense that they have read a different iteration of part one of *Don Quijote* than Sansón Carrasco has ("Apocryphal Part One").

21 Childers, *Transnational*, 239n9; and Henry, *Signifying Self*, 134.

22 Thacker, "La figura," 122.

23 Thacker, 123.

24 Thacker's radical reinterpretation of this scene was the germ of my thinking about *El rufián dichoso*. In the princeps, "Curiosidad" when referring

to herself uses a masculine noun – "soy tu amigo" ("I am your [male] friend"; 1228) – and a masculine adjective: "[Q]uedo satisfecho en parte" ("I am partly satisfied"; 1306). Although many editors fix this language by removing its cross-gendered valence, Thacker argues persuasively that to do so is a mistake. In Thacker's reading, the scene is a comical exchange between old friends: one, Curiosidad, a punctilious queen who is rather taken aback at his preening friend's new look, and Comedia, who seems to be trying a little too hard to please her new friends (128–9). I agree with Thacker that the scene may be quite funny; I also agree with Velasco and Fuchs that Cervantes's representation of gender ambiguity is not *only* funny.

25 Thacker, "La figura," 124.

26 Cervantes, *El rufián dichoso*, 1206.

27 Fuchs, *Passing for Spain*, 9.

28 In *El rufián dichoso*'s final verses, Ciudadanos or citizens crassly stumble over one another to despoil Cruz's body for relics. Lope stages the desire to take a bit of the body of the saint as a relic with rather more decorum in the third act of *San Isidro Labrador*.

29 De Armas Wilson, "Passing the Love," 15.

30 Cervantes, *El rufián dichoso*, 380–1.

31 Or it *nearly* is. As Sonia Velázquez pointed out to me in a personal communication, Lugo does not faithfully tell her story. He recasts it (and recasting is the predominant trope of the play).

32 Cervantes, *El rufián dichoso*, 249. Anderson observes that "the only stage directions that mention performers" in Cervantes's theatre "refer to female characters" ("Mothers," 34). These mentions simultaneously draw our attention to the presence of female performers and circumscribe their activity.

33 Fuchs, *Passing for Spain*, 22.

34 Cervantes, *El rufián dichoso*, 2598–9. Fathers or "padres" in the play refers equally to pimps and priests.

35 Cervantes, *Don Quijote*, 1.33. Although it was the infanta Antonomasia who was transformed into a bronze monkey ("jimia de bronce"), it is Lugo/Cruz who, according to Antonio, is made of bronze: "[D]e bronce el cuerpo" (*El rufián dichoso*, 1318).

36 Cervantes, *El rufián dichoso*, 195.

37 Cervantes, 1245–7.

38 Cervantes, 1661, 1651.

39 Cervantes, 200–1. All the nymphs could be played by men – which is what Thacker and Rosa Rivero contend – but, as I mention above, it is possible that two could be played by women. The fact that we can be certain that the nymphs are not all played by women differentiates this scene from that of the *dueñas barbudas* (bearded duennas); as Sherry Velasco notes, critics

disagree about whether the *dueñas* are played by men or women (*"Dueña Dolorida,"* 236–7).

40 Cervantes, *El rufián dichoso*, 758–61.

41 Cervantes, 723.

42 Harvey, *Ventriloquized Voices*, 15.

43 Cervantes, *El rufián dichoso*, 757, 1055–7.

44 De Armas Wilson, "Passing the Love," 17.

45 Cervantes, *El rufián dichoso*, 886–7; emphasis mine.

46 Cervantes, 201; emphasis mine. Thacker goes as far as to suggest that Comedia – dressed in the modern style – might be played by the same female actor who played Antonia ("La figura," 126).

47 Cervantes, *El rufián dichoso*, 200. Zugasti points out that Cervantes hews closely to his source texts and that finding irony in these passages may be a function of our ignorance of the antecedent hagiography ("Algo más sobre las fuentes," 506). However, Zugasti's work also helps call attention to the fact that Marieta's hagiography describes a "multitud de mozuelas en corro" ("gathering of many girls"), whereas Cervantes describes men "vestidos como ninfas, lascivamente" ("lasciviously dressed as nymphs"). Both Childers's argument that these passages indicate the "lack of conviction Cervantes felt regarding these scenes" ("Ese tan borrado sobrescrito," 258) and Zugasti's demonstration that these scenes are drawn from history, precisely as the *acotaciones* indicate, are, I believe, necessary to understand *El rufián dichoso*.

48 Cervantes, *El rufián dichoso*, 201.

49 Fuchs, *Passing for Spain*, 28; and Velasco, "Dueña Dolorida," 230. There is more work to be done on the relationship between the *dueñas barbudas* and *El rufián dichoso*. For example, the Duke and Duchess's magical steed Clavileño is here one day, the next in France, and after that in Potosí – "hoy está aquí y mañana en Francia y otro día en Potosí" (*Don Quijote*, 2.40) – and Comedia, in *El rufián dichoso*, describes her art as a map that jumps effortlessly from Germany to Guinea (1259–60).

50 Cervantes, *El rufián dichoso*, 201.

51 Cervantes, 1817, 1824–5.

52 Cervantes, 1855–6.

53 Antonio, ocular witness to Cruz's life, is consistently the star of what ineluctably strike the modern reader as *El rufián dichoso*'s queerest scenes: moments that display a tender, secretive, and playful relationship between Antonio and Ángel. The two play together in the garden alone (at "bolas," "en el jardín … a solas"; 2364–7); Antonio is abashed when caught, out of breath, trying to teach Ángel the rudiments of fencing (2374–410). Antonio and Ángel's furtive pleasure revolves around the slurping of two eggs – bringing to mind Galdos's *Fortunata y Jacinta*, in which Fortunata's earthy

eroticism is emblematized by her eating a raw egg ("¿No lo ve usted?…
Un huevo crudo") – and an intensity that alternates between eagerness
("veslos aquí, no los niego") and coquettish withholding ("dilatando …
mercedes"). The intimacy between Antonio and Ángel is marked
typographically by Cervantes: to avoid confusing their abbreviated names
on the page, Cervantes explains that Ángel will be denoted simply by the
letter "A" ("señálase solo con la A"; Cervantes, *El rufián dichoso*, 1412).
54 Cervantes, 1862.
55 Cervantes, 1914, 1916.
56 Cervantes, 1944.
57 Childers, "Ese tan borrado sobrescrito," 255.
58 Cervantes, *El rufián dichoso*, 2088–91.
59 Cervantes, 2092–3.
60 Cervantes, 2100.
61 Cervantes, 2122–39.
62 Cervantes, 2155. Cruz likens the blood shed ("almagró") by Christ to
ruddle, the red ochre used to mark or smit sheep. Ana seems as much
like the "livestock" or prostitutes that Lugo the pimp kept as property
as she does the lost sheep of New Testament parable. Ana goes on to call
Cruz "padre," or father, which is, as Antonia explained to the Inquisitor, a
euphemism for pimp. There is no newness in this world.
63 Cervantes, 2166.
64 Cervantes, 2175.
65 Cervantes, 2176.
66 Cervantes, 2182–3.
67 Cervantes, 2197–8.
68 Cervantes, 2084–112.
69 Núñez Rivera, "*El rufián dichoso*," 144.
70 Cervantes, *El rufián dichoso*, 2651.
71 Wardropper, "*Don Quixote*," 1.
72 Gaylord, "True History," 218.
73 The Clérigo, present with Cruz and Antonio during Treviño's negotiation,
never again takes the stage.
74 Cervantes, *El rufián dichoso*, 2640, 2644.
75 Cervantes, 2221; and Childers, "Ese tan borrado sobrescrito," 256.
76 Cervantes, *El rufián dichoso*, 2227.
77 Cervantes, 2237–8.
78 Cervantes, *Don Quijote*, 2.39.
79 Cervantes, *El rufián dichoso*, 2271.
80 Cervantes, 2271.
81 Joaquín Hazañas y la Rúa provides a helpful historical context for
Cruz's swap: an account of another Cristóbal de la Cruz who proposed

to take on the weight of a dying woman's sins (71). This account is not *theologically* edifying, however; there is no reason that Treviño's sincere confession would not be sufficient to her salvation. If it were to have any biblical foundation, Cruz's swap – his credit for her debt, or his devotion for her sin – may have a New Testament antecedent in Romans 9:3, in which Paul says he wished he were "accursed from Christ for my brethren." The Dominican Alonso de Cabrera paraphrases Paul's desire as "mi resolución para comprarles su redención por mi mesma persona" (my determination to buy their redemption with my very self), which does not sound unlike Cruz's plan (Cabrera, *Libro*, 48). Cabrera is clear, however, that such a trade will not work because it confuses Christ's infinite capacity for love with human beings' finitude. For Cabrera, this is folly. The Jesuit António Vieira, also preaching on Romans 9:3, goes further. According to Vieira, believing that one human being might atone for another is "nunca imaginada locura" (unheard-of madness; Vieira, *Sermones*, 397), a phrase that nearly recalls the "jamás imaginada aventura de la dueña Dolorida" (the unheard-of adventure of the afflicted duenna; *Don Quijote*, 2.36).

82 Thomas Aquinas, *Moral Teaching*, 2.2, Q. 77, art. 1. Saquiel recalls, again, the ducal palace of *Don Quijote*, as Canavaggio points out (*Cervantès dramaturge*, 86).

83 Zugasti, "Algo más sobre las fuentes," 506–7. Contemporaneous biographies of the blessed (*beatos*) and others whose cults were celebrated but who were never canonized often contain the sort of dubious miracles that flirt with bad taste; see, for example, Camuñas's *Ecos posthumos*, especially the miracle of Juana drinking foul sputum (13).

84 Cruz's death is unceremoniously narrated by Luzifer: "¡Ea!, que expira ya" (Hey! He's biting the dust; 2672).

85 Cervantes, *El rufián dichoso*, 242.

86 Cervantes, *Don Quijote*, 2.70.

87 Cervantes, *El rufián dichoso*, 2696–7, 2736–9. This clinamen away from an expected destination – in this case, the ur-destination of Paradise itself – is typical of the play; Thacker, in describing act 1, sums up the feeling: "The audience has been led along a path towards a later scene only to have its expectations unfulfilled" ("Véote," 216).

88 Cervantes, *El rufián dichoso*, 2728–9, 2748–9.

89 Lucía Megías, "Los libros de caballerías," 322; and Sáez, *Alabada*, n.p.

90 Irigaray, *This Sex*, 171.

91 Cascardi, *Limits of Illusion*, 53.

92 Santos Discépolo, "Cambalache."

93 On Spanish history as haunted, see Pimentel, *Fantasmas de la ciencia española*.

REFERENCES

Anderson, Ellen M. "Mothers of Invention: Toward a Reevaluation of Cervantine Dramatic Heroines." *Bulletin of the Comediantes* 62, no. 2 (2010): 1–44. https://doi.org/10.1353/boc.2011.0012.

Arboleda, Carlos Arturo. *Teoría y formas del metateatro en Cervantes.* Salamanca: Universidad de Salamanca, 1991.

Baena, Julio. *Discordancias cervantinas.* Newark, DE: Juan de la Cuesta, 2003.

Cabrera, Alonso de. *Libro de consideraciones sobre los euangelios* [...]. Barcelona: Gabriel Graells y Giraldo Dotil, 1606.

Camuñas, Diego. *Ecos posthumos, que resuenan* [...] *Aclamatorios de las esclarecidas virtudes y heroycos empleos de la Venerable Madre Sor Juana de la Cruz* [...]. Murcia: Vicente Llofriu, [1699].

Canavaggio, Jean. *Cervantès dramaturge. Un théâtre à naître.* Paris: Presses Universitaires de France, 1977.

Casalduero, Joaquín. *Sentido y forma del teatro de Cervantes.* Madrid: Gredos, 1966.

Cascardi, Anthony J. *The Limits of Illusion: A Critical Study of Calderón.* Cambridge: Cambridge University Press, 2005.

Cervantes Saavedra, Miguel de. *Don Quijote.* 2 vols. Edited by Luis Andrés Murillo. Madrid: Clásicos Castalia, 1978.

Cervantes Saavedra, Miguel de. *El rufián dichoso, Pedro de Urdemalas.* Edited by Jenaro Talens and Nicholas Spadaccini. Madrid: Cátedra, 1986.

Childers, William. "'Ese tan borrado sobrescrito': The Deconstruction of Lope's Religious Theater in *El retablo de las maravillas* and *El rufián dichoso.*" *Bulletin of the Comediantes* 56, no. 2 (2004): 241–68. https://doi.org/10.1353/boc.2004.0000.

Childers, William. *Transnational Cervantes.* Toronto: University of Toronto Press, 2006.

Close, Anthony. "Comic Exemplariness in Cervantes' *Comedias.*" In *Essays on Hispanic Themes in Honour of Edward C. Riley,* edited by Jennifer Lowe and Philip Swanson, 64–103. Edinburgh: Department of Hispanic Studies, 1989.

de Armas Wilson, Diana. "'Passing the Love of Women': The Intertextuality of *El curioso impertinente.*" *Cervantes* 7, no. 2 (1987): 9–28.

Domínguez Caparrós, José. *Métrica de Cervantes.* Alcalá de Henares: Centro de Estudios Cervantinos, 2002.

Fox, Dian. "The Apocryphal Part One of *Don Quijote.*" *MLN* 100, no. 2 (1985): 406–16. https://doi.org/10.2307/2905745.

Friedman, Edward H. "Self-Fashion Show: Women in the Plays of Cervantes and Significant Others." In *Women Warriors in Early Modern Spain: A Tribute to Bárbara Mujica*. Edited by Susan L. Fischer and Frederick A. de Armas, 33–49. Newark: University of Delaware Press, 2019.

Friedman, Edward H. *The Unifying Concept: Approaches to the Structure of Cervantes' Comedias*. York, SC: Spanish Literature Publications, 1981.

Fuchs, Barbara. "Border Crossings: Transvestism and 'Passing' in *Don Quijote*." *Cervantes* 16, no. 2 (1996): 4–28.

Fuchs, Barbara. *Passing for Spain: Cervantes and the Fictions of Identity*. Urbana: University of Illinois Press, 2003.

Gallego Zarzosa, Alicia. "El despertar sexual de don Quijote: Construcción literaria y parodia erótica en el romance de Altisidora." *Calíope* 24, no. 2 (2019): 128–47. https://doi.org/10.5325/caliope.24.2.0128.

Gaylord, Mary M. "The True History of Early Modern Writing in Spanish: Some American Reflections." *Modern Language Quarterly* 57, no. 2 (1996): 213–25. https://doi.org/10.1215/00267929-57-2-213.

Gaylord Randel, Mary. "Proper Language and Language as Property: The Personal Poetics of Lope's *Rimas*." *MLN* 101, no. 2 (1986): 220–46. https://doi.org/10.2307/2905762.

González, Aurelio. "Espacio y dramaturgia cervantina." In *Memoria de la palabra: Actas del VI Congreso de la AISO*, edited by Francisco Domínguez Matito and María Luisa Lobato López, 897–904. Madrid: Iberoamericana Vervuert, 2004.

Harvey, Elizabeth D. *Ventriloquized Voices: Feminist Theory and English Renaissance Texts*. New York: Routledge, 1992.

Hazañas y la Rúa, Joaquín. *Los rufianes de Cervantes:* El rufián dichoso *y* El rufián viudo. Seville: Izquierdo, 1906.

Henry, Melanie. "Cervantine Theater as Counter-Perspective Aesthetic: Reconsidering *El rufián dichoso*." *Cervantes* 31, no. 2 (2011): 105–24. https://doi.org/10.1353/cer.2011.0020.

Henry, Melanie. *The Signifying Self: Cervantine Drama as Counter-Perspective Aesthetic*. London: Modern Humanities Research Association, 2013.

Irigaray, Luce. *This Sex Which Is Not One*. Translated by Catherine Porter and Carolyn Burke. Ithaca, NY: Cornell University Press, 1985.

Jones, Nicholas R., and Chad Leahy. "Introduction: Rethinking the Pornographic in Premodern and Early Modern Spanish Cultural Production." In *Pornographic Sensibilities: Imagining Sex and the Visceral in Premodern and Early Modern Spanish Cultural Production*, edited by Nicholas R. Jones and Chad Leahy, 1–16. New York: Routledge, 2020.

Lathrop, Thomas A. "Contradiction in the Quijote Explained." In *Jewish Culture and the Hispanic World: Essays in Memory of Joseph H. Silverman*, edited by Samuel G. Armistead and Mishael M. Caspi, 242–6. Newark, DE: Juan de la Cuesta, 2001.

Lucía Megías, José Manuel. "Los libros de caballerías en las primeras manifestaciones populares del *Quijote*." In *De la literatura caballeresca al Quijote*, edited by Juan Manuel Cacho Blecua, 319–46. Zaragoza: Prensas Universitarias de Zaragoza, 2007.

McKendrick, Melveena. "Writings for the Stage." In *The Cambridge Companion to Cervantes*, edited by Anthony J. Cascardi, 131–59. Cambridge: Cambridge University Press, 2002.

Núñez Rivera, Valentín. "*El rufián dichoso* entre verdades y fabulosos intentos." *Anales Cervantinos*, no. 49 (2017): 119–52. https://doi.org/10.3989/anacervantinos.2017.006.

Padilla, José. "'El rufián dichoso,' hoy." *Nueva Rivista*, 17 July 2017. https://www.nuevarevista.net/el-rufian-dichoso-hoy/.

Parker, Alexander A. *The Allegorical Drama of Calderón: An Introduction to the Autos sacramentales*. Oxford: Dolphin, 1943.

Pimentel, Juan. *Fantasmas de la ciencia española*. Madrid: Marcial Pons, 2020.

Profeti, Maria Grazia. "Cervantes, Lope y el teatro áureo." *eHumanista/Cervantes*, no. 1 (2012): 552–7.

Rosa Rivero, Álvaro. "La acción dramática en *El rufián dichoso* de Cervantes." *Hipogrifo* 6, no. 2 (2018): 233–45. https://doi.org/10.13035/H.2018.06.02.20.

Sáez, Alonso. *Alabada sea la Purissima Concepcion de la Madre de Dios* [...]. Seville: Francisco de Lyra, 1617.

Santos Discépolo, Enrique. "Cambalache." In *The Argentina Reader: History, Culture, Politics*, edited by Gabriela Nouzeilles and Graciela Montaldo, 266–7. Durham, NC: Duke University Press, 2002.

Schjeldahl, Peter. "Masters and Pieces: Leonardo, Michelangelo, and Munch." *The New Yorker*, 20 November 2017. https://www.newyorker.com/magazine/2017/11/27/masters-and-pieces-leonardo-michelangelo-and-munch.

Sontag, Susan. *Against Interpretation and Other Essays*. New York: Farrar, Straus and Giroux, 1966.

Talens, Jenaro, and Nicholas Spadaccini. "Introducción." In Miguel de Cervantes Saavedra, *El rufián dichoso, Pedro de Urdemalas*, edited by Jenaro Talens and Nicholas Spadaccini, 11–97. Madrid: Cátedra, 1986.

Thacker, Jonathan. "La figura de la Comedia en 'El rufián dichoso' de Cervantes." In *La comedia de santos: Coloquio internacional, Almagro, 1, 2 y 3 de diciembre de 2006*, edited by Felipe B. Pedraza Jiménez and Almudena García González, 121–34. Almagro: Universidad de Castilla-La Mancha, 2008.

Thacker, Jonathan. "'Véote, y no te conozco': The Unrecognizable Form of Cervantes's *El rufián dichoso*." *Hispanic Research Journal* 10, no. 3 (2009): 206–26. https://doi.org/10.1179/174582009X433176.

Thomas Aquinas. *The Moral Teaching of St. Thomas.* Translated by Joseph Rickaby. London: Burns & Oates, 1892.

Varas, Patricia. "*El rufián dichoso*: Una comedia de santos diferente." *Anales Cervantinos*, no. 29 (1991): 9–19. https://doi.org/10.3989 /anacervantinos.1991.409.

Vega Carpio, Lope de. *San Isidro Labrador.* In *Obras de Lope de Vega*, vol. 10, *Comedias de vidas de santos*, bk. 2, edited by Marcelino Menéndez Pelayo. Madrid: Atlas, 1965.

Velasco, Sherry. "The *Dueña Dolorida*: Policing Gender, Desire, and Entertainment." *Hispanic Review* 77, no. 2 (2009): 221–44. https://doi .org/10.1353/hir.0.0058.

Vieira, António. *Sermones varios traducidos en castellano de su original portugués.* Vol. 13. Madrid: Francisco Fernández, 1714.

Wardropper, Bruce W. "*Don Quixote*: Story or History?" *Modern Philology* 63, no. 1 (1965): 1–11. https://doi.org/10.1086/389723.

Williamsen, Vern G., and J.T. Abraham. "Vern's Miscellaneous Notes." Association for Hispanic Classical Theater. Updated 1 July 2002. http:// comedias.org/misc/vernsno.html.

Zimic, Stanislav. "La caridad 'jamás imaginada' de Cristóbal de Lugo (estudio de *El rufián dichoso* de Cervantes)." *Boletín de la Biblioteca de Menéndez Pelayo*, no. 56 (1980): 85–171.

Zugasti, Miguel. "Algo más sobre las fuentes de 'El rufián dichoso' de Cervantes." In *Locos, figurones y quijotes en el teatro de los Siglos de Oro: Actas selectas del XII Congreso de la Asociación Internacional de Teatro Español y Novohispano de los Siglos de Oro: Almagro, 15, 16 y 17 de julio de 2005*, edited by Germán Vega García-Luengos and Rafael González Cañal, 493–513. Almagro: Universidad de Castilla-La Mancha, 2007.

3 Of Players and Wagers: The Theatricality of Gambling for Salvation in *El rufián dichoso*

SONIA VELÁZQUEZ

In the rich analysis of the cultural importance of gambling in early modern Spain, Enrique García Santo-Tomás makes a fascinating remark, all the more so for its seeming self-evidence. Amid the myriad texts that were concerned with games and gambling, whether in fiction, in moralist treatises, or in legal and ecclesiastic proclamations, it was particularly the figure of the loser that concerned the authors, "for no winner becomes a useful topic to the writers of the time."[1] This assertion makes intuitive sense, especially within the logic of exemplarity – the application of past examples as models for action in the present – that structured political, religious, historical, and poetic discourses in the early modern period. García Santo-Tomás thus drops the subject there in order to focus on the ways in which the gambling den became an institution as familiar in urban peninsular settings as the brothel or the church and as important in the development of the bourgeois value of productivity.[2] In this chapter, I want to probe further into the question of winners and losers in order to understand why Miguel de Cervantes chose to make a consummate winner – a gambler who wins in this world by profiting from playing cards *and* secures salvation through a card game – the focus of his only religious play, *El rufián dichoso* (The Fortunate Rogue).[3] What sort of theatricality befits such a figure? And, if fiction in the early modern period found its justification in the Horatian dictum of combining didacticism with entertainment, what and how does a winning gambler teach a theatre audience? I will delve into these questions through a close reading of *El rufián dichoso* followed by the exploration of an unexpected parallel to the theatricality of Blaise Pascal's Wager in order to propose that both authors imagine a gambling winner in order to posit a more dynamic form of belief.

Of Drama: Losers and Winners

Let us return to the initial question: Why is it that the winner cannot be held as an exemplar to be imitated? Firstly, as a matter of definition, a winner in a game of *chance* cannot produce an imitable example. After all, winning (assuming an absence of cheating) is a matter of irreproducible luck, not will. Secondly, the gaming context itself problematizes the winner's exemplarity. Although according to moralists, play and games in general have a legitimate place in a well-ordered Christian republic as part of a healthy regime of alternation between work and rest, games of chance are uniquely suspicious because they encourage the illusion that humans could usurp God's power over contingency.[4] Moreover, the added element of unregulated profit inherent in gambling compounded the misgivings towards this activity. First, as with theatre, profit puts into question its very reason for being, its utility as *otium*, the opposite of *negotium*.[5]

More significantly, in the eyes of both secular and ecclesiastic authorities, the pursuit of easy money blinded players to their social and spiritual duties and invited a descent into vice that effectively animalized the player, turning him into a lone wolf willing to sacrifice self and kin at the altar of the win.[6] It is thus that Juan de Zabaleta (c. 1610–c. 1667) depicts the player who frequents the gambling den: "Sólo un animal hay en el mundo que, sin odio ni ira, quiere destruir al animal de su semejanza: éste es el hombre tahúr, y éste es el más cruel de todos los animales" (There is only one animal in the world that, without hatred or ire, will destroy its ilk: this is the gambling man, and this is the cruellest of all animals).[7] Going a step further, Pedro de Guzmán echoes Saint Anthony when he writes that "no se deue pues llamar Christiano, el que es dado al juego, pues haze vituperable el nõbre de Christo, y de Christiano" (one should not call Christian the person inclined to gambling for it renders reprehensible both Christ's name and the appellation of Christian).[8] This untethering from any community is what makes the audacity of extreme gamblers terrifying – and what makes great dramatic sense in the fiction of the period.

A perfect example of this is Ángela de Azevedo's *Dicha y desdicha del juego, y devoción de la Virgen* (Fortune and Misfortune in Gambling and Devotion to the Virgin).[9] Felisardo and María are poor but noble siblings, who find themselves orphaned and destitute thanks to their father's gambling addiction which cost him first his fortune, then his life, and finally that of his bereft wife. Without financial means, María has no dowry, and Felisardo is unable to convince his beloved Violante's father to consider him a proper suitor. Desperate at hearing the news that Violante is to marry rich Fadrique, Felisardo turns to the advice of astrologers who presage good fortune for him at the card table.[10] Then, faced with his opponent, Fadrique, "a great gambler" (2275), Felisardo is unable to step away from the table while he is ahead, and instead loses it all, including his sister, whose virtue he has gambled away. Although throughout the first two acts we have seen Felisardo act decorously the part of loving brother, faithful suitor, and devout follower of the Virgin Mary, his recklessness in gambling alone leads him to declare himself a great sinner, unworthy of divine help (2786). Felisardo's quick descent into sin – first idolatry, then greed and pride, finally despair – reaches a turning point when he invokes the devil and, feeling that he has nothing left to lose, reneges of God and His doctrine in order to get the treasure necessary to marry Violante. Tragedy is averted here only through the merciful intervention of the Virgin.

I use the word "tragedy" here deliberately, echoing the language of the play. Sombrero, Felisardo's servant, describes the situation as a lamentable tragedy, "triste tragedia" (2891), when the devil, angry at Felisardo's refusal to repudiate the Virgin Mary, spirits him away. Alone on the stage, a whimpering Sombrero wonders what his role should be given the calamitous turn of events: "¿Qué haré en tan triste tragedia?" (What shall I do [perform] in such a lamentable tragedy? [2891]). It would be tempting to interpret the use of the word "tragedia" here as mere amplifier of the adjective "triste." However, in the mouth of the *gracioso*, a character often associated with metatheatrical commentary, "tragedia" arguably points instead to specific theatrical expectations.[11] More precisely, it primes the audience to interpret what they have seen onstage in a tragic mode. This implies the depiction of an action of great magnitude that leads to the troubling and lamentable end of a noble person, whence the audience is to learn which actions to avoid in life.[12] The use of the word *tragedy*, then, reminds the viewer that while in the last act the miraculous intervention of the Virgin Mary may turn the story around, the misfortune brought about by the game – the skidding from virtue to great sinfulness – should not be forgotten.

Azevedo's play is interesting when thinking about gambling because its plot concerns not one, but two gamblers. Felisardo, the loser, follows a narrative arc marked by his brush with tragedy. Let us take a look now at the sort of drama that the winner's tale generates. First of all, it is notable that after the fateful game (which took place offstage, between the second and third acts), Fadrique disappears for roughly half of the last act. When he does return, his character is marked by a deep desire for vengeance on Felisardo for *his* impudent ambition to take everything away from Fadrique. Although he has won, Fadrique's actions onstage are still tied to those of the loser. While Felisardo gets several chances to express his confused emotions after the unfortunate game, Fadrique can only react angrily to Felisardo's temerity. Ultimately, it is this ire that finds condemnation in the play, not his gambling per se, even if he had been as reckless as Felisardo in having gambled all he owned. It is also significant that whereas María denounces Felisardo's blindness in his rash bid to take everything from his rival, there is no equal admonition for Fadrique, even if he, too, had been close to losing everything.[13] The closest the play comes to condemning the winner is through Violante's father, who expresses disgust at gambling itself, but in the end, he remains steadfast in his desire to unite his own fortune with Fadrique's through the latter's marriage to Violante (2649–60):

NUÑO: Yo de manera ninguna,
viendo que era jugador
(que mi condición repugna)
admitiera en casa mía
hombre que me la destruya.
Mas el ver que don Fadrique
el resto cobró, y que mudan
las costumbres los estados,
me está obligando a que cumpla
la palabra que le di.

(NUÑO: In no way would I,
seeing that he was a gambler
(which my nature abhors),
have admitted in my own house
a man who would destroy it.
But seeing that don Fadrique
recouped his lot, and that
habits change conditions,
I am obliged to keep
my word towards him.)

To sum up, then, although in *Dicha y desdicha del juego* it takes two to gamble, when it comes to drama, only the loser's fate seems to garner reflection and action onstage. I would like to suggest that this is largely because a tale of great loss finds a ready-made form and function in tragedy. The movement from peaceful beginnings to distraught endings, as López Pinciano puts it, maps nicely onto the curve of the fate of the losing gambler who begins, as Felisardo, with high hopes for a win, a height from which he can only fall to depths ready to be plumbed by the rest of the play. Moreover, at a functional level, the representation of the loser's woes and the consequences of his gambling folly lead to a didactically crisp message: gambling, product of "la curiosidad enemiga" (inimical curiosity), is to be avoided because in creating the conditions for an illusion of mastery, it provides the opportunity for the loser to imagine himself above the bonds that tie humans to one another and to the divine.[14] In contrast, the winner's plot lacks drama. In Fadrique's case, he begins rich and fortunate and ends that way. Not much to show onstage there.[15] It is conceivable that a gambler's starting point is nothing, a low point from which the player can only rise. However, as Violante's father notes, the promised path to upward mobility is often foiled by human imprudence.[16] A proper drama of the winner thus remains unimaginable in Azevedo's play.

Cervantes's Theatrical Gamble: A Play of Two Wagers

If *Dicha y desdicha del juego* can be rightfully called a "*comedia* famosa," it is thanks to the divine intervention of the Virgin Mary, who saves Felisardo on account of his lifelong devotion and to his ultimate unwillingness to renege of his love for her. The force of Felisardo's tragedy in the play's final act may well have been blunted by the *dea ex machina*, but this solution only intensifies the contrast between gambling as a dangerous curiosity that incites humanity's worst instincts, on the one hand, and the inscrutable mercy of heaven, on the other. In contrast, Miguel de Cervantes's *El rufián dichoso* does not draw its dramatic energy from the opposition between profane gambling and the possibility of salvation.[17] In fact, as we will see, he harnesses the structure of gambling – making calculations to stake something of value on the outcome of an event that is unknown in order to get a prize – to religious ends. Moreover, he raises the ante by offering to the audience not one, but *two* players who wager and win.

The play follows the fate of Cristóbal Lugo, a roguish student making mischief in Seville who succeeds, through one and the same bet, in earning back his money *and* saving his soul. Much like in Azevedo's play, the fateful gamble takes place offstage, but in contrast to it, the rest of *Rufián dichoso* traces the aftermath of Lugo's win. Those repercussions include, of course, the rogue's conversion. In this Cervantes follows the story as told by Juan de Marieta (*Historia eclesiástica*, 158), where the game is pivotal and leads, through introspection, to the rogue's conversion: "Ordenó el Señor que ganasse, y salido de alli pusose a considerar el camino que llebaua, y como de nueva luz visitado, abrio los ojos del entendimiento, y començo a retirarse de aquellas compañias malas" (The Lord arranged it so he would win, and once having left there [the gambling table], he reconsidered the path he was on, and as if he had been visited by a new light, he opened the mind's eye and he stepped away from evil companions).[18] Not only does Lugo leave behind his picaresque ways, but he humbly follows Inquisitor Tello de Sandoval when they both move to Mexico in the second act. There, living as a devout Dominican now known as Fray Cristóbal de la Cruz, his holiness will be revealed when he coaxes a dying woman who despairs of the love of God to wager in favour of God's grace. How does Cervantes turn these two wins into theatrical events, and what does the focus on the winners teach the audience?

These are slightly more focused versions of the questions at the heart of the polemic surrounding seventeenth-century hagiographic plays.[19] Working within a Horatian-Christian paradigm that found the justification of imaginative works in the balance between the useful and the pleasurable, *comedias de santos* typically walked a fine line between verisimilitude (and with it the expectations of truthfulness, decorum, and exemplarity) and an audience's taste for dramatic action (love intrigues, the antics of a *gracioso*, etc.), as well as for what today we would call special effects, such as devils and angels flying with the aid of stage machinery. The question of how to make sanctity visible, a quality that as Anne Teulade has noted is best defined by negation, has thus haunted the reception of the *comedia de santos* from its beginnings.[20] Cervantes adds to this dramatic question by making a gambling winner become a saint whose defining miracle is another wager. Following Samuel Weber's understanding of theatricality as the staging of an alternative form of knowledge to philosophy's desire for completion, control, and meaningful action performed by autonomous selves, it is my contention that Cervantes's wagers foreground "a way of being moved."[21] This means each wager is a performance that pushes against the limits of autonomy, confounds the opposition of action and passivity and the self-containment of bodies. In contrast to the drama of the gambling loser, whose effects on the audience depend on a credible, coherent plot that confirms its expectations of representation (mimesis) and meaning (a recognizable moral), Cervantes's theatricality of the winner focuses on the willingness to dislocate oneself. It invites character, actor, and audience to imagine oneself, one's story, otherwise, all while maintaining nimble the articulations that bind us to others.

Let us turn then to the gambling scene. The first act of *El rufián dichoso* is a sequence of brilliantly sketched episodes showing Lugo's engagement now with the picaresque world of Seville, now with his master Tello de Sandoval, being true to his first appearance onstage wearing the garb of a student but carrying the weapon of a rogue. Lugo has just performed a marvellous deed, saving the pimp Carrascosa from going to prison, wondrously without shedding blood or using weapons, "sin sangre, sin hierro o fuego," as Lobillo, a fellow rake, puts it (995). And yet, instead of celebrating, Lugo's mind turns to other business (1002–6):

> Ir quiero agora a jugar
> con Gilberto, un estudiante
> que siempre ha sido mi azar,
> hombre que ha de ser bastante
> a hacerme desesperar.
> Cuanto tengo me ha ganado;
> solamente me han quedado
> unas súmulas, y a fe
> que, si las pierdo, que sé
> cómo esquitarme al doblado.

> (I want to go play now
> against Gilberto, a student
> who has always been my bad luck chip,
> man enough
> to bring me to despair.
> What I own, he has won from me;
> all I have left
> is a textbook of logic, and by my faith,
> if I lose it, I know
> how to quit myself twice over.)

Up to this point, the audience would have witnessed a very *dichoso* Lugo triumph, as he escapes capture by authorities, joyfully teases a baker into feeding his gang, and successfully deflects the scolding of his master. Yet, he is here, at the height of his powers in the Sevillian underworld, close to despair. His only source of unhappiness comes from playing cards with Gilberto, to whom he seems to have lost everything except for a textbook of logic, his *súmulas*.[22] The description of Gilberto as Lugo's *azar* – a losing card or stumbling block, according to Covarrubias – and its rhyming with *desesperar* (despair), signal that it is not clear whether Lugo's despair comes from financial loss, or because Gilberto is the only obstacle to Lugo having complete mastery of the picaresque world.[23] The desire for control is emphasized again in the ironic rhyme of his swearing, "a fe," with the assertion "*sé* / como esquitarme al doblado" (my emphasis). Cervantes thus sets Lugo up as if to follow the script of gambling as the occasion for hubris, sin, and perdition. This sense of foreboding is confirmed as we learn the details of his plan. Lugo wants to ensure his victory, but he declines the use of Lobillo's marked deck. Instead of depending on his skill at playing or at cheating, our *rufián* wants to tilt things in his favour by making the following daring wager (1015–19):

> ¡Largo medio es el que escoges!
> Otro sé por do se ataja.
> Juro a Dios omnipotente
> que, si las pierdo [las súmulas] al presente,
> me he de hacer salteador.

> (You've picked such a delayed tactic!
> I know of another shortcut.
> I swear to God Almighty
> that if I lose it [my textbook] presently,
> I shall become a highway robber.)

The move from rake to robber is not simply an incremental one. The vow to become a *salteador* does not just imply stealing from others to make a living. It entails living outside of society and betraying the confidence Tello had in him. Although Lagartija, the *gracioso* of the play, pledges to follow Lugo "al bien como a la maldad" (into virtue as much as into wickedness), Lugo's determination to cut ties is highlighted by his second refusal to join the rogues' celebration.[24]

When against everyone's expectations Lugo wins, he is the first to be surprised that his move to risk eternal salvation in order to win back his money actually worked. Yet, when queried by Gilberto about the unexpected win, Lugo laconically attributes it to the vagaries of fortune, "sucesos son de fortuna," he alleges.[25] Sebastián de Covarrubias writes that in the opinion of most people, the word *fortuna* refers to "lo que sucede a caso sin poder ser prevenido" (that which befalls by chance without being foreseen). And yet, while the odds of Lugo winning were low, his success was not entirely unanticipated. In fact, the expectation of a specific desired outcome (winning) that may or may not come to pass defines a wager and distinguishes it from a promise or a challenge.[26]

Indeed, at the end of act 1, once the protagonist is alone onstage, he recognizes that his turn of luck was neither a random occurrence nor the result of the turning of a fickle (and often blind) Wheel of Fortune. His conversion depends instead on his willingness to pause and take account of what has happened. It requires Lugo to recognize that he is neither an autonomous agent fully in control of his destiny, nor the puppet of forces beyond him, call them God or chance. What's more, his decision to change his life is still very much the result of an act of calculation as Lugo takes account of what has happened (1150–73):

> Solo quedo, y quiero entrar
> en cuentas conmigo a solas,
> aunque lo impidan las olas
> donde temo naufragar.
> Yo hice voto, si hoy perdía,
> de irme a ser salteador:
> claro y manifiesto error
> de una ciega fantasía.
> Locura y atrevimiento
> fue el peor que se pensó,
> puesto que nunca obligó
> mal voto a su cumplimiento.
> Pero, ¿dejaré por esto
> de haber hecho una maldad,
> adonde mi voluntad
> echó de codicia el resto?
> No, por cierto. Mas, pues sé
> que contrario con contrario
> se cura muy de ordinario,
> contrario voto haré,
> y así, le hago de ser
> religioso. ¡Ea, Señor;
> veis aquí a este salteador
> de contrario parecer!

> (I am all alone, and I want to
> take account of my actions by myself,
> even if the waves I fear drowning in
> should try to prevent me.
> I vowed today that if I lost
> I should become a highway robber;
> clear and obvious error
> of blind fancy.

Madness and daring
was the worst imagined
since it is no obligation to fulfil
an ill and evil vow.
And yet, does this erase my wicked act,
where my will threw the rest
on account of my greed?
Indeed not! And since I know
that opposite in opposite
finds often its cure,
I shall a counter-vow make:
And thus, I make it to become
a man of God. Hey, Lord:
See here, Lord, this repentant highway robber.)

Cervantes goes to great lengths to show that Lugo's triumph was not predicated on chance alone or even on *industria*.[27] That is why it is important that the rogue resolutely rebuffs his friend's offer to cheat using marked cards. Lugo wins, but it is not on account of his skills. And yet, his turn of luck is not random either. Instead, his gambling is volitional and relational: his resolution to devote his life to evil if he loses and the decision to engage in gambling are both forms of contractual agreement. He gambles that there is a God and that it is an interventionist divinity that cares about individual souls in order to win back his money. But, in turn, this initial wager gives rise to a second calculation. When by himself onstage he makes an accounting of his deeds good and bad, his desire to go all in is fuelled and he pledges his life to God. At this point, he renews his bonds with the Virgin Mary, his guardian angel, and the souls of Purgatory, asking that they intercede on his behalf before God. This gambling winner may have decided to change his life, but in the very moment he asserts his free will, he also becomes a suppliant to others. What Cervantes shows the audience here is the capacity of a human being to be moved, to redefine activity as reactivity, as Samuel Weber puts it.[28]

The insight gleaned from winning at a gambling game, namely, that there is more than the opposition of activity and passivity, is underlined in a scene that is sandwiched between Lugo's conversation with Gilberto immediately after his victory and the rogue's soliloquy where he accounts for his actions. Earlier in the first act, Lugo had rejected an anonymous lady who has come all covered, *tapada*, to proposition him. By chance, her husband passes by, and she panicked, but Lugo asks her not to speak or move while he deals with the husband. The rogue, taking a page from the Lope de Vega playbook, spins a *caso de honra*.[29] He tells the husband that he knows that someone is attempting to seduce his wife, but he also reassures him that she is so chaste and honourable that the seducer would have no chance. However, to be safe, Lugo proposes that the husband take his wife to the countryside. Lugo thus manages to save himself and the lady. Several scenes later, and immediately after Lugo's victory over Gilberto, the husband reappears. He insists on knowing the name of the man who wanted to stain his honour. He wants action; he thirsts for vengeance; he wants, in other words, to be the protagonist of a different sort of play. Lugo, however, calmly prevails over the man's curiosity as he convinces him to do nothing, that sometimes, the greatest action is non-action.

The last two acts of the play detail the now holy ex-rogue's newfound humility, his resistance to demonic temptations, and the working of a singularly unspectacular miracle. However, even in these seemingly more conventional acts, the engagement of play and the calculations of gambling have centre stage. The conversion, as we just saw, took place quietly without the intervention of any of the expected supernatural visions or miracles orchestrated by stage machinery. This stands in contrast to the taste for spectacle that characterizes many other stage conversions.[30] The fact that the theatrical in *El rufián dichoso* does not reside in the spectacular but in the relational informs also the choice Cervantes made for the representation of Father Cruz's signature miracle. Whereas Cervantes's sources credit flames engulfing the chapel where the Dominican friar was praying, the play focuses instead on a miracle as subtle as Lugo's own conversion.[31] What is more, this miracle depends, once again, on the structure of gambling, that is to say, on a calculation of risk, an appeal to self-interest, and above all on a willingness to engage in the game. A dying woman, doña Ana, laments her sinful life, and claiming that God cannot possibly pardon such iniquity, she despairs and refuses to clear her conscience through confession. Her sins exceed quantification in Cervantes's play, but they remain entirely unqualified, that is to say, we do not know their nature. In contrast, most identified historical sources for the play describe the sins as prideful vanity, although not necessarily sexual. This is important because unlike the legend of the conversion of Mary Magdalene, doña Ana's sins are not directly the result of misdirected love, but rather of a lack of trust in God's love, and as a result she does not have an available template for forgiveness. An unnamed priest initially attempts to remind her of the omnipotence of God, whose smallest part he claims could heal the greatest evil (1886–7), but his frantic logic exasperates her (1895–901):

> Matáisme, y cansáisos vos.
> ¡Bien fuera que Dios ahora,
> sin que en nada reparara,
> sin más ni más, perdonara
> a tan grande pecadora!
> No hace cosa mal hecha,
> Y así no ha de hacer aquesta.

> (You're killing me and tiring yourself out.
> How great would it be if God now,
> Without taking notice of anything,
> Without further ado, would forgive
> Such a great sinner!
> He does not perform wrongful deeds,
> Hence, he shall not do this [grant forgiveness].)

Doña Ana is as certain that she knows who and what she is (a "grande pecadora") as she is of what God can and cannot do. It is this certainty and her obstinacy in that (limited) knowledge, which translates into a lack of imagination and empathy, more than the specificity of her sins that mark her potential tragedy.

In the context of the Counter-Reformation's emphasis on the sacraments of penance and reconciliation, it is not surprising that the staging of the mystery of God's inscrutable will, especially when it comes to forgiving extraordinary sinfulness, should prove a privileged dramatic trope.[32] However, in contrast to plays such as Pedro Calderón de la Barca's *Devoción de la cruz* (Devotion to the Cross, 1636) or Tirso de Molina's *El condenado por desconfiado* (Damned for Despair, 1635), where each play's bandit (Eusebio and Enrico, respectively) is saved on account of his humility and the sincerity of his love, the reconciliation scene in Cervantes's play is mediated by yet another sort of gambling contract.

Father Cruz agrees to see doña Ana to persuade her to attend to her soul, and in contrast to the previous attempts, he succeeds. At the beginning, the lady continues to affirm that God does not exist for her and that she does not possess enough weapons (good deeds) to face a posthumous battle with the devil. Father Cruz deploys Biblical quotations in Latin, and garners strength from his trust in the Virgin Mary and the prayers of the onlookers onstage (including the priest who had failed earlier). However, in the end, his triumph over doña Ana's intransigence is not due to a persuasive theological argument, or even a clear visual manifestation of holiness such as an apparition or a miracle.[33] Instead, he asks her to consider the following: If she wagers her life on the possibility that things may be otherwise than she imagines, there *may* be hope for her, and if she proceeds to *perform* her part by accepting the sacrament of reconciliation, Father Cruz will take upon himself her sins (2085–91):

> Si te quieres confesar,
> Los montes puede allanar
> De caridad el exceso.
> Pon tú el arrepentimiento
> De tu parte, y verás luego
> Cómo en tus obras me entrego,
> Y tú en aquellas que cuento.
>
> (If you want to confess,
> Even the mountains can be levelled
> By the excess of charity.
> For your part, put in your repentance
> And you shall see then
> How I take to your deeds
> And you give yourself over to the ones I have told you about / count on.)

This description of the exchange of spiritual merit between sinner and holy man is marked by a language of calculation: of counting and accounting. The pun on the word *cuento* in the last line quoted refers both to an accounting of Father Cruz's good deeds and his counting on their efficacy, a nuance that echoes his earlier hope that while living a roguish life his prayers "darán buena cuenta de mí" (will give a good account on my behalf; 820). And yet, this spiritual math is thoroughly orthodox: forgiveness begins with contrition, the hatred of sin (which had perversely led the lady to despair), it is received in confession, and it is paid for in penance. In other words, doña Ana must wager that she may be wrong about God and about her own fate. But this gamble can only take her so far. The deal is sealed only when she agrees not only to wager but also to *perform*. This double play, as we shall see, was also central to Blaise Pascal's plan for moving the unbeliever towards God.

Cervantes's rendition of this episode emphasizes the contractual nature of doña Ana's reconciliation. Before reconciling herself with Christ and the church, she asks for guarantors ("fiadores," 2092) and witnesses ("testigos," 2109) to the deal she is about to make. In other words, Cruz does not offer her the *certainty* of salvation, only its *possibility* through the engagement of her will, that is to say, her recognition of herself as a player. Likewise, the contract she draws with him is not a pledge whose fulfilment will take place beyond the grave but rather a security that Father Cruz will not back out of his deal in this world. The "miracle" then does not reside in the most obvious aspect of the interaction of Father Cruz and doña Ana, that is to say, in the exchange of his good deeds for her bad ones. It is of a more subtle form: the real miracle is that a sinner who believed to be outside of grace realized that she was still in the game, so to speak.[34]

Thus far, I have shown that in *El rufián dichoso*, gambling and the language of calculation and risk no longer signify a desire for mastery and imply the dissolution of bonds to society and to the divine (the tragedy of the loser). Instead, through the staging of two wagers, the theatre becomes a space where it is possible to imagine oneself otherwise and to conceive of action as something other than remarkable exploit. Still to be addressed, however, is the question of exemplarity; that is to say, what exactly is it that the unspectacular theatricality of Lugo's conversion and doña Ana's salvation teach the audience. I would like to suggest that the play's didacticism is less propositional than pragmatic or even existential. This means that what the play aims to do is to *show* how to engage with the uncertainties of living in a contingent world rather than confine its message to a specific religious doctrine (of repentance, free will, etc.) or a moral *sententia* (gambling is harmful). In order to understand what this shift in focus means and what it has to do with the structure of gambling, we turn to what is perhaps the most famous example of imagining a gambling winner in a religious context: Blaise Pascal's Wager.

Pascal: A Wager and a Play for Salvation

The text of Pascal's Wager, where an unbeliever is brought over to the other side by proposing that he has nothing to lose and much to gain if he bets that God exists and lives accordingly, must have been so surprising to his contemporaries that it does not appear in the first edition of the fragments known as the *Pensées*.[35] In the eighteenth century, Voltaire's reaction shows that to use gambling to win over the unbeliever was still, if not scandalous, at least indecorous. The Encyclopedist writes of Pascal's Wager in the *Lettres philosophiques*: "Cet article paraît un peu indécent et puérile: cette idée de jeu, de perte et de gain, ne convient point à la gravité du sujet" (This entry seems a trifle indecent and childish; this idea of a wager, of loss and gain, ill befits the seriousness of the subject).[36] Still, the Wager can be seen as an attempt to accomplish the goal that the seventeenth-century philosopher set out in his reflections on the persuasive value of miracles to reach and "convince the whole man in body and soul" by turning to the realm of play – of games and gambling but also of play-acting – as a model.[37]

There are three folders of material containing Pascal's examinations of the persuasive value of miracles and Biblical prophecies to convince non-believers. However, he ultimately decided not to include these in what was going to be his Apology for Christianity but was never finished and became known after his death as *Pensées*. Having come to the conclusion that when it comes to the persuasive value of miracles, "il y a assez d'évidence pour condemner, et non assez pour convaincre" (there is enough evidence to condemn, and not enough to convince), Pascal nonetheless affirms their necessity.[38] Some sort of phenomenological sense of the divine is needed "because we must convince the whole man, in body and soul" ("à cause qu'il faut convaincre l'homme entire, en corps et en âme").[39] The basic premise in the Wager as in the section on miracles is that there are things whose nature exceeds our knowledge. But whereas in the discarded section the emphasis was still on proof (in a rhetorical sense if not epistemological), in the Wager, the emphasis is more pragmatic. Pascal concedes that if there is a God, he is infinitely incomprehensible, and this particular circumstance puts pressure on his reader to consider the situation in terms of *acting* (or possibly reacting) rather than of knowledge or belief.

What is the reader to do in light of uncertainty and truths that cannot be seen? How are we to act as the text would have it, "according to our natural lights" (selon les lumières naturelles)?[40] Because, as Pascal makes clear, not doing anything is already taking sides:

> Examinons donc ce point, et disons: Dieu est, ou il n'est pas. Mais de quel côté pencherons-nous ? La raison n'y peut rien determiner. Il y a un chaos infini qui nous sépare. *Il se joue un jeu*, à l'extrémité de cette distance infinie, où il arrivera croix ou pile: que gagerez-vous ? Par raison, vous ne pouvez faire ni l'un ni l'autre....
>
> « Le juste est de ne point parier ».
>
> « Oui ; mais il faut parier. Cela n'est pas volontaire vous êtes embarqué.... Voyons. Puisqu'il faut choisir, voyons ce qui vous *intéresse* le moins ».[41]

(Let us examine this point and say: either God is or he is not. But to which side shall we incline? Reason can determine nothing here. There is an infinite chaos that separates us. At the extremity of this infinite distance, *a game is being played* in which heads or tails will turn up. How will you wager? You have no rational grounds for choosing either way.

[The non-believer protests:] "The right thing is not to wager at all."

"Yes; but you must wager. It is not optional. You are committed [Vous êtes embarqué].… Since you must choose, let us see what is the less *profitable* option.")[42]

Not unlike Father Cruz does with doña Ana, Pascal convinces his interlocutor that it makes more sense, it is *more profitable*, of greater expected utility and interest, to wager in favour of the existence of God. The argument hinges on infinite gain versus nothing, and it has been hailed as one of the first examples of the application of mathematical probability and decision theories.[43] But this rational, sense-making proposition is not the end of the story. In a reversal in Pascal's drama of salvation, we get to hear the voice of the still sceptical non-believer respond to the appeal to bet wisely. I quote the exchange in full to give a sense of its theatrical character:

« Je le confesse, je l'avoue, mais encore… N'y a-t-il point moyen de voir le dessous du jeu ? »

« Oui, l'Écriture, et le reste, etc. »

« Oui, mais j'ai les mains liées et la bouche muette. On me force à parier, et je ne suis pas en liberté, on ne me relâche pas. Et je suis fait d'une telle sorte que je ne puis croire. Que voulez-vous donc que je fasse ? »

« … Travaillez donc, non pas à vous convaincre par l'augmentation des preuves de Dieu, mais par la diminution de vos passions. Vous voulez aller à la foi, et vous n'en savez pas le chemin ? Vous voulez vous guérir de l'infidélité, et vous en demandez les remèdes ? Apprenez de ceux qui ont été liés comme vous et qui parient maintenant tout leur bien: ce sont gens qui savent ce chemin que vous voudriez suivre et guéris d'un mal dont vous voulez guérir. Suivez la manière par où ils ont commencé : c'est en faisant tout comme s'ils croyaient, en prenant de l'eau bénite, en faisant dire des messes, etc. Naturellement même cela vous fera croire et vous abêtira. »

« Mais c'est ce que je crains. »

« Et pourquoi ? qu'avez-vous à perdre ?… »

« Ô ce discours me transporte, me ravit, etc. »[44]

("I confess it, I admit it. But still, … Is there no means of seeing what is in the cards?"

"Yes, Scripture and the rest, etc."

"Yes, but my hands are tied and my mouth is shut; I am forced to wager, and am not free.... I am made in such a way that I cannot believe. What then would you have me do?"

"... Work then, on convincing yourself, not by adding more proofs of God's existence, but by diminishing your passions. You would like to find faith and do not know the way? You would like to be cured of unbelief and ask for the remedies? Learn from those who were bound like you, and who now wager all they have.... Follow the way by which they began: they acted as if they believed, took holy water, had masses said, etc. This will make you believe naturally and mechanically."

"But this is what I am afraid of."

"And why? What do you have to lose?..."

"Oh! This discourse moves me, charms me, etc.")[45]

Philosophers have long been troubled by this exchange. Speaking from a perspective of logic, Daniel Garber objects that Pascal's deployment of the metaphor of the game and gambling does not constitute an argument for rational belief but rather a plausible consideration.[46] What's more, he questions the trustworthiness of the Pascalian suggestion of acting *as if* one believed as a way to bridge the gap between wanting to believe and actually believing, which for Garber constitutes nothing short of self-deception.[47]

And yet, read carefully, the summons to take stock of the circumstances and risk accordingly, followed by activation of the power of acting "as if" one believed, constitute for Pascal less a bid for self-deception than a pragmatic invitation to join the game first and then *play* the part: "Learn from those who were bound like you, and who now wager all they have.... Follow the way by which they began: they acted as if they believed, took holy water, had masses said, etc." This paradoxical *work of playing* is not only the way of those once non-believers who presumably now believe (and who, in this world can tell the difference between the two players anyway?) but it is also the characteristic of holiness, for nothing destroys it more thoroughly than a staunch assertion of its truthfulness and authenticity. This is why early modern historical saints rarely tout their holiness; to do so would be to turn it into self-idolatry.

To the impossibility of proving beyond all doubt the existence of God, Pascal responds by deploying the device of the wager. His goal is not so much to persuade the non-believer rationally or even rhetorically to believe blindly as much as to set the stage, *to put in motion a play for salvation* where the wagering non-believer becomes one more actor.[48] That is to say, the goal is to *engage* his interlocutor, to *move* him away from sceptical dithering and towards joining the circle of players. First as gamblers or *jugadores*, and then as actors, *comediantes* on life's stage, as it were.

Conclusion

The trouble with rationalist critiques of the Wager, from Voltaire's discomfort of mixing vulgar profit with serious matters, to Garber's fear of self-deception, stems largely from positing too stark an opposition between religion and the world. Voltaire cannot imagine that profane means may be used to religious ends. Garber's scepticism reads the "machine or beast-like" aspect of ritual repetition as self-deception unless accompanied by some transparent antecedent form of true belief: first grace, then action. Both Pascal and Cervantes before him turn that logic on its head and make use of the structure of gambling to posit a more dynamic vision of belief, one that allows for winning both here on earth and in the unknown. Moreover, as I hope to have shown, this reconsideration implies an emphasis on theatricality, on a form of action that is reactive, on the dislocation of certainties about self, story, and the world.[49]

Neither in *El rufián dichoso* nor in Pascal's Wager does grace manifest itself in spectacular eruptions or disruptions of the everyday (the realm of the miraculous), but it is also no longer possible to simply align gambling with spiritual blindness. Instead, grace is often nearly invisible, and it depends on a ruse of some sort or other to do its work. It surprises, and it moves us, and incites us to change course, to wager that we, too, can overcome ourselves and play at being otherwise. And what can be more theatrical than that?

NOTES

1 García Santo-Tomás, "Outside Bets," 149.

2 García Santo-Tomás, 150.

3 Cervantes's *Rufián dichoso* is the fourth of the eight full-length plays published in *Ocho comedias y ocho entremeses nuevos* (1615). The exact date of its composition is debatable, but it certainly postdates 1596, the publication date of the earliest historical sources Cervantes could have used for his adaptation: Juan de Marieta's *Segunda parte de la historia eclesiástica de todos los santos de España* and Agustín Dávila Padilla's *Historia de la fundación y discurso de la provincial de Santiago de México*. For a useful summary of the different hypotheses regarding the date of composition,

see Núñez Rivera, "Lectura de 'El rufián dichoso,'" 109–11. On Cervantes's sources, see Zugasti, "Sobre las fuentes de 'El rufián dichoso.'"

4 Rüdiger Campe distinguishes between sixteenth-century Catholic and Calvinist attitudes to games of chance. Calvinist doctrine made it possible to think of games of chance in line with a divine drawing of lots, that is to say, it returns the power of determination to God by making the results of the game the manifestation of God's decisions (Campe, *Game of Probability*, 28–34). García Santo-Tomás, for his part, notes that in spite of the declared moral suspicion against gambling, there were pragmatic and theoretical attempts to find a place for it in urban spaces as markers of social distinction, and in parallel to theatre, as evils that could be tolerated if harnessed for the greater good ("Outside Bets"). On the justifications of play and the association of literature with such legitimate leisure, see Scham, *Lector Ludens*.

5 Famously, jurist Cristóbal Suárez de Figueroa complained in *El pasajero* (1617) that theatre companies would stage *comedias de santos*, known for their stage machinery, as a way to attract an audience and make more profit (216–17). On the connection of theatre and gambling through the regulation of profit, see Bass, "Outside Bets," 165–6.

6 The brief mention in the gospels of Roman soldiers casting lots for Christ's clothing at the Crucifixion (Matt 27:35; John 19:23–24; Luke 23:34; and Mark 15:24; Coogan, *New Oxford Annotated Bible*), and especially Christ's words upon looking at them, "Father, forgive them, for they know not what they do" (Luke 23:34), becomes in the Middle Ages an allegory of the blindness to holiness caused by gambling. In the visual arts, the gambling soldiers are often depicted wholly absorbed in their vice, unaware of the historical intervention of God in human affairs. This blind obliviousness is contrasted with the grieving of Mary, attended by John the disciple and Mary Magdalene, a group that either looks in Christ's direction or whose eyes are closed in tears.

7 Scham, *Lector Ludens*, 9.

8 Guzmán, *Bienes del honesto trabajo*, 392. Here and elsewhere translations are mine unless otherwise noted.

9 The play appears in print together with two other Azevedo plays. Soufas bases her edition of *Dicha* on this edition, which has no date or place of publication, although she suggests that the plays must have been composed while Azevedo formed part of the court of Queen Isabel, who reigned from 1621 to 1644. I quote by line number from Azevedo, *Dicha*.

10 The association of Fortune with both astrology and games of chance, together with the rich symbolism of the figures printed on the cards themselves, often led to an association of gambling with idolatry (García Santo-Tomás, "Outside Bets," 159, 161).

11 On the *gracioso*'s multiple metatheatrical functions, see Nohe, "El gracioso como personaje metateatral."

12 In his influential *Philosophia antigua poetica* (1596), Alonso López Pinciano (*Filosofía*, 76–7) follows the Aristotelian distinction of tragedy from comedy, marking the differences thus:

> Es la primera de las diferencias que … la tragedia ha de tener personas graves, y la comedia comunes; y es la segunda que la tragedia tiene grandes temores llenos de peligro, y la comedia no; la tercera: la tragedia tiene tristes lamentables fines, la comedia no; la cuarta: en la tragedia quietos principios y turbados fines, la comedia al contrario; la quinta, que en la tragedia enseña la vida que se debe huir, y en la comedia la que se debe seguir; la sexta, que la tragedia se funda en historia, y la comedia es toda fábula …; la séptima, que la tragedia quiere y demanda estilo alto, y la comedia bajo.

> (The first distinction is that … tragedy must be about noble people and comedy about commoners; the second, tragedy is about frightful events full of danger, and comedy is not; the third, tragedy has lamentable endings while comedy does not; the fourth, tragedy has peaceful beginnings and distraught endings, in comedy it is the opposite; the fifth, tragedy teaches the sort of life to be avoided and comedy the sort of life to follow; the sixth, tragedy is based on history and comedy is all make-believe …; the seventh, tragedy asks for and requires a high style and comedy a lowly one.)

13 In Azevedo's play, the blindness typically associated with gambling is compounded by that inflicted upon the lover by Cupid (Azevedo, *Dicha*, 2993–6).

14 Azevedo, 2440.

15 The conflict in Fadrique's case emerges from the fact that he attempted to back out of a vow he made to the Virgin Mary in exchange for her protection while at sea. He had promised to marry the poorest girl in Lisbon, but he could not resist Nuño's offer of beautiful, rich Violante's hand.

16 Azevedo, *Dicha*, 2648–50. "Raro será el jugador / que por este trato suba, / habiendo muchos que bajan" (Uncommon shall be the gambler / who through this bargain climbs, / many more are those who descend).

17 Cervantes, *Rufián dichoso*, 365–467. All references henceforth are to line numbers of the play.

18 Other sources (Dávila Padilla, *Historia de la fundación*, 384) acknowledge divine intervention in Lugo's fortunate win, but the transformation is gradual: "Fue nuestro Señor servido para que no tuuiesse efecto tan infame proposito [to become a highway robber] … porque del todo no se

perdiesse el moço. Ganó entonces catorze o quinze reales, y despidio el proposito de ladron, aunque no las obras de moço perdido (It pleased the Lord that such an odious resolution [to become a highway robber] should not come to pass … so the young man should not be a wholly lost case. He won then fourteen or fifteen *reales* and he rejected the resolution to become a thief, though not the works of a stray young man.).

19 On the rhetorical characteristics of the genre in the context of the controversies surrounding the mixture of profane and religious elements in the *comedia de santos*, see Aparicio Maydeu, "A propósito de la comedia hagiográfica," "Preliminares." For a recent examination of the genre in a comparative context, France-Spain, see Teulade, *Le saint mis en scène*; for a psycho-critical approach to the appeal of the genre, see Llanos López, "Sobre el género de las comedias de santos."

20 Teulade, *Le saint mis en scène*. The saint is a figure characterized by spiritual perfection that, *pace* occasional contact with the supernatural via divine visions or the performance of miracles, manifests itself through a lack of ostentation. The saint is characterized by interiorized reflection, humility, and a general rejection of the trappings of the secular world – in other words, a *lack* of action.

21 Weber, *Theatricality*, 27.

22 On the importance of Aristotelian logic to the conversion of the rogue, see Delgado, "El itinerario moral de Cristóbal de Lugo."

23 Cervantes introduces this ambiguity. Dávila Padilla attributes Lugo's intention to become a robber to his impecunious condition (*Historia de la fundación*, 383).

24 Cervantes, *Rufián dichoso*, 1034.

25 Cervantes, 1096.

26 Campe quotes the seventeenth-century philosopher Samuel von Pufendorf's definition of a wager as "a reciprocal and conditional promise or bargain where chance plays a role, because whether or not an event or a thing exists does not depend on the player's efforts." He then goes on to explain the logic by placing it in the context of Roman law, which regulates "conditional contracts," in which both parties "bind their obligation to a future event that can occur or not occur and on which they have no influence" (*Game of Probability*, 32). A challenge, by contrast, implies the testing of another subject's abilities, rights, or existence. There is, so to speak, less skin in the game. For a reading of this scene in light of the picaresque and of Lugo's speech act as a challenge to God to prove his existence, see Henry, *Signifying Self*. As will become clear shortly, I contend that, as with Blaise Pascal's deployment of gambling as a structure for engagement with religion and the world, the question of proof or evidence is suspended in *El rufián dichoso* in favour of pragmatic action.

27 *Industria* may be translated as cleverness, skill, or diligence, but it carries in Spanish a slightly dubious connotation. Covarrubias defines it in his *Tesoro* as "la maña, diligencia y solercia con que alguno hace cualquier cosa con menos trabajo que otro" (the craftiness, diligence, and ability used by someone to do a particular thing with less effort than others). While Jesuits such as Gracián may have seen in *industria* deployable "tactics for perfecting and saving souls" (Kimmel, "No milagro, milagro," 435), in the context of games of chance and gambling it does not shed its negative connotations. In Azevedo's *Dicha*, for example, the word "industria" is used in the second scene of the first act by the devil to describe his efforts, always foiled by Mary's merciful jurisdiction (460); later it will be treated as a synonym of *ardid* (scheme) by Violante, referring to Felisardo's ploy to gamble (2311). Finally, Nuño describes it as the offspring of gambling: "Para ocupación del ocio / el juego inventó la industria; / mas esta curiosidad / así los hombres abusan" (As a way to employ leisure / gambling invented industry; / but this inquisitiveness / men abused so; 2638–41). In *El rufián dichoso*, the *gracioso* uses the adjective to refer ironically to highway robbers as sensible, industrious, and brave people ("personas que son cuerdas, / industriosas y valientes"; 1026–7).

28 Weber, *Theatricality*, 29.

29 Lope counsels that "Los casos de la honra son mejores, / porque mueven con fuerza a toda gente" (*Arte nuevo*, 134), advice that Victor Dixon renders thus: "Matters of honour are the best as subjects; / they powerfully move all kinds of folk" (Vega, "New Rules," ll. 327–8).

30 Ginés's soliloquy in the third act of Lope de Vega's *Lo fingido verdadero*, for example, is accompanied by heavenly voices and a miraculous vision that confirm his intuition that his soul would be saved by imitating truly the Christian martyrdom of the character he plays onstage (133). In contrast, Lugo has left the stage already when an angel and heavenly music confirm for the audience the veracity of the rogue's conversion at the end of the first act.

31 Marieta, *Historia eclesiástica*, 160; I should note that the play does have its share of supernatural sightings, of both the devilish (a squadron of lascivious nymphs dance around the praying friar) and the heavenly kind (in the last act, three saved souls welcome that of a deceased Cristóbal de la Cruz). However, it is significant that Father Cruz dismisses the former as a dream and is unaffected by the second since he is dead.

32 The role of grace and human freedom would, of course, divide Catholics and Protestants in the sixteenth century. The Council of Trent defined the Catholic Church's position declaring unequivocally that human freedom is not foreclosed by grace, a scenario that would be played over again onstage, most notably in the drama of what Parker called "santos y bandoleros" (saints and bandits). His groundbreaking study goes as far as to see this

particular plot line as a predominantly Spanish preoccupation ("Santos y bandoleros"). However, left unattended was the matter of how, specifically, grace and freedom will work together, and this omission opened the door to fierce debates within Catholicism between Jesuits and Dominicans; Augustianism and Thomism. In a succinct account of these controversies, Sullivan (*Tirso de Molina*) notes that by the late sixteenth century, the question of human freedom in its relationship to salvation not only "eclipsed all others in magnitude" (10) in Counter-Reformation Spain, but "the debate on grace even became a topic of tavern-room oratory" (30). However, by the time of the publication of Sebastián de Covarrubias's lexicon in 1611, the humanist demurely skirts the issue. After quoting Aquinas briefly under his description of the word *gracia*, as pertains to theology, Covarrubias states that "no es de mi instituto en esta obra seguir las materias, consulte escolásticos" (it is not within my competence or the objective in this work to treat these matters; consult the Scholastics). Similarly, Cervantes reassures the reader through the stage directions that the most unbelievable aspects of his play are also those that hewed closest to his historical sources. I would argue, that in doing so, Cervantes's play escapes the dramaturgy described by Sullivan in his work on Tirso as "predicated on dialectical oppositions (freedom versus destiny, certainty versus doubt, appearance versus reality, truth versus falsehood)" (*Tirso de Molina*, 10).

33 Kallendorf reads this scene as a humanist exorcism dependent on logos and Christian charity rather than on external aids such as holy water, a crucifix, incantations, and so on (*Exorcism and Its Texts*, 108–13).

34 Doña Ana's deathbed intransigence is not the only place in the Cervantine *œuvre* that a representation of a dying person unwilling to confess and save his or her soul is solved by a ruse. In the second part of *Don Quijote*, playful Basilio will fake his suicide and refuse to take the last rites until his rival has yielded to him in marriage the hand of his beloved Quiteria. Once he has secured Quiteria, Basilio springs back to life and everyone thinks they have witnessed a miracle. He corrects them, however, shouting that the events had not unfolded thanks to a supernatural intervention, but rather to very human *industria* (chap. 21). Seth Kimmel argues that in both prose and on the stage, theatricality's "power of artifice to compel belief was also to display the theological efficacy of religious representation" ("No milagro, milagro," 434). I am sympathetic to his argument, but my reading of Cervantes's play does not depend on a mimetic understanding of theatricality. Instead, what is at stake in the scene of doña Ana's repentance, I propose, is closer to what Roman Jakobson ("Linguistics and Poetics") described as the phatic function of language. At stake is the recognition of a shared premise, a way of engaging with the world, rather than the communication of any particular doctrine.

35 The famous fragment gets its name from just two paragraphs of a longer section in a bundle of reflections that Philippe Sellier, the text's most recent and careful editor, gathered under the heading of "Discourse on the Machine" (see his explanation in Pascal, *Les Pensées*, 466–7). All quotations of Blaise Pascal are taken from Sellier's edition, and I cite by fragment and page number; English translations are by Roger Ariew, and I cite by page number, since he follows Sellier's classification of Pascal's fragments in *Pensées*.

36 Voltaire, "Sur *Les Pensées*," 961.

37 On play as an important reference for Pascal's oeuvre, see Thirouin, *Le hasard et les règles*. Campe's second chapter also looks at the function of games in the Wager in order to argue, *pace* Ian Hacking and other historians of science, that although Pascal is lauded as the first to "tame chance" through the calculation of mathematical probability, the French philosopher does something more subtle: he makes a rhetorical use of the mathematical aspect of games in order to find in games a privileged site for engaging matters of serious concern.

38 Ariew, 116; Sellier, fr. 423, p. 332.

39 Ariew, 122; Sellier, fr. 430, p. 340.

40 Ariew, 212; Sellier, fr. 680, p. 469.

41 Sellier, fr. 680, p. 469; my emphasis.

42 Ariew, 212; my emphasis.

43 Hacking, *Emergence of Probability*.

44 Sellier, fr. 680, p. 471.

45 Ariew, 213–14.

46 Garber, *Pascal's Wager*.

47 An accessible version of Garber's claim that while the Wager may make rational sense when considering eternal salvation, it "isn't good enough for everyday life" (*Pascal's Wager*, 54–5) is presented in conversation with Gary Gutting in a piece published in the *New York Times* (Gutting, "Wanting to Believe").

48 Campe also speaks of this double movement in Pascal's Wager from the gambling and calculation itself to the "as-if" of the play acting suggested to the nonbeliever in order to set up Pascal as the lynchpin connecting a poetic model of probability based on rhetoric and the scientific calculation of risk. Such a collision, he argues, would devolve into the renewed sense of reality in the novel (*Game of Probability*, 67–72).

49 Although much has been written with regard to the question of "unity" in *El rufián dichoso*, what I mean by *dislocation* does not enter into the debates whether the play is a string of unconnected episodes or a coherent whole. What I mean by *dislocation* is the awareness by the characters and the audience that things could turn out differently than expected.

REFERENCES

Aparicio Maydeu, J. "A propósito de la comedia hagiográfica barroca." In *Estado actual de los estudios sobre el Siglo de Oro*, vol. 1, edited by Manuel García Martín, 141–52. Salamanca: Universidad de Salamanca, 1993.

Aparicio Maydeu, Javier. "Preliminares para una definición de la comedia religiosa en el siglo XVII." In *Actas del XI Congreso de la Asociación Internacional de Hispanistas*, vol. 3, *Encuentros y desencuentros de culturas: Desde la Edad Media al siglo XVIII*, edited by Juan Villegas, 169–76. Irvine: Regents of the University of California, 1994.

Azevedo, Ángela de. *Dicha y desdicha del juego y devoción de la Virgen*. In *Women's Acts: Plays by Women Dramatists of Spain's Golden Age*, edited by Teresa Scott Soufas, 4–44. Lexington: University Press of Kentucky, 1997.

Bass, Laura R. "'Outside Bets: Disciplining Gamblers in Early Modern Spain' by Enrique Garcìa [*sic*] Santo-Tomás." *Hispanic Review* 77, no. 1 (2009): 165–6. https://doi.org/10.1353/hir.0.0051.

Campe, Rüdiger. *The Game of Probability: Literature and Calculation from Pascal to Kleist*. Translated by Ellwood H. Wiggins. Stanford: Stanford University Press, 2012.

Cervantes, Miguel de. *Don Quijote de la Mancha*. Edited by Francisco Rico. Madrid: Real Academia Española, Asociación de Academias de la Lengua Española, 2004.

Cervantes, Miguel de. *Miguel de Cervantes: Comedias y tragedias*. Edited by Luis Gómez Canseco. 2 vols. Madrid: Real Academia Española, 2015.

Cervantes, Miguel de. *Rufián dichoso*. Edited by Valentín Núñez Rivera. In Cervantes, *Comedias y tragedias*, 1:365–467.

Coogan, Michael D., ed. *The New Oxford Annotated Bible*. Oxford: Oxford University Press, 2001.

Covarrubias, Sebastián. *Tesoro de la lengua castellana o española*. Edited by Ignacio Arellano and Rafael Zafra. Frankfurt am Main: Iberoamericana Vervuert, 2006.

Dávila Padilla, Agustín. *Historia de la fundación y discurso de la provincia de Santiago de México de la orden de predicadores*. 2nd ed. Brussels: Juan de Meerbecque, 1625.

Delgado, Manuel. "El itinerario moral de Cristóbal de Lugo en El rufián dichoso." In *Cervantes y su mundo*, vol. 3, edited by A. Robert Lauer and Kurt Reichenberger, 103–22. Kassel: Reichenberger, 2005.

Garber, Daniel. *What Happens after Pascal's Wager: Living Faith and Rational Belief*. Milwaukee: Marquette University Press, 2009.

García Santo-Tomás, Enrique. "Outside Bets: Disciplining Gamblers in Early Modern Spain." *Hispanic Review* 77, no. 1 (2009): 147–64. https://doi.org/10.1353/hir.0.0039.

Gutting, Gary. "Can Wanting to Believe Make Us Believers?" *Opinionator* (blog). *New York Times*, 5 October 2014. https://opinionator.blogs.nytimes .com/2014/10/05/can-wanting-to-believe-make-us-believers/.

Guzmán, Pedro de. *Bienes del honesto trabajo y daños de la ociosidad.* Madrid: Imprenta Real, 1614.

Hacking, Ian. *The Emergence of Probability: A Philosophical Study of Early Ideas about Probability, Induction and Statistical Inference.* London: Cambridge University Press, 1975.

Henry, Melanie. *The Signifying Self: Cervantine Drama as Counter-Perspective Aesthetic.* London: Modern Humanities Research Association, 2013.

Jakobson, Roman. "Linguistics and Poetics." In *Style in Language*, edited by Thomas A. Sebeok, 350–77. Cambridge, MA: MIT Press, 1960.

Kallendorf, Hilaire. *Exorcism and Its Texts: Subjectivity in Early Modern Literature of England and Spain.* Toronto: University of Toronto Press, 2003.

Kimmel, Seth. "'No milagro, milagro': The Early Modern Art of Effective Ritual." *MLN* 128, no. 2 (2013): 433–44. https://doi.org/10.1353 /mln.2013.0014.

Llanos López, Rosana. "Sobre el género de las comedias de santos." In *Homenaje a Henri Guerreiro: La hagiografía entre historia y literatura en la España de la Edad Media y del Siglo de Oro*, edited by Marc Vitse, 809–26. Frankfurt am Main: Iberoamericana Vervuert, 2005.

López Pinciano, Alonso. *Filosofía antigua poética.* In Sánchez Escribano and Porqueras Mayo, *Preceptiva*, 71–80.

Marieta, Juan. *Segunda parte de la historia eclesiástica de España.* Cuenca: Pedro del Valle, 1596.

Nohe, Hanna. "El gracioso como personaje metateatral: Funciones y desarrollo a lo largo del Siglo de Oro." *Hipogrifo* 6, no. 1 (2018): 663–79. https://doi.org/10.13035/H.2018.06.01.44.

Núñez Rivera, Valentín. "Lectura de 'El rufián dichoso.'" In Cervantes, *Comedias y tragedias*, 2:97–111.

Parker, Alexander A. "Santos y bandoleros en el teatro del Siglo de Oro." *Arbor*, nos. 43–4 (1949): 395–416.

Pascal, Blaise. *Les Pensées.* Edited by Philippe Sellier. Paris: Classiques Garnier, 1999.

Pascal, Blaise. *Pensées.* Translated by Roger Ariew. Indianapolis: Hackett, 2005.

Sánchez Escribano, Federico, and Alberto Porqueras Mayo. *Preceptiva dramática española del Renacimiento y el Barroco.* Madrid: Gredos, 1965.

Scham, Michael. *Lector Ludens: The Representation of Games and Play in Cervantes.* Toronto: University of Toronto Press, 2014.

Suárez de Figueroa, Cristóbal. *El pasajero.* Vol 1. Barcelona: Promociones y Publicaciones Universitarias, 1988.

Sullivan, Henry W. *Tirso de Molina and the Drama of the Counter Reformation*. Amsterdam: Rodopi, 1981.

Teulade, Anne. *Le saint mis en scene*. Paris: Cerf, 2012.

Thirouin, Laurent. *Le hasard et les règles. Le modèle du jeu dans la pensée de Pascal*. Paris: J. Vrin, 1991.

Vega, Lope de. *Arte nuevo de hacer comedias*. In Sánchez Escribano and Porqueras Mayo, *Preceptiva*, 125–36.

Vega, Lope de. *Lo fingido verdadero. Revista de la Asociación de Directores de Escena de España*, no. 87 (2001): 109–39.

Vega, Lope de. "New Rules for Writing Plays at This Time." Edited by Victor Dixon. 2009. Emothe Biblioteca Digital. http://emothe.uv.es/biblioteca/textosEMOTHE/EMOTHE0116_NewRulesForWritingPlaysAtThisTime.php

Voltaire. "Letter Twenty-Five: On the *Pensées* of M. Pascal." In *Philosophical Letters: Letters Concerning the English Nation*, edited by John Leigh and translated by Prudence Steiner, 101–23. Indianapolis: Hackett, 2007.

Voltaire. "Sur *Les Pensées* de Pascal." In *Dictionnaire de la pensée de Voltaire par lui-même*. Edited by André Versaille, 957–71. Brussels: Éditions Complexe, 1994.

Weber, Samuel. *Theatricality as Medium*. New York: Fordham University Press, 2004.

Zugasti, Miguel. "Algo más sobre las fuentes de 'El rufián dichoso' de Cervantes." In *Locos, figurones y quijotes en el teatro de los Siglos de Oro: Actas selectas del XII Congreso de la Asociación Internacional de Teatro Español y Novohispano de los Siglos de Oro: Almagro, 15, 16 y 17 de julio de 2005*, edited by Germán Vega García-Luengos and Rafael González Cañal, 493–513. Almagro: Universidad de Castilla-La Mancha, 2007.

4 Writing to Rescue from Oblivion: The Phantasms of Captivity in *El trato de Argel*

JULIA DOMÍNGUEZ

The imposing city of Algiers plays a unique role in the collective memory of Spain during Cervantes's time. The city, long a focal point of Spain's struggle with the east, came to house thousands of Christian captives, whose personal experiences were recorded in *relaciones*, religious texts, and *informaciones*, as well as in drawings, etchings, and paintings. Such representations provided different perspectives on both Christian and Muslim cultures abroad and offered contested versions of the same reality. As an illustration, in the exhibition *Miguel de Cervantes: De la vida al mito (1616–2016)* celebrated at the Biblioteca Nacional in Spain that commemorated the fourth centenary of the writer's death, the public had the opportunity to contemplate the view of Algiers depicted in the *Civitates orbis terrarum* created by Georg Braum and Frans Hogenberg in 1575. In the drawing, one could clearly see a city that, judging by its organization, its buildings, and the existence of an interior and exterior wall, boasted one of the most developed urban societies of the time, a somewhat idyllic vision of a city established from the memories recorded in the textual accounts.[1] In contrast, in another depiction of the city dated from just a few years earlier, in 1563, and preserved in the General Archive of Simancas, Algiers is presented from a very different perspective.[2] Its creator clearly imposed a more personal imprint that "no quiere tanto dibujar un plano exacto de la realidad como mostrar los puntos flacos de una ciudad que tenía fama de ser inexpugnable"[3] (He does not want so much to draw an exact map of reality as to show the weak points of a city that had a reputation for being impregnable).[4] The intentional visible manipulations of the mental image of the same city in both drawings is an evident illustration of an act of memory as a re-presentation, as elucidated by Andreas Huyssen in *Twilight Memories*: "It does not require much theoretical sophistication to see that all representation – whether in language, narrative, image, or recorded sound – is based on memory. Re-presentation always comes after.... The past is not there in memory, but it must be articulated to become memory."[5]

Similarly, in *El trato de Argel* (c. 1580),[6] the act of recollection of Cervantes's time as a captive in Algiers yields an articulation and re-enactment of memories through the presentation of distinct mental images revealed in dramatic form. As a result, the plot of the play, the portrayal of the captivity of Christians in Muslim North Africa at the end of the sixteenth century, embodies what I call the theatricality of memory. The play's main actions and themes reveal Cervantes's own experience in Algerian captivity after spending six years as a soldier in Italy.[7] Those recollections, captured within the plot of the play, coincide with the testimonies of Cervantes's companions described in Antonio de Sosa's *Topographia e historia general de Argel* (1612).[8] Through the intertwining of reality and fiction – by following classical and medieval resources as well[9] – the play draws on these historical accounts and weaves them into a fictional dramatic rendering of captivity.

The play narrates the vicissitudes of two Christian captives in love, Aurelio and Silvia, who, victims of the passion of their Muslim masters, Zahara and Yzuf, suffer the conditions of captivity and lack of freedom in Algiers. The play also includes other characters' interspersed stories that portray the harsh and humiliating mental and physical conditions of captives and their spiritual and social dilemmas under confinement during Hasan Pasha's first term as ruler of Algiers (1577–80). The apparent fragmented and scattered plot in *El trato de Argel* includes captives, renegades, masters, slaves, corsairs, parents, children, a devil, a lion, and two allegorical figures: Necessity and Occasion. While the variety of characters and actions can be distracting to an audience, the interjection of so many plot twists accurately reflects how human memory functions with its paradoxes, power, and limitations, particularly after traumatic experiences.[10] When one remembers, there is not just one single image, but rather several from which the experience is recomposed, transformed, and distorted. Cervantes, aware of the fragility of memory and the relative value of this faculty to accurately render the past – a theme that appears again and again in his literary work[11] – instead determines to theatricalize the past in order to guarantee its existence and rescue it from oblivion.[12] Hence, the integration of so many characters and themes was an attempt at providing form, function, veracity, and persistence to the past while also underscoring the human conditions of survival. By doing so, *El trato de Argel* legitimizes and reinforces the significance of singular memory acts and reduces the danger that they will be erased or fall into what Huyssen calls "cultural amnesia."[13]

Once back in Spain, Cervantes reconstructs and re-presents the traumatic experience of his long five-year captivity. He does so by ascribing to the theories of the time regarding memory and recollection, and, more specifically, the art of memory that advocated for the use of the *imago agente*, that is, effective and persuasive images. The mental image, the basis of memory theory since classical antiquity, becomes a key element in his "cathartic evocation"[14] of the traumatic experience. Catharsis, following Aristotle in the *Poetics* (Lat. *catharsis*, Gr. κάθαρσις, *kátharsis*, "purge," "purification"), was a means by which theatre can have a purifying and liberating effect at the same time that it can arouse compassion, horror, and other emotions in the audience.[15] As a consequence, *El trato de Argel* is an excellent example of seeking catharsis through re-presentation of trauma.

The play becomes a rich setting to investigate the nature of these images, their power and their impact. I refer to Cervantes's dramatized response to captivity in *El trato de Argel* as a "phantasm," a concept first coined by Aristotle in the first book on memory, *Memoria et reminiscentia*, that would remain a dominant term for memory (Gr. *phantasmata*, Lat. *imagines*) up through the eighteenth century. Perhaps more importantly, a phantasm is metaphorical since, like a traumatic experience, memories haunt their victim as if they had a life of their own, as noted in Cathy Caruth's definition of trauma: "To be traumatized is precisely to be possessed by an image or event."[16] In his play, Cervantes reveals those "hidden phantasms" by re-presenting past experiences and becoming "el primero que re[-]presentase las imaginaciones y los pensamientos escondidos del alma" (the first to re[-]present the imagination and hidden thoughts of the soul) – just as he said he would in the prologue to his *Ocho comedias y ocho entremeses* (1615).[17] In order to analyse this act of revelation, I draw on the model of the art of memory – with its loci and *imagines* – and its particular preference for manipulating images of the past to show how Cervantes acutely reveals his personal experience of captivity to the audience through a dramatic re-presentation, a theatre of memory where mental images take on life.

**Cervantes and Early Modern Memory: *El trato de Argel*
as a Theatre of the Mind**

As one of the most influential writers in early modern Europe, perhaps it should not be surprising that Cervantes's work reflects the general understanding of the different theories of memory during the time.[18] During the Middle Ages and up through the Renaissance, scientifically, memory was considered the treasurer of all sciences. Physiologically, physicians believed memory to be an interior sense located in one of the three ventricles, at the back of the brain, without which the other interior "faculties," intellect and imagination, could not function properly. In art, philosophy, and literature, the goddess Mnemosyne was considered the mother of the highly praised nine Muses. As a result of the legacy of the Platonic tradition, *remembering* was synonymous with knowing. Ethically, as part of the virtue of *prudentia*, memory was an essential part of the tripartite soul with which in future actions man could excel and improve his moral life. In rhetoric, memory was a critical instrument to study, write, and speak properly in public. Furthermore, to speak of memory in the time of Cervantes was to speak not only of the inner workings of the brain (*natural memory*), the intricacies of the soul, and the construction of the self, but also to address ways to improve memory's capacity through trained recollection (*artificial memory*), powerful mnemonic images, and diverse tools of external memory such as books, libraries, commonplace books, *librillos de memoria*, and other places and objects that, as extensions of memory, attempt to preserve the past.

Given that innate natural memory was so venerated, artificial systems to improve it included specific techniques and strategies, many of which were contained in the various treatises in the art of memory. Devised in classical antiquity by Simonedes of Ceos, this art – also called artificial memory, *ars memorativa*, *ars memoriae*, or local memory – became part of the rhetorical method whereby a speaker could perfect his memory and conjure up long speeches through the creation of a mental architectonic design. Described by authors of the stature of Cicero, Quintilian, and the anonymous author of the *Rhetorica ad Herennium*, the technique required an orator to use his imagination to retrieve images (*imagines agentes*) that he had previously mentally placed in a set of places (loci).[19] After its evolution through the Middle Ages, the Renaissance art of memory was not restricted to storing and retrieving information, in fact, it acquired new dimensions. As studied by Frances Yates in *The Art of Memory*, these mental systems established links with rhetoric, religion and ethics, philosophy and psychology, the encyclopaedic knowledge concentrated in theatres and palaces, emblems, art and literature. The art became a social phenomenon that showed how mnemotechnics and their mental systems penetrated "into the lives of the urban middle classes, and even [played] a role in shaping one's daily habits."[20] In their introduction to *The Memory Arts in Renaissance England*, William E. Engel, Rory Loughnane, and Grant Williams speak of a "mnemonic epistème" to refer to the diversity and ubiquity of a mnemonic culture that fostered a cultural code based on a science of places and images.[21]

The evolution of the art of memory and its advent in the Renaissance in Spain helped writers theorize about the three-dimensionality of literature.[22] As Aurora Egido points out, artificial memory undoubtedly facilitated the production of mental schemas reflected in both artistic and literary works that led to endless possibilities: "Los ingenios de la máquina mnemotécnica produjeron un sinfín de posibilidades combinatorias, y favorecieron en la literatura toda clase de espacios alegóricos" (The ingenuity of the mnemonic machine produced endless combinatorial possibilities, and favoured all kinds of allegorical spaces in literature).[23] Artificial memory was widely embraced in society and it became a part of the instruction in universities and literary academies where poetic mnemonic exercises were carried out.[24] One of the most celebrated examples in this tradition is San Juan de la Cruz, who, as a result of his classes on logic, rhetoric, and mnemonics at the University of Salamanca, devised his *Cántico espiritual* mentally in prison where he memorized the first thirty stanzas of his work, and later put the poem to text.[25]

As one of the most representative authors of his time, Cervantes was part of this cultural *contaminatio* of the art of memory. A writer who recalls his own readings incessantly had to be familiar with the architectural and pictorial principles in the composition of places and images.[26] As in other contemporary works, Cervantes was quite familiar with such exercises of memory that generated mental spaces – in the style of virtual ones today[27] – and that relied upon the power of visual imagination. As a result, as studied by Egido[28] and Frederick de Armas, his narratives reveal the mental habits of that period that constantly appeal to memory, its spaces, and images. According to de Armas, Cervantes could have known Giambattista della Porta's *L'arte di ricordare*, published during his stay in Naples. In his work, dedicated to Philip II, the Italian scholar develops certain ideas that would have an impact on Cervantes's writings, such as the importance of places for memory images, the comparisons between the art of memory and the theatre, and the significance of strong images for memorizing.[29] More specifically, in regards to Cervantes and the use of images from Italian art, de Armas states that the writer's first endeavours to place images in his fiction can be found in his theatrical works, particularly in his early tragedy, *La Numancia*. More importantly, within the context of this essay, Cervantes "could well be acquainted with della Porta's dramatic works such as *La Turca* and could have related to the mnemonics of the writer to his theatre. The romance plot and the events of captivity could well have been an inspiration for Cervantes's *Trato de Argel*."[30]

With such treatises on memory in mind and himself a product of Spanish and Italian cultures that venerated and protected memory while seeking methods to improve it, Cervantes became a prisoner in Algiers where memory was the primary means of recording experience. Given the significance of places for mental images and the connection between the art of memory and theatre, he would have chosen this genre for the placement of strong mnemonic images from captivity and placed them in specific ways in *El trato de Argel*. The traumatic experience of captivity compelled him to write a play that inaugurated his career as a playwright.[31] As Antonio Rey Hazas states, the play is "el resultado literario de una experiencia vital insoslayable, imposible de olvidar, que había marcado para siempre su biografía y su quehacer literario" (the literary result of an unavoidable life experience, impossible to forget, that had forever marked his biography and his literary work).[32] In much the same way the mnemonist physically appears within the system he composes, Cervantes becomes a sort of stage director of the theatre of his own memory. I use the word *theatre* here echoing Giulio Camillo's use, that is, "The theater is that which makes visible, which projects outward, the stage spectacle overseen by memory inside of man."[33] Following Camillo's or Robert Fludd's theories on theatres of memory, these were constructs built on the idea that anyone entering could remember and contemplate universal knowledge by uniting man's inner universe, his microcosm, with the outer universe, the macrocosm.[34] Based on this idea, William Shakespeare's Globe was inspired by Fludd, with the words "All the world's a stage" "tak[ing] on a new meaning as we begin to see the *Globe Theater* as indeed a *Theater of the World*, presenting the history of the Microcosm within the Macrocosm."[35]

For Cervantes, who expressed on numerous occasions his fondness for theatre,[36] these words represent what drama was intended to be, as evidenced by Don Quixote during his encounter with a company of actors: "Espejo de la vida humana, ejemplo de las costumbres e imagen de la verdad" (A mirror of human life, an example of customs and the image of truth).[37] In this sense, Cervantes takes his personal experience, the microcosm, and transforms *El trato de Argel* into a macrocosm, a reflection of the whole Algiers experience. This idea is clearly reflected in the closing lines of the play when Aurelio speaks of *El trato de Argel* as a "trasunto de la vida de Argel" (a reflection of life in Algiers),[38] that is, an imitation and a reflection of survival in the Algerian city, *trasunto* understood here as a re-presentation of the writer's memories of the city now transposed to the stage. By projecting his interior space towards the exterior, the writer reveals his mental theatre – a mental architecture – and invites the spectator to metadramatically participate in the captivity experience as if it were a "retablo de las maravillas" (tableau of wonders).[39] In the end, the audience is transported beyond the real space of the stage into the "memoryscapes"[40] of the writer.

The Loci of Captivity

As a reflection of the space of Algiers, the stage becomes an extension of memory where the spectator witnesses the locative projection of the captive's trauma. This dramatic rendering reveals the spatiality of memory,[41] a conceptual metaphor that describes memory as a receptacle, a treasury of mental images.[42] This conceptualization comes from the treatises on classical rhetoric, in which memory commonly appears described in terms of its spatiality – such as Aristotle's *Topica* in the Greek tradition – and divided into loci where images are positioned in a precious treasure house, a thesaurus (Lat. *thesaurus*). One important consequence of the art of memory was the existence of complex mental systems that advocated for creating topographical structures or spatial dispositions of memory such as the Augustinian "vast palaces of memory" or Saint Teresa's "castillo interior" (interior castle). Texts begin to be perceived in architectural terms, as reflected in the use of titles containing the words *plaza*, *jardín*, *teatro*, or *hospital* (square, garden, theatre, hospital). Cervantes uses metaphorical spaces that are full of symbolism such as the Black Forest of *La casa de los celos*, the valley of the Cypreses in *La Galatea*, or in *Don Quixote*, the cave of Montesinos,[43] or the Sierra Morena mountains.

Through his initial *compositio loci*, the writer follows one of the most important precepts of the art of memory, that of carefully selecting and describing specific places to create the desired effect, in this case that of revealing the captive's delicate mental condition. As a result, the mental loci of captivity will always be described in tandem with the inhospitable and cruel conditions in the city and as a reflection of the difficult and distressing situation in which captives find themselves. Cervantes makes the urban setting a protagonist of the play not only by elevating it in the title but also through spatial dimensions meant to underscore the captives' personal thoughts. In the monologue that opens the play, Aurelio equates his mental state to common loci associated with captivity, that is, confined and restricted places endowed with strong negative connotations that remind the audience that there is no way out: "¡Triste y miserable estado, / triste esclavitud amarga, /

donde es la pena tan larga / cuan corto el bien abreviado! / ¡Oh, purgatorio en la vida, / infierno puesto en el mundo / mal que no tiene segundo, / estrecho do no hay salida" (Sad and miserable state, / sad bitter slavery, / where the pain is so enduring / how short the abbreviated good! / Oh, purgatory in life, / hell imposed upon the world / evil that has no second, / straits with no way out).[44] The monologue sets the tone for the play by serving as "trasunto" of the state of the captive – "a mental purgatory" – that plays out onstage. The art of memory taught one to carefully select and describe specific spaces according to the distinction between *topotesia* (imaginary places or *ficta loca*) and *topographia* (real or typical places). Such overlapping of places – real and imagined – yields multidimensional spaces where a real place is presented as a reflection of the captive's *loci mentales*, stressing the relationship between the mental state of captivity and the external world. Lina Bolzoni speaks of the ways in which the art of memory facilitated a "mirroring relationship between the mind and writing ... between mental places and textual places, between inner experience and the external world."[45] When Aurelio connects the negative connotations of Algiers to the inner experience of captivity, which he describes as "caos" (chaos) and "hondo valle" (deep valley), the mirroring relationship immediately recalls the well-known religious reference "in hac lacrimarum valle" (valley of tears) from the *Salve regina*. In another instance, distressed forces of nature are seen as the contributing cause of suffering for an entire family of Christian captives. The spectator contemplates a desolate mother, broken in pain at the irremediable loss of her children, who screams: "[H]ase oscurecido el cielo, / turbado los elementos, / conjurado mar y vientos, / todos en tu desconsuelo" (The sky has darkened, / the elements disturbed, / sea and winds conjured, / all in your grief). Once again, the writer links the inner turmoil to the outer world, providing an intimate window onto the captive's suffering and despair.

Algiers acquires symbolic and allegoric value and a multiplicity of meanings that recall common loci of the arts of memory that were also well known to the audience, particularly with respect to their topographical disposition. More specifically, Cervantes projects the Algerian experience within a spatial structure that symbolizes hell and purgatory – Christian metaphorical and symbolic spaces whose visual structure was known to audience members from depictions in churches or images in artistic works, including treaties of the art of memory that facilitated their memorization. In their versions of the art of memory, several writers saw religious concepts as excellent teaching opportunities. In his *Thesaurus artificiosae memoriae* (1579), Florentine Dominican friar Cosimo Rosselli featured diagrams designed to visually recollect the road to salvation in Heaven or to condemnation in Hell.[46] Similarly, in the *Congestorium artificiose memorie* (1520) the German Dominican Johannes Romberch observes Paradise, Purgatory, and Hell as unmistakable loci of memory.[47] As an emblem of these two symbolic places, Aurelio's opening monologue specifically calls Algiers a "purgatorio" (purgatory) and "infierno" (hell). And the metaphorical value of hell and purgatory transcends explicit speaking parts in the play. For María Antonia Garcés the inclusion of the number seven in the title of the play to refer to the number of years of captivity – and not the actual five years Cervantes spent there – underscores the religious allegory of the hellish experience of captivity: *Comedia llamada* trato de Argel, *hecha por Miguel de Cervantes questuvo* [sic] *cautivo en él siete años* (Comedy called the trade of Algiers, by Miguel de Cervantes who was [sic] captive in it for seven years). Garcés sees a link between the religious symbology of the number seven and Aurelio's allusion to the mental spatiality of purgatory, "which in turn, summon contemporary images of purgatory, with its seven tiers of mountains."[48] The number seven must have triggered another set of associations for the spectator, that of the seventh circle of Dante's Inferno from the *Divina commedia*,[49] known as a symbol of suffering, thus stressing "the visions of purgatory and hell on earth."[50] Similarly, Garcés, paraphrasing Stanislav Zimic, sees correspondence between the scenes represented in the four acts and the four spheres of Dante's Inferno – a known representation often featured in the *ars memorativa*:[51] "'the abysmal verticality of an *Inferno*' symbolically represented by a city completely surrounded by the desert and the sea, an inferno also recalled by the eternal sufferings and punishments of the captives."[52]

It does not seem accidental to me that Cervantes invokes well-known loci that were unmistakably known to the public. Doing so gives the playwright the opportunity to elicit a whole series of associations between the conditions of captivity and the social anxieties surrounding the afterlife. In this case, such recollection occurs as prescribed by Aristotle's laws of association,[53] and connects the ethical aspect of the art of memory that was so crucial to the Council of Trent (1545–63) to the individual experience. In Spain, the use of frightening imagery and symbolic places were carefully integrated into ecclesiastical teachings to bolster Counter-Reformist arguments for orthodox practices.[54] The *ars memorativa* would hold special importance for even the staunchest supporters of the Counter-Reformation such as the Jesuits who believed in the *compositio loci* and mnemonic power of images for religious conversion. As a result, certain places, such as Paradise and Hell, became fully charged with great symbolism as found in images of catechisms, and the art of memory was a key strategy to learn it all.

For many captives, memory is a blessing that provides refuge from their imprisonment, while also a curse that constantly reminds them of a past that no longer exists – and which they may never experience again: "Being disposed of everything that had given a meaning to their life," as Garcés notes.[55] Deprived of liberty in their current situation, the captives constantly look to their past with nostalgia and contrast it with their current tormented life. As an illustration, Silvia compares the prosperity that characterized her previous life with her current real and figurative poverty: "Dicen que fui rica un tiempo / pero toda mi riqueza / se ha vuelto en mayor pobreza / y ha pasado con el tiempo" (They say I was rich / but all my wealth / has become greater poverty / and has vanished with time).[56] Similarly, for Sayavedra, memory is the cause of much pain: "[E]stas cosas volviendo en mi memoria / las lágrimas trujeron a los ojos, / forzados de desgracia tan notoria" (These things coming back to my memory / brought tears to my eyes, / forced from such notorious misfortune).[57] For these characters, remembering is not just a personal experience; it is also part of a social practice. For example, in a dialogue with Sayavedra, another captive, Pedro, now a renegade, justifies his decision to convert to Islam to escape the horrible circumstances to which Christian captives are subject.[58] Sayavedra proclaims nostalgia for better times under Charles V and expresses discontent with Philip II's political approach to the Mediterranean conflict – which is very similar in tone to the letter that Cervantes wrote to Mateo Vázquez to denounce the situation of captives in Algiers.[59] Likewise, Aurelio sentimentally recalls the mythical time of the "Edad Dorada" (golden age), when there was neither war nor the avarice that promoted the trade of captives.[60]

The Power of the Mnemonic Image

Once specific loci have been strategically embedded in the play, a series of intruding images in succession reveal the experience of captivity. These images, like the loci, reinforce the physical and psychological suffering through multiple references to the confinement of both body and soul. Aurelio laments his lack of words to describe his state: "no llegará cuanto digo / a un punto de lo que siento" (how much I say / will not reach the point of how I feel).[61] Beyond dialogue, Cervantes leaves it to the audience to fill in the gaps through a series of poignant images: slavery is represented with constant allusions to the yoke around the neck; the lack of freedom is portrayed through the persistent images of imprisonment – *hierros*, mazmorras, cadenas (irons, dungeons, chains) – scarcity is dramatized through a lack of clothing – the "hábito de esclavo" (slave garb) – and characters refer to faith several times over as a "roca" (rock) in order to represent the spiritual strength against temptations that could lead to apostasy and sodomy. The most striking and persistent images include continuous weeping, tears, and sorrow that represent the captives' undermined hopes, their fear of the cruel punishments, the terrible consequences of the captive trade, and the ever-present threat of oblivion at the hands of the authorities in Spain. Leaving these images to speak for themselves, the states of deprivation, hardship, and humiliation of the captive's life are reinforced repeatedly. Their constant repetition, carried out by different characters in distinct scenes throughout the play, is a significant strategy drawn from the art of memory, here designed to make strongly negative images impact the audience.

Although a particular term for traumatic experience did not exist during the sixteenth and seventeenth centuries,[62] in his *Topographia*, Sosa speaks of "los muchos y muy grandes dolores interiores, que la alma de un cautivo padece, viéndose en tan desdichado estado" (the many and very great interior agonies that the soul of a captive suffers, seeing himself in such a wretched state).[63] Throughout *El trato de Argel*, Cervantes constantly refers to a psychological state dominated by "sufrimiento" (suffering), "castigo" (punishment), or "pena" (sorrow) that haunts the captives. Cathy Caruth describes such a state of trauma as being "possessed by an image or event" as a response to a violent incident.[64] Psychologists and psychiatrists coincide in their description of trauma as "a response to an overwhelming event or events which take the form of repeated, intrusive hallucinations, dreams, thoughts, or behaviours stemming from the event."[65] In Cervantes's works, images appear almost uncontrollably as a result of the force of the trauma,[66] as Garcés states: "The story of this traumatic experience continuously speaks through Cervantes's fictions. His oeuvre *is haunted by images of captivity*: cages of all sizes, Christian captives, galley slaves, and female prisoners."[67] Like his other literary works, *El trato de Argel* becomes an exercise of reconstruction and revelation of the writer's traumatic experience from images stored in memory and brought forth with blunt force.

Cervantes attempts to repair the emotional distress and personal trauma through the theatricality and force of the images in order to "construct an observatory into human interiority, to create an opening through which one can see the gallery of phantasmata that inhabits the internal space."[68] In her analysis of *El trato de Argel*, Garcés notes how critics have emphasized the force of the writer's memories. Cotarello Valledor speaks of "pintura viva de los sufrimientos del cautiverio" (living portrait of the sufferings of captivity),[69] Astrana Marín describes the "relación viva, doliente y trágica de las torturas del cautiverio de Argel" (living, suffering and tragic narration of the tortures of the captivity of Algiers),[70] and Zamora Vicente points out the "presencia viva de una memoria dolorida" (living presence of a painful memory).[71] The constant and intruding images from the past engraved in memory haunt the playwright and further underscore the popular belief in the force of the mental image.

During Cervantes's time, images stored in memory were believed to have an extraordinary power on mind and body. In his discussions on the art of memory, Aristotle writes that mental images, especially in dreams, re-enact and have a life of their own, as if they were performing.[72] Consequently, Aristotle highlighted the autonomy and force of mental images and their capacity to act internally and influence the senses. The notion that one could be possessed by a phantasm coming to life actually existed during Cervantes's time:

> There is a rich tradition of classical philosophy and medicine that conceives of images through which we know and remember as *phantasmata*, as something that acts internally but also retains a sensory status.... It is easy to imagine how centuries of experience in memory techniques have given scholars some idea of the complex nature of mental images and their capacity to inhabit their creators, to come alive and escape their control.[73]

The uncontrollable nature and powerful strength of the image[74] required iconoclastic means to erase or weaken them, the remedy for which can be traced to the *ars memorativa* and its counterpart, the *ars oblivionalis* (the art of forgetting). As studied by Bolzoni, the belief in the mental capacity to forget was explained in treatises designed to help the afflicted do away with images that haunted them. For example, Giovanni della Porta advocated for the application of ointments to the back of the brain. Giovanni Fontana in *De oblivion*, suggested that one should mentally cover with a piece of cloth images they would like to forget, destroy them in a mental fire, or even visualize them sleeping or dead. Cosimo Rosselli in *Thesaurus artificiosae memoriae* preferred to mentally throw them out the window. Lambert Schenkel's *Gazophylacium artis memoriae* proposed conjuring violent storms or an armed gang that would destroy images, or, if that did not work, visualizing the loss of images through their suicide. Filippo Gesualdo in *L'arte di scordare*, drawing on xenophobic fears from the period, suggested that images be hunted by Turks or pagans. Without a doubt, the most astonishing and dangerous of all these remedies was the idea of reheating the back of the skull to melt the image and make it disappear.[75]

Given his knowledge of the workings of memory and aware of the complex nature that the effects of a memory could have on the spectator, Cervantes manipulates images to make them more memorable for his audience. He seems to be following the same psychological directives found in the *Rhetorica ad Herennium*, whose anonymous author advocated for novel and surprising images – *imagines agentes* – rather than anything ordinary. As the author explains, active and easily memorable images will have the greatest impact and will be remembered longer: "We ought, then, to set up images of a kind that can adhere longest in memory. And we shall do so if we establish similitudes as striking as possible; if we set up images that are not many or vague but active (*imagines agentes*),"[76] as when in everyday life one sees "things that are pretty, ordinary, and banal, we generally fail to remember them, because the mind is not being stirred by anything novel or marvellous. But if we see or hear something exceptionally base, dishonourable, unusual, great, unbelievable, or ridiculous, that we are likely to remember for a long time."[77]

Mindful of an image's mnemonic power, Cervantes had an extraordinary ability to draw forth images of great intensity that are meant to remain in the memory of his readers (and spectators) throughout the centuries, as Edward Riley has stated in reference to *Don Quixote*: "A piece of verbal discourse (and initially nothing else) has evoked an image in the minds of individual readers clearly enough for them to recognize immediately visual reproduction."[78] Like the novel, *El trato de Argel* becomes a gallery of images of an extraordinary visual intensity carefully stored in Cervantes's memory and revived in dramatic settings with strong doses of pathos.[79] The constant presence of horror and macabre touches, the captives' fear of the Muslims, the persistent allusion to crying and sorrow, and, in particular, Hasan Pasha's cruelty and impiety all enjoin to project vivid images and instil trepidation in the audience.

One of the most dramatic and memorable scenes of the play is without a doubt the real-life martyrdom of a Valencian priest, Miguel de Aranda. Aranda's death at the hands of an angry mob of Algerians was a revenge killing for the Inquisition's earlier public execution in Valencia of a moor named Alicax around 1576.[80] Both deaths were recorded in the *Topographia*, and Cervantes may have read about them, or, as Canavaggio maintains, it is also likely that Cervantes witnessed Aranda's execution first-hand in Algiers, then dramatized the death in *El trato de*

Argel: "[L]apidado y quemado ante sus ojos" (Stoned and burned before his eyes).[81] What makes the scene so significant is that all the techniques of the art of memory are at work in arranging the dramatic action: the *compositio loci*, the placement of images *agentes*, the power of visualization, and the Aristotelian laws of association all come together in the description of the act of revenge. The scene begins with the entrance of a young captive, alone and dressed in the habit of a slave. He enters the stage visibly dumbfounded and in shock due to having witnessed some horrible and cruel event that is still unknown to the audience. In an attempt to calm him down, Leonardo reveals his name: "Sebastián, dinos qué tienes, / que hablas razones tales" (Sebastián, tell us what happened, / why do you speak like this).[82] The choice of the name Sebastián,[83] that of one of the best-known martyrs in Christendom, clearly appeals to the audience's collective memory and, in the style of *memoria mandare*, they are prompted to make the necessary connections to Sebastián's description of Aranda's horrible torture and death. He begins by setting the scene, particularly through the contrast between two demarcated places to which he will situate opposing respective images: "¡Oh, España, patria querida!, / mira cuál es nuestra suerte, que, si allá das justa muerte, / quitas acá justa vida!" (Oh, Spain, dear homeland! / Look at our fate, that, if you give just death there, / here you take just life).[84] This division reinforces the collective memory of the captives, "el allá" (there) in Valencia in contrast to "el acá" (here) in Algiers characterized as "maldito lugar" (damned place). The split also exposes the bilocated memory of every captive who is caught between two different places and subject to the memories of here and there, which is accentuated by the constant presence of pairs of opposites as noted by Sebastián's narration of the execution (misericordia vs. crueldad, muerte vs. vida, etc.; mercy vs. cruelty, death vs. life, etc.).

Considering the lack of stage directions for this scene, the description of the martyrdom is done following the precepts of the *Rhetorica ad Herennium*, which advocates for the use of active images "that can adhere longest in memory" and which endows them with a series of pivotal characteristics. As the anonymous author describes it, the more elaborate the image, the better it is fixed in memory: "If we assign to them exceptional beauty or singular ugliness; if we ornament some of them, as with crowns or purple cloaks, so that the similitude may be more distinct to us; or if we somehow disfigure them, as by introducing one stained with blood or soiled with mud and smeared with red paint, so that its form is more striking, or by assigning certain comic effects to our images, for that, too, will ensure our remembering them more readily."[85] Cervantes's strategy for keeping the horror in memory's consciousness long after the initial tragedy includes a series of techniques to amplify the dismay of the scene even though the execution is never dramatized. Indeed, the entire death is described through Sebastián's eyes who makes it as real as possible for the audience through vivid and realistic descriptions that disfigure Aranda. We are told that the priest was chained, bloodied, and wearing a torn cassock ("vestido roto y cadenas"). Sebastián is careful to note Aranda's facial expression at the time of death along with the positioning of his hands, his neck, and the gestures of terror – tactics fully in line with those of other theorists such as Leporeus, who recommended the animated use of gestures and facial expressions to help one remember.[86] The images have such strength and autonomy that they even speak for themselves and elicit the memory and compassion of the audience. For example, Sebastián's description of the priest being burned alive is reinforced by verbs that denote movement to mirror the voracious fire that devours his clothes: "[V]ase arrugando el vestido / con el calor violento / y el fuego, poco contento / busca lo más escondido" (His robe curls up / from the violent heat / and the fire, not content, / pursues what is most hidden).[87] Techniques like this were highly regarded. Juan de Aguilera, in his *Ars memorativa* (1536), demands movement from images, and El Brocense states the importance of "imágenes de seres vivos en movimiento pues de esta forma excitarán más vigorosamente la memoria" (images of living beings in motion will more vigorously excite memory).[88]

As Sebastián tells it, the priest faced the hordes of the city of Algiers alone, thus highlighting the loneliness of the martyr in such dire circumstances: "A ningún lado miraba / que descubra un solo amigo, / que todo el pueblo enemigo / en torno le rodeaba" (He didn't find a friend / anywhere he looked, / the entire enemy / surrounded him).[89] Although in the account of Aranda's martyrdom, Sebastián is not alone as he recollects the events of martyrdom, his description emphasizes the solitude of the priest to make it more dramatic and memorable. The use of solitude lends greater dramatic force, which tends to be the case in the most pivotal scenes in *El trato de Argel*. In addition to Sebastián's monologue, for example, the opening scene with Aurelio or the scene of the fleeing captive and the lion all tend to highlight loneliness and despair. Indeed, according to the author of the *Rhetorica ad Herennium*, solitude keeps images sharp and makes them more memorable: "It will be more advantageous to obtain backgrounds in a deserted than in a populous region, because the crowding and passing to and fro of people confuse and weaken the impress of the images, while solitude keeps their outlines sharp."[90] As a result, Cervantes draws on the popular image of the martyr "solo entre 2000 ladrones" (alone among 2,000 thieves)[91] in his own "Calvario" (Calvary), which inevitably brings to the viewers' collective memory the crucifixion of Christ on the Golgotha hill with a "ladrón" on either side. In the play, Sebastián describes the figure of the "martyr" using the religious symbolism of the "passion" of Christ with objects such as the crown, the cross, the image of Golgotha, walking alone, surrounded by enemies.

The description of the martyrdom also relies heavily on the power of visualization – as described also by Aristotle in *De memoria et reminiscentia* – whereby "el ojo de la mente recorr[e] las imágenes de una manera lenta, ordenada y analítica" (the mind's eye slowly reviews the images in ordered and analytical fashion).[92] As a result, Sebastián insists on what has been seen: "[Y]o he venido a referiros, / lo que no pudistes ver, / si os lo ha dejado entender, / mis lágrimas y suspiros" (I came to tell you / what you could not see yourselves / so you can understand / my tears and sighs).[93] Once again, Cervantes does this by composing a text that functions in a fashion parallel to the way memory works, "for it is possible to produce something before our eyes, *as those who set things out in mnemonic systems and form images of them.*"[94]

Conclusion

Given his humanistic training and his knowledge of rhetoric, the writer must have been familiar with the art of memory, the power of the image and the potential for its manipulation in literature, especially in theatre, and the ability to use memory and image to create dramatic moments. As previously seen, the relationship between memory and theatre is not new and it was commonly shown in the classical art of memory as well. As an illustration, in *De oratore*, Cicero considered it useful to put theatrical masks on the concepts, transforming them into active images in memory, in *imagenes agentes*.[95] Likewise, in his *Ars memorativa* Juan de Aguilera recommends that "si quieres acordarte de algo previamente conocido, pero incorpóreo, tanto que se trate de una sustancia como de un accidente, has de fingir una imagen sensible y corporal" (if you want to remember something previously known, but incorporeal, whether it is a substance as if by accident, you have to fake a sensitive and corporal image).[96] Cervantes boasted that he was the first to reveal the hidden or buried internal workings of the soul: "[F]ui el primero que representase las imaginaciones y los pensamientos escondidos del alma, sacando figuras morales al teatro" (I was the first to represent the imagination and hidden thoughts of the soul, bringing moral figures to the theatre). In *El trato de Argel*, the two figures that appear to tempt Aurelio in the name of the Devil as a result of Fátima's enchantment, Occasion and Necessity, become interior voices, those that Cervantes probably heard many times, now represented onstage to denote a "spiritual conflict," as Edward Riley has stated,[97] and which Armando Cotarelo y Valledor defines as "productos psíquicos" (psychic products).[98] As the power of the mnemonic image moved away from the *ars memoriae* and aligned with the plasticity of the Renaissance mind, Yates highlights the transcendence of the art of memory in the creation of images that emerged in art and literary works: "For when people were being taught to practise the formation of images for remembering, it is not so difficult to suppose that *such inner images might not sometimes have found their way into outer expression*."[99]

El trato de Argel is an excellent example of the theatricality of memory clearly derived from the art of memory and its techniques. When invoking the memory of his own captivity, the writer literally presents the places (loci) in his mind on the stage along with the images (*imagines*) evoked by those places. Despite their fallibility and imperfections, memories were an inevitable source of creativity for Cervantes, and he understood the power that memory provided him for literary creation, for imagination, as well as its important role in the cognition process.[100] *El trato de Argel* therefore represents the loci and *images* not of one captivity but many. In order to disclose the experience of captivity, make it memorable, and literally place it before his audience, Cervantes employs a sequence of strategies meant to engage the audience and expose the hardships of captivity: a topographical memory that leads to a text composed of spatial dimensions, an inherent theatricality of images, patterns that repeat by withdrawing and returning, the associative capacity of memory in the midst of trauma, and the imitation of models drawn from memory. Thanks to these techniques, the catalogue of places and mental images drawn from his trauma, treasured in the space of his memory, reveals how personal experiences come to life on the stage.

NOTES

1　The image can be found in the archives of the Biblioteca Nacional and in the catalogue of the exhibition with the title *Miguel de Cervantes: De la vida al mito (1616–2016)*, 84.

2　I take the reference from José Manuel Lucía Megías, who also compares both images although with a different purpose (Lucía Megías, *Juventud*, 189–92).

3　Lucía Megías, 190.

4 All translations are my own unless otherwise indicated.

5 Huyssen, *Twilight Memories*, 2–3.

6 Geoffrey Stagg ("Date and Form") dates the composition of the play to 1577; Franco Meregalli ("De *Los tratos de Argel* a *Los baños de Argel*") to 1580; Canavaggio (*Cervantes*) to between the years 1581 and 1583; and Vaccari ("Noticias") to 1584.

7 The ship carrying the writer back to Spain in 1575 was taken by Barbary pirates and Cervantes was held in Algiers from 26 September 1575 until 19 September 1580, until he was ransomed five years later.

8 Published thirty years after Sosa's captivity by Diego de Haedo in Valladolid.

9 As Lina Bolzoni states in her study of Renaissance theories on memory, "Writing means above all remembering," and Cervantes's extensive literary production engages with different acts of remembering (Bolzoni, *Gallery of Memory*, xv). Bolzoni's words find their echo in *El trato de Argel*, where Cervantes demonstrates his prodigious recollection of a multitude of literary and artistic works, and his uncanny ability to integrate them meaningfully into the play to reveal the vicissitudes of captivity through the intertwining of reality and fiction. There are many noteworthy examples of Cervantes's use of previous source material. Fátima's incantation of Aurelio's love for Zahara (Cervantes, *Trato*, 2.1420–75) is already found in Virgil's *Aeneid* and Ovid's *Metamorphoses* and later can be traced to *La Celestina* (see note 1420 by Ojeda Calvo, Cervantes, *Trato*, 961). References to Phaedro's *The Ass and the Lyre* – ("[A]nsí entiende él del amor / como el asno de la lira" (That's how he understands love / like the ass the lyre; Cervantes, *Trato*, 1.155–6) – are also present as is the classical belief in the Fates through "el hilo que se corta" (the thread that is cut; Cervantes, *Trato*, 1.41). Even more commonplace references such as nautical metaphors from classical antiquity – "[C]omo el que en rota nave y mar airado / se halla solo, sin saber do hay puerto" (Like the one who in a broken ship and angry sea / is alone, without knowing where there is a port; Cervantes, *Trato*, 2.1356–7; see note 1357 by Ojeda Calvo in Cervantes, *Trato*, 959) – point to Cervantes's own experience navigating the Mediterranean world, and would also have been known to the audience. Moral literature, too, is central, itself imitating both classical and biblical models and clearly pointing to medieval literary tropes, such as the topic of martyrdom found in the death of the Valencian priest in the play (Cervantes, *Trato*, 1.520–686) and the use of the anchor image to symbolize the faith of the Christian martyr (Cervantes, *Trato*, 1.587–90). Throughout the play there are also references to the inconstancy of the Wheel of Fortune and its effect on captivity – "¿[Q]uién podrá bajar lo que tú una vez subiste?" (Who will be able to lower what you once

uploaded?; Cervantes, *Trato*, 1.71–2); "[A]unque tamaña mudanza / hace
Fortuna en mi estado" (Although such a change / makes Fortune in my
state; Cervantes, *Trato*, 2.1095–6) – and the character Occasion is portrayed
exactly as they appeared in Alciato's emblems: "[Y] la melena /
de mis pocos cabellos" (And the mane / of my sparse hair; Cervantes,
Trato, 3.1676–7). Drawing on the Byzantine novel, Cervantes also creates a
fictional universe fostered by the love affairs of Moors and Christians (see
Ojeda Calvo, "Lectura," 163). Absent the original sources, these examples
reveal exactly how valued memory was in the early modern period.

10 See Garcés, *Cervantes in Algiers*; and Domínguez, 'Escenarios.'"

11 See Domínguez, "Imaginar mundos."

12 Chartier, *Author's Hand*, 34. Through writing, Cervantes records his story
in history and gives voice to captivity, constantly playing with the tension
between history and memory as forms of re-presentation of the past.

13 Huyssen, *Twilight Memories*, 1.

14 "[The play] is the vehicle for a cathartic evocation of his own life as a slave
in Algiers" (McKendrick, "Writings," 138).

15 Aristotle, *Poetics*, 1449b12–34.

16 Caruth, *Trauma*, 4–5.

17 Cervantes, *Comedias*, 1:12.

18 See Domínguez, "Cervantes," "Internal Senses."

19 As Cicero describes it "One could thus prepare the mind as a written
statement thereby controlling the delivery as through reading from an
imaginary text" (Beecher, "Recollection," 372).

20 Bolzoni, "Play of Images," 21.

21 Engel, Loughnane, and Williams, "Introduction," 11.

22 In Spain, the art of memory became evermore acknowledged in society,
and intellectuals of various stripes saw the great utility of its techniques
and principles, as studied extensively by Fernando Rodríguez de la
Flor and Luis Merino Jerez.

23 Egido, "La memoria y *El Quijote*," 7.

24 Egido, "La memoria ejemplar," 467.

25 Rodríguez de la Flor, "*Ars oblivionis*," 50.

26 These and many other sources show that the writer was amazingly able to
remember an impressive number of sources without having at hand the
original sources like books, manuscripts, or images. Nowhere is this more
poignant than in *Don Quixote*, where the author cites 104 mythological,
legendary, and biblical characters; 131 characters from chivalric and
pastoral novels; 227 historical personages; 21 famous animals; 93 books;
and 261 geographical places. The author seems aware of his own
exceptional memory. In the prologue to his *Comedias*, he flaunts his ability
to remember by stating that in his youth he memorized Lope de Rueda's

verses: "Por algunos [versos] que me quedaron en la memoria, vistos agora en la edad madura que tengo" (For some [verses] that remain in my memory, seen now in my mature age; Lathrop, "Introduction," xvii).

27 See Domínguez, "Imaginar mundos."

28 See in particular Egido's *Cervantes y las puertas del sueño*, "La memoria ejemplar," and "La memoria y *El Quijote*."

29 De Armas, *Quixotic Frescoes*, 28.

30 De Armas, 20.

31 I believe theatre lends itself to the revelation of a traumatic experience "that is not yet fully owned" (Caruth, *Trauma*, 151) and "that has not yet attained the form of narrative memory" (Caruth, 155).

32 Cited in Garcés, *Cervantes in Algiers*, 133.

33 Bolzoni, *Gallery of Memory*, 241.

34 On Camillo, see *La idea del teatro*; and on Fludd, see Yates, *Art of Memory*, chap. 15, "The Theatre Memory System of Robert Fludd" (320–41) and chap. 16, "Fludd's Memory Theatre and The Globe Theatre" (342–67).

35 Yates, "New Light," 21.

36 See Wardropper, "Comedias."

37 Cervantes, *Don Quijote*, 1.48.

38 Cervantes, *Trato*, 4.2530–1.

39 "Todo escenario del siglo de Oro es un retablo de maravillas que se ofrecen, con la esencial ayuda de la palabra, al enajenado espectador para su instrucción y deleite" (Every stage of the Golden Age is a tableau of wonders that are offered, with the essential help of the word, to the alienated spectator for their instruction and delight; Arellano, "Valores," 413).

40 Hiscock, *Reading Memory*, 17.

41 There are two types of metaphors used to designate memory. On one hand, metaphors that link memory to the spatiality where all kinds of metaphorical spaces arise such as the tree, the field, the labyrinth, the garden, or the jungle – wide and disorderly – and in contrast, a more ordered and confined space such as the house. On the other hand, there is a second group of metaphors related to writing, being par excellence, the wax tablet and the book, considered technologies of memory. See Carruthers, *Book of Memory*, 31–55.

42 Cervantes utilized examples that illustrated how memory was conceived in spatial terms. For example, in *El rufián viudo llamado Trampagos*, Escarramán speaks of a story "digna de atesorarla en mi memoria" (worth treasuring in my memory; Cervantes, *Entremeses*, 134), and in *La Galatea* memory is described as "tesorera y guardadora del objeto que los ojos miraron" (treasurer and keeper of the object that the eyes looked upon; Cervantes, *La Galatea*, 292). In *Don Quixote*, Sancho listens carefully to

the knight, trying to "conservar en la memoria sus consejos, como quien pensaba guardarlos" (keep his advice in memory, as someone who will keep them; Cervantes, *Don Quijote*, 2.43, 973) and in the play by Aurelio with the idea of "ocupar la memoria" (occupy memory; Cervantes, *Trato*, 3.1786).

43 Egido, *Cervantes y las puertas del sueño*, 222.

44 Cervantes, *Trato*, 1.1–8.

45 Bolzoni, *Gallery of Memory*, xviii.

46 Rosselli, *Thesaurus*, 12, 27v.

47 See Yates, *Art of Memory*, 94.

48 Garcés, *Cervantes in Algiers*, 137. As studied by Henry Sullivan (*Grotesque Purgatory*), the allegory of purgatory was linked to the Counter-Reformation and the doctrines of the Catholic Church, and it must have been well known to the spectators of the play.

49 With regard to the influence of Dante in Cervantes, see Avery, "Elementos dantescos," "Elementos dantescos (segunda parte)."

50 Garcés, *Cervantes in Algiers*, 136.

51 These four spheres are given as "Incontinence, Violence, Ordinary Fraud, and Treacherous Fraud, with their respective circles" (Garcés, 138). Garcés also notes Zimic's assertion that all forms of violence depicted in the seventh circle of Dante's Inferno are "represented in detail in the scenes of captivity in Algiers: tyranny, homicide, suicide, blasphemy, sodomy, and usury" (139).

52 Zimic, quoted in Garcés, 138.

53 The process echoes Aristotle, whose laws of association dictate in what manner memory is elicited: "This is exactly why we hunt for the successor, starting in our thoughts from the present or from something else, and from something similar, or opposite, or neighbouring. By this means recollection occurs" (Aristotle, *On Memory*, 54).

54 The doctrines of Trent will also appear when Sayavedra tries to convince Pedro of the consequences of apostasy (see Cervantes, *Trato*, 4.2069–279).

55 Garcés, *Cervantes in Algiers*, 150.

56 Cervantes, *Trato*, 2.1179–80.

57 Cervantes, 1.408–10.

58 Cervantes, 4.2069–278.

59 Cervantes, 1.393–452.

60 Cervantes, 2.1313–78.

61 Cervantes, 1.23–4.

62 A relatively new diagnosis in the 1980s whose term dates back to the nineteenth century – previously known as shell shock, combat stress, delayed stress syndrome, and traumatic neurosis – trauma has been traced back in different cultures by numerous scholars. There are enough

reasons to believe that post-traumatic stress disorder indeed existed before the nineteenth century; however, according to Judith Pollmann, "What the early modern world did not have was a psychological theory to account for the lasting damage such experiences can produce or to explain the re-emergence of painful memories later in life" (*Memory*, 185). Pollmann laments the scarcity of this type of historical documents that actually illustrate the articulation of trauma during the time. There is no doubt that early modern people definitely considered traumatic experience worthy of being remembered, and Cervantes's play is an illustration.

63 Sosa, *Topographia*, 136.

64 Caruth, *Trauma*, 4–5.

65 Caruth, 4.

66 In fact, most theories and studies on trauma coincide in pointing out the idea of the image as being difficult to control: "Inaccessible to conscious recall and control" (Caruth, *Trauma*, 151); "Vivid, uncontrollable … persistent and debilitating" (Fernyhough, *Pieces of Light*, 181); "The uncontrollability of the memories sustaining the trauma" (Fernyhough, 182).

67 Garcés, *Cervantes in Algiers*, 1; my emphasis.

68 Bolzoni, *Gallery of Memory*, xxii.

69 Cited in Garcés, *Cervantes in Algiers*, 133.

70 Cited in Garcés, 133.

71 Cited in Garcés, 133.

72 "In fact, some people have actually experienced such dreams, e.g. those who judge that they are arranging a given set of items according to the system for memorizing them" (Aristotle, *Dreams*, 87).

73 Bolzoni, *Gallery of Memory*, 131. See also Freedberg, *Power of Images*.

74 The uncontrollable power of images was indeed well known at the time. In fact, the archbishop of Bologna, Gabriele Paleotti, in his *Discorso intorno alle imagini sacre e profane* (Discourse on Sacred and Profane Images, 1582) – where he refutes the Protestant condemnation of sacred images and favours their use in Catholicism – uses the art of memory and the power of its images as an example to prove the effect that images had on the individual: "As to memory, what shall we say? We know that so-called artificial memory consists mostly in the use of images. Thus, it is no wonder that sacred images refresh the memory all the more" (cited in Bolzoni, *Gallery of Memory*, 131).

75 See Ciavolella, "Eros."

76 Cited in Yates, *Art of Memory*, 10.

77 Cited in Yates, 9.

78 Riley, "*Don Quixote*," 108.

79 For Carruthers, memory is "hexis or pathos in that 'is a state or affection …
  that follows on perceiving, apprehending, experiencing, or learning' – all
  of which require the production of phantasms" (Carruthers, *Book of
  Memory*, 85).
80 Cervantes, *Trato*, 1.491–686.
81 Canavaggio, *Cervantes*, 75.
82 Cervantes, *Trato*, 4.479–80.
83 See Zmantar, "Miguel de Cervantes" for the meaning of the names in the
  play.
84 Cervantes, *Trato*, 1.477–8.
85 Cited in Yates, *Art of Memory*, 10.
86 Morcillo Romero, "El *Ars memorativa*," lxxxvii.
87 Cervantes, *Trato*, 1.631–4.
88 Cited in Merino Jerez, *Retórica*, 188.
89 Cervantes, *Trato*, 1.575–8.
90 [Cicero], *Rhetorica*, 211.
91 Cervantes, *Trato*, 1.558.
92 Bolzoni, "Espectáculo," 11.
93 Cervantes, *Trato*, 1.683–6.
94 Cited in Bolzoni, *Gallery of Memory*, 131; my emphasis.
95 Yates, *Art of Memory*, 17.
96 By doing so, Aguilera gathered "la tradición medieval de gran interés
  para las representaciones plásticas de cosas espirituales y aludiendo a
  los emblemas de Alciato" (the medieval tradition of great interest for the
  plastic representations of spiritual things and alluding to the emblems of
  Alciato; Muñoz Delgado, "Juan de Aguilera," 185).
97 Riley, "*Pensamientos escondidos*," 631.
98 Cotarelo y Valledor, *El teatro de Cervantes*, 216.
99 Yates, *Art of Memory*, 91–2; my emphasis.
100 See Domínguez, "Janus Hypothesis."

REFERENCES

Arellano, Ignacio. "Valores visuales de la palabra en el espacio escénico del
  Siglo de Oro." *Revista Canadiense de Estudios Hispánicos* 19, no. 3 (1995):
  411–43.
Aristotle. *Aristotle on Memory*. Edited by Richard Sorabji. London: Duckworth,
  1972.
Aristotle. *Aristotle on Sleep and Dreams*. Edited and translated by David
  Gallop. Oxford: Oxford University Press, 1991.
Aristotle. *The Poetics of Aristotle*. Edited by S.H. Butcher. London: Macmillan, 1902.

Avery, William. "Elementos dantescos del Quijote." *Anales Cervantinos*, no. 9 (1961–2): 1–28.

Avery, William. "Elementos dantescos del Quijote (segunda parte)." *Anales Cervantinos*, nos. 13–14 (1974–5): 1–28.

Beecher, Donald. "Recollection, Cognition, and Culture: An Overview of Renaissance Memory." In *Ars Reminiscendi: Mind and Memory in Renaissance Culture*, edited by Donald Beecher and Grant Williams, 367–426. Toronto: Center for Reformation and Renaissance Studies, 2009.

Bolzoni, Lina. "El espectáculo de la memoria." In Camillo, *La idea del teatro*, 9–40.

Bolzoni, Lina. *The Gallery of Memory: Literary and Iconographic Models in the Age of the Printing Press*. Translated by Jeremy Parzen. Toronto: University of Toronto Press, 2001.

Bolzoni, Lina. "The Play of Images: The Art of Memory from Its Origins to the Seventeenth Century." In *The Enchanted Loom: Chapters in the History of Neuroscience*, edited by Pietro Corsi, 16–65. Oxford: Oxford University Press, 1991.

Camillo, Giulio. *La idea del teatro*. Edited by Lina Bolzoni. Translated by Jordi Raventós. Madrid: Siruela, 2006.

Canavaggio, Jean. *Cervantes*. Translated by Mauro Armiño. Madrid: Espasa, 1987.

Carruthers, Mary. *The Book of Memory: A Study of Memory in Medieval Culture*. Cambridge: Cambridge University Press, 2001.

Caruth, Cathy, ed. *Trauma: Explorations in Memory*. Baltimore: Johns Hopkins University Press, 1995.

Cervantes Saavedra, Miguel. *Don Quijote de la Mancha*. 2 vols. Barcelona: Crítica, 1998.

Cervantes Saavedra, Miguel. *Entremeses*. Edited by Nicholas Spadaccini. Madrid: Cátedra, 1995.

Cervantes Saavedra, Miguel. *La Galatea*. Edited by Francisco López Estrada and Maria Teresa López García-Berdoy. Madrid: Cátedra, 1995.

Cervantes Saavedra, Miguel. *Miguel de Cervantes: Comedias y tragedias*. Edited by Luis Gómez Canseco. 2 vols. Madrid: Real Academia Española, 2015.

Cervantes Saavedra, Miguel. *El trato de Argel*. Edited by María del Valle Ojeda Calvo. In Cervantes, *Comedias y tragedias*, 1:909–1004.

Chartier, Roger. *The Author's Hand and the Printer's Mind*. Translated by Lydia G. Cochrane. Cambridge: Polity, 2014.

Ciavolella, Massimo. "Eros and the Phantasms of Hereos." In *Eros and Anteros: The Medical Traditions of Love in the Renaissance*, edited by Donald A. Beecher and Massimo Ciavolella, 75–85. Toronto: University of Toronto Press, 1992.

[Cicero]. *Rhetorica ad Herennium*. Translated by Harry Caplan. Cambridge, MA: Harvard University Press, 1954.

Cotarelo y Valledor, Armando. *El teatro de Cervantes: Estudio crítico*. Madrid: Revista de Archivos, Bibliotecas y Museos, 1915.

De Armas, Frederick A. *Quixotic Frescoes: Cervantes and Italian Renaissance Art*. Toronto: University of Toronto Press, 2006.

Domínguez, Julia. "Cervantes and the Mother of the Muses: Views of Memory in Early Modern Spain." In *Cervantes and the Early Modern Mind*, edited by Isabel Jaén and Julien Jacques Simon, 118–37. New York: Routledge, 2021.

Domínguez, Julia. "Los escenarios de la memoria: Psicodrama en *El trato de Argel* de Cervantes." *Bulletin of the Comediantes* 61, no. 1 (2009): 1–23. https://doi.org/10.1353/boc.0.0010.

Domínguez, Julia. "Imaginar mundos: Memoria y ciencia ficción en la obra de Cervantes." *Cervantes* 40, no. 2 (2020): 33–51. https://doi.org/10.1353/cer.2020.0016.

Domínguez, Julia. "The Internal Senses in *Don Quixote* and the Anatomy of Memory." In *Beyond Sight: Engaging the Senses in Iberian Literatures and Cultures, 1200–1750*, edited by Ryan D. Giles and Steven Wagschal, 47–65. Toronto: University of Toronto Press, 2018.

Domínguez, Julia. "The 'Janus Hypothesis' in *Don Quixote*: Memory and Imagination in Cervantes." In *Cognitive Approaches to Early Modern Spanish Literature*, edited by Isabel Jaén and Julien Jacques Simon, 74–90. Oxford: Oxford University Press, 2016.

Egido, Aurora. *Cervantes y las puertas del sueño: Estudios sobre* La Galatea, El Quijote *y* El Persiles. Barcelona: PPU, 1994.

Egido, Aurora. "La memoria ejemplar y *El coloquio de los perros*." In *Cervantes: Estudios en la víspera de su centenario*, edited by Kurt Reichenberger, 2:465–82. Kassel: Reichenberger, 1994.

Egido, Aurora. "La memoria y *El Quijote*." *Cervantes* 11, no. 1 (1991): 3–44.

Engel, William E., Rory Loughnane, and Grant Williams. "Introduction." In *The Memory Arts in Renaissance England: A Critical Anthology*, edited by William E. Engel, Rory Loughnane, and Grant Williams, 1–32. Cambridge: Cambridge University Press, 2016.

Fernyhough, Charles. *Pieces of Light: The New Science of Memory*. London: HarperCollins, 2013.

Freedberg, David. *The Power of Images: Studies in the History and Theory of Response*. Chicago: University of Chicago Press, 1991.

Garcés, María Antonia. *Cervantes in Algiers: A Captive's Tale*. Nashville: Vanderbilt University Press, 2002.

Hiscock, Andrew. *Reading Memory in Early Modern Literature*. Cambridge: Cambridge University Press, 2011.

Huyssen, Andreas. *Twilight Memories: Marking Time in a Culture of Amnesia.* London: Routledge, 1995.

Lathrop, Thomas. "Introduction." In *Don Quijote*, edited by Thomas Lathrop, ix–xlviii. Newark, DE: Cervantes & Co., 2005.

Lucía Megías, José Manuel. *La juventud de Cervantes: Una vida en construcción.* Madrid: Edaf, 2016.

McKendrick, Melveena. "Writings for the Stage." In *The Cambridge Companion to Cervantes*, edited by Anthony J. Cascardi, 131–59. Cambridge: Cambridge University Press, 2002.

Meregalli, Francisco. "De *Los tratos de Argel* a *Los baños de Argel*." In *Homenaje a Casalduero: Crítica y poesía*, edited by Rizel Pincus Sigele and Gonzalo Sobejano, 395–409. Madrid: Gredos, 1972.

Merino Jerez, Luis. *Retórica y artes de memoria en el humanismo renacentista.* Cáceres: Universidad de Extremadura, 2007.

Miguel de Cervantes: De la vida al mito (1616–2016). Madrid: Acción Cultural Española, 2016.

Morcillo Romero, Juan José. "El *Ars memorativa* de G. Leporeo (estudio, edición crítica, traducción, notas e índices)." PhD diss., Universidad de Extremadura, 2015.

Muñoz Delgado, Vicente. "Juan de Aguilera y su *Ars memorativa* (1536)." *Cuadernos de Historia de la Medicina Española*, no. 15 (1975): 175–89.

Ojeda Calvo, María del Valle. "Lectura de *El trato de Argel*." In Cervantes, *Comedias y tragedias*, 2:156–70.

Ojeda Calvo, María del Valle. "Notas complementarias a *El Trato de Argel*." In Cervantes, *Comedias y tragedias*, 2:564–94.

Pollmann, Judith. *Memory in Early Modern Europe, 1500–1800.* Oxford: Oxford University Press, 2017.

Riley, Edward. "*Don Quixote*: From Text to Icon." *Cervantes*, no. 8 (1988): 103–15.

Riley, Edward. "The *Pensamientos escondidos* and *Figuras morales* of Cervantes." In *Homenaje a William L. Fichter: Estudios sobre el teatro antiguo hispánico y otros ensayos*, edited by David Kossoff and José Amor y Vázquez, 623–31. Madrid: Castalia, 1971.

Rodríguez de la Flor, Fernando. "*Ars oblivionis* (Arte del olvido)." *Cuadernos Hispanoamericanos*, no. 527 (1994): 45–56.

Rodríguez de la Flor, Fernando. "Estudio introductorio." In *Fénix de Minerva o arte de memoria*, edited by Fernando Rodríguez de la Flor, vii–lii. Valencia: Tératos, 2002.

Rosselli, Cosimo. *Thesaurus artificiosae memoriae* […]. 1578. Hathitrust Digital Library.

Sosa, Antonio de. *Topographia, e historia general de Argel* […]. Edited by Diego de Haedo. Valladolid: Diego Fernández de Córdova y Oviedo, 1612.

Stagg, Geoffrey. "The Date and Form of *El trato de Argel*." *Bulletin of Hispanic Studies* 30, no. 120 (1953): 181–92.

Sullivan, Henry W. *Grotesque Purgatory: A Study of Cervantes's* Don Quixote, *Part II*. University Park: Pennsylvania State University Press, 1996.

Vaccari, Debora. "Noticias de unos comediantes de finales del siglo XVI y *El trato de Argel* de Cervantes." *Teatro de palabras. Revista de teatro áureo*, no. 7 (2013): 357–76.

Wardropper, Bruce W. "Comedias." In *Suma cervantina*, edited by J.B. Avalle-Arce and E.C. Riley, 147–69. London: Tamesis, 1973.

Yates, Frances A. *The Art of Memory*. Chicago: University of Chicago Press, 1966.

Yates, Frances A. "New Light on the Globe Theater." *New York Review of Books*, 26 May 1966, 16–22.

Zamora Vicente, Alonso. "El cautiverio en la obra cervantina." In *Homenaje a Cervantes*, edited by Francisco Sánchez-Castañer, 2:237–56. Valencia: Mediterráneo, 1950.

Zimic, Stanislav. *El teatro de Cervantes*. Madrid: Castalia, 1992.

Zmantar, Francoise. "Miguel de Cervantes y sus fantasmas de Argel." *Quimera*, no. 2 (1980): 31–7.

5 Captivating Music, Memory, and Emotions in *Los baños de Argel*

SHERRY VELASCO

Halfway through the second act of Cervantes's captivity play *Los baños de Argel* (The Bagnios of Algiers, written between 1590 and 1610; published in 1615),[1] a group of Christian captives are granted a temporary reprieve from their labours and allowed to visit the garden of Agi Morato. The captives intend to spend their precious temporary freedom to "danzar, cantar y tañer / y hacer nuestras cabriolas" (dance, caper about, sing and play our instruments), in the hope that music might prove a salve for their suffering during a brief retreat in what must have been a lovely natural setting.[2]

Among the captives are an older Christian Morisco father (El Viejo) and his two young sons, Francisco and Juan.[3] The young boys are dressed in the expensive garb of the *garzones*, which in captivity narratives of Cervantes's time would have indicated their status as slaves intended for the sodomitic pleasure of their Algerian masters.[4] Immediately aware of the meaning of the boys' sensual clothing, their father laments that their garb is more appropriate for "regocijo y de fiestas" ("revelry and celebrations") than for hard labour, and he prays that God will let his sons die rather than have them thus defiled.[5] Also dressed in the lavish clothing of the *garzones* is the captive Ambrosio. Four other captives bring guitars and a rebec, further signalling that their reprieve will be a musical one.[6] A few of the captives are also carrying additional *garzón* garments and Turkish capes, as if expecting that the singers and players will find enjoyment from the luxury garments – a sign of upper nobility from the popular game of canes (*juego de cañas*) in Spain.[7] After all, their master (the Cadí) has practically ordered them to enjoy themselves: "[E]s la intención / del cadí que nos holguemos, / y que los viernes tomemos / honesta recreación" ("The Cadí wants us to take our ease and enjoy honest sport on Fridays").[8]

Music's Power to Control Emotions

While music has received relatively little attention in Cervantes's work, its polyphonic presence has not gone unnoticed. In recent years, musicologists, historians, and literary scholars have considered music in Cervantes's prose, poetry, and drama from a wide range of perspectives. However, all agree that the author had a keen interest in arranging music and sound to entertain as well as fine-tune the emotional responses of his readers, spectators, and listeners.[9]

The musical recital that took place on the way to the garden might be understood as a straightforward scene designed as a pleasurable reprieve for the captives – and audiences, who may also have experienced it thus. A close reading of the scene reveals more. As other scholars have pointed out, Cervantes was well acquainted with the dominant theories of how various tonalities – instrumental and vocal – were believed to affect listeners' psyches. Ancient theories of musical modes still held sway throughout the sixteenth and part of the seventeenth century. Along with Plato, Aristotle's theory of musical modes and their effect were still taken seriously, and Aristotle maintained that plaintive music would produce sadness in the listener. As he explains in the *Politics*: "The effect of some [modes] will be to produce a sadder and graver temperament; this is the case with the mode called the Mixolydian."[10] Assessing the Lydian modes to be sorrowful and languid, Plato banned this sombre music because, as Juan Eusebio Nieremberg summarizes in his meditation on music, "afligía al ánimo con tristeza" (it afflicted the soul with sadness).[11] To dramatize Plato's point, Nieremberg recounts an anecdote of a famous musician known for his ability to control listeners' emotions simply by changing the mode of the music played: "Entristecíolos al principio con un son grave y bajo, que, mudándole luego, los regocijó de modo que querían saltar de contento" ("At first he made them sad with a deep and low sound and then changed it to make them so joyful they wanted to leap from happiness").[12]

Musical commentary among the captives in the garden soon reveals a nuanced acoustic exploration of the power of music – especially the singing voice – to stimulate certain emotions (such as joy) and distract listeners from others (pain, fear, grief, among others). Given the thoughtful preparations, which involved gathering festive clothing and instruments for a private – albeit sanctioned – garden party, we might expect to hear lively melodies and rhythms conducive for dancing. It may come as a surprise when the elegantly clad Ambrosio redirects the festivities by suggesting that they start with sad music – "[C]omencemos tristemente" ("Let us begin sadly") – requesting specifically a mournful ballad lamenting the pain of captivity composed by their companion Julio.[13] Ambrosio tells his companions that the sombre *sound* of the music will have a positive effect on the group of singers/listeners: "[T]iene aquel *tono triste* / con que *alegrarnos* solemos" ("It has that sad tone that cheers us up").[14] Some recent studies by psychologists and neurobiologists have shown that sad music has a positive effect on listeners, apparently because it triggers nostalgia, and nostalgia is often associated with positive feelings, but this was not the common assumption at the time.[15]

It is quite likely that the instrumentation and the music composition had changed sufficiently since Aristotle's time that sad-sounding music had quite a different effect on seventeenth-century listeners than it did for Aristotle and his countrymen. In fact, a closer look at the literature at the time reveals that some early modern musicians, theologians, and philosophers were beginning to recognize certain positive effects of sad music. Cervantes's Ambrosio could very well have been on the cutting edge of new musical interpretations when he proposed that they begin with sad songs. In a chapter on sadness in his 1538 *The Passions of the Soul* (*De anima et vita*), Juan Luis Vives asserts that the comradery of communal expression of one's sadness can lessen the pain: "But their sadness is alleviated because they find some consolation in the fact that they are not the only miserable ones, and that others feel sorry for their misery."[16]

Beyond its importance for group solidarity and survival, sad music may also acquire an aesthetic value that helps victims cope with their trauma through art, what some call the "tragedy paradox" or "the seemingly contradictory idea that humans work to minimize sadness in their lives, yet find it pleasurable in an aesthetic context."[17] While we do not have a musical score that would allow us to reproduce the kind of sound that Ambrosio wished them to perform and listen to, the "tono triste" that would raise their spirits may refer to a slower tempo, softer sound levels, and the use of the minor mode that is not only experienced as beautiful but perhaps cathartic.

In a similar way, Cervantes's text suggests that the sombre lyrics that accompany the plaintive melody of the first of three songs in the musical gathering offer a purgative function, preparing the captives for the festive dancing that was meant to follow:

Cantan este romance:
A las orillas del mar,
que con su lengua y sus aguas,
ya manso, ya airado, llega

del perro Argel las murallas,
con los ojos del deseo
están mirando a su patria
cuatro míseros cautivos
que del trabajo descansan;
y al son del ir y volver
de las olas en la playa,
con desmayados acentos
esto lloran y esto cantan:
¡Cuán cara eres de haber, oh dulce España!

([They sing this ballad]
On the shores of the sea,
whose bay and waters
reach the walls of that infidel Algiers
now turbulent, now calm;
four wretched captives,
resting from their labors,
with eyes of longing
look to their homeland,
and to the tone of the ebb and flow
of the waves on the shore,
in faint voices they sing and lament:
How dear you are to attain, o sweet Spain![18]

In his study *Cervantes: Música y poesía*, Juan José Pastor Comín reminds us that this original ballad was inspired by a sonnet (set to music by Juan Navarro) included in the *Cancionero Musical de Medinaceli* (c. 1569), with the most direct appropriation in the refrain "¡Qué cara eres de haber, oh dulce España."[19] Pastor Comín speculates that Cervantes would have known the musical score by Juan Navarro (1530–80), whose homophonic music (música golpeada) in the verse "where the sea was pounding" ("do la mar batía") establishes some of the semantic and acoustic possibilities for subsequent versions.[20] Cervantes scholar Jean Canavaggio reads the first song as a multitasking rendition of the melancholic atmosphere of captivity.[21] As a moment of rest, it provides a necessary pause between tense altercations before and after the musical reprieve. Furthermore, Canavaggio argues, the seemingly contradictory sad music that offers joy provides an apt transition from the gravity of Ambrosio to the spontaneity of Francisco in the second song – which the scholar interprets as a shared attitude where the despair of captivity converges with Christian hope.[22]

Recalling Memories of a Mother's Song

As mentioned earlier, at least one recent study of the effects of sad music on listeners conducted at the Free University of Berlin reached the tentative conclusion that of the 772 subjects who were asked to describe their feelings when listening to what we normally think of as sad music, 76 per cent said that the music made them nostalgic. This unexpected discovery ("surprisingly, nostalgia rather than sadness is the most frequent emotion evoked by sad music") led the psychologists who conducted the study to conclude that listening to sad music can lead to beneficial emotional effects such as allaying negative emotions and providing consolation.[23] One can hardly rely on just one sample, of course, and a free person listening to sad music in twenty-first-century Berlin would have quite a different reaction to nostalgia than a young captive in seventeenth-century Algiers. Yet it is notable that just as the singers conclude the final note of the captivity ballad, Francisco (the younger of the two boys dressed in the *garzón* apparel) asks his father if they might sing the song that the boys' mother used to sing back home in Spain. That the boy – by turns miserable and angry in the play – would want to find succour in a song his mother sang to him is not surprising. The father's response to Francisco's question is silence, so the boy asks him if he does not want them to sing the song. When Francisco follows up with "¿Qué dice? / ¿No quiere, padre?" ("What do you say? Don't you want to father?"), the patriarch evades the questions with one of his own: "¿Cómo decía el cantar?" ("How did the song go?")[24]

Before considering Francisco's brief tune reminding his father of the maternal song in question, let's pause to reflect on what is lurking behind the awkwardly enigmatic interaction between the father and son. Returning to Juan Luis Vives, this time to his chapter on memory and recall, his attention to the role that age plays certainly would explain, in part, the father's silence and the son's quick and accurate ability to recall the tune and lyrics: "What is seen and heard at an early age is stored for a longer duration and more fully; for at that time the mind is free of worries and thoughts."[25] Of course, Vives is not alone when he points out that "old people have difficulty in grasping and retaining things on account of their age."[26] However, if age were the only factor at play in the tense moment between father and son, it wouldn't account for what seemed to have triggered in Francisco the memory of his mother's singing voice and song. Did a particular semantic or sonic feature of the captives' ballad (such as a vocal performance accentuating the "desmayados acentos" ["faint voices"] of the intradiegetic captive singers) lead to the thought of that specific tune sung by the mother?[27] For theorists such as Vives, sound (as well as sight, touch, taste, and smell) are effective prompts for memory recall: "When some happy event befalls us and is accompanied by some sound or voice, we are delighted when we hear the same sound again. If it is a sad event, we feel sad."[28] Although in Francisco's case both the cue (the captivity ballad) and the event (his mother's song) are musically produced, it remains unclear how he could recognize the same or similar sound again if it were folded into the collective and divergent voices of the group.

Listening to the well-known refrain from the popular song that Francisco sings, we might consider whether the link between the first two songs that triggers the maternal memory is found in the lyrics – as opposed to a unique materiality or "grain" of the voice: "Ando enamorado, / no diré de quién; / allá miran ojos / donde quieren bien" ("I am in love, / with whom I won't say; / eyes look where they love, / where they love full well").[29]

If Francisco's memory recall is based on a semantic connection, the verses "con los ojos del deseo / están mirando a su patria" ("with eyes of longing / look to their homeland") in the captives' ballad surely brought to mind "allá miran ojos / donde quieren bien" ("eyes look where they love, / where they love full well") in the popular tune sung by his mother and reproduced by her son at the gathering.[30] In fact, this is the connection that the father makes, as he redirects their attention away from the amorous subtext of the mother's song back to the captives' woeful nostalgia for Spain: "Bien al propósito fuera, / pues que los del alma miran / desde esta infame ribera / la patria por quien suspiran, / que huye y no nos espera" ("The song is fitting, since the eyes of the soul gaze from this cursed shore to the homeland for which they sigh, which retreats and awaits us not").[31]

Although Francisco seems to find comfort in the memory of his mother's singing, the father's initial silence hints at his own conflicted recollection of his absent wife and her song. Even though the text does not tell us what had happened to her, Francisco mentions later that "lo postrero que mi madre / me enseñó quiero decir, / que es bueno para el morir" ("the last thing that my mother taught me, which is good for dying"), thereby implying that she had died.[32] The "Old Man's" pregnant pause also invites a reflection on the divergent ways in which father and son process the music memory of the beloved wife/mother that would not have surprised some early modern music practitioners. Juan Bermudo, in his 1555 *Declaración de instrumentos musicales*, for example, questions why the same music can produce such different emotional responses in listeners:

> Porque la Musica siendo una causa produze diversos effectos. A unos entristece y a otros alegra. Aunque en parte estos effectos contrarios sean causados de la disposicion y contrariedad de los modos; pero la principal causa de estos effectos contrarios es disposicion del hombre. Assi que si el hombre esta alegre, con la Musica se alegra mas; y si triste, con la Musica augmenta su tristeza.

> (Because music, as a single cause, can produce various effects. Although, in part, these contrary effects may be caused by the nature and opposition of the modes; but the principal cause of these contrary effects is the disposition of the individual. So if the person is happy, with music he will become happier; if he is sad, music will increase his sadness.)[33]

Following Bermudo's theory that one's present emotional state has a greater impact on how we respond to music than does the mode of the music, then the father's anxiety about his son's future in captivity would preclude a more positive or at least sentimental response to the mother's song.

Echoes of the Sopranos: Mother, Child, and la señora Catalina

When Francisco sings his mother's song, the absent Morisca mother acquires a kind of acoustic presence through her young son's high-pitched voice. To put it differently, the mother's voice is auralized (the listening version of "visualize") when reproduced by the treble vocalizations of her son, whose voice has not yet changed and is thus most likely in the soprano or mezzo-soprano range. The voice of the absent mother, while ephemeral, has been stored, retained, and recalled in the son's aural memory, allowing him to reproduce it for his immediate audience.

The exceptional sound of Francisco's singing ability did not go unacknowledged, as fellow captive Julio enthusiastically applauds his voice as "estremado" ("excellent").[34] In the same breath, Julio turns to Ambrosio, instructing him to sing what appears to be his "signature song," with what he describes as a voice that can calm the seas with "gusto infinito" or infinite pleasure: "Canta tú, Ambrosio, un poquito / lo que sueles a tus solas, / que te escucharán las olas / del mar con gusto infinito" ("Now you sing, Ambrosio, a bit of what you usually sing alone, for the waves of the sea will hear you with infinite pleasure").[35]

In keeping with Ambrosio's initial preference for sad sounds, his favoured song is a popular *zégel* with melancholic lyrics bemoaning how emotional appearances are deceiving while the affective truth resides beneath the surface:

Aunque pensáis que me alegro,
conmigo traigo el dolor.
Aunque mi rostro semeja
Que de mi alma se aleja
La pena, y libre la deja,
Sabed que es notorio error:
Conmigo traigo el dolor.
Cúmpleme disimular
Por acabar de acabar,
Y porque el mal, con callar,
Se hace mucho mayor,
Conmigo traigo el dolor.

(Although you think I'm happy,
I carry my pain inside.
Although my face shows
Grief leaving my soul
And setting it free, know
That it's a clear mistake:
I carry my pain inside.
I must pretend
So I can end my end,
And because silent woes
Grow apace,
I carry my pain inside.)[36]

The attentive listener can detect a familiar message shared by Francisco's rendition of his mother's tune and Ambrosio's popular song. In the mother-son song, the desiring subject withholds the identity of the object of their affections: ("no diré de quién" ["with whom I won't say"]). The truth about this desire must be accessed visually: look where I'm looking, as the gaze will give it away. If the mother's song announces, "I won't tell," then Ambrosio's message implies, "Keep silent and pretend" – regardless of the pain. What, then, are the beautiful voices of Francisco and Ambrosio not telling us? The audience already knew (as do readers of the play, thanks to repeated and insistent stage directions) that Ambrosio's message is pitch perfect: "his" external façade of a captive in fancy *garzón* garments belies the truth that the role of Ambrosio is cross-sex cast. This particular *garzón* is played by an actress identified multiple times in the text as la señora Catalina.

In essence, theatregoers and readers of the play alike would have recognized the visual and aural features that link Francisco and Ambrosio/Catalina: first, because they are the only two featured soloists in this scene and are both dressed in the eye-catching yet coded garments of the *garzones*; and secondly, it is reasonable to assume that they both had a high voice associated with the "boy soprano" and most female singers.

The soprano-range voice explains, in part, why Cervantes insists that the role of a young man – in particular a *garzón* – be played by a woman. Likewise, even though the role of Ambrosio is not a female character in the diegesis who must disguise herself as a man to achieve a desired goal, with Catalina playing the part of a *garzón*, the audience could enjoy a visual and aural fetish of the extradiegetic *mujer vestida de hombre*.

That Catalina (as Ambrosio) has relatively very few lines to memorize suggests that the appeal of casting la señora Catalina resides in her singing voice and her stage presence. The most productive and audible advantage of casting a woman to play the role of the youthful Ambrosio is undoubtedly achieved through the high voice – difficult for most male actors unless performed in falsetto or by a prepubescent actor like the boy playing Francisco. Nonetheless, this still doesn't explain why Cervantes insisted on a particular woman – "la señora Catalina" – for this role. Furthermore, the specificity of this cross-sex casting is significant since it is the only time in any of Cervantes's dramatic works that he identifies a particular individual by name to play a role. Without a doubt, the author left nothing to chance with this casting choice, as he repeats three times in the stage directions of a relatively short scene (and as well as in the initial list of characters) that la señora Catalina would play this role.

Who was la señora Catalina?

So, who was "la señora Catalina" and why does Cervantes single *her* out to play Ambrosio? Most scholars have assumed (following Astrana Marín) that "la señora Catalina" was Catalina Hernández Verdeseca, wife of the successful actor-director-manager Pedro Gaspar de Porres.[37] This *autor* had purchased two of Cervantes's plays years earlier during the 1580s. When Cervantes was drafting *Los baños* between 1606 and 1610, perhaps he hoped to entice Gaspar de Porres to produce this play by designating a specific role for his wife. If this were the case, his strategy was unsuccessful since there is no record of the popular director-manager having produced it.

Given the importance of the *garzón* costume for her role as Ambrosio, it is significant that Hernández Verdeseca was active in the financial and creative transactions necessary for acquiring the luxury outfits that were so expensive yet so important for the success of most performances. Although there are no references to Catalina having belonged to the regular cast of any theatre company during the late sixteenth or early seventeenth centuries, theatre scholar Evangelina Rodríguez Cuadros claims that Catalina Hernández Verdeseca was among a group of actresses known for their extravagant costumes onstage, especially for the performances during Corpus Christi.[38] That Gaspar de Porres's wife had a reputation based, in part, on her elegant wardrobe is not surprising given her husband's extensive involvement and investment in luxury fabrics in the vibrant clothing trade.[39] This expertise and experience would undoubtedly come in handy when performing the role of Ambrosio dressed in stylish *garzón* attire, since actresses owned and performed in their own costumes onstage, and from her insider's position in the clothing industry she would have had access to similar garments for male roles.[40]

Catalina's absence from the cast list of professional theatre companies points to a career onstage based on her singing abilities instead of the dramatic chops required for non-musical roles. There is a glimpse of Catalina as a celebrity singer in Julio's almost fan-like devotion to Ambrosio when he requests his "greatest hit" and gushes that "his" voice has a kind of supernatural power over the rhythmic motions in nature: "Canta tú, Ambrosio, un poquito / lo que sueles a tus solas, / que te escucharán las olas / del mar con gusto infinito" ("Now you sing, Ambrosio, a bit of what you usually sing alone, for the waves of the sea will hear you with infinite pleasure").[41]

Is Cervantes arranging, in part, the musical setting through casting in this scene to ensure that the soprano voices of Francisco and Ambrosio/Catalina produce a kind of aural fetish for some theatregoers?[42] If so, what do we know about these voices and their impact on the audience? For their part, moralists such as Juan Ferrer were gravely troubled by the provocative and lustful message that actresses' singing voices could communicate to listeners captivated by an intangible yet forceful influence of the musical features:

Con cantares de *buenas y suaves voces*, que algunas destas mujercillas tienen, ... porque una razón dicha en verso bueno, cantada con *una dulce voz,* tiene no se qué que lleva y arrebata el ánimo y con una voluntaria violencia, cautiva el corazón del oyente… ¿Qué será, viendo por vista de ojos y oyendo con nuestros oídos tantas cosas, cuantas en una comedia incitan al torpe deleite?

(With good and pleasurable voices that some of the so-called "ladies" have … because an idea spoken in a fine verse, sung with an inviting voice, has something indefinable that transports and takes hold of the soul with a spontaneous fury that takes the listener's heart prisoner…. What will happen, when looking with our eyes and listening with our ears to so much onstage that incites sinful pleasure?)[43]

Articulated by theatre detractors as good, pleasurable, sweet/inviting, satisfying, and feminine (*buenas, suaves, dulces, blandas, deliciosas,* and *afeminadas*), these voices seem consistent with the "soprano fetish" of the seventeenth century described by Susan McClary in her study *Desire and Pleasure in Seventeenth-Century Music*. Characterized as an "addiction" and an "insatiable appetite for high voices" that gave an advantage to female singers, McClary remarks that as a result "very little music was written for performance by tenors or basses during the seventeenth century. The soprano voice ruled."[44]

In Spain, critics of the actresses singing and dancing onstage were particularly concerned by the mesmerizing effect that left the audience spellbound by what ecclesiastics recognized as both exceptional and sinful music:

Porque la dulce armonía de los instrumentos, la destreza y *suavidad* de las voces, la conceptuosa agudeza de las letras, la variedad y *dulzura* de los tonos, el aire y sazón de los estribillos, la gracia de los quiebros, la suspensión de los redobles y contrapuntos hacen tan *suave y deliciosa* armonía que tiene a los oyentes suspensos y como hechizados.

(Since the pleasing harmony of the instruments, the skill and delight in the voices, the conceptual wit of the lyrics, the variety and sweetness of the tones, the airiness and perfection of the refrains, the charm of the trills, the lift of the repetitions and counterpoints create such pleasurable and satisfying harmony that it holds the listeners as if spellbound.)[45]

Even Saint Augustine claims to have become so entranced by an awe-inspiring voice that he became deaf to the spiritual message of the song – reminiscent of the "oyentes suspensos y como hechizados":

I also know that there are particular modes in song and in the voice, corresponding to my various emotions and able to stimulate them because of some mysterious relationship between the two…. Yet when I find the singing itself more moving than the truth which it conveys, I confess that this is a grievous sin, and at those times I would prefer not to hear the singer.[46]

For feminist philosopher Catherine Clément, the real danger of the diva's irresistible voice in opera is that "the music makes one forget the plot."[47] As Mary Ann Smart notes: "In her [Clément's] quest to reveal the darkly misogynistic aspects of opera's plots, she depicts music as a sort of siren song that lures us to wallow in the operatic experience while forgetting the violence done to women. Despite the obfuscating spell cast by the music, we are ultimately affected by these fatal messages."[48]

The Hidden Truth beneath Garzón Clothing

Of course, Francisco's "estremado" (singular, excellent) voice may, for some, also mesmerize and distract as well as attract ears. What, then, is his music making us forget? One possibility is introduced at the very start of the scene. The first lines address head-on the problematic sign of the *garzón* attire. When the aging father sees his boys for the first time after being sold to an Algerian judge (Cadí) with a particular attraction for beautiful boys, the patriarch is horrified by the sight of the *garzón* clothing. Juanico reassures him: outer trappings like clothing can be changed, but inner truths are impenetrable:

VIEJO:
¿No son mis prendas aquéstas?
¿Cómo vienen adornadas
de regocijo y de fiestas?
Prendas por mi bien halladas,
¿qué bizarrías son estas?
Harto costoso ropaje
es éste….
JUANICO:
Padre, no le pene el ver
que hemos vestido trocado,
que no se ha podido hacer
otra cosa; y, bien mirado,
de aquesto no hay que temer,

porque si nuestra intención
está con firme afición
puesta en Dios, caso es sabido
que no deshace el vestido
lo que hace el corazón.

(OLD MAN:
Are these not my jewels? Why are they dressed for revelry and celebrations? My happily found treasures, what finery is this? These are very
  expensive clothes....

JUANICO:
Father, don't cry over our change of clothes, there was no way around it; and,
  if you think about it, there's nothing to worry about, for if our love of God
  stands firm, everyone knows clothes can't undo what the heart does.)[49]

The father's fears, however, are well founded in the play. In act 1 we learn of the Cadí's attraction for young boys when the Algerian officials discuss the newly arrived captives from Spain: "Cadí: ¿Hay muchachos? / Yzuf: Dos no más; / pero de belleza estraña, / como presto lo verás. / Cadí: Hermosos los cría España." ("Cadí: Are there any young lads? Yzuf: Only two; but of a rare beauty, as you'll soon see. Cadí: Spain makes some beauties").[50] The old father overhears this conversation, and his anxiety is palpable in almost every inter-action he has for the duration of the play. In the scene preceding the private musical gathering, the father confesses his worries to the Sex-ton – and to the heavens: "Más cautiverio y más duelos / Cupieron a mis dos niños, / Por crecer mis desconsuelos. / Conservad a estos armiños / En limpieza, ¡oh limpios cielos! / Y si veis que se endereza / De Mahoma la torpeza / A procurar su caída, / Quitadles antes la vida / Que ellos pierdan su limpieza" ("More captivity and sorrows befell my two sons, to increase my grief. Preserve the chastity of those ermines, O chaste heavens! And if you see that Mohammedan lewd-ness rise to make them fall, take their lives from them before they can be defiled").[51]

In a somewhat ironic and metatheatrical variation on a similar scene in Lope de Vega's adaptation (*Los cautivos de Argel*) of Cer-vantes's earlier captivity play (*Los tratos de Argel*), the father and Sex-ton are confronted by two or three young Moors, whose only function here is to taunt the Christian captives. The Sexton, a religious official with venomous views of Muslims in Algiers (both young and old), responds to the Algerian boys with violent curses and insults largely focused on sodomy and other vices: "¡Oh hijo de una puta, / nieto de un gran cornudo, / sobrino de un bellaco, / hermano de un gran traidor y sodomita! / … ¡Tú morirás, borracho, / bardaja fementido; / quínola punto menos, / anzuelo de Mahoma, el hideputa!" ("O son of a whore, grandson of a great cuckold, nephew of a rogue, brother of a great traitor and sodomite!… You will die, you sot, you lying bugger; you don't play with a full deck, you're the bait of Mohammed, that whoreson!").[52]

The Sexton's threats and invectives are extreme but do not vary greatly from the standard propaganda from other Christian religious officials in Algiers – the most famous being the Portuguese cleric Antonio de Sosa, who provides the most detailed account of life in Algiers at the time when he and his friend Cervantes were held captive in the infamous city. Like the Sexton in *Los baños de Argel*, Sosa presents Muslims in Algiers as perverse sodomites who prey on vulnerable Christians. In his *Topografía de Argel*, the only *garzones* who are characterized as victims are the young Christian captives tempted or forced to don the fancy garb and partake in other sinful activities: "Los de mas todos viven una vida bestial de puercos animales, dandose continuamente a la crapula y lujuria, y particularmente a la hedionda y nefanda sodomía, sirviendose de mozos christianos cautivos que compran para ese vicio, que luego visten a la turquesca." ("The rest of the Algerians live a bestial life of swine, constantly giving themselves over to licentiousness and lechery, and particularly to the heinous and revolting act of sodomy, abusing young boys, captive Christians whom they buy for this vice and later dress in the Turkish mode").[53] As Adrienne Martín notes in her critical study of early modern perceptions of sexual deviance as the ultimate threat to Spanish Christianity in Algiers, the stakes were certainly high: "What better call to action to Spanish Christians and to the monarch? The imprisoned slaves must be ransomed at all costs in order to save them from Islamic 'promiscuity' and the threat of apostasy."[54]

To this end, in the middle of his vitriolic tirade, Sosa unexpectedly turns his attention to the musical practices – both instrumental and vocal – of some of these men in Algiers. Again, Sosa's analysis is fraught with prejudice:

Algunos, mas muy raros tañen vihuelas a su uso, que son como media calabaza de cuello largo, partida toda por el medio, de manera que el hueco de retumba y se causa el son, es redondo, y tan hondo como la mitad de la cabeza de la calabaza partida.[55] En este tal instrumento atan hasta tres cuerdas que tocan muy desacordamente, sin artificio o gracia alguna y lo mismo es del canto, que parece mas aullido de lobos que voz humana de hombres y las canciones son compuestas en rima; mas generalmente todas muy sucias y torpes en alabanza de muchachos y garzones, a los cuales festejan y dan musica publicamente como a las mas requebradas damas del mundo.

(Some men, albeit few, play a form of guitar that is like a halved pumpkin with a long neck and split entirely down the middle, so that the echo is round where it booms and causes the sound, as hollow as the half of the head of a split gourd. They pluck up to three strings of this instrument played very discordantly and with little grace or skill. The same applies to their singing, which seems more the howling of wolves than the human voice of men. And their songs are composed in verse but generally these verses are all filthy and obscene in praise of the boys and *garzones*, whom they celebrate and for whom they play music in public as if they were the most desired ladies in the world.)[56]

What stands out in Sosa's biased critique is the convergence of illicit sexual desires and the sound of "local" music in Algiers – which includes instrumental and vocal features as well as the semantic messages in the crafted lyrics. Not surprisingly, the musical sonority of sodomitic desire is cacophonous, bestial, and performed *for* – and not *by* – the *garzones*. Conversely, in Cervantes's treatment of *garzones* and music, the stylish boys (whether played by a boy actor or cross-dressed actress) are themselves producing pleasant and harmonious vocal sounds.

For all the talk of the idealized Arcadian destination, we never actually make it to the garden. The three songs in this scene are performed on the road – the group stops to sing a capella while working their way through the streets of Algiers towards the garden near the marina on a Friday. Three of the young captives are dressed as *garzones* – and others seem poised to join them, given the pile of *garzón* garments they are carrying for the festivities. Some theatregoers (those who had seen, read, or heard Christian perspectives about captivity in Algiers) would find these details troublesome. Here is what Sosa has to say:

Acostumbran entonces los arraeses y leuentes, vestir muy ricamente a sus garzones (que son sus mujeres barbadas) de vestidos de damasco, raso y terciopelo.… Y tienen por punto de honra y contienda entre si, de quien mas numero tiene de garzones, mas hermosos y mas bien vestidos y para esto los embian a manadas y en compañías a pasear el Xuma [Friday] y otros dias por la ciudad y a la marina y campaña; reputando esto a una gran pavonada y gloria muy particular que es la cosa mas notable y mas digna de llorar.... La sodomía se tiene como dijimos por honra, porque aquel es mas honrado que sustenta mas garzones y los celan mas que las propias mujeres y hijas sino es a los viernes.

(Both the captains and lewends are given to richly dressing up their *garzones* (who are actually bearded women) with clothes of damask, satin, and velvet. These young men ... are more pampered than the most refined and beautiful women. A point of honour and rivalry among the Turks is who has the larger number of *garzones*, the most handsome, and the best dressed. To this end, the Turks send them in droves to stroll about the city on Fridays and other days, as well as down to the seashore and out to the country. They regard this as a great way to have fun and a very particular form of glory. And of all the practices in the world which could be seen or imagined, this one is enough to make one weep (that such a thing should occur among men, in public and with such great shamelessness).... Sodomy, as we said, is considered honourable, because he who can support the most *garzones* is the more honoured for it. He is envied for this even more than for his own wives and daughters, when on Fridays and holidays he displays his boy-loves very richly dressed.)[57]

Surely Cervantes was aware of the significance of the luxury attire of the *garzones*, as they stroll through the streets of Algiers en route to the marina and countryside on a Friday. It is conceivable, then, that the group of captives in Cervantes's play could be mistaken for *garzones* parading for the pleasure of their adoring captors during a Friday excursion.

Like Sosa, the aging Morisco father is acutely anxious about the visual temptation that his youthful boys donning beautiful clothing posed for the men in Algiers with transgressive desires. Yet, his quick reaction to his wife/son's tune downplays the amorous innuendo of the song in favour of a nostalgic gaze that desires home and country. Although he does not comment directly on the material qualities of his son's voice, could the father's angst here point to an acoustic anxiety (conscious or not) based on an aural fetish produced by the soprano voice? In other words, after hearing his son's voice, does the father intuit an aural eroticism that poses an even more dangerous threat to his son's chastity – given that sound travels indiscriminately to all ears (even the "wrong" ears), passing through physical barriers that visual objects like fancy clothing cannot?

For all the unique excellence of Francisco's and Catalina's voices, what exactly is heard (or not heard) and how these sounds transform emotions tell us more about the listener than the singer. Sosa hears the music and voices of Turks and renegades in Algiers as animalistic and grating. Yet Cervantes would have us hear the voice of the Morisco nephew of a renegade in Algiers (Yzuf) as exquisite, perhaps an angelic siren song foreshadowing his imminent martyrdom in act 3.

Given that the power of music to influence emotions is traced, in part, to the personal and culturally determined experiences of the listener, we cannot ignore the importance of the audience as listeners. It is not by chance that both Francisco and Ambrosio/Catalina sing popular songs that would have been familiar to, perhaps even a favourite of, the audience. Again, the moralists were painfully aware of the influence of popular music on theatre productions as well as the sway of adapted compositions onstage (such as the captivity ballad) on the receptive public. Not surprisingly, this two-way music production relied on how attentive the listeners were and their capacity to store, retain, and recall acoustic information, as ecclesiastic Juan de Mariana traces through public and private spaces: "Los cantarcillos torpes tomados de las plazas, bodegones y casas públicas, con tonadas que sirven al tal propósito, *se reducen a la memoria* con gravísimos perjuicios de las costumbres y tanto mayor mal que de los teatros pasan a las plazas y a las casas particulares, *fijados en la memoria* con la torpeza como con engrudo" (The lewd little songs that come from plazas, taverns, and brothels to the stage, where they are then *stored in the memory* of the audience with serious harm to their behaviours. It's even worse when these tunes are carried from the theatre back to the streets or private homes, having been lewdly *fixed in their memory* as if with glue).[58]

Although Juan de Mariana understands the convergent relationship between music and memory, he accounts for only one (illicit) response to the profane songs performed onstage. This is where Cervantes's play models a much more nuanced understanding of the personal and political implications of music, memory, and emotions. The playwright does not tell us directly which musical feature(s) of a song may trigger specific affective responses. Like Vives, Cervantes was keenly aware that certain details of our memories are archived by our ears and eyes, even when we are not consciously aware of the process: "… things that come in from the external sources by way of the two senses of hearing and seeing. Although these things go unheeded, they are passed immediately to the memory."[59] What for Saint Augustine and Catherine Cléments is the sinister consequences of being distracted by the sublime voices in profane or sacred spaces and for Vives is the unconscious (or repressed) aural and visual information that enters the memory unheeded, for Cervantes these music memories invite those alert members of the audience to consider the uncertain fate of absent Morisca mothers and prepubescent boys in captivity.

NOTES

1 The *baños* were the prisons that housed captives and slaves.
2 Cervantes, *Los baños de Argel*, 528; *Bagnios of Algiers*, 45. All quotes from *Los baños de Argel* are from Sevilla Arroyo's edition of *Teatro completo*, and all translations – unless otherwise noted – are from Barbara Fuchs and Aaron J. Ilika's *"The Bagnios of Algiers" and "The Great Sultana": Two Plays of Captivity*.
3 Although Cervantes does not specify that the old father and his family are Moriscos, I follow Javier Irigoyen-García and others, who argue that the captive family's renegade uncle Yzuf is modelled after the parallel Morisco character Francisco in Lope de Vega's *Cautivos de Argel*. See Vega Carpio, *Los cautivos de Argel*, 171; and Irigoyen-García, "La música ha sido hereje," "El problema morisco."
4 The 1734 *Diccionario de autoridades* defines *garzón* as "el joven, mancebo o mozo bien dispuesto" (a young and attractive man or boy; *Diccionario de autoridades*, s.v. "garzon"). The *garzones* were often assumed to be the young lovers of sodomites. See also Garcés, *Early Modern Dialogue*, 278; and Martín, "Images of Deviance."
5 Cervantes, *Los baños de Argel*, 527; *Bagnios of Algiers*, 44.
6 A rebec is a medieval string instrument played with a bow and descended from the Arabic *rebab* (Garcés, *Early Modern Dialogue*, 326).
7 See Irigoyen-García, *"Moors Dressed as Moors."*
8 Cervantes, *Los baños de Argel*, 528; *Bagnios of Algiers*, 46. See also Martín, "Images of Deviance."
9 See Alustiza, "La música en las obras de Cervantes"; Avello, "Música en el *Quijote*"; Baker, "Sonic Expectations"; Calvo-Manzano, *El arpa en la obra de Cervantes*; Diego, "Cervantes y la música"; Espinós, *El "Quijote" en la música*; Gasta, "Señora"; Gutiérrez del Arroyo, "La música en Cervantes"; Haywood, "Cervantes and Music"; Irigoyen-García, "La música ha sido hereje"; Istel and Baker, "Music"; Lambea, "Procesos intertextuales"; Leal Pinar, *La música en el Quijote*; Pastor Comín, *Cervantes*, "Música y literatura"; Querol Galvadá, *La música en las obras de Cervantes*; Roda, *Los instrumentos músicos*; Salazar, *La música de Cervantes*; and Velasco, "From Spain to Algiers," "Music, Sex, and Politics."
10 Aristotle, *Politics*, 310.
11 Plato, *Republic*, 93–5; and Nieremberg, *Oculta filosofía*, 47.
12 Nieremberg, *Oculta filosofía*, 46–7.
13 Cervantes, *Los baños de Argel*, 529; *Bagnios of Algiers*, 46.
14 Cervantes, *Los baños de Argel*, 530 (emphasis mine); *Bagnios of Algiers*, 47.
15 See Sachs, Damasio, and Habibi, "Sad Music"; and Taruffi and Koelsch, "Music-Evoked Sadness."

16 Vives, *Passions of the Soul*, 97. See also Noreña, *Juan Luis Vives*.

17 Sachs, Damasio, and Habibi, "Sad Music."

18 Cervantes, *Los baños de Argel*, 530 (emphasis in original); *Bagnios of Algiers*, 47.

19 Pastor Comín, *Cervantes*, 38.

20 Pastor Comín, 38–9, 42.

21 Canavaggio, *Cervantès dramaturge*, 320.

22 Canavaggio, 320. See also Pastor Comín, *Cervantes*, 37.

23 Taruffi and Koelsch, "Music-Evoked Sadness."

24 Cervantes, *Los baños de Argel*, 531; *Bagnios of Algiers*, 47–8 (translation modified).

25 Vives, "De Anima et Vita," 29.

26 Vives, 30.

27 "Los baños de Argel," 530; *The Bagnios of Algiers*, 47.

28 Vives, "De Anima et Vita," 29.

29 Cervantes, *Los baños de Argel*, 531; *Bagnios of Algiers*, 48. See Barthes, "Grain of the Voice."

30 Cervantes, *Los baños de Argel*, 530–1; *Bagnios of Algiers*, 47–8.

31 Cervantes, *Los baños de Argel*, 531; *Bagnios of Algiers*, 48. See also Irigoyen-García, "El problema morisco."

32 Cervantes, *Los baños de Argel*, 548; *Bagnios of Algiers*, 65.

33 Bermudo, *Declaración*, 59; translation mine. See also Lozano Virumbrales, "De efectos y afectos," 313.

34 Cervantes, *Los baños de Argel*, 531; *Bagnios of Algiers*, 48.

35 Cervantes, *Los baños de Argel*, 531; *Bagnios of Algiers*, 48.

36 Cervantes, *Los baños de Argel*, 531 (emphasis in original); *Bagnios of Algiers*, 48 (emphasis in original).

37 Gaspar de Porres (Porras; 1550–c. 1615): "Spanish actor-manager. Performing between 1585 (when he bought two plays from Cervantes) and 1608, Porres was probably the most important and prosperous impresario of his day. His company played throughout the country, and employed several actors famous later. A close associate and friend of Lope de Vega, he bought and first performed dozens of that author's plays, twelve of which he published, with Lope's help, in Madrid in 1614" (Dixon, "Porres"). See also Astrana Marín, *Vida ejemplar*; Cotarelo y Valledor, *El teatro de Cervantes*; Canavaggio, *Cervantès dramaturge*; and Cervantes, *Los baños de Argel*.

38 Rodríguez Cuadros, *La técnica del actor*, 618. See also Díaz de Escovar and Lasso de la Vega, *Historia del teatro español*, 735.

39 Irigoyen-García, "Moors Dressed as Moors," 77.

40 Theatre scholar Lola González, conversely, argues that the Catalina mentioned in the text is unlikely to be Catalina Hernández Verdeseca,

given that there are no references to this Catalina in any theatre company or performance documentation from the early modern period. González's hypothesis argues that the mysterious señora Catalina is most likely the actress Catalina Eugenia de Torres, wife of the actor Juan Bautista de Angulo, who is believed to be the entertainer characterized in *El coloquio de los perros* as the most humorous actor on stage. Catalina de Torres acted in the companies of Antonio Granados in 1604, Alonso de Heredia in 1607, and Hernán Sánchez de Vargas in 1610. See González, "Y mientras tanto escribía el Quijote (1605)," 240.

41 Cervantes, *Los baños de Argel*, 531; *Bagnios of Algiers*, 48.

42 In reference to music in *Don Quixote*, Christina Baker argues that "Cervantes uses his writing to become the purposeful creator of aural environments, and as such, is not just an author, but also a sound designer" ("Sonic Expectations," 67). See also Smith, "Shakespeare as Sound Artist" for his work on Shakespeare as sound designer.

43 Cited in Cotarelo y Mori, *Bibliografía*, 252; emphasis and translation mine.

44 McClary, *Desire and Pleasure*, 94–6.

45 Ignacio de Camargo, cited in Cotarelo y Mori, *Bibliografía*, 123–4; emphasis and translation mine.

46 Saint Augustine, *Confessions*, 238–9.

47 Clément, *Opera*, 10. See also Cavarero, *For More than One Voice*, 123–30.

48 Smart, "Introduction," 4.

49 Cervantes, *Los baños de Argel*, 527; *Bagnios of Algiers*, 44–5.

50 Cervantes, *Los baños de Argel*, 504; *Bagnios of Algiers*, 23.

51 Cervantes, *Los baños de Argel*, 522–3; *Bagnios of Algiers*, 41.

52 Cervantes, *Los baños de Argel*, 523; *Bagnios of Algiers*, 42.

53 Sosa, *Topographia*, 15; *Topography*, 148.

54 Martín, "Images of Deviance," 12.

55 Garcés identifies this "vihuela" or guitar to be the *rabab* or *rebeb*, "a string instrument of the viola family used in North Africa and the Middle East. One of the key instruments of Arabic-Andalusian music, the rabab was the favorite instrument of the Ottoman Empire, heard in all parts, from the palace to the teahouse" (*Early Modern Dialogue*, 326).

56 Sosa, *Topographia*, 15; *Topography*, 149; translation emended.

57 Sosa, *Topographia*, 17v–18, 38; *Topography*, 159, 239.

58 Cited in Cotarelo y Mori, *Bibliografía*, 434; emphasis mine.

59 Vives, "De Anima et Vita," 30.

REFERENCES

Alustiza, Juan B. de. "La música en las obras de Cervantes." *Estudios Musicales*, no. 1 (1917): 7–25.

Aristotle. *Politics*. Translated by Ernest Barker. Edited by R.F. Stalley. Oxford: Oxford University Press, 1998.

Astrana Marín, Luis. *Vida ejemplar y heroica de Miguel de Cervantes Saavedra*. Vols. 3–4. Madrid: Reus, 1952.

Avello, Ramón. "Música en el *Quijote*, música sobre el *Quijote*." In *El Quijote: IV Centenario 1605–2005*, edited by Jesús Menéndez Peláez, 85–98. Madrid: KRK, 2005.

Baker, Christina. "'Where There's Music There Is'…: Manipulating Sonic Expectations in *Don Quixote*." *Romance Notes* 56, no. 1 (2016): 67–79. https://doi.org/10.1353/rmc.2016.0018.

Barthes, Roland. "The Grain of the Voice." In *Image, Music, Text*, translated by Stephen Heath, 179–89. New York: Hill & Wang, 1977.

Bermudo, Juan. *Declaración de instrumentos musicales*. Osuna: Juan de Leon, 1555.

Calvo-Manzano, María Rosa. *El arpa en la obra de Cervantes:* Don Quijote *y la música española*. Valladolid: Junta de Castilla y León, 1999.

Canavaggio, Jean. *Cervantès dramaturge. Un théâtre à naître*. Paris: Presses Universitaires de France, 1977.

Cavarero, Adriana. *For More than One Voice: Toward a Philosophy of Vocal Expression*. Translated by Paul A. Kottman. Stanford: Stanford University Press, 2005.

Cervantes, Miguel de. *"The Bagnios of Algiers" and "The Great Sultana": Two Plays of Captivity*. Edited and translated by Barbara Fuchs and Aaron J. Ilika. Philadelphia: University of Pennsylvania Press, 2010.

Cervantes, Miguel de. *Los baños de Argel*. In *Teatro completo*, edited by Florencio Sevilla Arroyo, 477–588. Barcelona: Penguin, 2016.

Clément, Catherine. *Opera, or The Undoing of Women*. Translated by Betsy Wing. Minneapolis: University of Minnesota Press, 1999.

Cotarelo y Mori, Emilio. *Bibliografía de las controversias sobre la licitud del teatro en España*. Granada: Universidad de Granada, 1997.

Cotarelo y Valledor, Armando. *El teatro de Cervantes*. Madrid: Revista de Archivos, Bibliotecas y Museos, 1915.

Díaz de Escovar, Narcisco, and Francisco de P. Lasso de la Vega. *Historia del teatro español: Comediantes, escritores, curiosidades escénicas*. Vol 1. Barcelona: Montaner y Simón, 1924.

Diccionario de autoridades. Madrid: Real Academia Española, 1726–39. https://apps2.rae.es/DA.html.

Diego, Gerardo. "Cervantes y la música." *Anales Cervantinos*, no. 1 (1951): 5–40.

Dixon, Victor. "Porres (Porras), Gaspar de (1550–c.1615)." In *The Oxford Companion to Theatre and Performance*, edited by Dennis Kennedy, 477. Oxford: Oxford University Press, 2010.

Espinós, Victor. *El "Quijote" en la música*. Barcelona: Consejo Superior de Investigaciones Científicas, 1947.

Garcés, María Antonia. *Cervantes in Algiers: A Captive's Tale*. Nashville: Vanderbilt University Press, 2002.

Garcés, María Antonia, ed. *An Early Modern Dialogue with Islam: Antonio de Sosa's* Topography of Algiers *(1612)*. Translated by Diana de Armas Wilson. Notre Dame: University of Notre Dame Press, 2011.

Gasta, Chad M. "'Señora, donde hay música no puede haber cosa mala': Music, Poetry, and Orality in *Don Quijote*." *Hispania* 93, no. 3 (2010): 357–67.

González, Lola. "Y mientras tanto escribía el Quijote (1605). Cervantes y el teatro." In *Cervantes y su mundo*, vol. 2, edited by Kurt Reichenberger and Darío Fernández-Morera, 227–43. Kassel: Reichenberger, 2005.

Gutiérrez del Arroyo, Fernando. "La música en Cervantes." *Boletín de la Institución Libre de Enseñanza* 2, nos. 53–4 (2004): 31–44.

Haywood, Charles. "Cervantes and Music." *Hispania* 31, no. 2 (1948): 131–51. https://doi.org/10.2307/334144.

Irigoyen-García, Javier. *"Moors Dressed as Moors": Clothing, Social Distinction, and Ethnicity in Early Modern Iberia*. Toronto: University of Toronto Press, 2017.

Irigoyen-García, Javier. "'La música ha sido hereje': Pastoral Performance, Moorishess, and Cultural Hybridity in *Los baños de Argel*." *Bulletin of the Comediantes* 62, no. 2 (2010): 45–62. https://doi.org/10.1353/boc.2011.0015.

Irigoyen-García, Javier. "El problema morisco en *Los baños de Argel*, de Miguel de Cervantes: De renegados a mártires cristianos." *Revista Canadiense de Estudios Hispánicos* 32, no. 3 (2008): 421–38.

Istel, Edgar, and Theodore Baker. "The Music in *Don Quixote*." *Musical Quarterly* 13, no. 3 (1927): 434–50.

Lambea, Mariano. "Procesos intertextuales y adaptaciones musicales para las aventuras de Don Quijote." In *Actas del VIII Congreso de la Asociación Internacional del Siglo de Oro*, edited by Anthony Close, 399–405. Madrid: Iberoamericana, 2006.

Leal Pinar, Luis F. *La música en el Quijote*. Guadalajara: Llanura, 2006.

Lozano Virumbrales, Luis. "De efectos y afectos en la música." In *Accidentes del alma: Las emociones en la Edad Moderna*, edited by María Tausiet and James S. Amelang, 307–44. Madrid: Abada, 2009.

Martín, Adrienne L. "Images of Deviance in Cervantes's Algiers." *Cervantes* 15, no. 2 (1995): 5–13.

McClary, Susan. *Desire and Pleasure in Seventeenth-Century Music*. Berkeley: University of California Press, 2012.

Murray, D.J., and Helen Ross, trans. "Vives (1538) on Memory and Recall." *Canadian Psychology / Psychologie canadienne* 23, no. 1 (1982): 22–31. https://doi.org/10.1037/h0081226.

Nieremberg, Juan Eusebio. *Oculta filosofía: Razones de la música en el hombre y la naturaleza*. Edited by Ramón Andrés. Barcelona: Acantilado, 2004.

Noreña, Carlos G. *Juan Luis Vives and the Emotions*. Carbondale: Southern Illinois University Press, 1989.

Pastor, Juan José, and Sergio Barcelona. *Por ásperos caminos: nueva música cervantina*. Toledo: Universidad de Castilla-La Mancha, 2005.

Pastor Comín, Juan José. *Cervantes: Música y poesía. El hecho musical en el pensamiento lírico cervantino*. Vigo: Editorial Academia del Hispanismo, 2007.

Pastor Comín, Juan José. "Música y literatura: la senda retórica. Hacia una nueva consideración de la música en Cervantes." *Revista de Musicología* 27, no. 2 (2004): 1190–8. https://doi.org/10.2307/20798028.

Plato. *The Republic*. Translated by Desmond Lee. Introduction by Melissa Lane. New York: Penguin, 2007.

Querol Galvadá, Miguel. *La música en las obras de Cervantes*. Alcalá de Henares: Centro de Estudios Cervantinos, 2005.

Roda, Cecilio de. *Los instrumentos músicos y las danzas en el* Quijote: *Conferencia leída en el Ateneo*. Madrid: B. Rodríguez, 1905.

Rodríguez Cuadros, Evangelina. *La técnica del actor español en el Barroco: Hipótesis y documentos*. Madrid: Castalia, 1998.

Sachs, Matthew E., Antonio Damasio, and Assal Habibi. "The Pleasures of Sad Music: A Systematic Review." *Frontiers of Human Neuroscience*, no. 9 (2015): 404. https://doi.org/10.3389/fnhum.2015.00404.

Saint Augustine. *Confessions*. Translated by R.S. Pine-Coffin. New York: Penguin Classics, 1961.

Salazar, Adolfo. *La música de Cervantes y otros ensayos*. Madrid: Ínsula, 1961.

Smart, Mary Ann. "Introduction." In *Siren Songs: Representations of Gender and Sexuality in Opera*, edited by Mary Ann Smart, 3–16. Princeton, NJ: Princeton University Press, 2000.

Smith, Bruce R. "Shakespeare as Sound Artist." In *The Routledge Companion to Sounding Art*, edited by Marcel Cobussen, Vincent Meelberg, and Barry Truax, 351–61. New York: Routledge, 2016.

Sosa, Antonio de [Haedo, Diego de]. *Topographia e historia general de Argel* [...]. Valladolid: Diego Fernandez de Cordova y Oviedo, 1612.

Sosa, Antonio de. *Topography of Algiers*. In Garcés, *Early Modern Dialogue*, 81–272.

Stackhouse, Kenneth A. "Beyond Performance: Cervantes's Algerian Plays, *El trato de Argel* and *Los baños de Argel*." *Bulletin of the Comediantes* 52, no. 2 (2000): 7–30. https://doi.org/10.1353/boc.2000.0014.

Taruffi, Liila, and Stefan Koelsch. "The Paradox of Music-Evoked Sadness: An Online Survey." *PLoS ONE* 9, no. 10 (2014): e110490. https://doi.org/10.1371/journal.pone.0110490.

Vega Carpio, Lope Félix de. *Los cautivos de Argel*. Edited by Natalio Ohanna. Barcelona: Castalia, 2017.

Velasco, Sherry. "From Spain to Algiers: Morisco/Muslim Sounds in the Western Mediterranean." *Journal for Early Modern Cultural Studies* 18, no. 3 (2018): 96–128. https://doi.org/10.1353/jem.2018.0025.

Velasco, Sherry. "Music, Sex, and Politics in *Don Quixote*." In *Sexo y género en Cervantes / Sex and Gender in Cervantes: Essays in Honor of Adrienne Laskier Martín*, edited by Esther Fernández and Mercedes Alcalá Galán, 133–52. Kassel: Reichenberger, 2019.

Vives, Juan Luis. "De Anima et Vita: Book Two, Chapter Two on Memory (Memoria) and Recall (Recordatio)." Translated by D.J. Murray and Helen Ross. In Murray and Ross, "Vives (1538) on Memory and Recall."

Vives, Juan Luis. *The Passions of the Soul: The Third Book of* De Anima et Vita. Translated by Carlos G. Noreña. Lewiston, NY: Edwin Mellen Press, 1990.

6 In the Name of Love: Cervantes's Play on Captivity in *La gran sultana*

ANA LAGUNA

Reliable Western accounts of the Ottoman world were rare in the early modern age, especially with regard to an alluring courtly institution like the harem. As an exotic and "inaccessible cavern," this space generated immense curiosity, yearning, and contempt among Western audiences.[1] In 1665, for example, the British ambassador Paul Rycaut (1629–1700) observed that while "the Western knight consumes himself with combats, watching, and penance to acquire the love of one fair Damsel, here [in Turkey], an army of Virgins make it the only study and business of their life to obtain the single nod of invitation to the Bed of their Great Master."[2] Regretful of the freedoms that Ottoman lords enjoyed in these pleasure chambers, and clearly untroubled by concerns of female captivity, the ambassador considered his clichéd view of the space as proof of the excessive expectations that Western culture had placed on *male* lovers.

Judgments on the harem were usually more political than personal, however, since Western observers had elaborated the myth of oriental tyranny precisely through the orgiastic sex assumed to occur within its walls. Sexual dissoluteness operated in these reports as a "metaphor for power corrupted" and projected the underlying prejudice of the image onto the entire Ottoman establishment.[3] While views of this nature conveyed a long and apparently irreconcilable clash of Eastern and Western material and symbolic (erotic) systems, in what follows I examine how a play like Cervantes's *La gran sultana* (c. 1608) neutralizes some of their most striking East–West divides through its layered examination of the idea of captivity. By removing the curtain that separates the most guarded space of the Ottoman court from public view, Cervantes portrays the harem as a domain not so radically different from other early modern Christian households and headquarters. Rather than presenting the idyllic pleasure island that Rycaut envied, Cervantes turns this chamber into a porous Mediterranean microcosm, heavily punctuated by the political and racial frictions stirring the world of the 1600s and by the domestic pressures – especially surrounding the idea of marriage – affecting its social orbits.

Far from supporting simplistic Western fantasies about polygamous lords, *La gran sultana* presents an Ottoman ruler just as devoted to his beloved (Catalina) as the Western knights that Rycaut complained about, who consumed themselves with combats and penance in hopes of earning the love of their ladies. While this depiction of the Ottoman Sultan – often identified with Suleiman I (1494–1566) and Murad III (1546–95) – appears to project Western Petrarchan and courtly conventions, a deeper, intertextual reading of Cervantes's play in context reveals intriguing amatory and domestic parallels between the disparate shores of the Mediterranean Sea. In this reading – which will also consider the novel *El celoso extremeño* and the interlude *El juez de los divorcios* – a play like *La gran sultana*, traditionally considered an elegy to cultural tolerance, integration, and hybridity, also carries an unsettling reminder of the powerful patriarchal structures that, superseding all other racial and religious divides, pervaded the Eastern *and* Western Mediterranean cultures.[4]

A Daring Theatrical Perspective

Cervantes's play approaches the Ottoman world inside out, placing the opening scene outside of the palace. It is there, in the streets of Istanbul – or Constantinople, as it was known in English at the time of Ottoman rule – that we first meet two renegades, Salec (a Turk) and Roberto (a Christian), as they witness "the lavishness and majesty" with which the Sultan's entourage is entering the Hagia Sophia Mosque.[5] Their conversation informs us not only of the impressiveness of the cortege – which comprises more than six thousand soldiers on horse and on foot ("De pie y de a caballo")[6] – but also of the different Islamic and Christian perspectives at play among onlookers like them. While some, like Roberto, are free to gaze upon the magnificent procession, those, like Salec, who observe Islamic law and custom are not allowed to. This peculiarity forces Roberto to describe, incredulously – "no creo la verdad" ("I can't believe the truth")[7] – the splendour of the scene to Salec, giving his audience, too, the opportunity to mentally reconstruct the Ottoman opulence that the play is conjuring, a magnificence later portrayed by Ottoman artists like Konstantin Kapıdağlı (figure 6.1).[8]

While the theatrical ambition of the scene may reveal Cervantes's imperfect awareness of stage limitations, it also anticipates the main

Figure 6.1. Konstantin Kapıdağlı, *Ottoman Sultan Selim III* (1789). Oil on canvas. Topkapı Sarayı Müzesi, Istanbul (Inv. 17/163), courtesy of Wikimedia Commons.

structural elements of the play, such as the delicate balance between what is to be seen or concealed, what to believe or discredit, and what to cherish or fear. The Sultan's imposing display of power contrasts with news of a hidden crime committed against him deep in his court by one of the eunuchs guarding the harem, Rustán. Daring to disrupt the culture of staged affairs that rules the court, the eunuch is accused of keeping from the Sultan's view the most prized member of his inner domain, Catalina. This is an act of treason that he is bound to pay for with his life.[9]

Rustán's attempt to protect Catalina is not an isolated act of compassion; Catalina herself will also risk her good standing with the Sultan when she advocates for Rustán's forgiveness and for the liberation of fellow captives like Zaida/Clara and Zelinda/Lamberto. From the beginning, spectators are presented with empathetic actions that publicly and privately defy easy stereotypical attributions of the Ottoman world, like the callous depravity of the harem's custodians or the ruthless competition among its constituents.[10] Our first glimpse of the seraglio presents it as an erotic locus, but one where fellowship and solidarity are somehow able to elude – albeit temporarily – the control of the Ottoman official machinery.

As the play unfolds, our understanding of this space evolves. Although still infused with an erotic charge – given the ruler's desire to meet Catalina first, and to urgently enjoy her love afterwards – the harem increasingly appears wrapped in an aura of domesticity that escaped commentators like Rycaut.[11] The Sultan's insistence on meeting Catalina, marrying her, and making her the mother of Ottoman "lions" distances this inner chamber from the idea of a pleasurable island and instead brings it closer to the generic, domestic space of other Western European courts.[12]

Viewed from this perspective, as a site for domestic female containment, this Cervantine harem may also have a familiar feel for those readers or spectators aware of the existence of a similar space in two of his other works, the interlude *El viejo celoso* and the exemplary novel *El celoso extremeño.* In both texts, and under the pretence of a cautionary tale against jealousy, Cervantes brings the interplay of marriage, indulgence, and captivity to the Spanish Christian shores by locating the novel, *El celoso extremeño*, in no less than the commercial capital of the Spanish empire, Seville.

The protagonist of *El celoso* is not a Sultan, but a plain, rich *indiano* that, after achieving a dubious fortune in the Americas, confines his young wife (Leonora) with several slaves he buys to keep her company. As an Ottoman lord would do, the *indiano* restricts wife and slaves to the house and shields them "from any contact with men," following the prescribed identification of chastity with enclosure shared by both Christian and non-Christian social norms and creeds.[13] Cervantes "exemplary" novel explicitly emphasizes the harem-like associations of the space:[14] the fact that the protagonist, Carrizales, is called "el gran señor," the appellative used for the Ottoman Sultan; the narrator's description of his "fortress-like house" as a "serrallo," also guarded by a black eunuch slave; and, above all, the strange parity between his wife, Leonora, and Carrizales's "bozales" slaves, which several protagonists remark on. "Leonora *andaba a lo igual* con sus criadas, y se entretenía en *lo mismo que ellas*" ("Leonora *treated her maids as equals*, whiling away the time *in the same pursuits*"),[15] says the narrator, reinforcing soon afterwards an uncommon parallelism rife with sexual innuendo:[16]

Íbase a sus negocios, que eran pocos, y con brevedad daba la vuelta y encerrándose, se entretenía en *regalar a su esposa y acariciar* a *sus* criadas,

que todas le querían bien por ser de condición llana y agradable, y sobre-
todo, por mostrarse tan liberal con todas.[17]

(He attended business affairs, which were few, quickly returning home,
and locking himself inside, would spend his time indulging his wife and
pampering [caressing] her [his] maids, who were all rather fond of him
because of his unaffected and pleasant character, and especially, because
he was so generous towards them all.)[18]

That key verb, *acariciar* (to caress), erased in the translation but present
in the original, provides a powerful indication that the house, though
a prison for the wife, can contain a paradise of indulgence for a husband who apparently sees little difference between his wife and his
slaves. The occupants of this harem-like space do not count (at least
initially) on the disinterested help of the guardian eunuch. Everything
inside this indulgent island works as expected, as designed by the *indiano* lord, Carrizales. At the heart of the Christian world, the traditional
and somatic ontology of captivity – racial and violent – is echoed by
the invisible bond of marriage. Or, put in another way, the existence of
this kind of restrictive and indulgent household in a Catholic context
illustrates the deep deterioration of the social institution, marriage, that
allows the existence of this kind of arranged confinement; marriage
was, after all, supposed to regulate the sexual relationships contained
within the domestic framework.

The Harem as a Trans-Mediterranean Development:
Bringing Marriage to the Rocks

One of the most scandalous implications of *El celoso extremeño* is that
a "Catholic pleasure chamber" on the western banks of the Mediterranean can be concealed by a textual curtain, by the fable-like tone of
the story. But as current scholarship reveals, the over-permissive opera-
tion of Carrizales's harem-like "household," successfully veiled from
modern readers, may have been quite obvious to Cervantes's contemporaries. It was apparently too prevalent in his society. As Allyson Poska
has shown, regardless of ethnic background, class, or social register,
"concubinage and consensual unions flourished at all levels of the social
hierarchy despite ecclesiastical sanctions and secular punishments."[19]
This new range of sexual attachments was as prominent among the
powerful as among the needy; while it provided "an alternative to conventional marriage for male nobles whose families denied them their
chosen partner in order to secure or preserve patrimony," it allowed

the peasantry "much more flexibility than Church-sanctioned marriage," precisely at a time when that flexibility increased the chances of overcoming hardship.[20] In a southern city like Seville, humble women caught at the crossroads of financial fluctuations and structural deficiencies were clear-eyed about their poor choices, plainly acknowledging for example – even in their Inquisition trials – that "to be the concubine of a white man was better than to marry a mulatto."[21]

Seville's slave population, "the largest in the Spanish kingdoms,"[22] favoured the widespread sexual exploitation of female slaves and servants, to the point that "during the sixteenth century, between 80% and 90% of black women were not married, but had one or two children," and children that were mixed-race were largely "born from a female black slave and a male white Christian."[23] Yet, between 1559 and 1648, only 174 people were prosecuted for "fornication" issues, and those that were, (unsurprisingly) were overwhelmingly poor, mulatto, and *Morisco* male peasants.[24] Powerful white men like Carrizales seemed immune to any kind of punitive inquiry or restraint.[25] Spanish writers sensitive to these ongoing dynamics did not need to look into distant Ottoman secret chambers to recognize the currency of these extramarital unions and the power imbalance at play within them.[26] The significance of this kind of arrangement apparently "became vividly clear as European men journeyed around the globe as part of early modern exploration and expansion" and experienced in their own lives and families the other human cost of constant military and exploratory campaigns.[27]

In Spain, in a city like Seville, these social dynamics, including human displacement and financial disparity, soon translated into growing marginal populations with alarming rates of child abandonment and prostitution. Even households that supposedly had family structures in place often denoted the deterioration of the foundational idea (and praxis) of marriage.[28] This was a crisis long in the making; by the mid 1500s, marriage had become "an embattled institution" throughout early modern Europe.[29] While in Catholic Europe, the Council of Trent (1545–63) tried to remedy this weakness by turning it into a sacrament, secular European institutions (in both Catholic and Protestant countries) issued new edicts and royal decrees aiming to "discipline reproduction according to ever tightening patriarchal principles."[30]

Perhaps one of the most straightforward indications of the frail state of affairs regarding marriage was the quite desperate call to women by moralists like Juan Luis Vives to disobey the plea for love. "A lover should be listened to no more than one who casts spells or a poisoner," Vives firmly states in his *Education of a Christian Woman* (*De institutione feminae christianae*, 1523), warning his readers that such a poisoner would first approach them "smoothly and persuasively" in order to "praise their beauty" and later claim that "he is perishing of his uncontrollable love" for them.[31] According to Vives, the process does not end well for the female victim, since the "girl," as Vives calls her (obviously never considering the case of a full-grown, autonomous woman), will surely be abandoned, forgotten, and even killed.[32] Vives argues that the best way to survive and heal from such abandonment is to avoid it in the first place. To that purpose, he insists on recognizing the signs of deceit: "How did he plead his case?" Vives presses on: "Did he say that he was captivated by your good qualities? Then what? That he would die unless he had you? Now we know the reason for those tears."[33]

It would be hard to ignore how faithfully the protagonist of *La gran sultana* follows this courtship playbook; as soon as the Sultan meets Catalina, he praises her "rare" and "divine beauty," placing her next to Allah and above mere mortals like him ("Al par de Alá en sus asientos ... clara estrella, / dando leyes desde allá, / que con reverencia y celo / guardaremos los del suelo"; "Wouldn't it have been better to put her at Allah's side ... another bright star. Issuing laws from thence, which we shall keep on earth with the same reverence and zeal as those Mohammed gave?").[34] As if he were now Catalina's slave, the Sultan repeatedly claims that his will is fully subjected to hers ("a vuestra voluntad / tan sujeta está la mía"; "my will is subjected to yours").[35]

This approach matches the Petrarchan leverage – the song of deceit, as Vives calls it – used by the Sultan. Seeing this protagonist so well versed in this topos constitutes a clear cultural projection on Cervantes's part, since "Ottomans did not read Petrarch."[36] While the eastern shores of the Mediterranean had also produced a robust literature of love in the form of treatises, theories, and public prescriptions on the sentiment, Ottoman letters did not refer to Petrarch – perhaps because they did not need to, as they relied on Hafezism, a poetic trend described as "an extreme form of Petrarchism" due to its tendency to marginalize and idealize the beloved (who is not always a female figure).[37] In short, Ottoman love literature was just as effusively mystical, poetic, and objectifying as that of the Western world. Moreover, Ottoman poets did not limit themselves to the benign effects of the emotion but also warned of its destructive consequences:[38] "Yield not the soul to pang of Love," warns the revered Azerbaijani poet Fużūlī (Muhammad bin Suleiman, 1494–1556), "for Love's the soul's fierce glow / That Love's the torment of the soul doth all the wide world know."[39] A transcultural anxiety about the ambivalent effects of love similarly concerned male poets and amorous devotees on both sides of the White Sea (as Mediterranean dwellers called it).

Being seated in deeply patriarchal structures (like their Christian counterparts), Ottoman amatory discourses, despite their poetic value, similarly omitted or constrained the voice and agency of women. In this catalogue of similarities, if there is one difference that stands out between East and West, it is the fact that almost no Ottoman lover would in his love pleas – regardless of how passionate they were – declare himself to be a "slave" of his beloved. Ottoman lovers did not frequently relinquish the power of their symbolic or material empire to their objects of affection. "With my sword," claims the victorious Ahmed I, "I have conquered many and many a shore; / Still I sigh sorely, Ah! To conquer more!"[40] In a society whose political body was fully dedicated to military conquest, and in which an Ottoman fighter or leader distinguished himself by his victories, the poetic platitude of a captive of love did not find much expression.[41]

Cervantes nonetheless makes his Sultan a champion of the courtly and Petrarchan idiom, as he emphatically claims to have capitulated to love in the most *Triumphus Cupidinis* fashion. Love, not he, is the conqueror here that brings under its yoke other "gods and near-divine men" and demands total obedience to this lady:[42]

A cuanto quieras querer
obedezco y no replico.
Suelta, condena, rescata,
absuelve, quita, haz mercedes,
que esto y más, señora, puedes:
que Amor tu imperio dilata.[43]

(I obey and do not dispute whatever you might want. Set free, condemn, ransom, absolve, strip away, grant favours, for you can do this and more, my lady. Love expands your empire.)[44]

Vives had tried to inoculate his reader against the charms of this tempting idiom, which claims total servitude to the beloved: "Make sure *you're not captured* by his words, for the two of you will perish together."[45] Vives was not the only moralist to remind the young of the fleeting nature of desire, but he is particularly significant here precisely because he fixates on this image of captivity, warning his female readers of the ease with which these feeble male "love's captives" turn their beloveds into "captive preys" themselves.[46] In fact, he argues that the greatest reward that his advice will render his young female readers is the possibility of avoiding such captivity altogether, because "if you have not yet been captured … you will not be captured, and if you are already caught...you will escape."[47] Of course, Vives ironically asks these women to free themselves from these extramarital dangers by entering into an equally unsatisfying experience – the strenuous, domestic confinement of marriage – which hardly represents a great escape.

But Vives's exposure of the real-world consequences that a poetic convention could render did not escape a much older (and male) reader like Cervantes. The forty editions that *Institutione* saw before 1600 made this crossing of paths almost unavoidable.[48] As usual, Cervantes takes the criticism of the Petrarchan conceit one or two steps further by invoking it in a play like *La gran sultana*, in which a true captive – who happens to be the beloved, Catalina – factors into the equation.

The Sultan's commitment to achieving, as a faithful servant, the impossible for Catalina soon proves to be as unreliable as the empty promises of the lovers that Vives warned about. The only thing she asks for herself in the entire play is to be given three days to reflect on the proposal of married life that the Sultan is presenting to her. "Tres días me han de acabar" (three days will kill me),[49] he retorts, grudgingly acquiescing to the demand, only to immediately command Rustán to start announcing the nuptials: "Entra, Rustán; da las nuevas / a esas cautivas todas / de mis esperadas bodas" ("Go, Rustán; tell the news of my longed-for wedding to all those captive women").[50]

The inconsistency of this amatory trope is reinforced through a similar invocation by another character, Madrigal, probably the most unheroic protagonist of the play. We learn of the Spaniard's love affair in a casual conversation with Andrea, the spy, as they both remember how Madrigal refused to be rescued a few years back. He had given romantic reasons for remaining in Constantinople some years prior, claiming that his soul had surrendered to an Arab lover, and as a result he had been subjected to a different kind of captivity: "[R]endida el alma ... con un nuevo *cautiverio*, y nuevas leyes" ("Chained ... in a new captivity and new laws").[51] Now, years later, he tells Andrea that this is still the case, that he is still a prisoner of love to (apparently) the same woman: "[A]ún *todavía estoy cautivo*, todavía la fuerza poderosa de amor tiene sujeto a mi albedrío" ("I still have the yoke around my neck, *I'm still a captive*, the great power of love still rules over me").[52] However, when he is suddenly and finally liberated by the Sultan and is free to return to Spain, he shows in his emotional farewell a deeper attachment to the city than to his supposed lover, whom he does not mention at all:

> ¡Adiós, Constantinopla famosísima!
> ¡Pera y Permas, adiós! ¡Adiós, escala,

Chifutí y aun Guedí! ¡Adiós, hermoso
jardín de Visitax! ¡Adiós, gran templo
que de Santa Sofía sois llamado … ![53]

(Farewell, famous Constantinople! / Pera and Permas, farewell! / Farewell, Chifutí and Guedí stairs! Farewell, fair garden of Visitax! Farewell, great temple [known as] St. Sophia … !)[54]

At the end of the day (and the play), being a metaphoric love-captive, like Madrigal and the Sultan, versus being a truly imprisoned human, like Catalina, are two quite different things.

For that reason, if Cervantes's proudly Christian character, Catalina, is as defiant against Islam as she appears to be, and so intent on keeping her virtue from the "infernal serpiente" (hellish serpent; v. 825) that the Sultan represents for her, she would be well aware of the prescriptions and warnings issued by a counsellor like Vives. After all, the moralist had written his *Education of a Christian Woman* precisely at the request of another embattled and hyper-Christian Catalina, who was also married to an infidel, the protestant Henry VIII.[55] We can only speculate on how many of these referents were fresh in Cervantes's mind when he composed this play; did he think of the Catholic and Spanish princess Catalina, imprisoned in the English court, when designing this Christian captive in the Turkish one? The possibility only adds to the rich and evident correlation of cultural allusions in the play, which converge in a complex, multidimensional idea of captivity. Such confluence allows Cervantes to employ one of his favourite narrative tools: using a metaphor or specific symbol against itself in order to expose its artificiality and perniciousness.

Whether as pernicious metaphor or sad reality, captivity is then a pivotal motif in *La gran sultana*.[56] In the play, freedom is both openly and subtly denied Catalina, even if she does not seem to understand its full permanence until the last act when, misinterpreting the Sultan's orders, she believes she has been freed like the rest of the captives. As she rushes to kiss the Sultan's feet, "overwhelmed with happiness" at the news of her liberation, an exulting Sultan – who, as Leyla Rouhi has noted, shows little remorse for his decision – corrects her error while resorting once again to hyperbolic language to justify his decision: "[L]a merced que quise hacer / y, si la queréis saber, / a los esclavos se extiende, / y no a ti, que eres señora / de mi alma, a quien adora / como si fueses su Alá" ("The favour I granted does not include you; and, if you must know, it extends to the slaves, not to you, mistress of my soul, which adores you as if you were its Allah").[57] This unwillingness to consider her freedom contrasts with the eagerness with which he, the Sultan, considers the liberation of almost anybody else in the chamber. Even when a Christian tailor – the captive who happens to be Catalina's father – is brought to the harem, the ruler generously offers *him* freedom and good pay for his service: "Libertad por galardón, / y gran riqueza os daré" ("I'll reward you with your liberty and great wealth").[58]

The Sultan's supposed willingness to respect Catalina's sexual freedom can also be cast into doubt in this context. Regardless of his explicit commitment to earn her consent ("Como a mi esclava, en un punto / pudiera gozarte agora; / más quiero hacerte señora, / *por subir el bien de punto*"; "As my slave, I could possess you in a minute; but I want to make you my lady, *to increase my happiness*"),[59] Catalina finds herself three months pregnant at the end of the play, which calls into question whether the Sultan really resisted his impulses or not.[60] An attentive reader can only be sceptical of the extent of Catalina's power and agency throughout the play in light of the constant orders (not choices) that the Sultan gives over her person; from the name she is allowed to have to the dress she is adorned with, each of these elements is not decided by her but authorized by him: "Doyte la preeminencia" ("I henceforth give you that privilege");[61] "Vestídmela a la española" ("Dress her for me in the Spanish fashion").[62] Even the celebrated permission that the Sultan gives Catalina to continue practicing Christianity ("He de ser cristiana"; "I shall remain a Christian") – which critics agree constitutes one of the most memorable proofs of the ruler's humanity and tolerance – also comes in the form of a directive rather than a choice: "Sélo" ("Be one").[63] There is simply no way to elude or revert the sets of decisions that the Sultan continues to make for her.

Unlike other vibrant and victorious characters in Cervantes's opus, such as Marcela, Dorotea, and the little gypsy girl Preciosa, whose intelligence and eloquence allow them to earn the aims of their desires, Catalina, despite the power she is claimed to have, is never able to even minimally alter the fate the Sultan has set for her, as he himself acknowledges: "A tu fortuna / no hay dificultad alguna / que la pueda contrastar" ("no obstacle can impede your fortune").[64] Even more unsettling is the fact that no one can tell how long that fortune will last; it could be more reversible than expected, as Catalina explicitly acknowledges: *"Tantas alabanzas siento / que me han de servir de ultraje / pues siempre la adulación / nunca dice la razón / como en el alma se siente, / y así, cuando alaba, miente"* ("I fear *so many praises will only serve to insult me*, for flattery never says what the soul feels, and thus lies when it praises").[65]

Two other members of this Spanish-Turkish harem, Zaida/Clara and Zelinda/Lamberto, reinforce this inconsistency, as Zaida claims that what the Sultan calls love is only sexual appetite ("tan presto se le fue de la memoria / la singular belleza que adoraba? / El suyo no es amor, sino apetito"; "How is that? Did he so soon forget the singular beauty he adored? His is not love, but lust").[66] Likewise, Zelinda advances that the *Grand Señor*'s prompt change of heart, whether attributable to his service to the state or not, is not out of character ("¿Pues cómo? ¿El Gran Señor vuelve a su usanza?"; "What is this? Does the Great Signor go back to his habits?").[67]

All these considerations weigh considerably on Catalina, whose persistent – and, for some, bothersome – gloominess is obvious throughout the play. She is far from the joyful woman that Cervantes seems to have taken as his historical reference, Roxelana (1502–58), the famous Christian slave whom the sultan Suleiman I (1494–1566) called "Hurrem" (cheerful) when he married her – apparently having freed her first – in 1531.[68] Unlike Catalina, Roxelana was tenderly in love with the Sultan, at least according to the surviving letters that she wrote to him: "I console myself with these memories in your absence. I am low when you are away. No one can ease my pain."[69] Catalina, in turn, is simply and conventionally beautiful and persistently despondent at the thought of her suitor and husband, whose presence, as "the minister of my torment," she blames for her pain.[70]

It is out of this anguish that she considers committing suicide, resembling those religious and secular martyrs, from St. Lucía and St. Inés to Lucrezia Borgia, who preferred death to seduction or defilement at the hands of suitors, invaders, and enemies of the faith.[71] But this possibility is also taken away from her. After reminding his daughter that "que por lo menos estás, / hija, en pecado mortal" ("you must realize, to your disadvantage, that you are in mortal sin, my daughter"),[72] her father recalls the sinfulness of suicide and the condemnation that it carries.[73] Though subject to a life of captivity and sexual entanglement with a man she clearly does not love, she lacks the essential condition of a forced conversion in order to assume the role of a martyr, a desire she intimates in her very first encounter with the Sultan. In that scene, Rustán tries to dissuade her from such extreme measures by declaring her free from sin, arguing that "cuando la fuerza va / contra razón y derecho / no está el pecado en el hecho, / si en la voluntad no está" ("when force trumps reason and right, then there is no sin in the deed if there is none in the intent").[74]

But both Rustán and her father may miss the ultimate point of her martyrdom, which in this case represents freedom rather than salvation: "Mártir soy en el deseo" (v. 2035) and "la luz que guía / al cielo al más pecador, / en mi tiniebla algún día; / y desta *cautividad* … adonde reino ofendida me llevará arrepentida / a la *eterna libertad*" ("I would wish to be a martyr.… I trust that the light that guides the greatest sinner to heaven shall shine brightly on my darkness one day and take me repentant from this *captivity* where I reign aggrieved to *eternal liberty*").[75] Acting almost as a judicial witness, her father simply contests her eligibility to claim this prize, since showing no signs of physical force meant, in his mind, that she had complied willingly, having fallen prey to the "licenciosa vida, desta pompa y majestad" ("licentious life, this pomp and majesty") of the Ottoman court.[76]

The notion of martyrdom, connected with the Ottoman world, constituted an incredibly delicate and malleable subject that, as Maria Antonia Garcés, Diana de Armas Wilson, Barbara Weissberger, and Steven Hutchinson have shown, is deeply ingrained in Cervantes's opus. In a society like the Ottomans', where jarring punishments were enacted on an almost daily basis, the supposed immolation of a character who not only is not bound to be punished or killed, but is actually given permission to practice her chosen religion and is elevated to the status of Sultan, seems fatuous at best.[77] However, when Catalina's anguished justification of her self-annihilation is taken into account, her claim of a different and secular martyrdom can be better understood. When realizing what a life of submission and sexual obligation to the Sultan would entail, she explicitly resolves to live this mortification in silence: "[H]aré lo que fuere de mí, / y en silencio, en mis recelos, / daré voces a los cielos" ("I shall do what I can, and in silence and my apprehension, I shall cry out to the heavens").[78]

This silent outcry is the only form of resistance that is left to the captive. The Sultan acknowledges that this inner space, the private assertion of will, is beyond his influence – "a tu cuerpo, *por agora*, / es el que mi alma adora / …¿Tengo yo a cargo tu alma / o soy Dios…?" ("For now, my soul adores your body as if it were its very heaven. Am I in charge of your soul or am I God…?")[79] – a statement traditionally considered as another example of *his* magnanimity.[80] The acknowledgment also echoes an underlying debate taking place in both Christian and non-Christian Europe, one tied to the ongoing crisis of marriage: how to reconcile the biblical injunction that in marriage "two become one" with the patriarchal preconceived notions of authority and superiority of the husband in such a union. As Leon Battista Alberti had reminded his readers, "The civil law today and the religious authorities as well declare that marriage is not so much a mating of bodies as a union of will and of mind, and for this reason consider marriage a sacrament and a religious tie."[81] Patriarchal discourse had escaped this paradox of reconciling the "unity" of equals with the "supremacy" of the husband by simply editing out the female voice, agency, and subjectivity from love or marital discourses. But as the sixteenth century unfolded, and female authors started to populate the literary scene, a growing recognition of the inner resistance in female and individual consciousness led to a search for alternatives to traditional elisions and dichotomies. *La gran sultana* accelerated this search by exposing the contradictory messages of patriarchal ideas on love, order, and hierarchy unevenly united in the triumphant but unsatisfactory marriage of its main protagonists.

The Theatrics of Marriage and Martyrdom in Cervantes

The issue of subjection or captivity within the normative and sanctioned institution of marriage is one of the most subtle and intriguing explorations of Cervantes's opus. The author may press the subject through exotic settings – like the Ottoman court here in *La gran sultana* – or concealed, domestic spaces – like the Catholic "harems" in the novel *El celoso extremeño* – leaving his sharpest indictments to the most irreverent and irrelevant channels, like the interlude. In the *Juez de los Divorcios* (The Divorce Court), Cervantes delves into this idea of marriage as a form of captivity, this time showing how it affects husbands as well. In the interlude, an old man describes to the judge his mood as he entered into marriage, comparing himself to a captive entering a prison like the one ruled by a Calabrian like "Uchalí" (Uluj Ali):[82] "[E]ntré en su [mi mujer] poder *como quien entre en el de un cómitre calabrés a remar galeras* de por fuerza" (I entered her house [power] *like a captive enters the service of a Calabrese owner to become a lifetime rower*).[83] For this character, divorce is described as a liberating intervention, equivalent to freeing someone from a frightening prison: "[A]lzándome de esta carcelería" (Taking me out of this jail).[84]

In the interlude, marriage is consistently described not only as a prison, but also as a place of martyrdom; that same old man claims, "veinte y dos años ha que vivo con ella *mártir*" (it's been twenty years that I have lived with her as a martyr), reminding the judge that returning him to his wife "será de nuevo entregarme al verdugo que *me martirice*" (would take me back to the executioner who tortures me).[85] In such a short theatrical piece, Cervantes emphatically reiterates this association of marriage with captivity and martyrdom (or self-cancellation), showing this time how it not only affects women in vulnerable positions, like Catalina or Leonora, but even brave and respectable – "well-dressed" – soldiers. The "soldado" that shows up next confides in the magistrate that granting his wife the divorce that she seeks would liberate him from his prison, as if a sort of miracle had taken place; "pensando que me castiga" (thinking that this is a punishment), he concedes, "[M]e *sacará de cautiverio* como si por milagro se librase *un cautivo de las mazmorras*" (You will liberate me from this captivity, as if a miracle had freed a slave from his dungeon).[86] Obviously, this idea of marriage as a life sentence has value in and of itself in the context of a short and funny theatrical piece. But against the backdrop that I have revealed in this essay, the persistent idea of domestic captivity and even martyrdom points to the deadly, scarring experiences to which the men and women of the 1600s were too often exposed: war imprisonment – in the case of men like Cervantes – and domestic or sexual servitude – in the case of the many wives, servants, and concubines that were regulars in the corral's audience.

Despite the occasional reminders of moralists to recognize that no partner in a marriage had any ownership over the other, on both sides of the Mediterranean shores, Catholic, Protestant, and Islamic societies designated the husband as the proprietor of the family goods.[87] A writer like Cervantes, who set so many of his works in disparate locations, used his literary platform as a cultural laboratory, where he explored the consequences of and alternatives to that patriarchal norm. Just as his female characters, including Marcela, Dorotea, Leonora, and Catalina, are sometimes capable and at other times incapable of manipulating such convention, Cervantes provides choices to the husbands; while Carrizales – having been tricked and dishonoured by all the women and the guardian of his *serallo* – contradicts all patriarchal expectations by choosing to liberate his female prisoners, including his wife Leonora (only the evil Duenna fails to receive his generosity), the Sultan of *La gran sultana* takes a very different route, freeing almost all Christian captives except the one who pleaded for their freedom, Catalina.[88] Unlike Carrizales with Leonora, the Sultan does elevate Catalina over the rest of the slaves and concubines of the harem: "[A] esas cautivas todas," commands the Sultan to Mamí, "… como a cosa divina, / … les dirás / sirvan y adoren de hoy más / a mi hermosa Catalina" ("Mamí, bring me … the captives from the seraglio so that they may vow their obedience to the Sultana").[89] However, he never confers to her the ultimate distinction: freedom. As the musical adage goes, this is the kind of ruler who would send his fully armed battalion to remind his people (or in this case, his wife) of his love.[90]

To this Sultan, and to such a husband, perhaps Catalina would have liked to argue what a very "free" Mariana tells her husband in *The*

Divorce Court when he suggests they go their separate ways, splitting their goods and locking themselves up in separate monasteries (male and female). Furious by the offer, she responds:

> ¡Malos años! ¡Bonica soy yo para estar encerrada!… [E]ncerraos vos … que yo estoy sana, y con todos mis cincos sentidos cabales y vivos, y quiero usar dellos a la descubierta, y no por brújula, como quínola dudosa.[91]

> (No way! I am no good being locked up!… You do that … if you wish … for I am healthy, and have my five senses [am in my right mind] and I want to use them in plain sight, without a compass or secrecy.)

Regardless of the continent (hence the curious mention of the "compass"), creed, state, or condition, protagonists like her want to be able to act "a la descubierta" (in plain sight), that is, without the covert operations that captives like Cervantes needed (when seeking their freedom in Argel) or that wives in Constantinople or Seville employed (when trying to "do their things discretely," without being uncovered).[92] Regardless of the location, Cervantes contests in myriad ways, and with a plurality of voices, formats, and contexts, the idea of captivity, be it political or domestic. Critics have often commented on Cervantes's dark view of love – on his manipulation of the Petrarchan idiom – without paying the same level of attention to his devastating critique of the prison of marriage in disparate corners of the globe.

The author's unusual subtlety may be responsible for that oversight. Masking a conclusion on the subject by placing it at the beginning of the interlude, Cervantes states through this same protagonist, Mariana, that "[e]n los reinos y en las repúblicas bien ordenadas, había de ser limitado el tiempo de los matrimonios, y de tres en tres años se habían de deshacer o confirmarse de nuevo, como cosas de arrendamiento" (in orderly kingdoms and republics, marriage should have an expiration date, requiring it, like all contracts, to be cancelled or renewed every three years; fols. 220v–221r). Marriage, like a lease, like love perhaps, should be frequently renegotiated according to the change of seasons, sentiments, and inclinations of both parties. The only thing more insidious than failing to do so, as *La gran sultana* reminds us, is to negate freedom in the name of love.

NOTES

1 In 1786, the Baron de Tott called the harem an "inaccessible Cavern" (*Memoirs*, 70). Soon afterwards, Jacques Mallet du Pan declared "the

interior of *harems*" to be "the *first* object of the *curiosity* of Europeans every time there is a question regarding Turkey" (review of de Tott, *Mémoires*).

2 Rycaut, *History*, 69.

3 For an overview on the subject, see Ahmed, "Western Ethnocentrism"; Peirce, *Imperial Harem*; Boll, "Violating the Harem"; Infante, "Gendered Space"; and Hutchinson, *Frontier Narratives*.

4 Among these positive readings (arguing that the play constitutes an elegy to cultural tolerance, integration, and hybridity) are Jurado Santos, *Tolerancia*; Hegyi, *Cervantes and the Turks*; Márquez Villanueva, *Moros, moriscos*; Mariscal, "*La gran sultana*"; Fuchs, *Passing for Spain*; and Castillo, "¿Ortodoxia cervantina?" Some of the most favourable assessments have been moderately or drastically contested by, among others, Díez Fernández, "Sin discrepar"; Alcalá Galán, "Erotics of the Exotic"; Kluge, "Twisted Turquoiseries"; Hutchinson, *Frontier Narratives*; and Rouhi, "Radical Re-assessment." Ultimately, as Hutchinson reminds us, while *La gran sultana* presents "flashes of truth by exaggerating or inverting all the common stereotypes about the Ottoman court ... to get at this truth we have to work through all the playful distortions and falsifications that the play presents us with" (*Frontier Narratives*, 16–17, following Alcalá Galán, "Erotics of the Exotic," 27–9).

5 Cervantes, *La gran sultana*, vv. 1–70; "*The Great Sultana.*"

6 Cervantes, *La gran sultana*, v. 55.

7 Cervantes, *La gran sultana*, v. 53; *The Great Sultana*, 130.

8 García Lorenzo, "Cervantes," 207–8.

9 As the Sultan contends, "Flaca disculpa me das / de la traición que me has hecho" (*La gran sultana*, vv. 544–5 [You give me but a weak excuse for the treachery you've committed against me, the greatest ever seen; *The Great Sultana*, 143]).

10 For assessing these stereotypes, see Peirce, *Empress*, 9–10.

11 As Peirce notes, "It was not sex, however, that was the fundamental dynamic of the harem, but rather family politics" (*Imperial Harem*, 3).

12 The Sultan tells Catalina, "has de parir, Catalina, hermosísimos leones" (*La gran sultana*, vv. 1220–1 [You will bear beautiful lions; *The Great Sultana*, 158]).

13 Throughout the early modern age, as Stallybrass famously summarized, "the ideal woman has been disciplined by cultural codes that require a closed mouth (silence), a closed body (chastity) and an enclosed life (domestic confinement)" ("Patriarchal Territories," 127). This well-known Western ideal is now being contextualized beyond traditional European contexts in enlightening ways. Banerjee's *Burning Women* has explored how the expansive patriarchal norm fed off the early modern exploratory journeys around the globe through the exposure to disciplinary practices

like the sati, making such norms more constrictive rather than more flexible and permissive. Fox and Lewis have studied how the *Querelle des Femmes* impacted early modern Judaic communities (*Many Pious Women*).

14 As noted by Infante, "Gendered Space," 255.

15 Cervantes, "El celoso extremeño," 182 (emphasis added); *Jealous Old Man*, 155.

16 In fact, the slaves speak of the lady whom they are supposed to serve, apparently showing more independence and agency than her: "No serían polvos de sueño para él, sino de vida *para todas nosotras*, y para la pobre de mi señora Leonora, su mujer" ("El celoso extremeño," 9; emphasis added [It wouldn't be a sleeping draught for him so much as an elixir of life *for all of us* and for my poor Mistress, Leonora, his wife; *Jealous Old Man*, 168; emphasis added]). One of the main protagonists, the seducer Loaysa, recognizes this sense of equality when he addresses all the women (Leonora and slaves) as one: "Yo, *señoras mías* – dijo a esto Loaysa – no vine aquí, sino con la intención *de servir a todas vuesas mercedes* con el alma y con la vida" ("El celoso extremeño," 118; emphasis added [I, *my good ladies*, said Loaysa at this point, did not come here with any other intention than *to serve your honourable selves* with my heart and soul; *Jealous Old Man*, 167; emphasis added]). In Laguna, "Exemplar Case of Jealousy," I read this short novel as a compendium of the seven deadly sins.

17 Cervantes, "El celoso extremeño," 1; emphasis added.

18 Cervantes, *Jealous Old Man*, 156; emphasis added.

19 Poska, "Upending Patriarchy," 197. See also Pike, *Aristocrats*, 180, 183; and Franco Silva, *La esclavitud en Sevilla*, 37–44, 217–18. Also enlightening is Martín Casares, *La esclavitud en la Granada*, 65–89.

20 Poska, "Upending Patriarchy," 197.

21 Perry cites the trial of Agustina de la Sierra, probably a Morisca (Inquisición, Legajo 2075, no. 13), in *Gender and Disorder*, 121–2.

22 Fracchia, "African Slaves," 162. See also Cortés López, *Los orígenes*, 64–75.

23 Fracchia, "African Slaves," 164; and Franco Silva, *La esclavitud en Sevilla*, 215.

24 Perry, *Gender and Disorder*, 121.

25 As Hutchinson reminds us, in "Christian lands" like Spain, "there were far fewer opportunities for marriage and integration of slaves into the social domain, and it seems that the owners of Muslim slave women were subject to little restraint" (*Frontier Narratives*, 56).

26 To see how widespread this concubinage was, see Phillips, *Slavery*, 87–9.

27 Poska, "Upending Patriarchy," 198.

28 In Seville, "officials regarded *seduction and abandonment* as one of the major causes for the problem of wandering women" (Perry, *Gender and Disorder*, 59), but in trying to tackle the growing number of unmarried mothers

and illegitimate children, laws disproportionately penalized women and minorities, leaving intact the roots of the problem and reinforcing the double standard (Boyle, *Unruly Women*, 5–9; and Juárez-Almendros, *Disabled Bodies*, 17–55).

29 Sperling, "Economics and Politics," 213.

30 Islamic countries, meanwhile, had already established efficient court systems that attended to a wide range of issues regarding marriage and divorce. See Sperling, "Economics and Politics," 215, 225–6. For a more detailed view, see Zarinebaf-Shahr, "Women, Law."

31 Vives, *Education*, 146–7.

32 "Examples are not rare," claims Vives. "No one is so inexperienced that he has not heard of or seen thousands of men who take advantage of girls and then consign them to a brothel, since they have never loved them. There are others who fell in love, and their burning love turned to deadly hatred, so they killed or strangled their mistresses. There is no city in which these things are not heard daily" (Vives, 148).

33 Vives, 147.

34 Cervantes, *La gran sultana*, vv. 649–55; *The Great Sultana*, 145.

35 Cervantes, *La gran sultana*, vv. 708–9; *The Great Sultana*, 147.

36 Andrews and Kalpakli, *Age of Beloveds*, 195.

37 Andrews and Kalpakli, 195–7.

38 Andrews and Kalpakli, 11.

39 Gibb, *Ottoman Literature*, 94.

40 Gibb, 38.

41 I am speaking of *ghâzî* fighters, following Wittek, *Rise of the Ottoman Empire*, 60. Sultans would poetically and politically capitalize on the popularity and prestige of these warriors, using the title (*ghâzî*) to legitimize their power and affirm their legendary virtues of military gentility, such as "courage, forbearance, generosity, [and] fidelity to kin" (Meri, *Medieval Islamic Civilization*, 153). See also Findley, *Bureaucratic Reform*, 109.

42 As in Petrarch's *Triumphus Cupidinis* (*Triumphs*, 1–10, 13). The message is consistent with Virgil's mandate "Let us submit to Love" (*Ecl.* 10.69).

43 Cervantes, *La gran sultana*, vv. 774–9.

44 Cervantes, *The Great Sultana*, 146.

45 Vives, *Education*, 147; emphasis added.

46 "Poor young girl, if you emerge from these encounters as a *captive prey*!" (Vives, *Education*, 144; emphasis added). See, for example, Dopico Black, *Perfect Wives*, 1–47; and Morant, "Hombres y mujeres."

47 This benefit is not put in gentle terms: "How much better it would have been to remain at home or to have a broken leg of the body rather than of the mind! I shall try to be of help, *if you have not yet been captured*, so that

you will not be captured, and *if you are already caught,* so that you *may escape*" (Vives, *Education*, 144; emphasis added).

48 Furey has explored in detail the consequences of seeing Vives's treatise (which appeared in Latin in 1524) translated into English in 1531 and subsequently "published in seven languages and nearly forty editions by 1600" ("Bound by Likeness," 30).

49 Cervantes, *La gran sultana*, v. 790; *The Great Sultana*, 148.

50 Cervantes, *La gran sultana*, vv. 804–6; *The Great Sultana*, 148. As Rouhi argues, "At no time does the Sultan ask for Catalina's hand in marriage, nor is she ever given the right of refusal" ("Radical Re-assessment," 6).

51 Cervantes, *La gran sultana*, v. 140; *The Great Sultana*, 141.

52 Cervantes, *La gran sultana*, vv. 494–5 (emphasis added); *The Great Sultana*, 140 (emphasis added).

53 Cervantes, *La gran sultana*, vv. 2925–9.

54 Cervantes, *The Great Sultana*, 152.

55 It is well known that Vives dedicated his work to the "*Serenissimae Angliae Reginae*," Catherine of Aragon (1485–1536), given that this was her commission. Fischer and de Armas remind us that the Queen may not have been completely satisfied with the result, given that she entrusted Erasmus with writing pretty much the same treatise. As a result, Erasmus published just a couple of years later, in 1526, his *Christiani Matrimonio Institutio* (Fantazzi, "Other Voice," 15). Fischer and de Armas highlight that here, "rather than pre-marital chastity, Erasmus focuses on partnership and mutual understanding," and while Erasmus still follows a patriarchal prerogative, "unlike Vives, who envisions marriage as a kind of paternalistic despotism, Erasmus advocates intellectual exchange between spouses" ("Rethinking," 8).

56 Kluge reads this captivity within a religious framework – what she names an "underlying eschatological schemata" ("Twisted Turquoiseries," 163). For an expanded view of eschatology, see Grieve, "Conversion."

57 Cervantes, *La gran sultana*, vv. 2426–31; *The Great Sultana*, 159–60.

58 Cervantes, *La gran sultana*, vv. 1787–8; *The Great Sultana*, 169.

59 Cervantes, *La gran sultana*, vv. 1282–4 (emphasis added); *The Great Sultana*, 164 (emphasis added).

60 Rouhi, "Radical Re-assessment," 6.

61 Cervantes, *La gran sultana*, v. 1198; *The Great Sultana*, 157.

62 Cervantes, *La gran sultana*, v. 1789; *The Great Sultana*, 169.

63 Cervantes, *La gran sultana*, v. 1239; *The Great Sultana*, 157.

64 Cervantes, *La gran sultana*, vv. 1223–5; *The Great Sultana*, 157.

65 Cervantes, *La gran sultana*, vv. 2195–9 (emphasis added); *The Great Sultana*, 181 (emphasis added). This praise is also quite constricted to Catalina's extraordinary beauty, which is a synonym for her husband's delight. Like

Zaida and Zelinda later, female protagonists in Cervantes's play
are taken literally at face value, in ways that do not always benefit them.
Cognizant of this fact, Zelinda, in a moment of anguish, asks Zaida,
"¿[N]o será bien afearnos / los rostros?" (Cervantes, *La gran sultana*, v.
2590 [Should we disfigure (uglify) our faces?; *The Great Sultana*, 187]). Just
like in the Christian world, as María de Zayas would critically put on
display one generation later, the "curse of beauty," in Marina Brownlee's
words, continued to determine the destiny (or fate) of a woman (*Cultural
Labyrinth*, 116).

66 Cervantes, *La gran sultana*, vv. 2555–7; *The Great Sultana*, 188.

67 Cervantes, *La gran sultana*, v. 2552; *The Great Sultana*, 188.

68 For questions about Roxelana's freedom, see Peirce, *Empress*, 126, 132–3.
It is not surprising that Cervantes would use this particular moment in
history, when the union of Suleiman and Roxelana eroded the differences
between East and West by making marriage an expectation for Ottoman
rulers. The precedent was "still at work in their [Suleiman and Roxelana's]
children and grandchildren's generations. A more peaceful system of
identifying the next sultan began to emerge from transformation in the
practice of succession-by-combat" (Peirce, 17).

69 Two of Roxelana's letters are reproduced in Montefiore's *Written in
History*, 77–87. I am here taking Roxelana as the most probable historical
inspiration, but there are many others, as Smith has noted ("*La gran
sultana*," 69–70). For the influence of Roxelana as a historical figure in
Cervantes's age, see Pinto-Muñoz, "Roxelana."

70 "Si yo de consentimiento / pacífico he convenido / con el deste descreído,
/ *ministro de mi tormento*, / todo el Cielo me destruya" (Cervantes, *La gran
sultana*, vv. 1985–9; emphasis added [If I have peacefully assented to this
unbeliever, *this minister of my torment*, may all heaven destroy me, and may
your blessing become a curse to me, for my perdition; Cervantes, *The Great
Sultana*, 175; emphasis added]).

71 For more on the incidence of these figures – St. Lucía and St. Inés – in
Cervantes's age, see Fernández Cordero, "Vírgenes, mártires y doctoras,"
534–7.

72 Cervantes, *La gran sultana*, vv. 2011–12; *The Great Sultana*, 175.

73 Of course, this duality is implied in what Ferguson calls "the moral
complexities of martyrdom," since on the one hand, dying for the Catholic
faith constitutes "a route to supreme glory for Christians," but on the
other hand it can entail "a temptation to pride entailing the premature
abandonment of earthly labors" (*Dido's Daughters*, 298).

74 Cervantes, *La gran sultana*, vv. 1114–17; *The Great Sultana*, 175. Rustán
argues that "peca el que hace la fuerza, no el que la recibe" (Cervantes,
La gran sultana, vv. 1127–8 [The sinner is the one who compels, not the

one compelled; *The Great Sultana*, 155]). Exploring the eschatological implications of the idea of martyrdom in the play, Kluge believes that, "faced with the deadlock situation, father and daughter finally agree to opt for the classic Stoic-Christian solution: inner resistance and the patience of the righteous" ("Twisted Turquoiseries," 162).

75 Cervantes, *La gran sultana*, vv. 2041–7 (emphasis added); *The Great Sultana*, 175 (emphasis added).

76 Cervantes, *La gran sultana*, v. 1982; *The Great Sultana*, 175.

77 See Hutchinson's detailed assessment on the matter in *Frontier Narratives*, 129–52. See also Garcés, *Cervantes in Algiers*, 67–123; *Early Modern Dialogue*, 37–67; and Weissberger, "Es de Lope."

78 Cervantes, *La gran sultana*, vv. 1154–6; *The Great Sultana*, 156.

79 Cervantes, *La gran sultana*, vv. 1239–40, 1242–3; *The Great Sultana*, 158.

80 Mariscal, *"La gran sultana,"* 200.

81 Alberti, *Family*, 128.

82 Often mentioned in Cervantes, as in *La gran sultana*, 541–2. For more on Uluj Ali (or Occhiali)'s story and Cervantes, see de Armas Wilson, "For Love of the White Sea."

83 Cervantes, *El juez*, fol. 221v; emphasis added. All quotations are from this edition. Translations are my own.

84 Cervantes, fol. 221v.

85 Cervantes, fol. 221v; emphasis added.

86 Cervantes, fol. 122r [222r]; emphasis added.

87 Sperling concludes her trans-Mediterranean study of "marital property arrangements" with the complaint of a Florentine woman from the fifteenth century, Alessandra Strozzi, that "he who takes a wife wants women" ("Economics and Politics," 215). While not all the Catholic, Protestant, and Islamic states that Sperling covers were as extremely unfavourable to the wife's side as Florence, they all reflected the patrilineal logic that systematically and disproportionally benefited the husband.

88 The only one who does not receive freedom and some form of pension is the "mala" (wicked) and "malvada" (perfidious) Duenna Marialonso, who is left "pobre y defraudada de todos sus malos pensamientos" (Cervantes, "El celoso extremeño," 220 [poor and cheated in all her ill-conceived ambitions; *Jealous Old Man*, 184]).

89 Cervantes, *La gran sultana*, vv. 805, 808–11; *The Great Sultana*, 159.

90 From "You'll Be Back," the seventh song from act 1 of the musical *Hamilton* (2015). Music and lyrics by Lin-Manuel Miranda.

91 Cervantes, *El juez*, fol. 221v.

92 This is the famous conclusion that reaches don Fadrique, one of the most famous protagonists of María de Zayas's short novel *El prevenido, engañado* (Forewarned but Not Forearmed), as he learns to value women that are

discreet, first because "son virtuosas" (they are virtuous), and second because if they are not, "*hacen sus cosas con recato* y prudencia" (they go about their business prudently and quietly; *Novelas amorosas y ejemplares*, 340; my translation).

REFERENCES

Ahmed, Leila. "Western Ethnocentrism and Perceptions of the Harem." *Feminist Studies* 8, no. 3 (1982): 521–34. https://doi.org/10.2307/3177710.

Alberti, Leon Battista. *The Family in Renaissance Florence, Books One–Four*. Edited and translated by Renée Neu Watkins. Long Grove, IL: Waveland Press, 2004.

Alcalá Galán, Mercedes. "Erotics of the Exotic: Orientalism and Fictionalization of the Mooress in the Early Modern Mediterranean." *Journal of Levantine Studies* 2, no. 1 (2012): 11–40.

Andrews, Walter G., and Mehmet Kalpakli. *The Age of Beloveds: Love and the Beloved in Early-Modern Ottoman and European Culture and Society*. Durham, NC: Duke University Press, 2005.

Banerjee, Pompa. *Burning Women: Widows, Witches, and Early Modern European Travelers in India*. New York: Palgrave Macmillan, 2016.

Boll, Jessica. "Violating the Harem: Manipulation of Spatial Meaning in Cervantes's 'La Gran Sultana.'" *International Journal of the Humanities* 9, no. 5 (2012): 137–47. https://doi.org/10.18848/1447-9508/CGP/v09i05/43168.

Boyle, Margaret E. *Unruly Women: Performance, Penitence, and Punishment in Early Modern Spain*. Toronto: University of Toronto Press, 2014.

Brownlee, Marina S. *The Cultural Labyrinth of María de Zayas*. Philadelphia: University of Pennsylvania Press, 2000.

Castillo, Moisés R. "¿Ortodoxia cervantina?: Un análisis de *La gran sultana, El trato de Argel* y *Los baños de Argel*." *Bulletin of the Comediantes* 56, no. 2 (2004): 219–40. https://doi.org/10.1353/boc.2004.0013.

Cervantes Saavedra, Miguel. *"The Bagnios of Algiers" and "The Great Sultana": Two Plays of Captivity*. Edited and translated by Barbara Fuchs and Aaron J. Ilika. Philadelphia: University of Pennsylvania Press, 2010.

Cervantes Saavedra, Miguel. "El celoso extremeño." In *Novelas ejemplares*, edited by Juan Bautista Avalle Arce, 2:173–221. Madrid: Castalia, 1982.

Cervantes Saavedra, Miguel. *La gran sultana*. Alcalá de Henares: Centro de Estudios Cervantinos, 1995. http://cervantes.uah.es/teatro/sultana/sultana.html.

Cervantes Saavedra, Miguel. *The Jealous Old Man from Extremadura*. In *Exemplary Stories*, translated by Lesley Lipson, 150–84. Oxford: Oxford University Press, 1992.

Cervantes Saavedra, Miguel. *El juez de los divorcios*. Edited by Florencio Sevilla Arroyo. Alicante: Biblioteca Virtual Miguel de Cervantes, 2001. https://www.cervantesvirtual.com/nd/ark:/59851/bmc8p5z0.

Cortés López, José Luis. *Los orígenes de la esclavitud negra en España*. Madrid: Mundo Negro, 1986.

de Armas Wilson, Diana. "For Love of the White Sea: The Curious Identity of Uludj Ali." In *Goodbye Eros: Recasting Forms and Norms of Love in the Age of Cervantes*, edited by Ana Laguna and John Beusterien, 221–9. Toronto: University of Toronto Press, 2020.

Díez Fernández, José Ignacio. "'Sin discrepar de la verdad un punto.' *La gran sultana: ¿Un canto a la tolerancia?*" *Lectura y Signo*, no. 1 (2006): 301–22. https://doi.org/10.18002/lys.v0i1.1081.

Dopico Black, Georgina. *Perfect Wives, Other Women: Adultery and Inquisition in Early Modern Spain*. Durham, NC: Duke University Press, 2004.

Fantazzi, Charles. "Introduction: Prelude to the Other Voice in Vives." In Vives, *Education of a Christian Woman*, 1–42.

Ferguson, Margaret. *Dido's Daughters: Literacy, Gender, and Empire in Early Modern England and France*. Chicago: University of Chicago Press, 2007.

Fernández Cordero, María Jesús. "Vírgenes, mártires y doctoras. Los sermones de Santas de Fr. Cristóbal de Avendaño (1569–1629)." *Estudios Eclesiásticos* 84, no. 330 (2009): 513–53.

Findley, Carter V. *Bureaucratic Reform in the Ottoman Empire: The Sublime Porte, 1789–1922*. Princeton, NJ: Princeton University Press, 1980.

Fischer, Susan L., and Frederick A. de Armas. "Introduction: Rethinking the Early Modern Spanish Woman, from Victim to Warrior." In *Women Warriors in Early Modern Spain: A Tribute to Bárbara Mújica*. Edited by Susan L. Fischer and Frederick A. de Armas, 1–30. Newark: University of Delaware Press, 2019.

Fox, Harry, and Justin Jaron Lewis. *Many Pious Women: Edition and Translation*. Berlin: De Gruyter, 2011.

Fracchia, Carmen. "The Place of African Slaves in Early Modern Spain." In *The Problem and Place of the Social Margins*, edited by Spicer A. and Stevens Crawshaw, 158–80. Oxford: Routledge, 2016. https://eprints.bbk.ac.uk/12337/1/12337.pdf.

Franco Silva, Alfonso. *La esclavitud en Sevilla y su tierra a fines de la Edad Media*. Seville: Diputación Provincial, 1979.

Fuchs, Barbara. *Passing for Spain: Cervantes and the Fictions of Identity*. Urbana: University of Illinois Press, 2003.

Furey, Constance. "Bound by Likeness: Vives and Erasmus on Marriage and Friendship." In *Discourses and Representations of Friendship in Early Modern*

Europe, 1500–1700, edited by Maritere López, 29–44. London: Taylor & Francis, 2016.

Garcés, María Antonia. *Cervantes in Algiers: A Captive's Tale*. Nashville: Vanderbilt University Press, 2002.

Garcés, María Antonia, ed. *An Early Modern Dialogue with Islam: Antonio de Sosa's* Topography of Algiers *(1612)*. Translated by Diana de Armas Wilson. Notre Dame: University of Notre Dame Press, 2011.

García Lorenzo, Luciano. "Cervantes, Constantinopla, y *La gran Sultana*." *Anales Cervantinos*, no. 31 (1993): 201–13. https://doi.org/10.3989/anacervantinos.1993.386.

Gibb, E.J.W. *Ottoman Literature: The Poets and Poetry of Turkey*. Washington, DC: M. Walter Dunne, 1901.

Grieve, Patricia. "Conversion in Early Modern Western Mediterranean Accounts of Captivity: Identity, Audience, and Narrative Convention." *Journal of Arabic Literature* 47, nos. 1–2 (2016): 91–110. https://doi.org/10.1163/1570064x-12341319.

Hegyi, Ottmar. Cervantes and *the Turks: Historical Reality versus Literary Fiction in "La gran sultana" and "El amante liberal."* Newark, DE: Juan de la Cuesta, 1992.

Hutchinson, Steven. *Frontier Narratives: Liminal Lives in the Early Modern Mediterranean*. Manchester: Manchester University Press, 2020.

Infante, Catherine. "Gendered Space and the Place of Women in Cervantes's *La gran sultana*." In *Sexo y género en Cervantes / Sex and Gender in Cervantes: Essays in Honor of Adrienne Laskier Martín*, edited by Esther Fernández and Mercedes Alcalá Galán, 243–59. Kassel: Reichenberger, 2019.

Juárez-Almendros, Encarnación. *Disabled Bodies in Early Modern Spanish Literature: Prostitutes, Aging Women and Saints*. Liverpool: Liverpool University Press, 2018.

Jurado Santos, Agapita. *Tolerancia y ambigüedad en "La gran sultana" de Cervantes*. Kassel: Reichenberger, 1997.

Kluge, Sofie. "Twisted Turquoiseries: Emulation and Critique in Miguel de Cervantes' *La gran sultana Catalina de Oviedo*." *Nordic Journal of Renaissance Studies*, no. 16 (2019): 147–72.

Laguna, Ana. "An Exemplar Case of Jealousy. Cervantes's *Jealous Old Man from Extremadura*: Fall and Rise of an Operative Principle." *Hispanófila*, no. 143 (2005): 1–18.

Mallet du Pan, Jacques. Review of *Mémoires du Baron de Tott sur les turcs et les tartares*, by François Baron de Tott. *Mercure de France*, no. 127 (1784): 160.

Mariscal, George. "*La gran sultana* and the Issue of Cervantes' Modernity." *Revista de Estudios Hispánicos* 28, no. 2 (1994): 185–211.

Márquez Villanueva, Francisco. *Moros, moriscos, y turcos de Cervantes: Ensayos críticos*. Barcelona: Bellaterra, 2013.

Martín Casares, Aurelia. *La esclavitud en la Granada del siglo XVI: Género, raza y religion*. Granada: Universidad de Granada, 2000.

Meri, Josef W., ed. *Medieval Islamic Civilization: An Encyclopedia*. Vol. 1. New York: Routledge, 2006.

Montefiore, Simon Sebag. *Written in History: Letters That Changed the World*. London: Orion, 2018.

Morant, Isabel. "Hombres y mujeres en el discurso de los moralistas. Funciones y relaciones." In *Historia de las mujeres en España y América Latina*, edited by Rosa Ríos Lloret, 27–61. Madrid: Cátedra, 2005.

Peirce, Leslie P. *Empress of the East: How a European Slave Girl Became Queen of the Ottoman Empire*. New York: Basic Books, 2017.

Peirce, Leslie P. *The Imperial Harem: Women and Sovereignty in the Ottoman Empire*. Oxford: Oxford University Press, 1993.

Perry, Mary Elizabeth. *Gender and Disorder in Early Modern Seville*. Princeton, NJ: Princeton University Press, 1990.

Petrarca, Francesco. *The Triumphs of Petrarch*. Translated by Ernest Hatch Wilkins. Chicago: University of Chicago Press, 1995.

Phillips, William D., Jr. *Slavery in Medieval and Early Modern Iberia*. Philadelphia: University of Pennsylvania Press, 2013.

Pike, Ruth. *Aristocrats and Traders: Sevillian Society in the Sixteenth Century*. Ithaca, NY: Cornell University Press, 1972.

Pinto-Muñoz, Ana. "Roxelana in the Spanish Golden Age." *eHumanista*, no. 19 (2011): 375–89.

Poska, Allyson M. "Upending Patriarchy: Rethinking Marriage and Family in Early Modern Europe." In Poska, Couchman, and Melver, *Women and Gender in Early Modern Europe*, 195–212.

Poska, Allyson M., Jane Couchman, and Katherine A. Melver, eds. *The Ashgate Research Companion to Women and Gender in Early Modern Europe*. Burlington: Ashgate, 2013.

Rouhi, Leyla. "A Radical Re-assessment of Miguel de Cervantes's *La gran sultana*." Preprint, submitted 2019. https://www.academia .edu/41100538/A_Radical_Re_assessment_of_Miguel_de_Cervantes _La_gran_sultana.

Rycaut. Paul. *The History of the Present State of the Ottoman Empire*. London, 1689.

Smith, Paul Lewis. "*La gran sultana doña Catalina de Oviedo*: A Cervantine Practical Joke." *Forum for Modern Language Studies* 17, no. 1 (1981): 68–82. https://doi.org/10.1093/fmls/XVII.1.68.

Sperling, Jutta Gisela. "The Economics and Politics of Marriage." In Poska, Couchman, and Melver, *Women and Gender in Early Modern Europe*, 213–33.

Stallybrass, Peter. "Patriarchal Territories: The Body Enclosed." In *Rewriting the Renaissance: The Discourses of Sexual Difference in Early Modern Europe*, edited by Margaret W. Ferguson, Maureen Quilligan, and Nancy J. Vickers, 123–44. Chicago: University of Chicago Press, 1986.

Tott, Baron de. *Memoirs, Containing the State of the Turkish Empire and the Crimea, during the Late War with Russia* [...]. London: G.G.J. and J. Robinson, 1786.

Virgil. *Eclogues, Georgics, Aeneid, Books 1–6*. Edited by G.P. Goold. Translated by H. Rushton Fairclough. Cambridge, MA: Harvard University Press, 1999.

Vives, Juan Luis. The *Education of a Christian Woman: A Sixteenth-Century Manual*. Edited and translated by Charles Fantazzi. Chicago: University of Chicago Press, 2000.

Weissberger, Barbara F. "'Es de Lope': Child Martyrdom in Cervantes's *Los baños de Argel*." *Cervantes* 32, no. 2 (2012): 143–70. https://doi.org/10.1353/cer.2012.0019.

Wittek, Paul. *The Rise of the Ottoman Empire: Studies in the History of Turkey, Thirteenth–Fifteenth Centuries*. Edited by Colin Heywood. London: Taylor & Francis, 2013.

Zarinebaf-Shahr, Fariba. "Women, Law, and Imperial Justice in Ottoman Istanbul in the Late Seventeenth Century." In *Women, the Family, and Divorce Laws in Islamic History*, edited by Amira El Azhary Sonbol, 81–96. Syracuse, NY: Syracuse University Press, 1996.

Zayas, María de. *Novelas amorosas y ejemplares*. Edited by Julián Olivares. Madrid: Cátedra, 2000.

7 Revolving Sets: Spatial Revelations in the *entremeses*

ESTHER FERNÁNDEZ AND ADRIENNE L. MARTÍN

The year 1615 was a transcendent one for Cervantes, marking the publication of both the second part of *Don Quixote* and his collected dramatic works, *Ocho comedias y ocho entremeses nuevos, nunca representados* (Eight Plays and Eight Interludes, New and Never Performed). This particularly auspicious year for literary history brought to light two milestones in different genres that share the concept of theatricality as one of their main conceptual and literary underpinnings. Naturally, theatricality is manifested in precise ways in the second part of his dramatic oeuvre, the *entremeses*.

The staging of these brief one-act farces is simple, with minimal stage machinery or props. They depend on stock popular characters from the lower strata of society (the fool, the devious student, the jealous husband, the ignorant rustic, the unfaithful wife, the trickster), situations (often a ruse in which an unfaithful wife deceives her doltish husband, or a wily student cheats a bailiff), and themes (sham magic, erotic tricks, the world upside down, forced marriages, the inversion of social conventions and values).[1] Nonetheless, as Carolyn Lukens-Olson recently pointed out, Cervantes's *entremeses* "are as imaginative, ironic, funny and modern as his *Don Quixote*."[2] Without a doubt, his are far more complex in their composition, internal structure, and messaging than the conventional early modern *entremés*. These innovations are due especially to their highly individualized and often urban rather than rustic characters and settings, combined with rapid-fire dialogues composed of language that ranges from underworld slang as in *El rufián viudo llamado Trampagos* (Trampagos, the Widower Pimp) to the duplicitous doublespeak utilized by Chanfalla in *El retablo de las maravillas* (The Marvellous Wonder Show), the type of stylized and captivating rhetoric used by the wily student in *La cueva de Salamanca* (The Cave of Salamanca), and the rustic speech used by ignorant villagers in *La elección de los alcaldes de Daganzo* (The Election of the Aldermen in Daganzo). Given this increased diversity of voice and character, combined with a plot structure and social critique that often transcend the generally simple comic incidents that habitually characterized the genre, Cervantes's works obviously challenge the confines of the standard *entremés*.[3] For the above reasons and others akin to them, Cervantes's *entremeses* have become "the most distinguished pieces in a dramatic genre that has flourished in Spain for centuries"[4] and the theatrical quintessence of his oeuvre over time. Recent literary history has in fact tended to rank Cervantes's *entremeses* above his *comedias*, while the author himself implicitly equalled the artistic value of both by publishing eight of each genre together, at a time when playwrights rarely published their works and the *entremés* was particularly ill regarded.

This chapter focuses on one aspect of the guiding concept of our book – Cervantine theatricality – as exhibited in these brief but brilliant works. To begin we acknowledge with other Cervantes critics that the commercial failure of his dramatic works propelled him to create in their place a highly theatrical and metatheatrical narrative style.[5] Cory Reed, for example, has noted that Cervantes readdressed his unperformed drama to a reading public and explores precisely what made his *entremeses* inadequate for the stage and rich in novelistic elements, remarking that he "fuses the popular theatrical form of the traditional *entremés* and the more thematically profound composition of character and plot found in prose narrative. His characters are more complex and individualized, his situations suggest possible psychological interpretation and his thematic content invites socio-historical analysis."[6]

Thus, instead of completely renouncing drama composed strictly for the stage, the novelist used the safe and liberating terrain of the page to rehearse experimental approaches to the concept of theatricality, some of which were undoubtedly too radical both thematically and formally for his time. As Jesús Maestro explains: "La dramaturgia cervantina resultó ser un discurso ético y estético para la posteridad mucho más que para su propio tiempo. Sus contemporáneos estaban demasiado alienados como para ser capaces de percibir el mensaje de libertad – de libertad contra corriente – que emanaba de sus obras" (Cervantes's dramaturgy turned out to be an ethical and aesthetic discourse for posterity much more than for his own time. His contemporaries were too alienated to be able to perceive the message of freedom – freedom as countercurrent – that emanated from his plays).[7] That said, it must be acknowledged that even though his *entremeses* were not performed, and perhaps were too radical for his time, they nevertheless were read and copied by other writers who found inspiration in his characters, situations, and verbal wit.

As Eugenio Asensio claims in the introduction to his edition of the *entremeses*, Cervantes "influyó hondamente en la tonalidad irónica, en la amalgama de realismo e imaginación que caracteriza a Quiñones de Benavente y otros autores de su tiempo" (had a profound influence on the ironic tone, the mixture of realism and imagination that characterizes Quiñones de Benavente and other authors of his time).[8] Be that as it may, many of the same social messages to which Maestro and Asensio allude – critiques of the obsession with purity of blood, unequal marriages, the repression of women, and the importance of free will – as well as characteristically Cervantine literary techniques such as self-referentiality, dialogism, heteroglossia, the constant presence of meta-literature, and a sophisticated and deeply serious humour above all else – distinguish his *entremeses* from the norm. All of these motifs and techniques are especially relevant and significant for today's audiences, reading public and literary critics.

Moreover, their condensed structure and the critical and spectacular way in which Cervantes's *entremeses* dialogue with one of the most representative dualities of the baroque (and another of Cervantes's favourite themes) – the illusion/disenchantment antithesis – has over time forged them a reputation of canonicity. Within this unique dramatic framework of the *entremeses*, our analysis approaches the essence of their theatricality as a characteristic firmly anchored in social reality. That is to say, through the play of opposites (reality/fiction, illusion/disillusion, lies/truth, mystery/revelation), we posit that Cervantes proposes a critical view of his time through a demystifying lens and frames it in a highly reflexive sense of *burla* or mockery.[9]

If with the *entremeses* Cervantes intends to innovate and take risks in the field of theatre monopolized at the time by audience tastes informed by Lope de Vega's *comedia nueva*, as is generally believed, the writer must be able to break with these internalized structures. In other words, Cervantes would have to apply the principle of *tabula rasa* in order to construct his theatrical vision, which was far removed from contemporary dramatic expectations. The widely quoted proclamation made by our author in the "Prólogo al lector" (Prologue to the Reader) in his *Ocho comedias y ocho entremeses* about a bare theatre, devoid of all stage decor and machinery, reveals his nostalgic admiration for an artistic simplicity based on the play's message and not on its aesthetics. Cervantes as creator of interludes uses a complete "empty space" à la Peter Brook to fabricate illusions through a comic theatricality that he immediately deconstructs before his audience/readership, thereby exposing the grotesque although normalized social reality in which they are firmly anchored. Ironically, it is in these very acts of revelation where the "seriousness of his art and thought" reside.[10]

Since Cervantes was unable to participate fully in the physical and material – that is performative – world of theatre, a distinguishing characteristic of his theatricality is the fact that he depends exclusively on language to create his dramatic worlds. For example, in *El retablo de las maravillas* both the entire *entremés* and the play-within-a-play that Chanfalla constructs are oral, invisible, and non-existent. Héctor Brioso Santos analyses extensively this particularity of *El retablo*, remarking that "el *vacío* o la *no-comedia* serían justamente el ardid de representar lo que en realidad no existe" (the *void* or *non-comedia* would be precisely the trick of representing what does not really exist).[11]

Besides this liberating reliance on language's inner qualities to create drama because the constraints of live performance can be disregarded, the free manipulation of a variety of unseen (by audiences) spaces becomes another main driver of Cervantes's dramatic agenda. The author uses the domestic and rural spheres, and especially a variety of urban settings such as streets, plazas, and marketplaces, to deploy interactive spectacles that ridicule social and institutional power and simultaneously involve the spectator in this reflexive mockery.[12] In this regard, Aurelio González's interpretation of the scenic space of the *entremeses* is illuminating:

> Del espacio elemental e indeterminado de *El juez de los divorcios* se llega al espacio complejo de la comedia en *La cueva de Salamanca*, graduando la complejidad espacial en los otros entremeses con los espacios extensivos e innovando en *El retablo de las maravillas*. Me parece que Cervantes presenta toda una propuesta de la espacialidad en el teatro a partir del género entremesil.

> (From the elemental and indeterminate space of *El juez de los divorcios* we arrive at the complex space of the *comedia* in *La cueva de Salamanca*, calibrating the spatial complexity of the other *entremeses* with the extensive spaces and innovating in *El retablo de las maravillas*. It seems to me that Cervantes presents a whole proposal of spatiality in theatre based on the *entremés* genre.)[13]

This attention to space sparked our interest to explore further Cervantes's "proposal of spatiality" in his *entremeses*, which we visualize as types of revolving sets, that is, animated scenarios that may have an initial meaning but acquire another as the play progresses. One such space is the domestic sphere – the home – in which the female protagonists operate in *El viejo celoso* (The Jealous Old Man) and *La cueva de Salamanca*, two interludes of adultery that mock the obsessive behaviour of controlling husbands. We suggest that both plots convert these particular domestic spaces into funhouses thanks to the protagonists' improvisations. By *funhouses*, we mean the type of amusement park attraction where playful devices such as halls of mirrors and spinning floors provide distorted, even grotesque visions of reality for the entertainment of the participants who wander through them. As in funhouses, the homes in these *entremeses* turn into playful spaces that are open to mockery and pleasure, allowing audiences to view the distortion of reality while the foolish male protagonists remain blind to it. At the same time, the messages to be taken from these works are profoundly serious.

Funhouses

It is significant to note how *El viejo celoso* and *La cueva de Salamanca* both begin by presenting the home as a prison, a distortion of domesticity if ever there was one. In the first playlet doña Lorenza bemoans her situation as a prisoner of her husband's obsessions to her neighbour Ortigosa: "No me clavara él las ventanas, cerrara las puertas, visitara a todas horas la casa, desterrara della los gatos y los perros, solamente porque tienen nombre de varón" (If only he wouldn't nail my windows shut, lock the doors, check on me all the time, and ban all dogs and tomcats from the house just because they are males).[14] Lorenza details her confinement further: "Siete puertas hay antes que se llegue a mi aposento, fuera de la puerta de la calle, y todas se cierran con llave" (Besides the street door, there are seven doors leading to my bedroom and he locks them all).[15]

Cañizares, for his part, also emphasizes this restrictive space when he proudly explains to his friend his strict surveillance measures: "[L]as ventanas, amén de estar con llave, las guarnecen rejas y celosías; las puertas, jamás se abren; vecina no atraviesa mis umbrales, ni los atravesará mientras Dios me diere vida" (The windows are not only locked, but shuttered and barred. The doors are never opened. No neighbour lady crosses my threshold, or ever will as long as God grants me life).[16] Of course the friend alerts audience-readers of the inevitability of Cañizares's fall into what he most fears by remarking: "[É]ste es de aquellos que traen la soga arrastrando, y de los que siempre vienen a morir del mal que temen" (This is one of those who go about with a noose around their neck and finally die from the disease they fear most).[17]

Up to this point, the house is presented as a closed, passive space, subject solely to male will and manipulated by it. It is not until the intervention of Ortigosa in collaboration with doña Lorenza and Cristina that the sealed domestic space opens up to become a chaotic and incoherent – and surprisingly explicit – representation of eroticism, behind closed doors. Cañizares's obsessive jealousy, similar to that of Carrizales in Cervantes's exemplary novel *El celoso extremeño* (The Jealous Extremaduran), is what causes the inevitable adultery and his downfall, whether he realizes it or not.

Thus, egged on by the other women, doña Lorenza proceeds to appropriate her confinement and fully enjoy her newfound intimacy by taking an active role in her seclusion and converting it into a space of seduction. The protagonist willingly closes her bedroom door as Cristina prompts her: "Señora tía, éntrese allá dentro y desenójese, y deje a tío, que parece que está enojado. LORENZA. Así lo haré, sobrina; y aun quizás no me verá la cara en estas dos horas" (Auntie, why don't you go into your room to calm down and leave uncle alone. He looks angry. LORENZA: I'll do just that, niece, and believe me, he won't set eyes on me for a couple of hours).[18] Jean Canavaggio has also noted the physical and representational aspect of the trick carried out by the protagonist in the following terms:

> Pero la burla no consiste únicamente en un adulterio fulminante cometido entre bastidores, sino en cómo la mujer llega a representarlo ante el celoso a pesar de la puerta que los separa: celebrando las gracias de un galán ..., comentando sus aptitudes amorosas ...; por fin, proclamando su descubrimiento del placer físico, un placer que, por culpa de la impotencia del vejete, le era hasta entonces desconocido....

> (But the trick consists not only of a devastating act of adultery committed behind the scenes, but also in how the woman performs it in front of the jealous husband, in spite of the door that separates them: celebrating the charms of a young ladies' man ..., commenting on his amatory skills ...; and finally proclaiming her discovery of physical pleasure, a pleasure that was unknown to her until then due to the old man's impotence....)[19]

Not until doña Lorenza is sexually satisfied does she open the door so that her lover can slip away, while she blinds Cañizares with a basin of water. The young wife finally breaks out of her imprisonment by loudly denouncing her unjust treatment: "Abre, Cristinica, y sepa todo el mundo mi inocencia y la maldad deste viejo" (Open the door, Cristina, and let the whole world know of my innocence and this old man's cruelty).[20] The spectator is then called upon to get involved in doña Lorenza's drama and to take part in it. For her this burlesque show of adultery functions as an "expresión de su libre albedrío y manifestación de desengaño contra el viejo malicioso y la infeliz vida matrimonial" (expression of her free will and manifestation of disillusionment with the malicious old man and her unhappy married life).[21] In this way she embodies one of Cervantes's choice themes: the importance of personal freedom and rejection of the abject submission of women to arbitrary male authority.[22]

Cañizares's home hosts the materialization and spectacularization of two anti-exemplary behaviours but its door remains open at the end of the play when nothing in the marriage is resolved. There is no closure, either for the house or the *entremés*; this is Cañizares and doña Lorenza's grim future as a couple. The task of closing the social and spectacular spaces falls to us. As readers and potential spectators, we must shut this household's doors knowing what is transpiring inside. We can either close this complex interior microcosm and forget about it or reopen it again to denounce what we have borne witness to inside.[23] Unlike in *El celoso extremeño* where Carrizales expiates his guilt by forgiving his young wife Leonora for adultery and then dying, without realizing that she was innocent all along, in the interlude there is no similar conflict resolution to the forced marriage. These complex and problematic domestic spaces, while approximating funhouses in their function as places that supply easy diversion for a public avid for light entertainment, become sites for profound investigations into Cervantes's concern with issues relating to marriage.

Magic Shows

La cueva de Salamanca shares characteristics with *El viejo celoso* in terms of the unjust social and economic consequences of marriage as a system of exchange. In both *entremeses* theatricality emerges sporadically within the domestic space. In *La cueva*, the household is once again constructed as a subversive stage where adultery becomes a sort of burlesque show, orchestrated this time by a student from Salamanca who pretends to be an enchanter. The first unseen but discursive space is the hayloft (*pajar*) in which the student hides and creates a backstage full of erotic suggestions.

The student manages to pass himself off as a necromancer in order to convince Pancracio that the sacristan and the barber, Leonarda's and

Cristina's respective lovers whom they were planning to meet, are devils. The lovers are forced to hide in the coal cellar to avoid being discovered by Pancracio when he returns unexpectedly in the middle of the night. Nonetheless, the student invites them in undisguised and concealed only by the power of a discursive hoax, so that they can continue with their original plan of having dinner with their lovers. The student, as Cristina foresaw, transforms the house into an extravagant stage where black magic represented by the invocation of the demons straddles a mundane dinner of lust and gluttony.

Similar scenes were very common in magic and hagiographic plays, where the earthly merged with the supernatural in a way that had become normalized.[24] However, for this type of scenario to be acceptable, the spectator, like Pancracio, has to renounce suspension of belief to reason. Indeed, Pancracio's watchful eye towards his honour and his wife's chastity is blinded by his curiosity and the opportunity to dine with two devilish figures, blurring the boundaries between reality and fiction. This farce of bewitchment exposes the irrationality of superstitions that were still deeply rooted in the society of the period and sometimes used as excuses to persecute minorities. The spectator/reader sees before his or her eyes the hasty fabrication of the trick and has no choice but to chuckle knowingly at the absurd situation.

The illusionist show in *La cueva de Salamanca* is repeated in *El retablo de las maravillas*, although in the latter the setting is deliberately theatrical in comparison with the other *entremeses* treated in this chapter. Here Chanfalla performs a showy and grotesque incantation in which he invokes the magical properties of the *retablo* that are conjured by the villagers' collective obsession with purity of blood. In this *entremés* there is no need for a physical backstage as in *El viejo celoso* and *La cueva de Salamanca*, or even for the presence of actors (such as the sham demons of *La cueva*). The supposedly magical set is created exclusively with words. As Francisco Ynduráin says in the preliminary study to his edition of Cervantes's dramatic works, "En el *Retablo* no hay magia, sino labia" (In the *Retablo* there is no magic, but loquacity).[25] The empty space that according to Brook is theatricalized by the simple act of an artist crossing it comes to life through the power of Chirinos and Chanfalla's words and the autosuggestion of the dim-witted rustics.[26] The spectacular space is subverted in a formal way by converting the show's spectators into puppets of an irrational system that is driven by fatuous social values. As Spadaccini notes in the introduction to his edition of the *entremeses*: "Los villanos 'espectadores' del retablo mágico que trae Montiel (Chanfalla) son cegados por sus propias inquietudes de legitimidad y por las palabras deslumbrantes (de Chanfalla y Chirinos) y los 'sonidos' desorientadores (de Rabelín) de los mistificadores" (The rustic "spectators" of the magical tableau brought by Montiel [Chanfalla] are blinded by their own concerns about legitimacy and by the dazzling words [of Chanfalla and Chirinos] and the disorienting "sounds" [of Rabelín] of the mystifiers).[27]

If *La cueva de Salamanca* can be understood as a critical questioning of magic and saint plays in whose extravagant miracles the rational and the irrational coexist naturally, *El retablo de las maravillas* can allude critically to the social messages widespread in rural plays or *comedias villanescas*. Lope de Vega's credulous rustic protagonists, who boast so much of their Old Christian heritage, are ridiculed by Cervantes as ignorant country bumpkins starring in their own show. In Cervantes's short drama, rural society is depicted as hopelessly fossilized in its obsessions and prejudices. As a result, the *Retablo* is a brilliant portrait of the Spain of the Austrias: a society totally preoccupied with appearances and bloodlines. Michael Gerli, and more recently Brioso Santos, have interpreted the theatricality of *El retablo de las maravillas* as a critique of the incongruous contents of the *comedia nueva*. Gerli writes that the interlude is

> cortada sobre las mismas hechuras de las piezas de Lope, esto es, con arbitrarios saltos de espacio y tiempo, la habitual irrealidad social y el caos incongruente y disparatado de motivos, temas y épocas – el toro de Salamanca, los ratones del Arca de Noé, el agua del río Jordán, osos, leones y el baile procaz de Herodías/Salomé confundidas entre sí – y todo ello verbal y oral más bien que visible o real, que solían exhibir las comedias y los dramas al uso.

> (cut from the same cloth as Lope's plays, that is with arbitrary leaps of space and time, the usual social unreality and the incongruous and nonsensical chaos of motifs, themes and epochs – the Salamancan bull, the mice from Noah's Ark, the waters of the River Jordan, bears, lions and the lewd dance of Herodias and Salome who are confused with each other – and all of it verbal and oral rather than visible or real, as usually occurred in comedies and dramas of the time.)[28]

In *El retablo de las maravillas* Cervantes engages deeply in social criticism, as well as the literary criticism Gerli points to. He openly presents to the reading audience a *mise en abyme* of an entirely irrational spectacular construction that cannot stand on its own feet when viewed from a rational point of view. The invisible space occupied by the *retablo* is indeed magical, a wonder show conjured by the villagers' obsession with establishing themselves as legitimately born Old Christians and to ward off the anguish of exclusion from the group.

Although magic does not enter into the plot, in *La elección de los alcaldes de Daganzo* Cervantes creates yet another magnificent portrait of human *stultitia*, here embodied by petty, corrupt authority figures and ignorant rustics who boast of their own ignorance and superficial piety. The four candidates offer their Old Christian purity of blood as the only decisive credential that qualifies them to occupy the office of alderman. The underlying notion is that purity of blood, a fundamental concept during the time, is sufficient to enable one to do anything; to have pure blood is to have everything. For this reason, all the candidates except Pedro de la Rana (a name that betrays his Converso lineage), claim to be Old Christians and boast of their ignorance and illiteracy to prove it. To be cultured or knowledgeable was considered suspect and Jewish, hence the villagers in *La elección* and *El retablo* are infected with the same urgent compulsion to prove their legitimacy and Old Christian blood. Significantly, Rana, the only reasonable candidate, remains silent on the issue.

Street Performances

A third type of Cervantine spectacle is the street performance by the underworld hero Escarramán at the end of *El rufián viudo llamado Trampagos*. Here we leave behind domestic interiors and the creation of ad hoc magic shows to focus on the space occupied by the urban underworld. Escarramán, known for being the "columna del hampa" (leader of the underworld) bursts onto the scene to interrupt the wedding celebration of the recently widowed Trampagos and the prostitute Repulida. Spadaccini (following Patricia Kenworthy) has interpreted this unexpected and spectacular entrance as a grotesque subversion of the traditional figure of the king in conventional *comedias*, who tends to appear at the denouement to re-establish social order and give his blessing to weddings between noble protagonists.[29]

Beyond this, Escarramán's entrance is spectacularly subversive in every possible way. He is first considered to be a revenant and those who contemplate him refer to him in terms of a supernatural presence, as a "visión" (vision), an "estatua" (statue), or a "fantasma" (ghost).[30] He then takes the spotlight to assert himself as a real being by relating the rather epic narrative of his misfortunes, whereupon he soon discovers that he has become a larger than life mythical figure. His theatricality at this very moment is created precisely in this fictional life that others have fashioned around him. He discovers that he has become an urban legend, omnipresent in the power of the word as he exists in numerous performative forms:

MOSTRENCA: Ya te han puesto en la horca los farsantes.

…

CHIQUIZNAQUE: Cántante por las plazas, por las calles;
Báilante en los teatros y en las casas;
Has dado que hacer a los poetas,
más que dio Troya al mantuano Títiro.

(MOSTRENCA: Actors have placed the hangman's noose around
Your neck

…

CHIQUIZNAQUE: They sing your praises in the streets and squares;
They dance in your honour in theatres and homes.
You've provided more material for poets
Than Troy did for Virgil.)[31]

In this lengthy scene the urban space of the underworld and the collective imagination envelop Escarramán's persona and elevate him into a living icon. Enrique García Santo-Tomás has pointed out in this regard:

El «bailarín fantasma» (Smith) de *El rufián viudo* se transforma ahora en un sólido personaje de extraordinaria rentabilidad dramática que, al tiempo que mantiene el carácter híbrido de su más inmediato predecesor – entre el folklore del truhan y su conversión en baile lascivo – logra madurar en un complejo arquetipo de doble rendimiento: Escarramán como «cabeça» (260) de los males de la hampa marginal de Sevilla del XVII, y como interlocutor de todas estas mismas lacras perpetuadas por un sistema corrupto.

(The "ghostly dancer" [Smith] of *El rufián viudo* is now transformed into a solid character of extraordinary dramatic profitability who, while maintaining the hybrid character of his more immediate predecessor – between the folklore of the rogue and his conversion into a lascivious dance – manages to mature into a complex archetype with a double capacity: Escarramán as leader of the ills of the marginal underworld of seventeenth-century Seville, and as the interlocutor for all the same vices that are perpetuated by a corrupt system.)[32]

As a creation of Quevedo's *jácaras* "Carta de Escarramán" and "Respuesta de la Méndez," Escarramán is a metapoetical presence in and of himself.[33] In *El rufián viudo* the character provides a spectacle of resurrection as the escaped bandit is reborn from the ashes of his symbolic death as a galley slave. In this way, he represents the triumph of life over death, as does Trampagos's swift and self-serving replacement of Pericona with Repulida. Escarramán's entrance onstage becomes a climactic metatheatrical solo marked by his spectacular appearance, his narration of his life, and his final dance performance. In fact, in his stage directions Cervantes requires that this character be a dancer: "Tocan la gallarda; dánzala ESCARRAMÁN, que le ha de hacer el bailarín" (They play the Gallarda and ESCARRAMÁN, played by a dancer, dances it).[34] Seen in this way, it could be argued that Escarramán's larger than life mythical theatricality cannot be bound within enclosed spaces. For this reason, if Trampagos sheds his mourning garb to marry Repulida, Escarramán – faithful to his literary existence – will cast off his slave chains to dance the Gallarda. In this way Cervantes grants his character total freedom of expression in the environment where he belongs, the city streets.

Illusory Backstages

As befits unperformed theatrical works that have been redirected to a reading public, the backstage becomes a space that, doubly hidden, opens widely to the imagination. It is a space whose dimensions can grow or shrink at the playwright's or director's will, whose location can be literally anywhere, and whose imaginary stage has no limitations, spatial or otherwise. Author, director, and audiences can let their imagination fly, and words create impossibilities, magical spaces, illusions, and permit performances that for a variety of reasons could not otherwise be staged openly before a live audience.

Because the most notable among these backstage scenes in Cervantes's interludes is the openly erotic one performed by doña Lorenza in *El viejo celoso*, we return to that work here. In this scene we experience the young wife's reaction as she relishes the fruits of an illicit encounter with her young lover whom the neighbour Ortigosa has managed to sneak into Cañizares's house concealed in a tapestry. The scene is both invisible and auditory, joyful and liberating for the female protagonist and tension-filled for the cuckolded husband who doubts whether to believe his ears. Taking place in doña Lorenza's bedchamber, behind a closed and presumably bolted door (sealed this time by doña Lorenza herself rather than by her jailor husband), the scene calls attention to its own hiddenness: what transpires backstage is concealed from the other characters, from the assumed audience, and from readers. The scene's very invisibility invites all these onlookers within and outside the text to apply their imagination and construct the backstage scenario in which the frustrated young wife finally discovers the joy of sex. Any false morality is cast aside and mocked since doña Lorenza was forced into marriage by her parents against her will and for money, and to a man several times her age who is not only impotent but, probably because of his lack of sexual prowess, excessively jealous.

Regarding wealth and its dysfunction as a foundation for marriage, Lorenza laments vehemently at the beginning of the interlude: "¡Que malditos sean sus dineros, fuera de las cruces, malditas sus joyas, malditas sus galas, y maldito todo cuanto me da y promete! ¿De qué me sirve a mí todo aquesto, si en mitad de la riqueza estoy pobre, y en medio de la abundancia, con hambre? (To hell with his money except the crosses on the back, to hell with his jewels, to hell with his gifts and with everything he gives or promises me. What good is all that to me if in the midst of riches I am poor, and surrounded by abundance, hungry?)[35] That is, wealth cannot be the basis for a healthy marriage nor heal the inequities of a forced one. As we have pointed out, this theme is dear to Cervantes and he will return to it insistently in his works. Lorenza and Cañizares's union is utterly devoid of physical intimacy (hence her hunger), as is that of Leonora and Carrizales in *El celoso extremeño*. Such sterility is also suggested in the unhappy marriage between the Vejete (old man) and Mariana in *El juez de los divorcios* (The Divorce Court Judge). As a response to such flawed and unnatural misalliances, Cervantes intimates that matrimony should be based on love, respect, and compatibility, of which sexual harmony for both partners is an essential element.

In *El viejo celoso*, after establishing the problem (the old man's impotence and resulting insecurity and jealousy), the solution for the wife is presented as adultery, which is rendered in surprising detail. Moreover, Cervantes assigns blame for this conjugal betrayal not to doña Lorenza but to her irrational husband, a clear inversion of social and literary conventions.[36] As befits their different genres, the misguided and tragic hero of *El celoso extremeño* is depicted as a ridiculous and risible cuckold in *El viejo celoso*. Hence in the interlude the backstage sex scene is presented as a logical (and humorous) consequence of the husband's irrational precautions, as Lorenza clearly delights in her newfound sensuality. She calls out to Cristina, who responds, along with Carrizales, from the stage:

LORENZA: ¡Si supieses qué galán me ha deparado la buena suerte! Mozo, bien dispuesto, pelinegro y que le huele la boca a mil azahares!

CRISTINA: ¡Jesús, y qué locuras y qué niñerías! ¿Está loca, tía?

LORENZA: No estoy sino en todo mi juicio; y en verdad que, si le vieses, que se te alegrase el alma.

…

CAÑIZARES: Lorenza, di lo que quisieres, pero no tomes en tu boca el nombre de vecina, que me tiemblan las carnes en oírle.

LORENZA: También me tiemblan a mí por amor de la vecina.

…

LORENZA: ¡Ahora echo de ver quién eres, viejo maldito, que hasta aquí he vivido engañada contigo!

…

LORENZA: Lavar quiero a un galán las pocas barbas que tiene con una bacía llena de agua de ángeles, porque su cara es como la de un ángel pintado.

(LORENZA: Cristina, if you only knew the lovely young man that my good luck has brought me! Young, handsome, dark-haired and his breath is as sweet as a thousand orange blossoms!

CRISTINA: Goodness, what childish nonsense! Are you mad, auntie?

LORENZA: I've never been saner, and truly, if you saw him, it would gladden your soul!

…

CAÑIZARES: Lorenza, say what you want but don't mention the word neighbour, it makes me shudder to hear it.

LORENZA: It makes me tremble too, but out of love for the neighbour.

…

LORENZA: Now I see who you really are, you damn old man, you had me fooled up till now!

…

LORENZA: I want to wash this young man's downy beard in a basin of perfumed water, because he has the face of an angel.)[37]

This scene of Lorenza's lovemaking has tremendous suggestive force because it communicates an erotic reality that, precisely because it is invisible, becomes much more powerful. All the action takes place backstage, "por dentro" the stage directions indicate,[38] and transpires in the time that it takes Lorenza to narrate what is happening. She deceives with the truth, teasing the other characters and the readers by telling and then denying, by shouting out her sensual and adulterous pleasure to all and afterwards insisting to Cañizares that she was simply joking and that he alone is guilty due to his obsessive jealousy:

"¡Mirad con quién me casó mi suerte, sino con el hombre más malicioso del mundo!… ¡Mirad en lo que tiene mi honra y mi crédito, pues de las sospechas hace certezas, de las mentiras verdades, de las burlas veras y de los entretenimientos maldiciones!" (Look who my bad luck married me to, the most malicious man in the world. Look how he treats my honour and my reputation. He turns suspicion into certainty, lies into truth, jest into earnest, and fun into cursing!)[39]

With respect to the morality of this *entremés* Cervantes is true to himself. Any immorality of the sex scene functions as a lesson to the unwise: such a denouement is the logical result of forced and unequal marriages when daughters' wishes are disregarded. Moreover, attempted female enclosure never ends well. This particular *entremés* with its ingenious verbal performance of a backstage scene of sexual intimacy provides a lesson to readers (the only audience possible): marriage can be a natural and positive institution only when it occurs between sexually active equals. This is a repudiation of the idea that imposed virginity for women and celibacy for men are superior states. In this brief scene and others, Cervantes dignifies eroticism as a natural impulse, thereby implicitly rejecting moralists' promotion of male celibacy and concomitant condemnation of women as the source of men's perdition.

As we pointed out in the section on funhouses, in Cervantes's works there are no facile solutions with respect to marital discord as are often found in the *comedia nueva*. *El juez de los divorcios*, for example, lacks *El viejo celoso*'s ready (if tricky) solution for an unhappy May–December marriage: the wife taking a young lover. Nor is the convent a satisfactory solution as in *El celoso extremeño*. Instead, the judge in *El juez* perpetuates what is a more realistic non-solution to Mariana and Vejete's loveless union: there is no reason to grant them a divorce, "quia nullam invenio causam."[40]

El viejo celoso is a brilliant farce, a comic masterpiece with a crucial theme that questions the Tridentine concept of marriage based on economic and social considerations rather than a woman's free and informed consent. It should be remembered that at this time the Catholic Church authorized the marriage of girls as young as twelve years old. As she tells Ortigosa at the beginning of the interlude, Lorenza's parents, who likely were aware of her aged groom's physical and sexual incapacity, married her off for money. For this reason, their marriage is fraudulent since Cañizares cannot fulfil the marital obligations authorized by Saint Paul for the purpose of procreation. Hence, he is subjecting his wife to the dangers of sexual incontinence. Similar to Carrizales in *El celoso extremeño* and Anselmo in the tale of impertinent curiosity (*el curioso impertinente*) in *Don Quixote*, Cañizares is the fabricator of his own dishonour.

Spatiality and the Cervantine *entremés*

Taken as a whole, what then is the role of space in Cervantine theatricality? Regarding Cervantes's control of staging and spatial considerations in his *entremeses*, Stanislav Zimic has pointed out that "a final de cuentas, la mezcla de espacios es el soporte en la representación del juego entre la realidad y la mentira, o tal vez mejor, entre la realidad y la ficción: el entremés es una parábola de la mentira" (ultimately, the combination of spaces is the medium for representing the play between reality and falsehood, or better yet, between reality and fiction: the *entremés* is a parable of the lie).[41] If we agree that Cervantes's interludes are fictive parables, we should also recognize that they have a purpose beyond mere comedic entertainment and that their humour is deeply complex. All Cervantes's works generate moral reflexion; in this sense his *entremeses* are no different from *Don Quixote* or the *Exemplary Novels*. Whether the spaces he uses are real or imaginary – Madrid streets, eroticized backstages, invisible wonder shows – they all serve a purpose and provide an implicit (never explicit) moral lesson that extends beyond individual behaviour.

If one agrees with William Egginton's definition of the *comedia* as an example of modern as opposed to medieval theatricality based on its three rearticulated elements of the modern stage – "The character as signifier, the stage as screen, and the imaginary but viable space"[42] – one could then argue that Cervantes takes his vision of theatricality even further – at least on the page. He does this, on the one hand, by demystifying in some of his works Lope de Vega's 1609 *Arte nuevo de hacer comedias* (The New Art of Writing Plays) and, on the other, by proposing new dramatic paradigms that account for a theatre that could not be performed.

In the context of this new paradigm, theatre would be much more an art of the imagination than it was for Cervantes's contemporaries. In this new "theatre" the spectator/reader has to play a much more active and creative role. As this essay has argued, the conceptual design of the spaces and their dramatic functioning is one of the keys to Cervantine drama. Thus, if with *Don Quixote* the novelist trains us to be engaged readers, with the *entremeses* he converts his spectators into scenographers of a drama that is conceived structurally. In these interludes, Cervantine theatricality is ultimately expressed through multiple micro scenarios filled with meanings that go beyond those habitually attributed to other components of drama.

NOTES

1 Asensio's *Itinerario del entremés* and his study in the *Suma cervantina* are still invaluable as general introductions to the genre's trajectory and to Cervantes's innovations with respect to character (greater numbers and more complex types), language (more expansive use of rhetorical devices and occasional verse), and resolution (greater complexity and fragile harmony achieved instead of the conventional ending in brawls). Lukens-Olson's "Ignominies of Persuasion" is a good recent updating.

2 Lukens-Olson, "Ignominies of Persuasion," 376.

3 These characteristics can perhaps be compared to the technological environment of the plays written by playwrights who were contemporaries of or successors to Cervantes. See in this regard García Reidy, "Technological Environment," in which he notes that the spatial properties and mechanical capacities of performance spaces influenced the ways playwrights and performers would think and embody their texts and that "the architectonic and technical foundation of performance spaces was an essential element in the creation of theatre." (59).

4 Honig, foreword to Cervantes, *Interludes*, x.

5 Lorenz, "Baroque Closet," 34.

6 Reed, "Novelization of Drama," 70.

7 Maestro, "Cervantes y el entremés," 531. Unless otherwise indicated, all translations herein are our own.

8 Asensio, "Introducción crítica," 46.

9 We could even argue that Cervantes develops in the *entremeses* the intellectual seed for what Ramón del Valle Inclán would term *esperpento*. The concept of *esperpento* refers to an aesthetic style in Spanish literature that uses distorted visions to criticize society. Cervantes's *entremeses* are in our view a concentrated form of *esperpento* that point out the grotesque and deformed reality of seventeenth-century Spain.

10 Zimic, "La ejemplaridad," 452.

11 Brioso Santos, "Cervantes frente a la comedia nueva," 726–7.

12 See Maestro, "Cervantes y el entremés."

13 González, "El espacio y la representación," 168.

14 Cervantes, *Entremeses*, 274. All quotations from Cervantes's *entremeses* are from Nicholas Spadaccini's edition. In translating the *entremeses* into English, we have benefitted greatly from the earlier translations by S.

Griswold Morley, Edwin Honig, and Charles Patterson. Each is unique and all have been invaluable in rendering difficult passages into English.

15 Cervantes, 275.

16 Cervantes, 277.

17 Cervantes, 279.

18 Cervantes, 285. Doña Lorenza will "perform" behind closed doors (thus offstage) a daring erotic scene that Américo Castro has described as "la forma más lúbrica y desvergonzada que registra la literatura española después de la cópula de Pármeno y Areúsa en la Celestina" (the most lubricious and shameless form recorded in Spanish literature after Pármeno and Areúsa's copulation in the *Celestina*; Castro, *El pensamiento de Cervantes*, 135).

19 Canavaggio, "Del *Celoso extremeño* al *Viejo celoso*," 596.

20 Cervantes, *Entremeses*, 287.

21 Chul, "La libertad femenina," 121.

22 Probably the best expression of this topic in Cervantes is the shepherdess Marcela's speech in *Don Quixote*, 1.14.

23 In the exemplary novel "El celoso extremeño," Cervantes focuses even more on the interior space represented by Carrizales's house, which is transformed into a microcosm that takes on a life of its own. In this regard, see Egginton, "How to Build a Baroque House," in *Theater of Truth*.

24 In addition to revealing a critique of superstition, *La cueva de Salamanca* also satirizes *comedias* of saints and magic that combined rationally contradictory worlds as a matter of course. This type of *comedia* was also accompanied by elaborate stage machinery and a whole battery of special effects of which Cervantes disapproved.

25 Ynduráin, "Estudio preliminar," lvii.

26 See Brook, *Empty Space*, 9.

27 Spadaccini, "Introducción," 66.

28 Gerli, *Refiguring Authority*, 106. See also Brioso Santos, "Cervantes frente a la comedia nueva."

29 Spadaccini, "Introducción," 19.

30 Cervantes, *Entremeses*, 139–41.

31 Cervantes, 139–40.

32 García Santo-Tomás, "El potencial dramático de Escarramán," 271.

33 Regarding Escarramán's multiple literary incarnations, see Checa, "*El rufián viudo* de Cervantes," 260–1.

34 Cervantes, *Entremeses*, 144.

35 Cervantes, 271.

36 Cervantes never condemns adulterous wives, as conventionally occurs in Golden Age *comedias* and novels, in which even innocent wives merely suspected of adultery are often tortured or murdered by their husbands. Among the most egregious examples are Calderón's so-called wife-murder

plays (especially *El médico de su honra*) and María de Zayas's *La inocencia castigada.*

37 Cervantes, *Entremeses*, 285–6.

38 Cervantes, 285.

39 Cervantes, 287.

40 Cervantes, 104.

41 Zimic, "*El retablo*," 160, quoted in González, "El espacio y la representación," 161.

42 Egginton, "Epistemology of the Stage," 398. This chapter reorganizes and updates much of the data contained in the foundational studies Shergold, *History of the Spanish Stage*; Díez Borque, *Sociedad y teatro*; and Rennert, *Spanish Stage.*

REFERENCES

Asensio, Eugenio. "Entremeses." In *Suma cervantina*, edited by J.B. Avalle-Arce and E.C. Riley, 171–97. London: Tamesis, 1973.

Asensio, Eugenio. "Introducción crítica." In *Entremeses*, by Miguel de Cervantes, edited by Eugenio Asensio, 7–49. Madrid: Castalia, 1976.

Asensio, Eugenio. *Itinerario del entremés: Desde Lope de Rueda a Quiñones de Benavente*. Madrid: Gredos, 1965.

Brioso Santos, Héctor. "Cervantes frente a la comedia nueva: *El retablo de las maravillas* y las maravillas del nuevo teatro." *eHumanista*, no. 38 (2018): 723–45.

Brook, Peter. *The Empty Space*. New York: Touchstone, 1968.

Canavaggio, Jean. "Del *Celoso extremeño* al *Viejo celoso*: Aproximación a una reescritura." *Bulletin of Hispanic Studies* 82, no. 5 (2005): 587–98. https://doi.org/10.3828/bhs.82.5.3.

Castro, Américo. *El pensamiento de Cervantes*. Madrid: Hernando, 1925.

Cervantes, Miguel de. *Cervantes's Eight Interludes*. Edited and translated by Charles Patterson. Milwaukee: Applause Theatre & Cinema Books, 2015.

Cervantes, Miguel de. *Entremeses*. Edited by Nicholas Spadaccini. Madrid: Cátedra, 2014.

Cervantes, Miguel de. *Interludes*. Translated by Edwin Honig. New York: Signet Classics, 1964.

Cervantes, Miguel de. *The Interludes of Cervantes*. Translated by S. Griswold Morley. Princeton, NJ: Princeton University Press, 1948.

Cervantes, Miguel de. "Prólogo al lector." In *Entremeses*, edited by Spadaccini, 91–4.

Checa, Jorge. "*El rufián viudo* de Cervantes: Estructura, imágenes, parodia, carnavalización." *MLN* 101, no. 2 (1986): 247–69. https://doi.org/10.2307/2905763.

Chul, Park. "La libertad femenina en los entremeses de Cervantes: *El Juez de los divorcios* y *El viejo celoso.*" *Anales Cervantinos*, no. 35 (1999): 111–25. https://doi.org/10.3989/anacervantinos.1999.006.

Díez Borque, José María. *Sociedad y teatro en la España de Lope de Vega.* Barcelona: Bosch, 1978.

Egginton, William. "An Epistemology of the Stage: Theatricality and Subjectivity in Early Modern Spain." *New Literary History* 27, no. 3 (1996): 391–413. https://doi.org/10.1353/nlh.1996.0033.

Egginton, William. *The Theater of Truth: The Ideology of (Neo)baroque Aesthetics.* Stanford: Stanford University Press, 2009.

García Reidy, Alejandro. "The Technological Environment of the Early Modern Spanish Stage." In *Science on Stage in Early Modern Spain*, edited by Enrique García Santo-Tomás, 58–78. Toronto: University of Toronto Press, 2019.

García Santo-Tomás, Enrique. "El potencial dramático de Escarramán." *Bulletin of the Comediantes* 56, no. 2 (2004): 269–87. https://doi.org/10.1353/boc.2004.0002.

Gerli, E. Michael. *Refiguring Authority: Reading, Writing and Rewriting in Cervantes.* Lexington: University Press of Kentucky, 1995.

González, Aurelio. "El espacio y la representación en los entremeses de Cervantes." *Cuadernos AISPI*, no. 5 (2015): 147–70.

Honig, Edwin. Foreword to Cervantes, *Interludes*, translated by Honig, xi–xxi.

Kenworthy, Patricia. "The Entremeses of Cervantes: The Dramaturgy of Illusion." PhD diss., University of Arizona, 1976.

Lorenz, Philip. "The Baroque Closet: Sovereignty and the 'Home Theatre' of Cervantes." In *Closet Drama: History, Theory, Form*, edited by Catherine Burroughs, 32–59. New York: Routledge, 2018.

Lukens-Olson, Carolyn. "The Ignominies of Persuasion in Cervantes's *Entremeses* (1615): An Overview of Cervantine Farce." In *The Oxford Handbook of Cervantes*, edited by Aaron M. Kahn, 376–90. Oxford: Oxford University Press, 2021.

Maestro, Jesús G. "Cervantes y el entremés, poética de una comicidad crítica." In *Con los pies en la tierra: Don Quijote en su marco geográfico e histórico: XII Coloquio Internacional de la Asociación de Cervantistas (XII-CIAC), Argamasilla de Alba, 6–8 mayo de 2005.* Edited by Felipe B. Pedraza Jiménez and Rafael González Cañal, 525–36. Cuenca: Universidad de Castilla-La Mancha, 2008.

Reed, Cory. "Cervantes and the Novelization of Drama." *Cervantes* 11, no. 1 (1991): 61–86.

Rennert, Hugo Albert. *The Spanish Stage in the Time of Lope de Vega.* New York: Hispanic Society of America, 1909.

Shergold, N.D. *A History of the Spanish Stage from Medieval Times until the End of the Seventeenth Century.* Oxford: Oxford University Press, 1967.

Spadaccini, Nicholas. "Introducción." In Cervantes, *Entremeses*, edited by Spadaccini, 13–76.

Ynduráin, Francisco. "Estudio preliminar." In *Obras de Miguel de Cervantes Saavedra*, vol. 2, *Obras dramáticas*, edited by Francisco Ynduráin, vii–lxxvii. Madrid: Atlas, 1962.

Zimic, Stanislav. "La ejemplaridad de los entremeses de Cervantes." *Bulletin of Hispanic Studies* 61, no. 3 (1984): 444–53. https://doi.org/10.1080/14753828 42000361444.

Zimic, Stanislav. "*El retablo de las maravillas*, parábola de la mentira." *Anales Cervantinos*, no. 20 (1982): 153–72.

PART TWO

Acts of Disclosure in Cervantes's Prose

8 *Coups de théâtre* in the *Novelas ejemplares*

B.W. IFE

I

In an interview for *The Times*, the award-winning British screenwriter and producer Jimmy McGovern was asked if he'd ever walked out of a play at the interval. "I've walked out of lots of plays," he replied. "When theatre is good it is very, very good, but when it is bad it is horrid. And 95 per cent of theatre is horrid. It consists of characters talking, talking endlessly, talking until, two hours later, a dark secret from the past is revealed and everybody then goes home." Not all plays are like that, of course, but it's hardly surprising that a man who made his reputation by writing crime and courtroom dramas (*Cracker*, *Accused*) should be hoping for something different when he goes to the theatre. Crime dramas are popular for good reason: the stakes are high; the action is fast-paced; the endings are morally satisfying.[1] And the idea that a play is a device for keeping the audience in the dark for as long as possible is a powerful one because it channels a profound contradiction at the heart of all narrative: good narrators conceal as much as they reveal. Classic crime drama balances these two imperatives to perfection. The longer the audience can be kept from finding out whodunnit, the more we enjoy the big reveal, the *coup de théâtre*. And once we've witnessed the moment of truth, we can all go home feeling morally satisfied.

This essay considers some strategies of concealment and revelation in an altogether different part of the genre spectrum: Cervantes's twelve short(ish) "Exemplary Novels" (*Novelas ejemplares*), published in Madrid in 1613. The four *novelas* from this collection that I want to discuss are all crime dramas in one form or another. In the order in which they appear in the published collection, they are: *La gitanilla* (The Little Gypsy Girl), *La española inglesa* (The English Spanish Girl),

La fuerza de la sangre (The Power of Blood), and *La ilustre fregona* (The Illustrious Kitchen-Maid).

The principal reason for treating these four *novelas* as a group is that they are all variations on the theme of captivity and redemption: in each of them a young woman, through no fault of her own, is displaced across a social, geographical, or religious boundary; her exceptional personal qualities of fortitude and integrity enable her to overcome the perils of her situation; and she is ultimately rescued (redeemed) by a man who is attracted to her precisely because of those exceptional personal qualities, as represented by her physical beauty. In each case, although the man is the narrative vector for her rescue, it is the beauty and integrity of the woman herself that trigger the process of her own redemption.[2] Cervantes returned time and again to this narrative and thematic framework, no doubt because it resonated so powerfully with his own experience of five years' captivity in Algiers and eventual redemption by the Mercedarian friars in 1580.[3]

What these four *novelas* also have in common is that the main driver of the plot is a crime and its consequences.[4] These women are not displaced by chance or ill fortune; they are victims of human (invariably male) malevolence. In two cases the crime is rape and in two others abduction. In two cases the fact that a crime has been committed is hidden from view and in two others it is apparent (to the reader, at least) from the outset. In all cases, the consequences of the crime are life-changing for the victim and her family, and the main plot line concerns both discovery (revelation) and restitution: how will the facts come to light and how will justice be done?

The crucial difference between Cervantes's search for a solution and that of a modern Gold Dagger award-winning crime writer is that Cervantes had no detective to help him work it out. If nineteenth- and twentieth-century crime fiction is a positivist celebration of deductive reasoning, Cervantes's early experiments with the genre are driven by a different imperative: the absolute necessity that truth must come to light. Cervantes has to take responsibility for his own procedural. It's his job as author to organize things so that the words of Matthew 10:26 can come to pass: "[F]or there is nothing covered that shall not be revealed; and hid, that shall not be known."

II

Cervantes did not, of course, write his *novelas* as plays, but the sudden, thrilling revelation of a hidden truth is only one of a number of features that they share with the dramatic literature of the period.[5] Cervantes's relationship with the theatre was passionate but largely unrequited. He only ever published one book of plays, the *Ocho comedias y ocho entremeses nuevos, nunca representados* (Eight Plays and Eight Interludes, New and Never Performed). They came out rather late in his career, in 1615, the same year as the second part of *Don Quijote* and after his reputation as a novelist had been established with the first part of *Don Quijote* in 1605 and the *Novelas ejemplares* in 1613. The *Ocho comedias y ocho entremeses* could well have been intended to cash in on that success.

A passion for drama is no guarantee of success in the competitive world of the commercial playhouse. Of the passion there can be no doubt. In *Don Quijote*, 2.11, Quixote meets a group of travelling players and tells them how much he was attracted to the theatre both as a boy and as a young man ("desde mochacho fui aficionado a la carátula, y en mi mocedad se me iban los ojos tras la farándula").[6] It's not difficult to hear Cervantes's own voice in this episode, wistfully projecting his love of the theatre onto his protagonist, and he retained a keen interest in the theatre throughout his life, even when the theatre failed to show much interest in him.[7] You can take Cervantes out of the playhouse, but you can't take the playhouse out of Cervantes.

In the prologue to the *Ocho comedias y ocho entremeses* this tension is played out at some length.[8] After a brief historical overview of the theatre in Spain, Cervantes admits that he had at one stage tried his luck as a playwright, claiming to have written some twenty or thirty plays that were well received, at least to the extent that no one threw anything, whistled, jeered, or caused a commotion.[9] But then he had other things to worry about ("tuve otras cosas en que ocuparme"), along came Lope de Vega, that "monster of nature" ("monstruo de naturaleza"), and the rest is history. By the time Cervantes went back to writing plays the world had moved on, and he couldn't find a producer willing to stage them.[10] So he locked them in a chest (where would early modern literature be without manuscripts locked in chests?) and consigned them to oblivion. Until now, that is: here they are again, marketed somewhat ambiguously as "new and unperformed," which is Cervantes's self-deprecating way of saying "old and unperformable."

The prologue to the *Ocho comedias y ocho entremeses* is itself an object lesson in concealing while revealing. It doesn't really tell us what we want to know: did he fall or was he pushed? Did he abandon the theatre because Lope was so much more successful than he was, or did he turn his hand to prose fiction because he could do things in prose that he couldn't do on the contemporary stage? Cervantes rather cleverly manipulates the chronology of the prologue to give the impression that he put aside pen and plays before that monster of nature, Lope, came on the scene: "[D]ejé la pluma y las comedias, y entró luego el monstruo de naturaleza."[11] This is unlikely, since Cervantes didn't return to Spain from Algiers until 1580, Lope was already active as a playwright in the 1580s, and by 1605, could publish a list of the 262 plays he had written by then. What is more likely is that Lope's popularity and commercial success, which Cervantes acknowledges, albeit grudgingly, must have been a powerful incentive for Cervantes to find another outlet for his talents.

Nevertheless, the prologue also gives a strong sense, as do the plays themselves, that Cervantes's dramatic imagination was pushing the contemporary playhouse and its audiences further than they were ready to go. He claims at one point to have been the first to attempt to stage the imagination and the hidden thoughts of the soul, bringing a moral dimension to the theatre ("fui el primero que representase las imaginaciones y los pensamientos escondidos del alma, sacando figuras morales al teatro").[12] This was a tall order, given the constraints of the contemporary playhouse, the dynamics of prevailing dramatic forms and the sheer popularity of Lope's own brand of fast and furious showmanship.

Live performance in a theatre can undoubtedly be exciting, uplifting, and entertaining, but it also suffered, then as now, from a number of drawbacks that did not necessarily suit Cervantes's literary ambitions.[13] Some of these were purely technical. There is a marvellous example of this in one of our quartet of *novelas*, *La fuerza de la sangre*, when Leocadia, who has just been abducted, raped, and locked in a darkened room, feels her way around the walls until she comes to a window, which she is able to open. In through the window comes the light of the moon ("el resplandor de la luna"),[14] by which she is able to take note of the contents, furnishings, and layout of the room. In particular, she spots a small silver crucifix, which she hides in the sleeve of her dress – not out of devotion or theft, Cervantes tells us, but as part of a clever plan ("no por devoción ni por hurto, sino llevada de un discreto designio suyo").[15]

The crucifix will turn out to be the key to Leocadia's redemption, and by shining the moonlight on it in this way Cervantes carries off a small *coup de théâtre*, a poignant moment of providence and hope, which would have been impossible in the seventeenth-century open-air theatre, in broad daylight. A good actor, miming day for night, could undoubtedly have led the audience to believe that she was feeling her way around a darkened room and could have drawn their attention to the significance of the crucifix in any number of ways; but the moment of illumination could not have been achieved with the kind of spotlight that would be a simple matter for a modern lighting designer and technical crew. It was so much easier for Cervantes to cue the moon by simply writing "entró el resplandor de la luna."

And therein lies the second drawback from Cervantes's point of view. Theatre is a collaborative undertaking and extremely resource intensive, even if the cast is kept to a minimum. Live theatre requires a producer/director, a venue, staff, actors, technical support; and it requires investment. The audience is limited by the size of the venue, and the income from the box office is limited by the number of performances and the price of entry. It was, and still is, an extremely risky undertaking, absolutely dependent on the ability and willingness of professionals to work together effectively. We have no way of judging Cervantes's record as a collaborator, but the evidence of his prose works certainly suggests that he may well have been a difficult client for a producer, wanting larger casts than were normal on the professional stage, and production values that would have stretched the capacity and budgets of contemporary producers, designers, and crew.

But there were other drawbacks of a different kind that might explain why Cervantes abandoned playwriting for prose fiction. For one thing, live performance was, and is, ephemeral. Once the production had finished its run, there was very little left to show: the author's manuscript, perhaps, or the prompt copy; some of the actors' parts (actors typically were given only their own part and cues, not the whole play, which would have been too costly to copy out in full, one for each actor); the costumes would probably have been repurposed and some of the props recycled back into store. Filming and streaming have given modern theatre productions an after-life, and even Shakespeare and Lope were quick to realize that they needed to publish their plays if they wanted to leave any kind of literary legacy; but otherwise playwrights were only ever as good as their next production.

Most significant for Cervantes would have been the nature of the audience, and the audience experience. Seventeenth-century audiences, in Spain as in England, were notorious for their lack of rapt attention.[16] Most were standing rather than seated, and playwrights constantly complained about disturbances caused by latecomers and early leavers. Actors had to work particularly hard to hold their audience's attention, often interacting with them through verbal repartee to draw them into the world of the play, as happens in modern open-air productions such as those at Shakespeare's Globe in London. The major drawback from the audience's point of view – leaving aside the hell of other people, with their coughing, spluttering, and constant distractions – was the fact that the performance was time-based. There were no action replays, no opportunity to pause and rewind. The audience simply had to proceed at the pace of the actors and pay as much attention as conditions in the playhouse would allow.

Under these circumstances, it's not difficult to see why Cervantes may have been drawn to the novel as a way of taking more control of the production and reception of his work. A printed book conquers time and space: it is available to anyone, anywhere, at any time; and as a physical object it embodies its own legacy. A novel is similarly unconstrained by time and place, technical limitations, or economic considerations. In a famous passage in *Don Quijote*, 1.47, Cervantes praises the wide open spaces of the novel, and its ability to provide "largo y espacioso campo por donde sin empacho alguno pudiese correr la pluma, describiendo naufragios, tormentas, rencuentros y batallas" ("a broad and spacious canvas on which the pen could wander unhindered, describing shipwrecks, storms, skirmishes and battles").[17]

Cervantes took full advantage of this potential, setting his novels in locations as far apart as the Aegean, the Caribbean, Iceland, and North Africa. In a printed book, he could have his cast of thousands and carry off his special effects without having to deal with actors, producers, stage carpenters, and scene painters.[18] What is more, private reading allowed his readers to pause for thought, giving them the chance to review and consider the implications of what they were reading, at leisure and at length. And books also gave private readers the opportunity to read aloud to themselves or to a group, creating a different kind of social event where one book could reach several listeners.

Nevertheless, as we have noted earlier, the attractions of the theatre were not lost on Cervantes, and it is not difficult to detect in his prose works clear evidence of a writer who was doing his best to have his cake and eat it too. The *Novelas ejemplares* represent his most ambitious, and successful, attempt to bring the rich drama of the playhouse into the quiet calm of the closet. This is not the place to document that process in full, but it is worth mentioning at least two salient features of Cervantes's approach to prose fiction that are clearly borrowed from the playhouse. First is the prevalence of dialogue in his novels. *Don Quijote* is an obvious example – at times it could almost be described as a novel in dialogue – but the last of the *Novelas ejemplares*, *El coloquio de los perros* (The Dialogue of the Dogs) goes the whole way: it's the perfect hybrid of a novel written entirely as a script, with absolutely no narrative at all.

Second is the prevalence in the novels of what Eduardo Olid Guerrero calls "disfraz": literally "disguise," but understood in its broadest sense to include the many facets of characters who take on multiple identities and/or roles. Just as an audience learns to understand and appreciate the creative distinction between the actor and the role, so too Cervantes's readers have to learn how to "see double" or even triple, as the characters (who are no longer embodied by actors but are brought to life by the readers themselves) change their names and costumes, disguise their voices, or shift the register of their speech.

One of Cervantes's greatest achievements is undoubtedly that of reconciling the advantages and drawbacks of live theatre and private reading to create a form of prose fiction that, as with Shakespeare, married literary ambition with dramatic thrust. It's not surprising, then, to find some of his most dramatic effects, his *coups de théâtre*, in his novels rather than in his relatively few surviving plays. But he went further, and brought the world of the playhouse into the novel not just to stretch its creative potential almost to breaking point, but actually to submit the conventions of the playhouse to creative destruction. I would argue that the *Novelas ejemplares* is the crucible in which this destruction takes place and, for that reason, have always maintained that this collection of twelve experimental novels constitutes Cervantes's true masterpiece.

III

The dates of composition of the individual *Novelas ejemplares* are uncertain, but the scholarly consensus is that the disposition of our quartet of crime novels is quite different from the order in which they appeared in 1613: first was probably *La española inglesa* (pre-1599); then *La gitanilla* (1601–6); followed by *La ilustre fregona* and *La fuerza de la sangre* (1608–10).[19] As we have seen, Cervantes returned to the theme of captivity and redemption several times, ringing the changes in terms of the geographical, political, religious, and social setting; the nature of the crime that precipitates the action; and, crucially, the means by which the hidden truth is revealed. If, indeed, *La española inglesa* is the earliest example of this narrative structure in Cervantes's short fiction, that would make perfect sense because it is, in a way, the baseline, the theme on which the others are variations.

La española inglesa is certainly the most extravagantly plotted of the four *novelas* in question. We are told at the outset about Isabela's abduction by the English during a raid on Cadiz, so there is no mystery about the crime itself. What is in question, though, is how she will be returned to her family and her native land. We follow Isabela's upbringing by an English recusant family in London; her introduction to the court of Elizabeth I; the Queen's imposition of a trial by ordeal on Ricaredo, the young Catholic Englishman who falls in love with Isabela; the

jealousy of the wicked Count Arnesto, sparked by Ricaredo's successful discharge of his mission; Isabela's poisoning and disfigurement by
Arnesto's mother; and Ricaredo's flight to Rome to avoid an arranged
marriage to a young woman and fellow Catholic from Scotland. These
are all good romance hurdles to put in the path of true love, but what
ensures that they are overcome is Ricaredo's twice-pledged love for
Isabela and his promise ("les daba su palabra") to join her in Cadiz
or Seville two years later.[20] Unless, that is, "some great obstacle, death
most probably" prevents his coming ("si deste término pasase, tuviesen
por cosa certísima que algún grande impedimento, o la muerte, que era
lo más cierto, se había opuesto a su camino").[21]

Little did he know how important that conditionality would turn out
to be. Repatriated back to Spain in the company of her parents and with
the financial assistance of the Queen, Isabela waits for Ricaredo to meet
her as promised, secure in the knowledge that he will be true to his
word. Her complexion even begins to recover its former beauty. Until
one day she receives a letter: Ricaredo is dead, killed by his rival, Count
Arnesto. Devastated, she determines to become a nun.

Except that the news of Ricaredo's death turns out to have been exaggerated. On the very day of her induction, exactly two years since they
had bidden each other farewell, Isabela, now looking radiantly beautiful and dressed in her finest, is about to cross the threshold of the convent of Santa Paula when a man, dressed in the costume of a redeemed
captive, cries out from the crowd: "¡Detente, Isabela, deténte ...!"
("Stop, Isabella, stop ...!")[22] It is, of course, Ricaredo, bang on time.

Readers who are aghast at this cynical manipulation of Isabela's emotions and their own may be assured that Cervantes goes on to explain
in some detail how Ricaredo came not to be dead after all. But for our
purposes, several things are striking about the plot of *La española inglesa*
and its delivery in what is, let us be clear, one of the finest examples of
prose romance in Western literature. The first is how genuinely shocking Cervantes contrives to make the news of Ricaredo's death, notwithstanding the conventions of the genre and their consequential effect
on the reader's expectations. The letter drops like a bombshell, just as
Isabel is rehearsing in her mind what she and Ricaredo will say to each
other when he arrives, the reasons he will give for his delay and the forgiveness and the embraces she will give him in return. The letter is from
Ricaredo's mother, Catalina, and the witness to Ricaredo's death is his
manservant Guillarte, both of them known to Isabela, both of them reliable. She has absolutely no reason to doubt that the contents are true.

And yet, and yet. Cervantes breaks the news in the form of a letter.
There is nothing unusual in that; indeed, short of Guillarte making the

journey in person, it is difficult to imagine how else the news could have reached Seville. But this is a *novela* in which the narrator does most of the heavy lifting. Dialogue is used rather sparingly and when it is, what is said carries genuine weight. When he interrupts the narrative to give us the text of the letter, verbatim, Cervantes performs one of his characteristic "French exits," quietly slipping into the background, leaving the characters to carry on without him. For a few moments he hands the narrative authority to the writer of the letter, Ricaredo's mother, and as we read what she says, we and Isabela become one – we and she read the same text at the same time, with the same eyes. This creates a powerful bond between us: we share the conviction that what the letter says is true.

But Cervantes has actually played a subtle trick on us. He forces us to buy into Isabela's misfortune while momentarily resiling from his role as guarantor of the truth. The contents of the letter are, in a sense, not his responsibility – they are the lady Catalina's. And we don't in fact have the verbatim text. The letter was actually written in English and what we have is a translation – *traduttore, traditore*, as Cervantes will demonstrate in *Don Quijote*, 2.62. Isabela does what anyone might do in the circumstances – she wonders if it can be true. But does she, as it were, (pro)test too much? The handwriting and the signature leave no doubt; she knows Guillarte to be "verdadero" – truthful. He had no desire or reason to "fingir aquella muerte" – make it up. Still less Ricaredo's mother – she had no reason to make it up or send her such sad news. "Finalmente, ningún discurso que hizo, ninguna cosa que imaginó le pudo quitar del pensamiento no ser verdadera la nueva de su desventura" ("No reasoning and nothing she could imagine gave Isabella cause to think that the news of her misfortune was in any way untrue").[23]

Cervantes pulls it off: he persuades us all that Ricaredo is dead while leaving behind a pile of clues to suggest that he may not be: "verdadero," "fingir," "fingido," "no ser verdadera"; the cumulative impact of the vocabulary tells its own story (see *La gitanilla* below). But why would he do this? A dead suitor and a heroine who becomes a nun would perfectly well right the wrongs perpetrated by the English, especially if Cervantes could have contrived a sticky end for the wicked Count Arnesto. But this way, Cervantes gets two revelations for the price of one: Ricaredo is revealed to be dead and then he is revealed to be alive, to great acclaim and general rejoicing. What is striking about Cervantes's handling of the two revelations is how different they are.

The final scene on the steps of the convent is both staged and "stagey" – in the playhouse Ricaredo would undoubtedly push his way through the groundlings shouting, "¡Deténte, Isabela, deténte …!" and it only needs a concluding jig to send the audience home happily and with all wrongs righted. What is more, however exasperated readers may feel at the impossible neatness of this happy ending, with the hero arriving to claim his bride just in the nick of time, no reader can reasonably claim to be surprised. Ricaredo said – *gave his word* – that he would be there in two years' time. If we can't believe that a man would do what he says he will do, when he says he will do it, we have to ask ourselves why not. It is precisely that promise that allows Cervantes to cover his back against the charge of excessive recourse to coincidence or narrative manipulation, a charge that many generations of readers of this text have made.

But, as we have seen, Ricaredo also covered his back: he promised that he would be there *unless* he was prevented from doing so by some great obstacle, most likely his death. Cervantes exploits the potential of that get-out clause to leverage the earlier revelation of Ricaredo's death. This is a much more subtle revelation, and not just because it is ultimately shown to be false. At one level, the false report of Ricaredo's death wrong-foots the reader and sets up the second revelation, filling the ending with surprise and delight. But at another level the false report shows, in retrospect, how well Cervantes has covered his back against another charge: that he has deliberately misled his readers, contrary to the common law requirement that narrators should at all times be reliable. Cervantes may reasonably claim that he left plenty of clues: all he asks is that his readers read what he has written with the same level of care and attention.

These two interlocking and conflicting revelations, one designed for the closet and the other for the playhouse, also remind us how relatively rare it is for a dramatist to mislead an audience as much as Cervantes misleads his reader in this *novela*. A trawl of Shakespeare's plays reveals very few instances of an audience not having been prepared in some way for a disclosure or revelation. The most obvious parallel with the ending of *La española inglesa* is the case of Hermione in *The Winter's Tale*; she is believed to be dead but appears in 5.3 in the form of a statue, which then comes to life. Similarly, in *The Comedy of Errors* the Abbess Emilia enters for the first time in 5.1 and reveals herself to be the wife of Egeon, in spite of the fact that she was thought to be dead. But these appear to be exceptions. The normal practice is for the audience to be in the know and the character to be in the dark. Pericles, for example, remains in total ignorance about the fate of his wife and daughter until the double recognition in 5.1 and 5.3, although the spectators have known everything all along. A similar trawl of Spanish plays has failed to identify a convincing example of a genuine revelation for which the audience is totally unprepared.[24]

If this is so, why is it so? One possible explanation is simply a matter of crowd control. As Cervantes notes in his prologue to the *Ocho comedias y ocho entremeses*, early modern audiences had a propensity to throw things if they were unhappy with what was happening onstage. Being deliberately misled could well have been grounds for unhappiness. They also had a habit of talking to each other and potentially spoiling the fun: it only needed one playgoer to give the game away and the whole thing would be ruined. Prose fiction read at home in private avoided some of these drawbacks.

But a better reason goes to the heart of dramatic theory as Cervantes and his contemporaries would have understood it. Sudden shifts of fortune, such as the arrival of the letter announcing Ricaredo's death, are often called *anagnorisis*, as described in chapter 11 of Aristotle's *Poetics*; but this is not strictly correct. As Aristotle makes clear, reversals of fortune are cases of *peripeteia*; *anagnorisis* (literally "un-unknowing") is the realization that follows the discovery. *Peripeteia* and *anagnorisis* work together to induce pity and fear.[25] What the dramatist is primarily concerned with, then, is the impact of a change of fortune on a character's understanding and consequent behaviour. The audience's appreciation of the character's response is clearer if they do not simultaneously have to process their own surprise and delight in response to a discovery. Paradoxically, the dramatic impact is sharper if the audience knows what's coming than if it does not.

What of the impact on Isabela of the revelation that Ricaredo is dead? One that causes real *admiratio* on the part of the reader:

> Acabada de leer la carta, sin derramar lágrimas ni dar señales de doloroso sentimiento, con sesgo rostro y, al parecer, con sosegado pecho, se levantó de un estrado donde estaba sentada y se entró en un oratorio, y hincándose de rodillas ante la imagen de un devoto crucifijo hizo voto de ser monja.

> (Having read the letter, without shedding a tear or displaying any sign of grief, with a tranquil face and apparently a tranquil heart, she rose from the dais on which she was seated and went into a little chapel, and, kneeling before the crucifix, she vowed to become a nun.)[26]

Characteristically, Cervantes speaks volumes with a simple adverb: "al parecer" (apparently). Her grief is all too real, but it is repressed in the service of a higher duty. Isabela would have entered the convent then and there had her parents not advised her to wait until the two years had fully elapsed that Ricaredo had set for his return, "que con esto se confirmaría la verdad de la muerte de Ricaredo, y ella con más seguridad podía mudar de estado" ("since this would confirm his death, and she would be able to become a nun fully assured of it").[27] What did they know that Isabela didn't?

IV

La española inglesa appears to be the earliest example of a *novela* in which Cervantes uses a discovery or revelation that is in some way problematic. The fake news of Ricaredo's death may well be just a case of prolonging the agony, submitting the heroine to one more test of her fortitude and wrong-footing the inattentive reader. But it is also Cervantes's explicit reminder to his readers that we must at all times be on our guard. There is a similar warning at the beginning of the *novela* that Cervantes chose to put right at the front of his collection in 1613: *La gitanilla*. This is also a *novela* about the consequences of an abduction, but this time Cervantes chooses to keep the fact(s) of that abduction secret until the end, when all will be revealed. Except that there are so many hints dropped in the first paragraph that any reader's suspicions should immediately be aroused.

The first paragraph tells us that, apparently ("Parece que" – the very first words), gypsies are born to be thieves ("ladrones"), are born to thieving parents ("ladrones"), are brought up among thieves ("ladrones"), study to be thieves ("ladrones"), and become fully qualified thieves ("ladrones"), and that "the desire to steal ["hurtar"] and stealing ["hurtar"] itself are in them essential characteristics."[28] An old woman, then ("pues" – a key word for Cervantes at all times), an expert in the science of thieving, brought up a young girl as her granddaughter. This young girl, Preciosa, turns out to be the most strikingly beautiful, outstandingly gifted, witty, intelligent, fair-skinned, blonde-haired gypsy that anyone has ever seen. Eight instances of words synonymous with "thief," seven of them in the (supposed) generalization about gypsies, and one applied to an old woman, "a member of that race," who is linked to that generalization by the word "pues." Why, then, in the face of so many hints, do so many readers cry "foul" when Preciosa turns out not to be a gypsy after all?

A revelation in this instance should be a simple task as, by the time Preciosa has demonstrated her talents, her virtue, her integrity, and her fortitude in the face of a challenging environment; by the time she has obliged her noble suitor, don Juan, to give up everything he holds dear, family, inheritance, and spend two years (!) living as a gypsy till he regains his senses; by the time she has done all that, there is very little left to reveal. If we have been paying attention, we should be fully aware that Preciosa is not who she appears to be. Yet she still has to be released by the narrative from the world in which she has been imprisoned.

The crucial link in a complex (and extremely chaotic) chain of events comes when don Juan, now called by his gypsy name, Andrés Caballero, is arrested, and in response to an insult, reverts to type and kills the soldier who insulted him. He is brought before the Corregidor, whose wife fails to recognize Preciosa as her long-lost daughter, Constanza de Azevedo y de Meneses. The old gypsy puts two lots of evidence before her, some baby clothes and a written affidavit detailing the circumstances of the theft. Perhaps the Corregidor's wife, doña Guiomar, knew her Aristotle: discovery by means of visible signs or tokens is "the least artistic form ... mostly used from sheer lack of invention."[29] But two tokens are not enough. Not to be intimidated, Cervantes allows himself a private joke and piles on two more, a birthmark and webbed toes. Only then does doña Guiomar realize that Preciosa is her daughter. Four-factor authentication just about does the job.

It gets worse. The Corregidor tortures don Juan, leaves him rotting in a dungeon long after he knows the true identity of the lovers, and pretends he is going to hang him once they are married. Even the priest he sends for refuses to marry them because the banns have not been read and there is no licence.[30] As revelations go, and certainly by playhouse standards, this is a shambles, not helped by the fact that the Corregidor seems determined to stage-manage the revelation himself, for maximum effect: "[Q]ue nadie sepa esta historia hasta que yo lo quiera" ("I charge you ... not to tell anyone of this story until I wish it").[31] Unfortunately, all he achieves is wobbly scenery and action that borders on farce. Nothing goes smoothly, and even the wedding is delayed by several weeks. No theatre audience would stand for that.

What is more, in an effort to tie up the loose ends, Cervantes only contrives to make them looser. The old gypsy gets off scot-free, but that is perhaps understandable as she has admitted the theft and by doing so has returned Preciosa to her family. She pretty much offers a plea bargain at the outset: "Si las buenas nuevas que os quiero dar, señores, no merecieren alcanzar en albricias el perdón de un gran pecado mío, aquí estoy para recibir el castigo que quisiéredes darme ..." ("If the good news that I wish to give you, sir and madam, does not deserve as a reward the pardon of a great sin of mine ...").[32]

Don Juan can't be allowed to stand trial for murder because that really would spoil the happy ending. In any case, the dead soldier's uncle, the mayor, knows he won't get justice now that the killer is about to become the Corregidor's son-in-law. He is given the promise ("la promesa") of 2,000 ducats to drop the case. That "promise" conceals as much as it reveals: did he get the money? Was he paid off or merely fobbed off? As for Juana Carducha, the jealous woman who frames Andrés and precipitates his arrest ... she is also let off. In a bizarre afterthought that Cervantes introduces with the immortal words "Olvidábaseme de decir ..." ("I forgot to say ..."), we are told that she confessed and was forgiven because, in the general happiness, "se enterró la venganza, y resucitó la clemencia" ("vengeance was buried and clemency triumphed").[33]

But perhaps the most disappointing aspect of this chapter of accidents is Preciosa's response to her anagnorisis. Gone is the cheerful, talented, spontaneous, self-confident, strong-willed Preciosa we have known and loved throughout the *novela*. As Constanza de Azevedo y de Meneses she too reverts to type: silent, submissive, and distinctly unenthusiastic about her new married status. Off with the motley.

V

When Cervantes returned to the theme of captivity and redemption in the years leading up to the publication of the *Novelas ejemplares*, the mood had become distinctly darker. *La ilustre fregona* is in many ways a counterpart to *La gitanilla*, but the crime has escalated from abduction to rape. Like Preciosa, Costanza, the illustrious kitchen maid who works in the Posada del Sevillano in Illescas, is exceptional, and she captures the attention by virtue of the qualities that make her exceptional. She simply looks after the silver, is modest, virtuous, and extremely beautiful. Her beauty and demeanour in context are clearly intended to mark her out as someone who is not who she appears to be. But in sharp contrast to *La gitanilla*, we are given no clue as to her true identity. Cervantes tells us at the outset that two young men, Carriazo and Avendaño, sons of noble, wealthy fathers, are the true protagonists of the *novela*, and they do indeed play a major role in guiding us to the inn and keeping us entertained while we are there. But the clue is in the title. It is Costanza that we need to keep in our sights.

By now, the attentive reader may have concluded that, as Avendaño is the man who is attracted to Costanza, he will be the one who will somehow reveal the truth about her origins. But even the most skilful readers will find themselves wrong-footed once again. After a great deal of pseudo-picaresque subplot, most of it generated by the wayward Carriazo, it is the Corregidor's son don Pedro, also in love with Costanza, who sets the ball rolling. His father, keen to know what all the fuss is about, appears at the inn, spots straight away that such a beautiful young woman should not be working in an inn and demands to know who she is and where she comes from. The innkeeper is bound to oblige. The explanation that follows is a narrative and, no doubt, a social commonplace, as we shall see in the case of Leocadia in *La fuerza de la sangre*. Fifteen years earlier a rich, noble lady in straitened circumstances and on a pilgrimage to Nuestra Señora de Guadalupe, had stayed at the inn, given birth to a young girl, and asked the innkeeper and his wife to take care of her. In consideration of which she had given them 200 gold escudos and two tokens. Costanza was the girl in question.

This explains a great deal but not everything. When two gentlemen arrive at the inn the following day, we might reasonably conclude that they are the fathers of Carriazo and Avendaño, come to call them to account for not doing their military service in Flanders as they said they would. The two men are indeed don Diego de Carriazo and don Juan de Avendaño, but they have not come in search of their sons at all. They have come to find Costanza. The Corregidor is called for and hears don Diego's confession: he is Costanza's father. He goes on to give an extraordinary account of the afternoon he stole up to her mother's rooms during the siesta and forced her on pain of public dishonour to remain silent while he raped her. The passage is remarkable for the way he recreates the sensuality of the hot, silent afternoon, the temptation offered by her beauty and solitude, and the frankness with which he admits that he "took her by force alone and against her will" ("yo la gocé contra su voluntad y a pura fuerza mía"); and that "she, exhausted, overwhelmed and in torment, either could not or would not say a word to me" ("Ella, cansada, rendida y turbada, o no pudo o no quiso hablarme palabra").[34]

Costanza's mother remains nameless and speechless throughout this *novela*, her story told only by the innkeeper and her rapist. But the Corregidor, another, more competent, master of ceremonies, stitches together a three-way marriage (Avendaño Jr. *m*. Costanza; Carriazo Jr. *m*. the Corregidor's [nameless] daughter; don Pedro, the Corregidor's son *m*. one of don Juan de Avendaño's [nameless] daughters). Tokens are exchanged, a dowry of 30,000 escudos is handed over, and there is general rejoicing. So that's alright then.

VI

If this series of revelations were not dark enough, *La fuerza de la sangre* shows Cervantes at his most *noir*, his most in-your-face. Not only is the crime evident from the outset, but the vicious rape of Leocadia by the rich, idle son of a well-born family in Toledo is narrated in graphic and chilling detail. Costanza's mother was a widow, but Leocadia is rendered unmarriageable by the rape, socially null and void. Her father, knowing that justice would be impossible and dishonour a certainty, advises her, in a remarkable display of sympathy and solidarity, to keep her counsel. She has the child with whom she is pregnant, in secret and with the full support of her parents. The little boy, Luis, is taken to the country to be nursed for four years until he is returned to the family home and brought up as nephew and cousin.

Luisico is seven when the discovery takes place that will kick start the solution to the crime. He is knocked down in the street by a horse and taken to the house of a nobleman who recognizes in the injured child the likeness of his own son. Leocadia, in turn, recognizes the room in which she had been raped. The crucifix comes into its own as a token, and the truth of the matter comes to light. Aristotle would have approved: the best form of discovery is "that which is brought about by the incidents themselves, when the startling disclosure results from events that are probable."[35] There is nothing more plausible than a child having an accident in the street and an elderly neighbour showing Christian charity by gathering up the child, taking him home, and calling for a doctor. And there is equally nothing implausible in his recognizing a family resemblance.[36]

So far, so good. But from this point on, the denouement of this *novela* becomes exceptionally problematic. The rapist's father recognizes his responsibility and calls his son Rodolfo back from Italy, but just when we might expect Rodolfo, at the very least, to get a severe dressing down and be made to face the consequences of his actions, his mother puts on a bizarre charade designed to make him fall in love with the woman he has wronged. It's an amazing piece of theatre: Leocadia appears at dinner in all her finery, in black velvet and diamonds, holding Luisico by the hand and preceded by two maids with candles in silver candlesticks, as if she were "alguna cosa del cielo que allí milagrosamente se había aparecido" ("as if she were something divine which had miraculously come among them").[37] It is a real *coup de théâtre* that in the playhouse would no doubt have used the discovery space to great effect. The performance does the trick in that Rodolfo is overcome by Leocadia's beauty, and when he marries her he does so from choice rather than obligation. But there is no hint of remorse, still less of punishment. A wrong is put right in socio-economic terms, but we look in vain for any sign of a moral reckoning.[38]

The fact that Rodolfo is both the cause of Leocadia's social exile and the (only possible) agent of her redemption makes *La fuerza de la sangre* the most compact and hard-hitting of Cervantes's variations on his theme. But the resolution is profoundly disturbing, as if social order is made to prevail at the expense of true justice.

VII

What do we make of all this? Not, surely, that Cervantes was incapable of wrapping things up more neatly and tidily than he sometimes does.

Nor that he couldn't summon up a Corregidor's wife who was capable of recognizing her own daughter (after all, he wrote a nobleman who managed to recognize his own grandson) or that he couldn't find a priest who would marry Preciosa and Andrés as expeditiously as he would have done on the stage of a *corral de comedias*. And certainly not that Cervantes could not have engineered a better, or at least a different, balance between social and moral outcomes.

Carroll B. Johnson reminded us some time ago that "we do violence to those specifically Hapsburg-era questions if we attempt to conflate them with the issues of here and now, and we similarly do violence to Cervantes if we ask him to address our specifically Reagan-Bush-Clinton-era problematics."[39] That was in 1998, but it's just as true now. Nevertheless, Cervantes often gives us an uncanny foretaste of our prevailing concerns. His advocacy for women of all ages and social classes is evident throughout, as is his treatment of excluded minorities. He is fascinated by questions of identity, is particularly hard on toxic masculinity and is an exemplary seeker after truth, a role model for a post-truth world.

But, ultimately, Cervantes is a product of his age, and he cannot be blamed for that. He writes, in the main, within a providentialist mindset. God works in mysterious ways, and without a hint of blasphemy, writers do too. Cervantes clearly found the parallels with authorship fascinating, but his pursuit of the truth through revelation was, as we have seen, invariably problematic. The process of engineering his revelations shows why, in the end, he distanced himself from the easy solutions of the contemporary playhouse. But his revelations, his novelistic *coups de théâtre*, go further and suggest that providential outcomes take their toll. Maybe Divine Providence, like entropy, is a zero-sum game. These *novelas* show us a writer who is saying: I can make some things come out well; maybe I can make most things come out well; but I can't make everything come out well. There will always be wrinkles, unresolved issues, residual cases of injustice or unfairness, unanswered questions. A happy ending always comes at a price.

NOTES

1 "Watching the Detectives," 74.
2 The inclusion of *La fuerza de la sangre* in this group was proposed by Ife and Darby in "Remorse, Retribution and Redemption." This *novela* is in many ways the most compact and powerful of the group because the man who rapes Leocadia is both the criminal and the agent of her (social) redemption (184). *El amante liberal* (The Generous Lover) also shares some

of the characteristics of these four, though Leonisa is rather less responsible for her own redemption than the other four heroines.

3 Garcés, *Cervantes in Algiers*.

4 Ife, "Miguel and the Detectives." See also Ife, "From Salamanca to Brighton Rock."

5 A number of writers have commented on the theatrical nature of Cervantes's prose fiction, of which the most systematic to date has been Olid Guerrero, *Del teatro a la novela*.

6 Cervantes, *Don Quijote*, 1:779. All references to *Don Quijote* are to the first volume of the Rico edition. For the implications of this passage, see Ife, "From Stage to Page," 105–7.

7 There is a strong parallel here with the career of Charles Dickens, whose early experience as a semi-professional actor stayed with him throughout his life and underpinned his success both as a novelist and as a performer in public readings of the most dramatic scenes from his novels. See Wilson, *Mystery of Charles Dickens*, especially chap. 5.

8 Cervantes, *Teatro completo*, 267–72.

9 Cervantes, 269–70.

10 Cervantes, 270.

11 Cervantes, 270.

12 Cervantes, 269.

13 These are discussed in more detail in Ife, "Drama as Novel," 356–7.

14 Cervantes, *Novelas ejemplares*, 309. References to the *Novelas ejemplares* are to the García López edition. English translations, when quoted, are from the Ife and Thacker edition of *The Complete Exemplary Novels*.

15 Cervantes, *Novelas ejemplares*, 309.

16 Ife, "Drama as Novel," 357.

17 Cervantes, *Don Quijote*, 1.601; *Don Quixote*, 441.

18 Parr has drawn attention to the difficulty of staging long journeys in the theatre, especially at sea, citing, for example, the Chorus in Thomas Heywood's *Fair Maid of the West* (c. 1597): "Our stage so lamely can express a sea / That we are forced by Chorus to discourse / What should have been in action" (Parr, "For his Travailes let the Globe witnesse"). I am grateful to Trudi Darby for this reference.

19 Cervantes, *Novelas ejemplares*, 726–35; and García López, *Cervantes*, 213.

20 Cervantes, *Novelas ejemplares*, 249.

21 Cervantes, 249.

22 Cervantes, *Novelas ejemplares*, 256; *Exemplary Novels*, 263.

23 Cervantes, *Novelas ejemplares*, 255; *Exemplary Novels*, 261.

24 I am grateful to Trudi Darby for her help with the Shakespearean examples and to Jonathan Thacker for giving some thought to and, at least

provisionally, confirming my suspicion that totally unprepared revelations are rare on the Spanish stage.

25 "A discovery is a change from ignorance to knowledge, and it leads either to love or to hatred between persons destined for good or ill fortune.... A discovery of this kind in combination with a reversal will carry with it either pity or fear, and it is such actions as these that, according to my definition, tragedy represents; and further, such a combination is likely to lead to a happy or an unhappy ending" (Aristotle, *Art of Poetry*, 46). The most authoritative discussion of Aristotelian principles in Cervantes is Riley, *Cervantes's Theory*, especially chap. 5.2, 179ff.

26 Cervantes, *Novelas ejemplares*, 255; *Exemplary Novels*, 261.

27 Cervantes, *Novelas ejemplares*, 255; *Exemplary Novels*, 261.

28 Cervantes, *Novelas ejemplares*, 27; *Exemplary Novels*, 5.

29 Aristotle, *Art of Poetry*, 16: 53.

30 For a more detailed discussion of this passage, see Ife, "Miguel and the Detectives," 357, 364–5.

31 Cervantes, *Novelas ejemplares*, 103; *Exemplary Novels*, 89.

32 Cervantes, *Novelas ejemplares*, 99–100; *Exemplary Novels*, 83–5.

33 Cervantes, *Novelas ejemplares*, 108; *Exemplary Novels*, 93.

34 Cervantes, *Novelas ejemplares*, 463; *Exemplary Novels*, 435.

35 Aristotle, *Art of Poetry*, 54.

36 I discuss family resemblance as a driver of plot in the *Novelas ejemplares* at greater length in Ife, "*Novelas ejemplares* (1613)."

37 Cervantes, *Novelas ejemplares*, 320; *Exemplary Novels*, 331.

38 For an extended discussion of this ending and a comparison with the more exigent outcome demanded in Middleton and Rowley's English treatment of this plot, see Ife and Darby, "Remorse, Retribution and Redemption."

39 Johnson, "Introduction," xviii.

REFERENCES

NB: This essay was written during the COVID-19 pandemic of 2020, when academic libraries in the UK were closed. The range of references is therefore more restricted than would normally be the case.

Aristotle. *On the Art of Poetry*. In *Classical Literary Criticism*. Edited and translated by T.S. Dorsch. Harmondsworth: Penguin, 1965.

Cervantes Saavedra, Miguel de. *The Complete Exemplary Novels*. Edited by Barry Ife and Jonathan Thacker. Oxford: Oxbow Books, 2013.

Cervantes Saavedra, Miguel de. *Don Quixote*. Translated by John Rutherford. Harmondsworth: Penguin, 2000.

Cervantes Saavedra, Miguel de. *Don Quijote de la Mancha*. Edited by Francisco Rico. 2 vols. Madrid: Real Academia Española, 2004.

Cervantes Saavedra, Miguel de. *Novelas ejemplares*. Edited by Jorge García López. Madrid: Real Academia Española, 2013.

Cervantes Saavedra, Miguel de. *Teatro completo*. Edited by Florencio Sevilla Arroyo. Barcelona: Penguin Random House, 2010.

Garcés, María Antonia. *Cervantes in Algiers: A Captive's Tale*. Nashville: Vanderbilt University Press, 2002.

García López, Jorge. *Cervantes: La figura en el tapiz*. Barcelona: Pasado & Presente, 2015.

Ife, B.W. "Drama as Novel / Novel as Drama." In *Cervantes – Shakespeare 1616– 2016: Contexto, Influencia, Relación*, edited by José Manuel González, José María Ferri, and María del Carmen Irles, 350–68. Kassel: Reichenberger, 2017.

Ife, B.W. "From Salamanca to Brighton Rock: Names and Places in Cervantes's *La ilustre fregona*." In *Essays in Honour of Robert Brian Tate*, edited by R.A. Cardwell, 46–52. Nottingham: University of Nottingham, 1984.

Ife, B.W. "From Stage to Page: *Don Quixote* as Performance." In *The Art of Cervantes in* Don Quixote: *Critical Essays*, edited by Stephen Boyd, Trudi Darby, and Terence O'Reilly, 93–118. Oxford: Legenda, 2019.

Ife, B.W. "Miguel and the Detectives: Crimes and Their Detection in the *Novelas ejemplares*." *Journal of Hispanic Research*, no. 2 (1993–4): 355–68.

Ife, Barry. "*Novelas ejemplares* (1613)." In *The Oxford Handbook of Cervantes*, edited by Aaron M. Kahn, 233–56. Oxford: Oxford University Press, 2021.

Ife, B.W., and Trudi L. Darby. "Remorse, Retribution and Redemption in *La fuerza de la sangre*: Spanish and English Perspectives." In *A Companion to Cervantes's* Novelas Ejemplares," edited by Stephen Boyd, 172–90. Woodbridge: Tamesis, 2005.

Johnson, Carroll B. "Introduction." In *Cervantes and His Postmodern Constituencies*, edited by Anne J. Cruz and Carroll B. Johnson, ix–xxi. New York: Garland, 1998. Reprint, London: Routledge, 2016.

Olid Guerrero, Eduardo. *Del teatro a la novela: El ritual del disfraz en las* Novelas ejemplares *de Cervantes*. Alcalá de Henares: Universidad de Alcalá, 2015.

Parr, Anthony. "'For his Travailes let the Globe witnesse': Venturing on the Stage in Early Modern England." In *Travel and Drama in Early Modern England: The Journeying Play*, edited by Claire Jowitt and David McInnis, 21–38. Cambridge: Cambridge University Press, 2018.

Riley, E.C. *Cervantes's Theory of the Novel*. Oxford: Clarendon Press, 1962.

"Watching the Detectives." *The Economist*, 27 June 2020, 73–4.

Wilson, A.N. *The Mystery of Charles Dickens*. London: Atlantic Books, 2020.

9 Captive Audiences: Performing Captivity in Cervantes's Prose Narrative

CATHERINE INFANTE

In the early 1580s Miguel de Cervantes's play *El trato de Argel* was performed in Madrid, vividly staging for the early modern Spanish public the lives of captives and the effects of human bondage in the Algerian corsair capital that Cervantes knew so intimately.[1] If we are to rely on what the author writes in his prologue to the *Ocho comedias*, this play was one of several that was well received by the audience, "sin que se les ofreciese ofrenda de pepinos ni de otra cosa arrojadiza; corrieron su carrera sin silbos, gritas, ni barahúndas" (without deserving an offering of cucumbers or other projectiles; they ran their course without whistles, shouts, or jeers).[2] Its possible reception aside, this play initiated the popular *comedias de cautivos* genre that Cervantes later revisited in *Los baños de Argel*, *El gallardo español*, and *La gran sultana*, plays where the fluid boundaries between lived experience and fiction allow the Mediterranean world to take centre stage.[3] It is well known that these dramatic works reveal underlying themes of captivity and bondage – aspects central to Cervantes's years in Algiers – presenting the life of the bagnio, harem, and frontier spaces with colourful details. Yet, because his later plays were not performed in early modern times, we cannot rely on the performance history and can only imagine how spectators may have reacted to these plays.[4] Unlike these dramatic texts, however, the theatricality of some episodes in his prose work exploring these same themes offers some clues about how the audience embedded within these theatrical acts could make meaning of these stories. In the performances of confinement and liberation in the episode of the false captives in the *Persiles* (3.10), along with the presentation of Maese Pedro (2.26) and the account of Ruy Pérez de Viedma (1.39–41) in *Don Quixote*, we see how the public both reacts to the events represented and influences their performance of captivity. This reaction exposes and unpacks some anxieties about bondage and freedom that deserve to be examined more closely. As we will see, Cervantes's orchestration of the theatricality of these episodes unveils the performative nature of recounting experiences of captivity and freedom, including the important role of the spectator in creating meaning from these performances in early modern Spain.

Before examining these three episodes, I want to call attention to the ways in which Christian captives' return and reintegration into Spanish society could be understood as a performance. Captives orally shared their experiences and visually presented themselves in front of an audience in what Erving Goffman has called a "presentation of self."[5] In these theatrical acts, the captives performed a certain role in front of engaged spectators in the early modern world. These individuals, as Daniel Vitkus reminds us, oftentimes verbally recounted their tales of misfortune numerous times to others before these improvised rehearsals were finally penned and fixed in print.[6] Spanish former captive Diego Galán, for example, admits on the first page of his captivity narrative that he only decided to write his account after having told his friends about his experience in Turkey, thus recognizing the important role of his listeners in influencing how his written narrative took shape. Of course, this oral recounting of captivity also recalls the fictional captive Ruy Pérez de Viedma, who offers an account of his days in Algiers to all of the attentive bystanders at Juan Palomeque's inn in *Don Quixote*.[7] Furthermore, many returning captives chose to present themselves before civil authorities and witnesses as part of the process of assembling their *información de méritos y servicios*, a bureaucratic document that attested to the captive's credibility and loyalty, both to the Spanish Crown and to their Christian faith. As in Cervantes's own *Información de Argel*, the process of composing this document oftentimes involved an oral interrogation of the witnesses in the presence of the captive and a scribe, among others. In this way, the transcribed report gave an account of the individual's "performance" as a captive, even if the resulting document was fixed in a specific legal genre that left little room for creativity.[8]

Aside from the ways in which captives publicly enacted their social identities to friends, family, and authorities before and after their return to Spain, the processions and ceremonies in which many of them were required to take part gave them another stage onto which to project their persona. Between 1561 and 1692, some ninety fundraising processions with ransomed captives took place in Madrid. For these spectacles, the town magistrate ordered the streets swept and watered, and balconies and awnings were adorned with the best decorations. The participating former captives washed themselves, changed their clothes, and rested before joining the procession, while the redeemers and other authorities dressed in their finest garments. People of all ages and social classes came to watch the ransomed captives pass by during these processions, which were accompanied by bells, hails to the Virgin Mary, fireworks, and other celebratory sounds.[9] Adjacent to all these "authentic" performances of captivity, other counterfeit displays of bondage competed for attention, as the false captives make clear in Cervantes's *Persiles*. The anonymous author of *Viaje de Turquía* and the former captive Juan de Olmedo, among others, criticized these imposters and suggested that documentary evidence that could be easily falsified could not validate a captive's status. Rather, it was the captive's linguistic proof – that is, their oral performance – that could distinguish a true captive from a counterfeit one.[10]

Performance, as Joseph Roach argues, "though it frequently makes reference to theatricality as the most fecund metaphor for the social dimensions of cultural production, embraces a much wider range of human behaviors. Such behaviors may include what Michel de Certeau calls 'the practice of everyday life,' in which the role of spectator expands into that of participant."[11] Over the last few decades, performance studies scholars have continued to highlight the centrality of the spectator within a theatrical act. Among these scholars, Susan Bennett insists on the essential relationship between performer and spectator, suggesting that "the audience becomes a self-conscious co-creator of performance."[12] Thus, the reciprocal bond between performer and spectator influences the evolution of the performance, allowing for different nuances each time it is staged. More recently, Jacques Rancière makes a case for how theatre audiences cannot be deemed just passive spectators. Rather, his "emancipated spectator" also acts and participates in the performance, thus breaking down the perceived barriers between performer and spectator.[13] Within the field of early modern Spanish theatre and performance studies, in particular, Catherine Connor (Swietlicki) has called attention to the audience's vital role in making meaning of their theatre experience. She pushes for more criticism that explores how different spectators with diverse life experiences could make polysemic or overlapping meanings out of the same play, especially considering the varied material conditions of each performance. That is to say, she asks how "meanings develop from co-production with spectators as subjects."[14] These notions about the audience's important role in a performance are fundamental for understanding the Cervantine episodes that I analyse in this chapter. The theatricality of Cervantes's prose, specifically in these examples that return to central themes of captivity and freedom, points to the spectators' active involvement and how this involvement contributes to the process of making meaning of the performance of captivity.

In particular, the episodes of Maese Pedro and the false captives both involve scenes of captivity and freedom staged by street actors whose livelihood depends on their ingenuity. The performers rely on their deceit to lead their audience to believe fiction as fact and, curiously, their spectacles also make use of props (Maese Pedro's divining ape and the false captives' painted canvas) that the performers claim to have acquired from freed Christian captives to embellish their theatrical acts. The audience judges and questions each performance, but when the truth finally comes to light, the acts end with conciliation between public and performer. Cervantes, as Forcione posits, "employs the confrontation of the narrating artist and the critical audience to examine the essential critical problem of verisimilitude and audience belief."[15] While these questions of truth and fiction are certainly central to these episodes, it is not a coincidence that Cervantes also uses the dialogue between performer and critical audience to explore questions of Mediterranean captivity and freedom in these passages, which are steeped in theatricality. Indeed, even in Ruy Pérez de Viedma's performance of captivity intercalated in *Don Quixote*, the characters at the inn become a critical audience that bears witness to his testimony while also evaluating and influencing his presentation. Focusing specifically on Cervantes's dramatic works in relation to trauma, María Antonia Garcés observes that "theater, of course, facilitates this encounter between the witness and the listener. The staging of Cervantes's drama thus made possible an encounter between the survivor and the listener (the spectator), so that an individual and a collective testimony could take place."[16] Thus, it is not fortuitous that the overt theatricality in passages related to bondage and freedom in Cervantes's prose fiction also forces the readers to consider how these episodes render captivity as a performance and reveal the vital role of the spectators in making meaning of the experience.

Let us begin with the episode of Maese Pedro. As soon as the puppeteer arrives at the inn, his future audience's predisposition towards his theatrical act is revealed. The innkeeper receives the itinerant mountebank with delight, exclaiming that he and his guests have a good night ahead of them. The innkeeper seems already aware of the popularity of Maese Pedro's puppet show on Melisendra's liberation, since he swiftly offers a preview to the other bystanders to drum up interest, claiming that it is "una de las mejores y más bien representadas historias que de muchos años a esta parte en este reino se han visto" ("one of the best and best-acted histories seen in this part of the kingdom for many years").[17] Don Quixote, on the other hand, first expresses some reservations about Maese Pedro, especially as concerns his "talking" ape. Nevertheless, after Maese Pedro's ambiguous response about the truth of Don Quixote's experience in the Cave of Montesinos, he finally comes around, expecting to see "alguna novedad" ("some surprises") in the marvellous show.[18] The fictional audience gathered at the inn is familiar with the legend of don Gaiferos's rescue of his wife Melisendra, which circulated orally and in popular *romances*. Likewise, Cervantes's own contemporaries may have seen or heard about similar performances, like the *Danza de Don Gayferos y rescate de Melisendra*, staged in 1609 during the festivities of Corpus Christi in Madrid (the same fateful year in which the expulsion of the Moriscos was underway) and in the years leading up to the publication of part 2 of Cervantes's *Don Quixote*.[19] Finally, the prelude that Maese Pedro includes before his own show reinforces the audience's favourable inclination to listen to and watch the travelling act. Before he begins to manipulate the pasteboard figures on his puppet stage, he creates rapport with Don Quixote and Sancho by incorporating their active participation as spectators in a sample act, using his fortune-telling ape to reveal some details about their past and who they are. These actions also encompass the "radical theatricality" of this episode that, as Bruce Burningham has illuminatingly argued, "ultimately mark the 'theatricality' not only of this segment, but of the novel as a whole."[20]

After the "Liberation of Melisendra" is underway, Maese Pedro and his assistant do not just manipulate the puppets and narration of their show; they also pull the strings on the audience's reception of their performance. The boy narrator controls the spectators' gaze, instructing them where and when to look at the action on the retable. He appeals to their sense of sight by urging them to focus on each puppet's movements, which are also emphasized by the characters in the play, who have their eyes set on the action as well: "No faltaron algunos ociosos ojos, que lo suelen ver todo" ("There was no lack of curious eyes, the kind that tend to see everything").[21] Of course, this also focuses the reader's attention on these same aspects of their play. At the same time, Maese Pedro influences how the spectators receive the show, adapting the performance for each particular audience and, as one can imagine, creating a different experience for the theatregoers each time. Before every performance in a new locale, Maese Pedro visits a nearby village to find out whatever specific things he can about the villagers and the place itself.[22] By knowing his audience, he can adapt the puppet show to try and please his spectators and keep them interested, in particular Don Quixote, knowing that he could (and would) intervene in the performance. After the first interruption, Maese Pedro implores his assistant to be attentive and tailor the show for the spectator. Later, when Don Quixote protests the sound of bells on the mosque tower, Maese Pedro stops the ringing, and the boy narrator incorporates flutes and drums, thus providing damage control and managing the audience's reception. I will return to these interruptions shortly.

Cervantes's constant preoccupation with a story's effect on its audience has led George Haley to suggest that the episode of Maese Pedro functions as an "analogue to the novel as a whole."[23] Focusing particularly on the themes of captivity and freedom that the puppet play unveils, Haley's thesis could be broadened to encompass Maese Pedro's show as an analogue to Cervantes's complete oeuvre, considering the significant impact of his years as a captive in Algiers on his writings, as Garcés has clearly shown.[24] Indeed, this is an episode that follows a striking list of other liberation scenarios from part 1, however unsuccessful some of them may have been.[25] The puppet show's action claims to be based on French chronicles and Spanish ballads and portrays how the reluctant don Gaiferos, reprimanded by the Emperor Charlemagne, finally decided to free his wife Melisendra, who was held captive in Spain by the Moors. Aside from the plot's action revolving around Melisendra's freedom, we cannot ignore the fact that some of the individuals involved in the puppet show are also linked in interesting ways to these key themes. Ginés de Pasamonte, disguised and playing the role of Maese Pedro, is actually one of the galley slaves from part 1 (1.22), who, after being freed from bondage himself, decides to stage a puppet show representing a character regaining her lost freedom. And, this episode's link to these questions comes up again in part 2, when Don Quixote compares the plan to rescue Don Gregorio in Algiers to don Gaiferos's liberation of his wife Melisendra, effectively tying the fictional story of Maese Pedro's puppet show to the very real world of Mediterranean captivity (2.64). Given the heightened theatricality of this episode, I am particularly interested in how the spectators embedded within the theatrical act could make meaning of this performance of confinement and liberation.

Don Quixote's inability to distinguish reality from fiction leads him to intervene violently in the play, irrevocably changing the course of Maese Pedro's puppet show and contributing a nuanced meaning to the performance. When Don Quixote takes the pasteboard figures for real Moors pursuing don Gaiferos and Melisendra, he begins to slash King Marsilio and his army until they are broken to pieces. Even after the puppeteer pleads with him to stop, Don Quixote is convinced that, as a good knight errant, he has been of service to the two lovers.

Only when he realizes what he has done does he offer to compensate Maese Pedro for the damages. In his study of theatre audiences, Marvin Carlson suggests that performances can inspire more "active resistance" than reading, for example, and that spectators thus create a new meaning that was not originally intended for a certain line or action of the performance.[26] Indeed, in a puppet show based on the legend of Melisendra's rescue, which the boy narrator claims "andan en boca de las gentes, y de los muchachos, por esas calles" ("are in the mouths of everyone, even children, on our streets"), Don Quixote's interventions redirect the action of the plot and point to novel conclusions.[27] Though Don Quixote intervenes most forcefully in this final interruption, it is difficult to consider his reaction here seriously, since he characteristically confuses truth and fiction. Instead, the nuanced meanings that the audience contributes to this particular performance can be traced to the first two ruptures in the plot's action, which I briefly mentioned earlier. In these cases, the spectator's resistance to some aspects of the storyline on Melisendra's captivity and liberation proposes what we might call a poetics of the performance of captivity.

Don Quixote interrupts the boy narrator, first, to protest the way in which he narrates the plot (including impertinent details that distract from the principal storyline) and, second, to correct the verisimilitude or historical truth (bells ringing on the mosque towers instead of the sound of drums and flutes). Unlike his final intervention, when he slips back into madness, these initial breaks in the action reveal concerns with how a story of captivity should be told or, in this case, performed. In studying the techniques, formal strategies, and ways of narrating captivity across a wide variety of texts in both the Old and New Worlds, Lisa Voigt shows how many authors sought to emphasize that their writings bearing witness to captivity were both truthful and entertaining. Certainly, in texts that presented distant and foreign lands that their audience had not personally experienced, it was equally important for authors to be able to declare the truthfulness of their accounts alongside the extraordinary nature of their tales.[28] Don Quixote's insistence on how Melisendra's rescue from captivity should be presented to the audience points to similar techniques that Cervantes employs to frame other related episodes. The narrator in the adventure of the false captives in the *Persiles*, for example, introduces the scene by insisting on the right balance of "variety" and "verisimilitude."[29] Furthermore, the boy narrator introduces the puppet play as a "true history," further linking the episode to other Cervantine performances of captivity, such as Ruy Pérez de Viedma's "true account," at the same time that he inscribes it within the framework of other "true histories" of pre-modern captivity.[30] These accounts that bring their truth claims to the forefront reveal some anxieties about the extent to which the audience could validate or discredit these assertions. More broadly, the spectators' active presence shows how the process of recounting captivity engages the audience in an act that is inherently performative. With a public that holds certain expectations about how captivity could or should be rendered, there could be palpable implications for not being believed, as the following episode illustrates.

The episode of the false captives in the *Persiles* (3.10) is reminiscent of the theatrical *entremés*, or what Forcione has called the "Interlude of the Counterfeit Captives," and presents two young men dramatically narrating what seem to be their adventures in Algiers to a large crowd in the town square.[31] Wearing the appropriate costume of recently ransomed captives, the two men make use of props, including a painted canvas spread out on the ground and two heavy chains displayed next to them, to make their performance more credible. The theatricality of the episode is heightened with sound effects when one of the showmen cracks his whip from time to time, piercing the spectators' ears and persuading them to keep their attention focused on the details of the painting, which depicts the captives rowing in a small galley under the command of the notorious Turkish corsair Dragut. One of the pseudo-captives, who speaks with a "voz clara y en todo estremo esperta lengua" (clear voice and an exceptionally eloquent tongue), seems to have experience performing, suggesting he may have rehearsed this show for other audiences.[32] In fact, the reader/audience soon learns that the two "actors" are indeed imposters, attempting to pass as authentic captives when actually they are students from Salamanca on their way to join the military troops in Italy and Flanders. They explain that they bought the painted canvas from other counterfeit captives and pieced together what they thought was sufficient information about Algiers to make their ruse look plausible. Even as the spectacle ends and their act is discovered to be fraudulent, the narrator suggests that the false captives will keep their show on the road as they head towards Cartagena.

Among those in the audience listening attentively to the performance are the two town mayors, who interrupt the young men's dramatic presentation. As the narrator is setting the scene for their theatrical act, he notes the presence of the bystanders and puts the spotlight on the elderly mayors, hinting at how these two spectators will soon emerge as actors and channel the play in another direction. One of them, a ransomed captive himself, begins to comment on the entertainers' discourse to his companion, finally interrupting the performance to interrogate some of the details about their alleged bondage in Algiers. When the mayor's questions to the so-called captives take the action off what is represented on the painted canvas, he uncovers their trickery. This interrogation to which the false captives are subjected by the mayor renders the plot more mobile and wide-ranging, especially since the captives initially support their account with the painted representation, a static image of a specific event in Algiers that has furthermore been reduced in size "porque lo pide así la pintura" (because the painting requires it).[33] The questions that the mayor asks the false captives shift this isolated scene to moments before and after the particular instance of persecution represented in the painting, providing a certain temporary mobility to the theatrical act. The captives' presentation that was originally focused on a specific moment is now expanded to include authentic facts and other episodes from captivity. The painted canvas used by the false captives is suddenly ineffective as proof of their supposed captivity, and a story that initially seemed well constructed is questioned by the mayor, revealing details that in the "particular" do not match the reality lived by the true captive during his years under duress in Algiers.

In the end, the mayor is completely in charge of the show, and the student-performers wish to go "offstage" and take their act elsewhere, as long as the mayor does not direct them to do otherwise. The spectators thus produce the "play" with the actors by contributing details and, to a certain extent, validating their livelihood, especially as the first mayor gives them "una lición de las cosas de Argel" (a lesson on Algiers) so that they can effectively enhance the verisimilitude of their performance.[34] The representation of captivity in this episode, as Barbara Fuchs notes, is "a long way from *El trato de Argel*, where the authenticity of the captive's experience served to cement a Christian Spanish identity. In the Spain depicted in the *Persiles*, the performance of captivity is far more common than the real thing; the currency of suffering has become disconnected from any real referent, and serves mostly to yield profits."[35] Ultimately, the public, including Periandro and his crew, are amazed by the ending of the "show" that the false captives and mayors have joined forces to present, revealing the important connection between actor and spectator – a former captive and his public – during the performance of captivity in early modern Spain.

In this episode of the false captives, the audience exercises its power to evaluate the performance of captivity with the greatest authority, creating the meaning of the theatrical act in collaboration with the "actors." The mayors interrupt the young students during their gig in the town square and respond to it by first interrogating and condemning them, and finally forgiving and rewarding them. As spectators, the two elderly men ultimately show how the audience puts the historical truth or verisimilitude of the performers' dramatic presentation to the test. In fact, the language used throughout the scene suggests that the mayors are much more than just a critical audience; instead, they adopt the role of judges, and the false captives acquiesce to their position as the accused on the verge of losing the freedom that they have supposedly just reclaimed. The dynamics of the performance are altered by the mayors' interruptions. The interlude's setting, with the false captives performing before the audience, is now transformed into an improvised tribunal, where the vocabulary and the roles adopted by the characters are radically changed from how the scene began. The pseudo-captives appear before the judges, who interrogate the alleged offenders ("da la cuerda," "mancuerda") until they pronounce their "sentencia" (sentence).[36] The false captives corroborate this characterization by naming one of them a "legislador de Atenas" (Athenian legislator) and finally insinuating that both of them are "jueces" (judges).[37] By interrupting the scene and participating actively in the performance, the spectators help draw attention to how the reintegration of captives – whether real or fake – into Spanish society could be performative in nature. In this case, the imposters initially depend on their public to validate their performance and lend credibility to their dramatic representation, which, as we know, produces the opposite effect and exposes the performance as fraudulent. The mayors' interventions also highlight the important role of the public in making value judgments about the verisimilitude of a captive's presentation of their experience of bondage and liberation, which could have serious consequences for these individuals.

Unlike the false captives' performance, which turned out to be blatant artifice, the captive Ruy Pérez de Viedma in *Don Quixote* (1.39–41) performs a "discurso verdadero" ("true account") of captivity for all the spectators at the inn.[38] This architectural space is, thus, transformed into a stage for the captive's performance, and as José Manuel Martín Morán has suggested, Cervantes uses theatrical scenes in *Don Quixote*, such as this one, to intercalate different stories that would otherwise be largely disconnected from the rest of the narrative. The inn paves the way for this theatricality to be amplified as different characters pass through the place and effectively become "actors" by recounting their tales or putting on a spectacle for the "audience." This demarcates the space of the inn between on- and offstage.[39] As soon as the captive, accompanied by Zoraida, enters the inn and appears onstage, the onlookers become quiet as if to watch a show. The narrator pays close attention to their costumes, helping to fix their roles and introduce the Mediterranean setting to the audience.

Ruy Pérez de Viedma addresses his public directly and instructs them to be attentive so that they will "hear" ("oirán") a true history of his adventures as a captive in Algiers.[40] The captive's emphasis on what his audience will "hear" is relevant for understanding this episode as a performance. Some scholars have advanced the idea that, during the Golden Age, the Spanish public more frequently went to the *corrales* to hear *comedias* than to see them. In his *Arte nuevo de hacer comedias* (1609), for example, Lope de Vega urges the public to listen attentively to the *comedias* because by hearing them the spectators will have a more thorough understanding of the plays. And, even in their discussion about literature in part 1 of *Don Quixote*, the priest remarks to the canon that an audience is pleased when they "hear" an artful and well-organized *comedia*.[41] Within this context, Ruy Pérez de Viedma's oral testimony could be interpreted as a theatrical act for a public eager to listen to his intriguing life story.

As the captive begins his staged account, the spectators sit down and quietly pay attention to his calm and collected voice. However, it is worth noting that some of the spectators also move into the limelight as they participate in piecing together the captive's experience, jointly producing his performance of captivity. Ruy Pérez de Viedma recounts his past, starting with his lineage and how he ended up in Algiers, but when he reaches his description of the fall of La Goleta and Tunis, he begins to intersperse the life stories of several other captives with his own experience. In this manner, the readers/spectators are told the fortunes and whereabouts of some three hundred captives who had the bad luck of falling into enemy hands – among them a certain Pedro de Aguilar. At the mention of this name, don Fernando and his friends look at each other with mutual understanding, and one of them, a "gentleman," interrupts the captive's tale, begging for a break in his personal history: "Antes que vuestra merced pase adelante, le suplico me diga qué se hizo ese don Pedro de Aguilar que ha dicho" ("Before your grace continues, I beg you to tell me what happened to this Don Pedro de Aguilar").[42] Ruy Pérez de Viedma answers the question by describing Pedro de Aguilar's escape from Constantinople in the company of a Greek spy, without knowing if he was successful in obtaining freedom or not. Don Fernando's friend divulges that he already knows the result of Pedro de Aguilar's escape attempt, since this man is his own brother. At this crucial part of the production, the spectator joins with the performer, and the gentleman begins to actively participate in the staged account of captivity. Ruy Pérez de Viedma invites him to take his place and recite two sonnets that mourn the loss of those African citadels and the soldiers who lost their lives.

So why does this gentleman interrupt the captive's performance and ask about the story of another captive when we can assume that he has already heard the first-person account from his own brother? In the episode of the false captives in the *Persiles*, the mayor also interrupts the performance to ask questions to which he already knows the answers, specifically so he can uncover the performers' deceitful act. In this case, however, the interruption helps to create a certain rapport between public and performer and lend credibility to the captive's tale.[43] The two enter into dialogue and take turns filling in the details about Pedro de Aguilar, each one corroborating the other's anecdotes. After the gentleman finishes reciting the first sonnet, Ruy Pérez de Viedma affirms "Desa mesma manera le sé yo" ("That is how I remember it, too"), and when he concludes the second one, the audience is pleased, and the captive is especially glad to receive news about his comrade.[44] This interlude in the captive's tale in which the two men come together – significantly, right before Ruy Pérez gets to the core of his story set in Algiers – hints at how the tale the captive is about to enact forms part of a collective, rather than individual, history of captivity in the Mediterranean. While Cervantes was not an eyewitness, María Antonia Garcés has shown how this passage was inspired by his personal experiences. In particular, Cervantes endured captivity in Algiers with survivors of the fall of La Goleta and Tunis, which likely explains his urge to incorporate this historical context into "The Captive's Tale" and suggests how he collaboratively reconstructs the lives of these soldiers in this episode.[45] Thus, the encounter between the captive-performer and his audience at this moment of the captive's soliloquy proves to be an important step in cementing the credibility of his account.

Reading "The Captive's Tale" as a performance demonstrates the entertainer's conscious preoccupation with the public's reception of his life story and how his spectators create meaning from it. When Ruy Pérez concludes the report of his captivity in Algiers, he immediately solicits feedback from his audience: "No tengo más, señores, que deciros de mi historia; la cual, si es agradable y peregrina, júzguenlo vuestros buenos entendimientos; que de mí sé decir que quisiera habérosla contado más brevemente, puesto que el temor de enfadaros más de cuatro circunstancias me ha quitado de la lengua" ("There is no more, Señores, of my story to tell you; you can judge for yourselves if it is unusual and interesting; as for me, I can say that though I would have liked to recount it more briefly, fear of tiring you made me omit more than a few details").[46] Without delay, don Fernando responds, praising the captive not only for the unusual and extraordinary events he has recounted but also for the way in which he has relayed that information to his listeners. It would not be unreasonable to assume that Cardenio and the other onlookers at the inn are also astonished by the captive's tale, since they affectionately offer their services to the captain, even if he does not want to accept their invitation.

Ruy Pérez de Viedma's constant concern with how he will be received by those at the inn, as Paul Michael Johnson has argued, is a result of what he calls the "specter of captivity," which manifests itself most significantly in the captive's "inconspicuous yet unmistakable expression of shame, an affect which induces him to be consciously discreet in his rhetorical self-presentation at the inn."[47] Yet, based on the public's response, the captive appears to have been successful in his performance, including just the right mix of details that are "peregrino y gustoso" ("unusual and interesting") to satisfy his audience and omitting other aspects that he judged might not bring them pleasure.[48] With a broad spectatorship that includes a priest, the brother of ex-captive Pedro de Aguilar, Don Quixote, characters of noble stature, such as don Fernando and Cardenio, and a range of strong women like Dorotea, Luscinda, and the innkeeper's wife, among others, the possibility exists for them to make varied meanings of the captain's public presentation, based on their own personal experiences.[49] Nevertheless, Ruy Pérez de Viedma seems to adapt his performance in a way that is well received and positions him favourably at the precarious moment of his reintegration into Spanish society upon his return from North Africa.[50]

In the three Cervantine episodes that I examine here, the presence of a critical audience makes visible the performative aspects of recounting tales of captivity and liberation. In these examples, the spectators play an important role in validating or questioning the verisimilitude of the performance and the way in which it is presented to the public, consequently developing the possible meanings of their theatrical acts. From Maese Pedro's puppet show on Melisendra's rescue to the false captives' and Ruy Pérez de Viedma's public presentations of captivity in Algiers – whether counterfeit or authentic – the performance of captivity is always influenced and motivated by the presence of engaged spectators. In this sense, these cases embedded within Cervantes's prose fiction gain more relevance if we consider them alongside other "real performances" of captives who presented themselves before the public as part of the process of repatriation and social readjustment to Spanish society that I alluded to at the beginning of this essay. In particular, Cervantes's own *Información de Argel*, which was drawn up in Algiers between 10 and 22 October 1580, unveils the public presentation of the recently freed captive before the Trinitarian priest Juan Gil and the apostolic notary Pedro de Ribera, in the presence of eleven witnesses who gave oral testimony (Antonio de Sosa, the twelfth witness, gave his in writing). Even though the *información de méritos y servicios* was a fixed genre that used a specific structure and vocabulary, it relied on witnesses to collaborate and orchestrate a certain representation before an audience, exposing a desire on the part of the ex-captive to be received favourably by the public.

The *Información de Argel* consists of introductory statements by Miguel de Cervantes, Juan Gil, and Pedro de Ribera, a questionnaire of twenty-five items composed by the former captive, followed by the witnesses' responses, and finally concluding with Juan Gil's and Pedro de Ribera's approbation. However, as Goodwin has suggested, if we read the questionnaire not just item by item but rather by interspersing the witnesses' responses after each question, flipping back and forth in the written transcript, "the theatricality of the hearing in front of Fray Juan Gil comes alive and we start to get a sense of drama, a drama orchestrated by Cervantes with the manifest purpose of presenting an image of himself to the Crown."[51] In effect, the theatricality of these public presentations, more in tune with how it may have actually taken place in Algiers, becomes more apparent by reading the *información* in this way than if we just read the resulting transcript in linear fashion. Furthermore, intimately tied to the ex-captive's performance is the question of verisimilitude and truth, a question that, as we saw, also emerges through the spectators' responses to the other Cervantine performances of captivity discussed in this chapter.[52] In Sebastián de Covarrubias's definition of *información*, he notes that it is "la relación que se hace al juez o a otra persona del hecho de la verdad" (the report that one gives to a judge or another person about the truth of the matter).[53] This "truth" is precisely what each witness in Cervantes's *Información* aims to authenticate orally with affirming statements repetitively beginning with "it is true that."[54] This sentiment is later echoed by Juan Gil in his closing statement, asserting the truthfulness of the hearing, including that all the witnesses are "personas de honra y de verdad ... y que sus testimonios no dirían sino la verdad en todo lo que han dicho y jurado" (people of honour and truth ... and that their testimonies would only tell the truth in everything they have said and sworn), finally validating the integrity of the whole process.[55]

This insistence on truth in the performance of captivity is obviously linked to the captives' anxieties and need to prove themselves before an evaluative public. Cervantes's *Información*, for example, documents his desire to present his behaviour as a captive in Algiers in a positive light in order to receive personal favour from the Crown.[56] These notarized affidavits were not required but were common practice for Christian captives who returned to Spain from slavery in other parts of the Muslim Mediterranean. Spanish authorities might view these captives with some suspicion if they could not present a clean image of their character during their time living among adherents of other religious beliefs.[57] At such a precarious moment of a captive's return and reintegration into Spanish society, the social consequences of not presenting a credible narrative or being believed would be too great a risk. The *Información de Argel*, thus, can be understood as a bureaucratic document that offers proof of Cervantes's exemplary behaviour in Algiers as an act of self-fashioning to protect him from possible accusations in an attempt to be received favourably by the Crown.[58] Reading these real-life public presentations and oral interrogations as performances, alongside the theatrical acts embedded in Cervantes's prose narrative, reveals the performative nature of portraying captivity and liberation to the early modern public. The spectators are instrumental in developing their narrative and identity, validating or contesting their story, and exposing the verisimilitude (or lack thereof) and historical truth of their presentation. Therefore, the episodes of Maese Pedro's puppet show, the false captives, and "The Captive's Tale" function as rehearsals to the very real world of Mediterranean captivity that was staged daily, uncovering the power of the captive audience to make meaning of these experiences.

NOTES

1 Stackhouse affirms that *El trato de Argel* was performed around 1584 but not published until 1784 ("Beyond Performance," 8). However, other scholars have suggested slightly earlier or later dates for the performance, including 1583 (Garcés, "Introduction," 42) and 1585 (García Martín, "Empathy," 141). On Algiers as a Mediterranean corsair capital, see Garcés, "Introduction."

2 Cervantes, "Prólogo," 12. All translations are my own, except when citing from Cervantes's *Don Quixote*. For this text, I have used Edith Grossman's English translation.

3 Rey Hazas, "Las comedias."

4 Indeed, Cervantes published his *Ocho comedias* (1615) without having them first performed on the early modern Spanish stage. *Los baños de Argel* was later adapted and staged in 1980 in Madrid by playwright Francisco Nieva, and *La gran sultana* was first performed in 1992 by the Compañía Nacional de Teatro Clásico. See Garcés, *Cervantes in Algiers*, 130, 281–2n. *El gallardo español* debuted in the summer of 1959, presented

by Georges Robert D'Eshougues and the Stage d'Art Dramatique in Oran. See Muñoz Caravantes, "Cincuenta años," 162; and Abi-Ayad, "Cervantes," 151.

5 Goffman, *Presentation of Self*, xi–76.

6 Vitkus, *Piracy*, 34. Levisi and Martínez also touch upon the interplay between the oral and written accounts of soldiers, some of whom were captives. See Levisi, "Golden Age Autobiography," 114; and Martínez, *Front Lines*, 40–53.

7 Bunes and Barchino, "Diego Galán," 15–16.

8 For information on these reports and the oral interrogations, I have relied on Sáez's critical introduction to Cervantes's *Información de Argel*, along with Tarruell's and Folger's studies. See Sáez, "Introducción"; Tarruell, "Memorias de cautivos"; Tarruell, "Prisoners of War"; and Folger, "Es benemérito." In Cervantes's case, in particular, his *Información*, which was drawn up in Algiers between 10 and 22 October 1580, reveals the oral character and polyphonic nature of the text, with all but one of his witnesses appearing in person before the scribe and redeemer. See Sáez, "Introducción," 37, 51.

9 Martínez Torres, *Prisioneros*, 99–105; Hershenzon, *Captive Sea*, 46, 89; and Friedman, *Spanish Captives*, 163.

10 Lozano-Renieblas, "El *mal latín*," 441.

11 Roach, "Culture and Performance," 46.

12 Bennett, *Theatre Audiences*, 21.

13 Rancière, *Emancipated Spectator*, 13.

14 Connor (Swietlicki), "*Preceptistas*," 426. Complementary to these studies is Bruce Burningham's *Radical Theatricality*, where he focuses on the dialogue between performers and spectators, specifically within the context of what he calls "jongleuresque performance."

15 Forcione, *Cervantes*, 172. See also Harrison, *La composición*, 101; Requejo Carrió, "De cómo se guisa una fábula," 873–4n; and Rupp, *Heroic Forms*, 192–3, for other perspectives on how Cervantes explores the question of verisimilitude, comparing the episode of Maese Pedro in *Don Quixote* with that of the counterfeit captives in the *Persiles*.

16 Garcés, *Cervantes in Algiers*, 12.

17 Cervantes, *Don Quijote*, 2.25, 234; *Don Quixote*, 624.

18 Cervantes, *Don Quijote*, 2.25, 239; *Don Quixote*, 628.

19 Brisset, "Imágenes del rapto," 206; and Ynduráin, "Estudio preliminar," lxii.

20 Burningham, "Jongleuresque Dialogue," 181.

21 Cervantes, *Don Quijote*, 2.26, 244; *Don Quixote*, 631.

22 It is worth noting that even the very act of scavenging for information to make the show more plausible also contributes to the performative nature of this episode, since the reader can imagine Maese Pedro rehearsing how

he will act and what he will stay to the villagers to obtain the information for his show.

23 Haley, "Narrator," 163.

24 Garcés, *Cervantes in Algiers*.

25 Wilson, "Chivalry," 250.

26 Carlson, "Theatre Audiences," 85–6.

27 Cervantes, *Don Quijote*, 2.26, 240; *Don Quixote*, 629.

28 Voigt, "La 'historia verdadera,'" 660, 670.

29 Cervantes, *Los trabajos de Persiles y Sigismunda*, 526–7. Various scholars have discussed this passage in relation to literary debates on verisimilitude and fiction. Among them, see Forcione, *Cervantes*, 170–86; Requejo Carrió, "De cómo se guisa una fábula"; Robbins, "False Captives"; and Voigt, "La 'historia verdadera,'" 664–6.

30 For an illuminating overview of how the rubric of "true histories" crops up in a wide variety of other early modern writings in Spanish from both the Old World and the New, see Gaylord, "True History." Within the particular context of captivity narratives, see Vitkus, "Barbary Captivity Narratives"; and Voigt, "La 'historia verdadera.'"

31 Forcione, *Cervantes*, 170. For readings of this episode as an *entremés*, see especially Casalduero, *Sentido*, 216–19; Forcione, *Cervantes*, 170–86; and Zimic, *Cuentos*, 139–47.

32 Cervantes, *Los trabajos de Persiles y Sigismunda*, 528.

33 Cervantes, 529.

34 Cervantes, 538.

35 Fuchs, *Mimesis and Empire*, 162.

36 Cervantes, *Los trabajos de Persiles y Sigismunda*, 531, 533, 536.

37 Cervantes, 535, 538.

38 Cervantes, *Don Quijote*, 1.38, 472; *Don Quixote*, 333.

39 Martín Morán, "Los escenarios teatrales," 38.

40 Cervantes, *Don Quijote*, 1.38, 472.

41 For a summary of the debates concerning how early modern publics went to "hear" versus "see" *comedias*, see Frenk, "Lectores y oidores," 71–3. For another illuminating example of how the verb "hear" (*oír*) and its derivative forms are used in *Don Quixote* to refer to seeing/being a spectator in the adventure of the lions, see Garcés, *Cervantes in Algiers*, 131, 158–9.

42 Cervantes, *Don Quijote*, 1.39, 482; *Don Quixote*, 340.

43 On the interruption of the captive's tale, see also Garcés, who significantly reads it as an inauguration to a "new chapter of the novel, one that includes the Algerian section of this tale, marked by the surname *Saavedra* and the apparition of the legendary Zoraida (*DQ* I, 40). The poems that mourn the fall of Tunis and La Goleta in *La historia del cautivo* thus point to

the frontier between autobiography and fiction, a frontier highlighted by a structural break in the narrative" (Garcés, *Cervantes in Algiers*, 220).

44 Cervantes, *Don Quijote*, 1.40, 483; *Don Quixote*, 342.

45 Garcés, *Cervantes in Algiers*, 223–6.

46 Cervantes, *Don Quijote*, 1.41, 513; *Don Quixote*, 368.

47 Johnson, "Soldier's Shame," 155.

48 Cervantes, *Don Quijote*, 1.38, 472; *Don Quixote*, 333.

49 For a consideration of how the material conditions, including who the spectator is, where they sit, and how they listen, among other factors, could influence each performance within the context of early modern Spain, see Connor (Swietlicki), *"Preceptistas."*

50 For another example of a captive's attempt to adapt his public presentation to a particular audience, see Rodríguez-Rodríguez, *Letras liberadas*, 64–5.

51 Goodwin, *Spain*, 201–2.

52 For other examples of how Cervantes explores the intersection of verisimilitude and truth in relation to plays on captivity, including *El gallardo español*, *Los baños de Argel*, and *La gran sultana*, see Sáez, "Introducción," 86.

53 Covarrubias, *Tesoro*, 1098.

54 The sixth witness, for example, uses "truth" ("verdad") nearly two dozen times in his testimony (Cervantes, *Información de Argel*, 169–76).

55 Cervantes, 205.

56 Cervantes, 121. Additionally, Garcés shows how Cervantes's *Información* attempts to protect him from Juan Blanco de Paz's "slander campaign" against him. See Garcés, *Cervantes in Algiers*, 99–106.

57 Garcés, 99.

58 Sáez, "Introducción," 67. On this subject, Carroll B. Johnson has proposed that the *Información de Argel* is Cervantes's "first attempt at self-fashioning," as well as his first work of prose fiction. See Johnson, "Algerian Economy," 211.

REFERENCES

Abi-Ayad, Ahmed. "Cervantes, Argel y el Mediterráneo." *eHumanista/ Cervantes*, no. 2 (2013): 146–55.

Bennett, Susan. *Theatre Audiences: A Theory of Production and Reception*. 2nd ed. London: Routledge, 2003.

Brisset, Demetrio E. "Imágenes del rapto de la doncella en rituales festivos ibéricos." *Revista de Dialectología y Tradiciones Populares* 43, no. 2 (2003): 201–22. https://doi.org/10.3989/rdtp.2003.v58.i2.156.

Bunes, Miguel Ángel de, and Matías Barchino. "Diego Galán, un cautivo de Toledo contemporáneo a Miguel de Cervantes." In *Relación del cautiverio y libertad de Diego Galán,* edited by Miguel Ángel de Bunes and Matías Barchino, 9–23. Seville: Espuela de Plata, 2011.

Burningham, Bruce R. "Jongleuresque Dialogue, Radical Theatricality, and Maese Pedro's Puppet Show." *Cervantes* 23, no. 1 (2003): 165–200.

Burningham, Bruce R. *Radical Theatricality: Jongleuresque Performance on the Early Spanish Stage.* West Lafayette, IN: Purdue University Press, 2007.

Carlson, Marvin. "Theatre Audiences and the Reading of Performance." In *Interpreting the Theatrical Past: Essays in the Historiography of Performance,* edited by Thomas Postlewait and Bruce A. McConachie, 82–98. Iowa City: University of Iowa Press, 1989.

Casalduero, Joaquín. *Sentido y forma de* Los trabajos de Persiles y Sigismunda. Buenos Aires: Editorial Sudamericana, 1947.

Cervantes Saavedra, Miguel de. *Don Quijote de la Mancha.* Edited by Luis Andrés Murillo. 5th ed. 2 vols. Madrid: Castalia, 1978.

Cervantes Saavedra, Miguel de. *Don Quixote.* Translated by Edith Grossman. New York: HarperCollins, 2003.

Cervantes Saavedra, Miguel de. *Información de Argel.* Edited by Adrián J. Sáez. Madrid: Cátedra, 2019.

Cervantes Saavedra, Miguel de. "Prólogo al lector." In *Miguel de Cervantes: Comedias y tragedias,* by Miguel de Cervantes Saavedra, edited by Luis Gómez Canseco, 1:9–15. Madrid: Real Academia Española, 2015.

Cervantes Saavedra, Miguel de. *Los trabajos de Persiles y Sigismunda.* Edited by Carlos Romero Muñoz. Madrid: Cátedra, 2004.

Connor (Swietlicki), Catherine. "The *Preceptistas* and beyond: Spectators Making 'Meanings' in the *Corral de Comedias.*" *Hispania* 82, no. 3 (1999): 417–28. https://doi.org/10.2307/346281.

Covarrubias Horozco, Sebastián de. *Tesoro de la lengua castellana o española.* Edited by Ignacio Arellano and Rafael Zafra. Madrid: Universidad de Navarra and Iberoamericana Vervuert, 2006.

Folger, Robert. "'Es benemérito para cualquier oficio': Cervantes interpelado." In *Actas selectas del VII Congreso Internacional de la Asociación de Cervantistas,* edited by Christoph Strosetzki, 353–62. Madrid: Centro de Estudios Cervantinos, 2011.

Forcione, Alban K. *Cervantes, Aristotle, and the* Persiles. Princeton, NJ: Princeton University Press, 1970.

Frenk, Margit. "Lectores y oidores en el Siglo de Oro." In *Entre la voz y el silencio: La lectura en tiempos de Cervantes,* 48–85. Mexico City: Fondo de Cultura Económica, 2005.

Friedman, Ellen G. *Spanish Captives in North Africa in the Early Modern Age.* Madison: University of Wisconsin Press, 1983.

Fuchs, Barbara. *Mimesis and Empire: The New World, Islam, and European Identities.* Cambridge: Cambridge University Press, 2001.

Garcés, María Antonia. *Cervantes in Algiers: A Captive's Tale*. Nashville: Vanderbilt University Press, 2002.

Garcés, María Antonia. "Introduction." In *An Early Modern Dialogue with Islam: Antonio de Sosa's* Topography of Algiers *(1612)*, edited by María Antonia Garcés, translated by Diana de Armas Wilson, 1–78. Notre Dame: University of Notre Dame Press, 2011.

García Martín, Elena. "Empathy, Catharsis, and Altruism in Cervantes's *Los tratos de Argel*, Read as a Redemptorist Play." *Cervantes* 38, no. 2 (2018): 129–64. https://doi.org/10.1353/cer.2018.0022.

Gaylord, Mary M. "The True History of Early Modern Writing in Spanish: Some American Reflections." *Modern Language Quarterly* 57, no. 2 (1996): 213–25. https://doi.org/10.1215/00267929-57-2-213.

Goffman, Erving. *The Presentation of Self in Everyday Life*. Garden City, NY: Doubleday, 1959.

Goodwin, Robert. *Spain: The Centre of the World, 1519–1682*. New York: Bloomsbury, 2015.

Haley, George. "The Narrator in *Don Quijote*: Maese Pedro's Puppet Show." *MLN* 80, no. 2 (1965): 145–65. https://doi.org/10.2307/3042607.

Harrison, Stephen. *La composición de* Los trabajos de Persiles y Sigismunda. Madrid: Pliegos, 1993.

Hershenzon, Daniel. *The Captive Sea: Slavery, Communication, and Commerce in Early Modern Spain and the Mediterranean*. Philadelphia: University of Pennsylvania Press, 2018.

Johnson, Carroll B. "The Algerian Economy and Cervantes' First Work of Narrative Fiction." In *Braudel Revisited: The Mediterranean World, 1600–1800*, edited by Gabriel Piterberg, Teofilo F. Ruiz, and Geoffrey Symcox, 207–28. Toronto: University of Toronto Press, 2010.

Johnson, Paul Michael. "A Soldier's Shame: The Specter of Captivity in 'La historia del cautivo.'" *Cervantes* 31, no. 2 (2011): 153–84. https://doi .org/10.1353/cer.2011.0022.

Levisi, Margarita. "Golden Age Autobiography: The Soldiers." In *Autobiography in Early Modern Spain*, edited by Nicholas Spadaccini and Jenaro Talens, 97–117. Minneapolis: Prisma Institute, 1988.

Lozano-Renieblas, Isabel. "El *mal latín* del episodio de los falsos cautivos del *Persiles*." In *Docta y sabia Atenea: Studia in honorem Lía Schwartz*, edited by Sagrario López Poza, Nieves Pena Sueiro, Mariano de la Campa, Isabel Pérez Cuenca, Susan Byrne, and Almudena Vidorreta, 433–44. Coruña: Universidade da Coruña, 2019.

Martín Morán, José Manuel. "Los escenarios teatrales del *Quijote*." *Anales Cervantinos*, no. 24 (1986): 27–46.

Martínez, Miguel. *Front Lines: Soldiers' Writing in the Early Modern Hispanic World*. Philadelphia: University of Pennsylvania Press, 2016.

Martínez Torres, José Antonio. *Prisioneros de los infieles: Vida y rescate de los cautivos cristianos en el Mediterráneo musulmán [siglos XVI–XVII]*. Barcelona: Bellaterra, 2004.

Muñoz Caravantes, Manuel. "Cincuenta años de teatro cervantino." *Anales Cervantinos*, no. 28 (1990): 155–90. https://doi.org/10.3989 /anacervantinos.1990.434.

Rancière, Jacques. *The Emancipated Spectator*. Translated by Gregory Elliott. London: Verso, 2009.

Requejo Carrió, Marie-Blanche. "De cómo se guisa una fábula: El episodio de los falsos cautivos en el Persiles (III, X)." In *Peregrinamente peregrinos: Actas del V Congreso Internacional de la Asociación de Cervantistas*, edited by Alicia Villar Lecumberri, 1:861–77. Palma de Mallorca: Asociación de Cervantistas, 2004.

Rey Hazas, Antonio. "Las comedias de cautivos de Cervantes." In *Los imperios orientales en el teatro del Siglo de Oro*, edited by Felipe Pedraza Jiménez and Rafael González Cañal, 29–56. Almagro: Universidad de Castilla-La Mancha, 1994.

Roach, Joseph. "Culture and Performance in the Circum-Atlantic World." In *Performativity and Performance*, edited by Andrew Parker and Eve Kosofsky Sedgwick, 45–63. New York: Routledge, 1995.

Robbins, Jeremy. "The False Captives and the Representation of History and Fiction in *Los trabajos de Persiles y Sigismunda*." *Bulletin of Spanish Studies* 81, nos. 4–5 (2004): 627–39. https://doi.org/10.1080/1475382042000254427.

Rodríguez-Rodríguez, Ana M. *Letras liberadas: Cautiverio, escritura y subjetividad en el Mediterráneo de la época imperial española*. Madrid: Visor Libros, 2013.

Rupp, Stephen. *Heroic Forms: Cervantes and the Literature of War*. Toronto: University of Toronto Press, 2014.

Sáez, Adrián J. "Introducción." In Miguel de Cervantes Saavedra, *Información de Argel*, edited by Adrián J. Sáez, 9–115. Madrid: Cátedra, 2019.

Stackhouse, Kenneth A. "Beyond Performance: Cervantes's Algerian Plays, *El trato de Argel* and *Los baños de Argel*." *Bulletin of the Comediantes* 52, no. 2 (2000): 7–30. https://doi.org/10.1353/boc.2000.0014.

Tarruell, Cecilia. "Memorias de cautivos, 1575–1609." In *Memòria personal: Una altra manera de llegir la història*, edited by Oscar Jané, Eulàlia Miralles, and Ignasi Fernández, 83–97. Barcelona: Bellaterra, 2013.

Tarruell, Cecilia. "Prisoners of War, Captives or Slaves? The Christian Prisoners of Tunis and La Goleta in 1574." In *Micro-spatial Histories of Global Labour*, edited by Christian G. De Vito and Anne Gerritsen, 95–122. London: Palgrave, 2017.

Vitkus, Daniel J. "Barbary Captivity Narratives from Early Modern England: Truth Claims and the (Re)construction of Authority." In *La guerre de course en récits. Terrains, corpus, series*, edited by Anne Duprat, 119–30. Paris: Projet CORSO, 2010.

Vitkus, Daniel J, ed. and comp. *Piracy, Slavery, and Redemption: Barbary Captivity Narratives from Early Modern England*. New York: Columbia University Press, 2001.

Voigt, Lisa. "La 'historia verdadera' del cautiverio y del naufragio en los imperios ibéricos." *Revista Iberoamericana* 75, no. 228 (2009): 657–74. https://doi.org/10.5195/REVIBEROAMER.2009.6601.

Wilson, Diana de Armas. "Chivalry to the Rescue: The Dynamics of Liberation in *Don Quijote*." *Cervantes* 27, no. 1 (2007): 249–65.

Ynduráin, Francisco. "Estudio preliminar." In *Obras completas de Miguel de Cervantes*, vol. 2, *Obras dramáticas*, edited by Francisco Ynduráin, vii–lxxvii. Madrid: Atlas, 1962.

Zimic, Stanislav. *Cuentos y episodios del* Persiles: *de la isla bárbara a una apoteosis del autor*. Pontevedra: Mirabel, 2005.

10 Painting into Theatre: "The Suicide of Lucretia" as a *tableau vivant* in *El curioso impertinente*

MERCEDES ALCALÁ GALÁN

In *El día de fiesta por la mañana y por la noche,* Juan de Zabaleta recounts a lady's visit to an elegant, luxurious house. After passing through a rich hall and a room with copies (*traslados*) of paintings, she comes to a third room dominated by a magnificent Flemish tapestry eloquently described as follows: "Entra luego en una sala que recibe la luz por cristales que están dando luz a la vivísima y hermosísima representación que hace una tapicería flamenca. En ella hallan los ojos una comedia sin voz de la historia que propone" (Then she enters a room that receives light from windows that illuminate the most vivid and beautiful representation made by a Flemish tapestry. Her eyes find in it a voiceless *comedia* of the story it tells).[1] The fact that the tapestry is considered a "representation" and a "voiceless *comedia*" of "the story it tells" and that this produces a theatre for the eyes is, it seems to me, an exact rendering of how tapestries – as well as paintings – can condense a story previously known to the viewer into a static scene.

This chapter reflects upon the dramatic dimension of painting and its ability to represent an entire story ("the story it tells") in a single scene that evokes it rather than summarizes it. Cervantes exploits this evocative capacity of painting in various ways. Indeed, although his narrative diversely combines theatricality and iconography, in this essay I want to explore the poetic technique of the *tableau vivant* in his works: pictorial "quotes" in which visual art is conjured up through the evocation of images whose motifs were represented obsessively by countless early modern artists. I will focus primarily on the analysis of "the suicide of Lucretia." This classical motif is staged in the passage from the interpolated novella *El curioso impertinente* in which Camila pretends to attempt suicide, knowing that she is being observed by Anselmo (*Don Quixote,* 1.35), in a splendidly metatheatrical scene. Other clear instances of *tableaux vivants,* or the staging of paintings whose theatrical character is marked by the presence of spectators within the narrative itself, include "Venus and Mars caught by Vulcan," depicted at the moment when Carrizales comes upon Isabela and Loaysa asleep after making love in the Porras de la Cámara version of *El celoso extremeño*; and "Susanna and the elders": represented in the scene where Dorotea bathes her feet in the river while being observed by the priest, the barber, and Cardenio, who are hidden behind bushes (*Don Quixote*, 1.28). I will refer later on briefly to the last two examples in order to contextualize the analysis of "the suicide of Lucretia" regarding the Cervantine literary technique of the *tableau vivant*. In these three cases Cervantes engages with the pictorial culture of his time through the staging of motifs represented in art, creating "pictures" that are acted out. The visuality of this "theatre of paintings" is reinforced because the narrative not only incorporates these pictorial quotes that were easily recognizable by the readers of his time, but also investigates and deepens the perception and reactions of the viewers of such scenes within the narrative.

The *tableau vivant*: Painting, Theatre, and Narrative

The genre of the *tableau vivant* reached its apogee at the end of the nineteenth century and consists of the staging of works of art with stationary actors who imitate paintings or sculptures "live." The fact that this practice was only belatedly considered a genre does not mean that inert staging of works of art did not exist much earlier in history. For example, in a letter dated 9 February 1813 addressed to the art historian Heinrich Meyer, Goethe describes the *tableau vivant* as "a hermaphrodite between painting and theatre."[2] Although it was of course not called by this name, there is documentation of its use since the Middle Ages,[3] and abundant evidence shows that it was a common practice during the early modern era, owing, for example, to the great public festivities that accompanied royal entrances.[4] The *tableau vivant* is an inherently paradoxical form of theatre, as it plays with the static nature of the work of art while capturing the essence of a story in a single scene. In the early modern era, plastic art is by definition inanimate, atemporal, and non-sequential, despite being able to "tell stories" in a profoundly different way than the arts based on words. Theatre, on the contrary, is a temporal art based on the representation of plays that tell stories in a sequential (though not necessarily chronological) order. The *tableau vivant* is constituted precisely in the impossible tension between plastic art and theatre. In itself, the staging of a painting is intriguing because it makes the permanent, ephemeral, and the inert, animate.

In the Cervantine passages mentioned above, the verbal images representing paintings (that in turn depict well-known stories) are what I call *tableaux vivants*: they are the verbal representation of acted paintings, despite the apparent anachronism of this term. Their interest resides in the fact that the characters do not "act" by dramatizing the story of Susanna and the elders – or that of Venus and Mars caught by Vulcan or that of Lucretia's suicide – according to original or contemporary textual sources; instead, what is dramatized in a *tableau vivant* is any painting that represents any of these three stories. It is a back-and-forth ekphrasis in which the relationship between the literary and the visual is interwoven in an extremely complex way. In the three selected passages, the literary imagination feeds on the pictorial imagination, and vice versa. The premise here is that Cervantes's characters dramatize the pictorial representation of a story in an intertextual twist in which painting and literature are intertwined.

Cervantes does not stage specific works of art but instead evokes the countless paintings that represent these motifs. The recognizability of this ekphrastic technique on the part of readers is essential for Cervantes's poetic artifice to have literary meaning and efficacy. Indeed, for the unannounced citation of a pictorial motif to be valid, it must be identified as such by the reader. As Fernando de la Flor affirms, the seventeenth century is ruled by an ocularcentrism that extends to all facets of life. However, I believe that the roots of the eminently philosophic culture of early modernity were firmly established by the sixteenth century.[5] The level of visual and artistic culture possessed by Cervantes's contemporaries was more than sufficient to enable them to identify the *tableaux vivants* inserted into his narrative. These pictorial quotes would have been recognized as such without difficulty.

To understand this Cervantine narrative technique, we must bear in mind that, despite the popular classes' lack of formal instruction, forms of visual culture were continually present in everyday life. The men and women of early modern Spain were familiar with an essentially codified culture in which iconography and symbols as well as references to mythology, sacred history, and the classical world were habitually displayed in public festivals and in civil and religious ceremonies. The manifestations of this highly codified visual culture were present in a myriad of heterogeneous spaces and situations such as the façades of palaces and churches, the triumphal arches erected on special occasions – royal entrances, for example – and in processions that exhibited a rich iconography.[6] When dealing with popular agency in the forms of visual culture of the Golden Age, Javier Portús and Miguel Morán Turina introduce the concept of "semantic discrimination" according to which all classes and estates of society have access to the same manifestations of the dominant culture. All enjoy the same theatrical works, the same public festivals, the same rituals, and even the same works of art – although with different degrees of understanding depending on their social and cultural level. It is essential to note that there was no cultural alienation to a degree that prevented the participation, within limitations, of the popular classes in a shared culture in which the recreation of motifs belonging to the classical tradition and the Bible were part of the common heritage.

It is also essential to recognize the importance of painting in Golden Age culture. In fact, men and women of Cervantes's time were immersed in a world devoted to art. Morán Turina affirms in this regard that "por pobre que fuera, no había hogar en aquellos tiempos que no estuviera adornado con pinturas" (no matter how poor it was, there was no home in those days that was not adorned with paintings)[7] to explain that

en el siglo XVII, la pintura estaba tan en la calle que en ella, en los aledaños de la plaza Mayor, de la puerta del Sol o de la plaza del Palacio, los madrileños podían comprar cuadros que se vendían en las aceras colgados de las paredes de las iglesias o de algunos edificios notables.

(in the seventeenth century, painting was so present in the streets that in them, in the vicinity of the Plaza Mayor, the Puerta del Sol, or the Plaza del Palacio, the people of Madrid could buy paintings that were sold on the sidewalk, hanging on the walls of churches or other important buildings.)[8]

Thus, in the era of Cervantes, works of art were not limited to those exhibited in churches and the ones that composed the great collections belonging to the monarchy and the nobility. Rather, in all towns of a certain size many art shops sold low-cost paintings of uneven quality that imitated the schools and artistic trends in vogue.

These paintings spanned all the genres of the time: devotional painting, portraits, still lifes, and landscapes, as well as representations of historical and mythological themes. For example, in *El donado hablador* Alonso de Alcalá Yáñez describes a shop painter in Toro who sold his mediocre paintings with secular themes at a low price:

Tenía costumbre de pintar la casa otomana, los emperadores romanos, los dioses de los antiguos. Y yo entonces ... reprehendía su trabajo y la vana curiosidad de algunos, diciéndole: «En verdad, señor, que no tanto me admiro de que vuesa merced pinte al Soldán, a Rosa su mujer, a Bayaceto, a Nero, a Julio César, a Júpiter y a Venus, sino de que haya tantos que los compren.»

(He would paint the Ottoman royal family, the Roman emperors, the gods of the ancients. And then I ... reprimanded his work and the vain curiosity of some paintings, saying: "In truth, sir, I am not so much amazed that you painted the sultan, his wife Rosa, Bayezid, Nero, Julius Caesar, Jupiter, and Venus, as that there are so many who buy them.")[9]

Indeed, the subjects painted by the great masters had become commonplace, almost banal, and easily recognizable. Another source of knowledge about historical or mythological painting was through *estampas* (prints) that were a cheap and widespread form of iconographic dissemination whose use was by no means limited to devotional purposes.[10] It is not necessary to dwell on the abundance of both literary and historical examples – for instance, those found among the items listed in wills – that attest to the familiarity with painting on the part of all social strata in the Golden Age.

The best window onto life in the Golden Age is the theatre. In this sense, the efficacy of Cervantes's *tableau vivant* technique in relation to his readers' ability to recognize pictorial citations is parallel to the use of art in the theatre, which also requires the public's active collaboration in order to function effectively. Both Emilio Orozco Díaz and Morán Turina have investigated art's presence in Golden Age theatre where, as is well known, paintings appear repeatedly, often as a central plot device. At times a lady's portrait is referenced but does not appear onstage.[11] Hence a painting is not seen by the spectators but, by being mentioned, needs no long description and serves to advance the dramatic action. The subject matter depicted in a painting that is spoken about can almost be automatically incorporated into the story. At other times, however, a painting does appear onstage. Curiously, in these cases the most common stage directions simply state the subject of the painting and add "como le pintan" (as painted). Morán Turina writes that the stock phrase

«como le pintan» es completamente usual en las acotaciones de las obras de teatro. La tradición iconográfica de la pintura – esa pintura que ... se encontraba en la calle y era objeto de discusión frecuente en la vida cotidiana– constituía un punto de referencia fundamental a la hora de concebir la propia acción dramática del teatro.

("as painted" is entirely normal in stage directions. The iconographic tradition of painting – the sort of painting that ... was seen in the streets and was the object of much discussion in daily life – constituted a fundamental point of reference when conceiving the dramatic action of theatre itself.)[12]

For his part, Emilio Orozco affirms that "[la imagen] se acomoda siempre a *cómo se pinta*, según nos dicen las acotaciones" ([the image] always corresponds to *how it's painted*, as the stage directions tell us).[13] Thus the pictorial image ceases to be a unique object, becoming instead a generic object according to the subject depicted. Theatre companies knew exactly what authors meant when they asked for a painting on a specific subject to appear onstage. The inventories made for wills are likewise explicit as they describe paintings by theme: a penitent Magdalene, a Venus and Adonis, a Mars.... This could be seen as an indication of what José Antonio Maravall characterizes as mass Baroque culture, which he describes as tawdry and "caracterizada por el establecimiento de tipos, con repetición estandardizada de géneros" (characterized by the establishment of types, with a standardized repetition of genres).[14]

Historical, mythological, or religious painting generally does not offer information but instead interprets, evokes, and re-presents a motif or theme that belongs to a cultural heritage that is renewed and activated with new works. Therefore, painting cannot be understood without a shared hermeneutical culture. For this reason, it is unnecessary to refer to a specific painting but to a motif repeatedly represented in art, reproduced in collections, copied ("trasladado") from the great masters and imitated in the painters' workshops and street stalls. In other words, there existed a collective memory of the conventional representations of those motifs or stories that entered into a codification assimilated by the popular use and consumption of paintings.

In both art and theatre – and especially in their intersection – we can discern the scope of Baroque visual culture among the popular classes. Cervantes's prose would not be possible without those two talents acquired by the readers of his time: familiarity with art and the skill of knowing how to be spectators of plays in which one often had to imagine what was being mentioned or suggested but not described. Theatre and the omnipresence of an intense visual environment enabled the men and women of the early modern period to become an audience prepared for the active use of the imagination.

Moreover, in a theatrical representation, the audience's collective experience generates an insurmountable kind of energy that is impossible to replicate by other means. For this reason, in these Cervantine *tableaux vivants* there are always characters who act, even without knowing it, and others who witness that representation and are absorbed by it. The gaze of the characters who compose an audience within the work is essential for the reader to activate an imaginary gaze upon these acted paintings. In the three scenes I mentioned, the analogy with the corresponding painting is as important as the fact that there are internal spectators through whom we, the readers, access the *tableau vivant*. There is an instant in which the scene coalesces in the retina of the character who looks on. Thus, in each of the three examples there is an added dimension in the action, one as essential as it is subtle, that is marked by the gaze that registers the scene and reacts with wonder. The amazement generated among the characters who observe is the emotional framework that isolates the *tableau vivant* from the rest of the action and connects it in a distinctive way to the reader.

These instances exploit the fact that painting has the uncanny ability to tell a story through a structural synecdoche that is exploited narratively, since the images it represents conjure an entire story. By using the technique of the pictorial quotation, Cervantes activates the power of art to make present, to evoke without narrating, without describing. These dramatic-pictorial quotes are more or less brief moments in which there is a transitory confluence between the quote and the context. Afterwards, the scene moves on and the plots separate and diverge irrevocably.

The collusion of art and theatre that occurs in the *tableau vivant* invokes and expands the limits of the artistic image, at the same time as it reveals art's inherent misalignment with the reality it imitates. In art the inert image fantasizes about the appearance of life it offers. The unalterable surface of the painting as object permanently captures the illusion of the ephemeral. In this regard W.J.T. Mitchell asserts that the image establishes dialectical relationships in various directions that go beyond the fact of being contemplated:

> It helps us to see why vision is never a one-way street, but a multiple intersection teeming with dialectical images, why the child's doll has a playful half-life on the borders of the animate and inanimate, and why the fossil traces of extinct life are resurrected in the beholder's imagination. It makes it clear why the questions to ask about images are not just "what do they mean?" or "what do they do?" but "what is the secret of their vitality?" and "what do they want?"[15]

For this reason, Cervantes's use of the image is critical due to its potential complexity and capacity to create connections, meanings, and relationships on different narrative levels. Thus, the dramatization of painting not only *does not* alleviate this estrangement between the inert and the living but also intensifies it, since the meta-representation in this geminated ekphrasis ends with a simulacrum radically contrary to that of artistic representation. Hence the work of art crystallizes its representation of the animate in an image while, paradoxically, its dramatization in the *tableau vivant* depends on the pretence that a living art – theatre – becomes a manifestation of the inert.

In chapters 55–6 of Rabelais's *Fourth Book*, we are told how Pantagruel's expedition when travelling through the confines of the glacial sea comes across the frozen words of a battle that occurred the year before at the onset of winter. The words, made of ice of different colours, as if they were crystals, randomly explode into sound as the adventurers melt them in their hands. I mention this suggestive image here to reflect on the nature of the pictorial quote in the three Cervantine scenes.

These *tableaux vivants* appear quite fleetingly in the narrative in which a painting or tapestry is dramatized. And in those moments, references to a story that is part of the pictorial culture of the time are "unfrozen."[16] The technique of the *tableau vivant* creates a certain cognitive dissonance in the reader-viewer since the pictorial quote refers to a story that is related to the plot through a complex representational game. The three stories that concern us are powerfully evoked through the visual-theatrical citation of the *tableaux vivants*. There is a moment when the plot and the story coincide, only to diverge later. Thus, for example, Venus, Mars, and Vulcan follow the sequence that their myth dictates while Carrizales, Loaysa, and Isabela embrace a different destiny; Lucretia's suicide extols her as a moral example while Camila will face her own destiny, just as Susanna is dragged into the abyss by those who contemplate her while, in contrast, it is the other people's gaze that will put Dorotea on the path of her reparation.

Nonetheless, the pictorial quote creates an identification, a similarity between the myth and the incidental existence, as it were, of the characters in the novel, granting them greater gravity by contagion, a kinship with a story capable of brushing against the archetype and receding from banality. The overlap between the painting's representation and the story that the characters live is another of Cervantes's techniques that enrich his literary discourse by means of connotation. Rabelais's frozen words serve as a simile since they are images archived by the collective imagination that unfreeze when acted out, momentarily connecting the vicissitudes of the characters' lives with a mythical story. The analogy with frozen words is reinforced by the fleeting nature of the acted image, just as the sound that erupts from ice crystals fades in an instant. This image also seems very apt to me because it expresses the liquid and immaterial character of sound and can be transposed into the immateriality of the *tableau vivant*, which, unlike a painting, yields up its permanence to become a temporal art.

These acted pictures profoundly alter the surface of the text as they inlay a different sort of discourse. On the other hand, the fact that they evoke paintings through a theatricalization inserted into the narrative creates a layering of different discourses, each with its own rules – the pictorial, the dramatic, and the narrative – that do not appear in sequence but are overlapping and simultaneous. In these quotes the resulting depth is not only conceptual but also discursive. The *tableaux vivants* involve a synergy of three discourses that are expressed as part of the narrative but are tangentially independent of it since their limits are always visible. We could use the metaphor of the frame of a painting to understand that, in effect, there is an interruption in the narrative, that the action acquires a sudden density and that the scene is collected and framed in the retina of the characters who are watching. Bakhtin writes that quotes behave like people doing their job without knowing they are being watched.[17] By applying this statement to *tableaux vivants*, I do not mean that the characters dramatizing the painting are or are not aware of being observed but rather that the pictorial quote evokes a story that is essentially foreign to the context in which it is cited. When V.N. Vološinov refers to the cited speech, he remarks that it is "an utterance that was originally totally independent, complete in its construction, and lying outside the given context."[18] He explains that the quote is only partially assimilated to the characteristics of the text that cites it. Indeed, a quote is inside and outside the discourse, being an element alien to the main text as well as part of it. Vološinov stresses that what is interesting about the quote is not so much the information it conveys as the fact that an "active relation" is established between the quote and its context. An essential aspect of citation is that quote and context cannot be understood independently. Thus, the tone and sense of the quote are always affected by the tone and sense of the context, and vice versa.

In Cervantes's *tableaux vivants*, everything said thus far about the quotation not only is applicable but also intensified in relation to verbal quotations that evoke visual language. The visual and the verbal are never equivalent, and it is precisely this lack of equivalence that implies the untranslatability of one to the other. The untranslatable leaves empty spaces of interpretative freedom that are filled by the reading imagination. As we shall see, Cervantes takes advantage of the enormous narrative potential offered by the *tableaux vivants*. In this regard, Foucault writes:

> But the relation of language to painting is an infinite relation. It is not that words are imperfect, or that, confronted by the visible, they prove insuperably inadequate. Neither can be reduced to the other's terms: it is in vain that we say what we see; what we see never resides in what we say. And it is vain that we attempt to show, by the use of images, metaphors, or similes, what we are saying; the space where they achieve their splendour is not that deployed by our eyes but that defined by the sequential elements of syntax.[19]

Before turning to the analysis of the motif of "the suicide of Lucretia" as this essay's main example of *tableau vivant*, it is essential to emphasize the role that the use of images played in the creation of popular culture. Biblical, mythological, and historical stories that became commonplace in early modern society, despite their narrative character, were primarily disseminated thanks to images, to artistic representation. Literary criticism tends to identify only sources and textual influences when it analyses literary works, and leaves behind the formidable presence of a prominent visual culture in the Golden Age. It is impossible to understand the work of Cervantes without recognizing that there is a natural convergence between textual and iconographic sources that have been intertwined throughout history in a gigantic skein of shared knowledge transformed into cultural memory. Cervantes's *tableaux vivants* are a consequence of this: images told with words of an amazing capacity to be imagined, as if they were coloured spheres of ice that, when thawed, explode into visions that tell stories known to all.

Of the three passages identified as examples, I will analyse the motif of Lucretia's suicide in *El curioso impertinente*. However, as already said, in order to understand this as a Cervantine narrative technique it is important to offer a brief outline of the other two. The first one is the motif of Mars, Venus, and Vulcan. In the Porras de la Cámara manuscript version of *El celoso extremeño* (c. 1604), Isabela and Loaysa consummate their love affair, guarded by the *dueña* after the husband has been administered a soporific ointment.[20] There is a clear parallel with the story of the adultery of Venus and Mars, whose classical antecedents, according to Pablo Martín Llanos, are established from the intertextual relationships between the eighth canto of the *Odyssey* (8.266–366) and the two times that Ovid narrates this adulterous relationship between the goddess of love and the god of war in the *Ars amatoria* (2.561–90) and in *Metamorphoses* (4.167–89). According to the classical myth, Venus is married to the deformed Vulcan who spends all night working in his forge. The lovers are wary of Apollo, god of the sun who dislikes secrets, and for this reason they assign Alectrion as guardian to warn them before dawn arrives. One night Alectrion falls asleep, and Apollo discovers the adultery and tells Vulcan, who in revenge weaves an invisible net in which he traps the lovers while they sleep. Caught in the net, they are exposed to the ridicule of the other gods, although ultimately forgiven. Alectrion is turned into a rooster for his negligence and is condemned to announce the dawn every day.

This story would be one of the most frequently represented in the art of the period for its suggestive eroticism. Until the early seventeenth century, Botticelli, Piero di Cosimo, Titian (see figure 10.1), Veronese, Tintoretto, Lavinia Fontana, Agostino Carracci, and Carlo Saraceni, among many other artists, dealt with the motif. Undoubtedly the pictorial imagination of this epoch is present in the development of this Cervantine episode. As will be remembered, Isabela (as she is called in this earlier manuscript) and Loaysa fall asleep at dawn while the *dueña* – the Cervantine version of Alectrion who is charged with guarding them – also falls into a deep sleep. Carrizales, whom the text explicitly compares with Vulcan – "[C]on la rabia que el celoso Vulcano buscaba a su querida, dejó las odiosas plumas" (With the rage that jealous Vulcan searched for his beloved, left his hateful bed [feathers])[21] – finds the lovers asleep. This scene constitutes a full-blown *tableau vivant* that the reader sees through the husband's eyes:

[Y] de allí, andando con maravilloso silencio, llegó a la sala donde la dueña dormía, y no hallando allí a Isabela, se fue a el aposento donde la dueña tenía su estancia, y abriéndole queditamente *vio lo que nunca quisiera haber visto*. Vio a Isabela en brazos de Loaysa, durmiendo entrambos tan a sueño suelto, como si a ellos se hubiera pegado la virtud del ungüento con que él había dormido. Sin pulsos quedó el viejo de la amarga *vista* de lo que *miraba*; la voz se le pegó a la garganta; secósele la lengua; los brazos se le cayeron de desmayado, y quedó como una estatua de mármol frío.

(And from there, walking with marvellous silence, he reached the room where the *dueña* was sleeping, and, not finding Isabela there, he went to the room where the *dueña* had her chamber, and, opening it quietly, *saw what he would never have wanted to see*. He *saw* Isabela in Loaysa's arms, both of them sleeping as soundly as if they had been under the effect of the ointment with which he had slept. The old man's pulse stopped at the bitter *sight* of what he was *looking at*, his voice stuck in his throat, his tongue dried out, his arms fell listless, and he seemed a statue of cold marble.)[22]

Figure 10.1. Titian, *Venus and Mars*, c. 1530. Kunsthistorisches Museum, Vienna.

This "bitter sight of what he was looking at" expresses how the scene is a visual quote isolated from the text, constituting an image nourished by the artistic imagination.

Cervantes takes up once again the theme of the visual representation of Venus's amorous passions in a more openly erotic scene, taking advantage of the licence allowed by the genre of the interlude. In *El viejo celoso* Lorenza indulges in a love affair with a gallant young man. In this case, Venus's lover is not the war-worn Mars but the adolescent Adonis. As I have written elsewhere, a tapestry directly related to the plot in various ways is essential in the interlude. Nonetheless, the surface of the closed door also acts as a canvas on which the old man imagines his wife's love affairs with the young lover: "I am referring here to the door behind which Lorenza encloses herself with her lover and behind which the young woman narrates the pleasurable details of her sexual encounter.[23] This is a verbal tapestry, or more accurately an eroticized tapestry in motion, a 'motion picture' in which Cervantes resorts to the evocative capacity of the discourse to turn into a sequence of mental images."[24]

Another obvious *tableau vivant* is the scene in which Dorotea appears for the first time in *Don Quixote*, bathing in the river.[25] As will be remembered, the priest, the barber, and Cardenio observe the scene, whose description unequivocally refers to the pictorial representation of "Susanna and the elders." Vincent Sellaer, Jan Massys, Paolo Veronese, and Tintoretto, among many other sixteenth-century painters, would portray this scene that combines the biblical theme with an erotic one, as shown in figure 10.2. This moment, when Dorotea's sexual vulnerability is expressed for the first time, is vital in her depiction. Contrary to the biblical heroine, Dorotea begins rebuilding her honour from that moment on. This scene evidences the visual quote and the superimposition of the two stories through visual memory.

Finally, the analysis of "Lucrecia's suicide" spans the second part of this chapter.

"The Suicide of Lucretia" as a *tableau vivant* in *El curioso impertinente*

In my view, the true sense of this novella within *Don Quixote* cannot be understood in all its complexity without considering the pictorial quote of Lucretia's suicide, which, more than offering an interpretive clue, provides the very key to the questions that the text raises. The Roman Lucretia is probably one of the most represented figures in the art of early modernity. Among many other artists, the Roman matron is depicted by Dürer, Titian, Giovanni Antonio Bazzi (Il Sodoma), Lucas Cranach the Elder, Sandro Botticelli, Joos van Cleve, Maestro del Papagayo, Giulio Romano, Rafael, Jan van Scorel, Tintoretto, Paolo Veronese, Guido Reni, Luca Cambiaso, Simon Vouet, Artemisia Gentileschi, Rembrandt, and Luca Giordano, to name only painters of the sixteenth and seventeenth centuries. Many of these works were reproduced in engravings and *estampas*, as well as recreated ad infinitum in painters' workshops.

The story of Lucretia, Collatinus's wife, tells of the suicide of a rape victim. Lucretia is admired for her beauty and virtue and celebrated as the perfect wife. Tarquin, the son of the Roman king, driven by love according to Ovid, or by lust according to Livy, or by the desire to destroy her reputation according to Cassius Dio, visits her and asks to stay, knowing that her husband is away.[26] In other versions of the story, Collatinus himself brags about Lucretia's virtue to Tarquin and other comrades-in-arms while they are in a military camp near Rome. They bet on whose wife best embodies the virtues that a Roman matron

Figure 10.2. Tintoretto, *Susanna and the Elders*, c. 1555. Kunsthistorisches Museum, Vienna.

should possess, and they decide to go to Rome and surprise them during the night. Indeed, Lucretia is the only one they find weaving as the others enjoy feasts and leisure while their husbands are at war. Collatinus wins the bet, and Lucretia is exalted for her virtues, although this is precisely what awakens Tarquin's irrepressible desire to possess her. Days later, betraying the trust of his friend and comrade-in-arms, he goes to Collatinus's home knowing that Lucretia will be alone. He asks to stay the night, and when everyone is asleep, he enters her room brandishing a sword. Lucretia prefers death to dishonour, but Tarquin threatens to kill her along with a slave and leave the two bodies naked on the marriage bed as proof that he executed them while they committed adultery in order to defend the honour of the absent husband and friend. Faced with this threat that would put an end not only to her life but also to the honour of her house, Lucretia surrenders herself to Tarquin. The next morning, she informs her husband and father of what happened, asking them to come with witnesses to make her confession public and remove it from the sphere of family privacy. She takes her own life, not without first publicly demanding revenge. Her suicide is interpreted as an act of supreme dignity and courage. The desire to avenge her initiated by Brutus inflames the Roman people, who end up overthrowing the monarchy and establishing the Republic. Thus, Lucretia's virtue and courage are recognized as the wellspring for the political changes that would lead Rome to the glory it attained during the Republic.

Therefore, according to this legend uncontested by history, the splendour of Rome would issue not only from an act of sexual violence but also from the sacrifice of a virtuous wife. As Cristina Martín Puente's exhaustive itinerary of the Greek and Latin sources attests, Lucretia's story spread swiftly through classical culture. The first author in prose to refer to Lucretia is the Roman Fabio Pictor, who wrote in Greek, and he would be the main source for Livy and Dionysius of Halicarnassus in that language. Cristina Martín Puente notes that other ancient authors of prose works on Lucretia include Cicero and Varro – and in Greek, Diodorus Siculus, Plutarch, and Cassius Dio. Seneca, Valerius Maximus, Tertullian, and Emporius also devote passages to the Roman matron. In verse Lucretia appears in Lucius Accius, Ovid, Livy, Martial, and Claudian.[27]

The fortune of the history of Lucretia would continue uninterrupted until the time of Cervantes, although Christianity would change the story's interpretation by casting doubt on the innocence of the Roman matron, as in Augustine. As we will see, this interpretive turn regarding her virtue would affect artistic representations of her rape and suicide in the early modern era. The *tableau vivant* of Lucretia is fundamental in *El curioso impertinente* because both stories, Lucretia's and Camila's, revolve around questions regarding the innocence or guilt of each woman. In both stories the husbands, Collatinus and Anselmo, want to prove their wife's worth. Collatinus makes a bet about who is the most virtuous wife and exposes her virtue publicly as a personal triumph, and this in turn awakens the lust and jealousy of the king's son. For his part, Anselmo wants to test Camila, repeatedly insisting that Lotario try to seduce her by being the instigator of his wife's adultery. Rape and adultery are two forms of debasement of the wife's body. These parallels between the two stories are revealed in the pictorial quote performed by Camila.

As will be recalled, in *El curioso impertinente* Anselmo asks his best friend Lotario to try to seduce his young wife Camila – beautiful, rich, noble, and deemed to be virtuous – to prove her true worth and integrity by passing a fidelity test. Lotario first resists such madness but then agrees, but with no intention of carrying it out. Yet when Anselmo spies on him and rebukes him for his inaction, Lotario resolutely woos her and she falls in love with him: "Rindióse Camila, Camila se rindió" ("Camila surrendered; Camila surrendered"),[28] says this exceptionally moralizing narrator. All goes well for the clandestine lovers until Lotario sees a young man – the maid Leonela's lover, as it happens – sneak out of the house. If Camila is capable of infidelity to her husband, he thinks, she can deceive him too. In a fit of jealousy, he betrays Camila by telling Anselmo that she has succumbed to him: "Sábete que la fortaleza de Camila está ya rendida, y sujeta a todo aquello que yo quisiere hacer della" ("You should know that the fortress of Camila has surrendered and submitted to everything I wished").[29]

Lotario designs a plan whereby Anselmo can see his disgrace with his own eyes and take appropriate revenge. Note the importance of "seeing" and how a theatrical performance is being prepared in which Camila, in good faith, would reveal her love for Lotario without knowing that she was signing her own execution:

> [H]az de manera que te quedes escondido en tu recámara, pues los tapices que allí hay y otras cosas con que te puedas encubrir te ofrecen mucha comodidad, y entonces verás por tus mismos ojos, y yo por los míos, lo que Camila quiere; y si fuere la maldad que se puede temer antes que esperar, con silencio, sagacidad y discreción podrás ser el verdugo de tu agravio.

> (Stay hidden in your antechamber, where there are tapestries and other things that can conceal you very comfortably; then you will see with your own eyes, and I with mine, exactly what Camila wants; and if it is the immorality that may be feared but is not expected, then silently, wisely, and discreetly you can punish the offense committed against you.)[30]

Shortly afterwards Lotario repents and confesses his betrayal to Camila, apprehensive about the grave danger he is exposing her to. Horrified at what he has done, Camila nonetheless devises a way to save herself. She tells Lotario to trust her and act as he normally would: "[Y] que a cuanto ella le dijese le respondiese como respondiera aunque no supiera que Anselmo le escuchaba" ("And respond to everything she said as he would if he did not know Anselmo was listening").[31]

Interestingly, Camila carries out the theatrical performance for Anselmo's eyes only. Everything will be done as Lotario had thought, but now the victim will not be an unwitting Camila but a deceived Anselmo who will believe that he sees, without being seen, a genuine scene in which his wife will show herself as she is. As I have written elsewhere, "Cervantes has Anselmo watch from his hiding place, believing that he is setting a ruse for Camila, while in fact she represents a lie in which she traps her jealous husband, who spies without knowing that it's all theatre designed for his gaze. We thus have a theatre in reverse in which truth and lie are mutually reflected in a sophisticated play of mirrors that would be impossible without a careful use of ekphrastic techniques and a narrative that explores to the limit the possibilities of the visual."[32] Anselmo's supposedly covert surveillance is the key to this *tableau vivant* in which the motif of Lucretia's suicide is to be performed, a motif that has been represented countless times in art and become commonplace. The day of the ruse arrives, and Anselmo hides behind the tapestries in the antechamber where he expects to witness his own dishonour. Knowing that she is being watched by her husband, Camila begins an ardent speech, dagger in hand, comparing herself to Lucretia and vowing to kill Lotario to cleanse her honour, which has been stained by his dishonest intentions. She asks her maid Leonela to summon Lotario in order to avenge her husband's honour. Meanwhile, Anselmo witnesses the scene from behind the tapestries, literally paralysed by curiosity:

> Todo esto escuchaba Anselmo, y a cada palabra que Camila decía se le mudaban los pensamientos; mas cuando entendió que estaba resuelta en matar a Lotario, quiso salir y descubrirse, porque tal cosa no se hiciese, pero detúvole el deseo de ver en qué paraba tanta gallardía y honesta resolución.

> (Anselmo listened to all of this, and each word Camila said changed his thoughts, but when he realized that she had determined to kill Lotario, he wanted to come out and show himself and prevent her from doing that; yet he was held back, however, by his desire to see the outcome of so gallant and virtuous a resolve.)[33]

After a series of laments, tears, fainting spells, and justifications of her marital honour, Camila assures Leonela that she does not intend to commit suicide like Lucretia – whom she describes as ingenuous – before taking revenge on Lotario for having defiled her honour with his lustful thoughts: "[Y]a que sea atrevida y simple, a tu parecer, en volver por mi honra, no lo he de ser tanto como aquella Lucrecia de quien dicen que se mató sin haber cometido error alguno y sin haber muerto primero a quien tuvo la causa de su desgracia" ("Because although in your opinion it is rash and foolish of me to defend my honour, I shall not go as far as that Lucretia who, they say, killed herself even though she had done no wrong, and without first killing the one responsible for her misfortune").[34] She insists on hyperbolizing her speech, intensifying the already extreme story of Lucretia in two ways. First, because she plans two deaths and not one: Lotario's and her own; and second, because in Lucretia's case there was a rape whereas in hers the alleged transgression is simply that Lotario has dared, unsuccessfully, to try to seduce her. Therefore we go from a rape to an attempt to engage in adultery and from the world of deeds to that of frustrated intent. She affirms that only blood can purify her honour: "Limpia entré en poder del que el cielo me dio por mío, limpia he de salir dél; y, cuando mucho, saldré bañada en mi casta sangre y en la impura del más falso amigo que vio la amistad en el mundo" ("I was pure when I came into possession of the man heaven gave me for my own; I shall be pure when I leave it behind, even if I am bathed in my own chaste blood and the impure blood of the falsest friend that friendship has ever known").[35]

This fiction that Camila performs for the concealed Anselmo lacks the public character of Lucretia's sacrifice. The latter commits suicide to establish the injury done to her family through the ignominy to her body as a legal recourse: she has made the injury public and, with her death, extracts a revenge that will bring an end to the Roman monarchy. This dimension of Lucretia's suicide has little relation to Camila's hyperbolic reaction that could border on the absurd. However, Anselmo's ostensible need to prove his wife's value is such that Camila's behaviour seems perfectly appropriate to him, and her plans for violence are proportionate: "Todo lo miraba Anselmo, cubierto detrás de unos tapices donde se había escondido, y de todo se admiraba" ("Anselmo watched it all, concealed behind the tapestries where he had hidden; and he was astonished at everything").[36]

Finally, after playing the role of the aggrieved wife to the extreme, Camila struggles with Lotario and, unable to wound him, stabs herself with the dagger in a mock suicide attempt, falling to the floor unconscious and covered in blood. This is the *tableau vivant* that articulates the whole story and that Anselmo observes while hidden behind the tapestries of his antechamber:

Y haciendo fuerza para soltar la mano de la daga, que Lotario la tenía asida [la daga], la sacó y, guiando su punta por parte que pudiese herir no profundamente, se la entró y escondió por más arriba de la islilla del lado izquierdo, junto al hombro, y luego se dejó caer en el suelo, como desmayada.

> Estaban Leonela y Lotario suspensos y atónitos de tal suceso, y todavía dudaban de la verdad de aquel hecho, viendo a Camila tendida en tierra y bañada en su sangre.

> (And struggling to free from Lotario's grasp the hand that held the dagger, she finally succeeded, aimed the point at a part of her body that she could wound, but not deeply, and plunged it in above her left armpit, near the shoulder; then she dropped to the floor as if she had fallen into a faint.

> Leonela and Lotario were dumbfounded, astonished at what had just happened and still doubting its reality although Camila lay on the floor, bathed in blood.)[37]

Despite believing that his wife has died, judging by the initial reaction of Leonela and especially of Lotario, who "comenzó a hacer una larga y triste lamentación sobre el cuerpo de Camila, como si estuviera difunta" ("began a long, melancholy lamentation over Camila's body, as if she were dead"),[38] Anselmo does not leave his hiding place and keeps observing, undaunted by the development of events:

> Atentísimo había estado Anselmo a escuchar y a ver representar la tragedia de la muerte de su honra, la cual con tan estraños y eficaces afectos la representaron los personajes della, que pareció que se habían transformado en la misma verdad de lo que fingían.

> (Anselmo had been very attentive as he heard and watched the performance of the tragedy of the death of his honour, which had been performed with such unusual and convincing affects by the actors that they seemed to have been transformed into the very parts they were playing.)[39]

Camila's "suicide" incorporates Lucretia's story into the text as a visual quote. At this moment the confluence of the two stories is total. Cervantes does not identify Camila with Lucretia *stricto sensu* but rather brings to the *Curioso* much more than the story of the Roman matron, incorporating the entire history of the myth's interpretation through the centuries. Thus, from the fifth century with Augustine of Hippo, Lucretia is not only an emblem of conjugal chastity but becomes the pretext to speculate on women's guilt when their bodies have been sexually abused. Augustine suggests that the idea that of the two, Tarquin and Lucretia, only Tarquin is an adulterer may well be false since there could be two adulterers, one using force and the other secretly consenting. And in the same passage he formulates his famous questions: "Si adulterata, cur laudata; si pudica, cur occisa?" (If she is an adulteress, why is she celebrated? And if she is chaste, why does she commit suicide?)[40] Jocelyn Catty points out that Roman culture is a culture of "shame" in which Tarquin's affront justifies suicide, which is interpreted as a vindication of family honour, while in Christian culture Lucretia's suicide is only understood from guilt ("Christian culture is, by contrast, one of guilt"), in which the emphasis on conscience led Christian commentators such as Augustine to seek a "guilty reason for suicide, such as enjoyment of the rape: 'she her selfe gaue a lustfull consent.'"[41]

In a similar vein, the fourteenth-century humanist Coluccio Salutati, in his *Declamatio Lucretiae* (c. 1367–91), put in Lucretia's own mouth the necessity of her suicide to free her spirit from her weak body capable of surrendering to lustful pleasure. This fictional Lucretia recreated by Salutati refers to the ethical disgust from the pleasure her body felt when she was raped: "That sad and unpleasing pleasure, of whatever sort it was, must be avenged by the sword…. Let the feeling be extinguished; too great are the powers of Venus for anyone who has had some experience of pleasure…. If I spare adultery, soon adultery will be pleasing, and then an adulterer will be welcome."[42] She insists on details that eroticize her experience as a victim, such as when she describes how Tarquin stroked her nipples "for the purpose of exciting lust."[43] Already in the early modern era, doctors and moralists believed that the biologically closed, enigmatic body of woman "lies" because it is indecipherable and causes an anxiety for not inscribing in body language the truth of what happens in the realm of the spirit. That is why a woman's guilt is assumed by default, and Christian culture would unquestioningly accept the shame that the victim of a sexual assault should feel.

Even at the scene of her suicide, artistic representations of Lucretia would reinforce this presumption of sensuality and lust. The unequivocally erotic character of Lucretia's pictorial representations is firmly anchored in the moral, psychological, and physiological arguments put forwards at the time that claim the virtual impossibility of the full and genuine innocence of women during rape. Indeed, Lucretia's story would open a longstanding debate about the almost inevitable corruptibility of the female spirit through the degradation of a body defiled by force.[44]

Two moments in particular in Lucretia's story would be represented in art: the rape and the suicide. Paradoxically, the supreme act of dignity in her suicide is eroticized in the iconographic tradition.

As of the early sixteenth century all European artistic schools show highly erotic images of a bare-breasted Lucretia. Jana Herrschaft and Gunnar Heydenreich, for example, in their study of Lucas Cranach the Elder's Lucretia in the Museo de Bellas Artes in Bilbao, observe that no fewer than thirty-five versions of Lucretia committing suicide are known to have been painted by him, all with exposed breasts and marked eroticism (see figure 10.3). What is more, his workshop produced twice as many "Suicides of Lucretia" (89). These authors ask why this pagan model of virtue is represented so erotically: "Las normas aparentemente tan contradictorias que hacen que la mujer de este cuadro oscile entre una lascivia provocadora y una rotunda castidad le confieren un atractivo erótico que podría inducir al espectador a pensar que ésta tal vez comparta con él una intención sexual" (The seemingly contradictory norms that make the woman in this painting waver between provocative lust and outright chastity give her an erotic appeal that could lead the [male] viewer to fantasize that she shares a sexual intent with him).[45]

However, the main question is how to understand the semantic change that Lucretia's suicide undergoes in its iconographic representation. This is all the more disconcerting when considering that, during this epoch, queens and noblewomen would identify with the figure of Lucretia to express their virtue as spouses. As shown in figure 10.4, for example, Lorenzo Lotto paints a newly married lady holding in her hand an engraving of Lucretia naked, piercing her chest with a dagger while pointing to a piece of paper on the table, on which is written: "[N]ec ulla impude Lucretia exemplo vivet" (taken from Livy's account of Lucretia's suicide: By Lucretia's example, no unchaste woman shall live).[46]

The answer to this question is directly linked to the profile of those who desired these works. Everything indicates that they were painted for the enjoyment of men who wanted them for their private chambers, a space of male intimacy in which the contemplation of female nudes was a widespread practice between collectionism and voyeurism. Philip II himself commissioned Titian for a *Tarquin and Lucrecia* (1571) for his private chambers, a painting of immense artistic merit and manifest eroticism that would have repercussions in the history of art. Copies from his workshop and various versions by the master himself as well as countless imitations have survived. Philip II was an avid art collector and admirer and patron of Titian, whom he would commission for the famous and patently erotic series of *Poesías* with a mythological theme for his private chambers. Ana Valtierra Lacalle maintains that Philip II commissioned these works to decorate a private chamber for his own

Figure 10.3. Lucas Cranach the Elder, *The Suicide of Lucretia*, c. 1525. Private collection.

enjoyment without having any "higher" intention, and adds that this "es exactamente lo mismo que Cranach hace al dedicarse a la pintura de género: satisfacer una demanda de pinturas eróticas por parte de 'aficionados' ofrecidas bajo el pretexto del prestigio cultural de su tema" (is exactly what Cranach does when devoting himself to genre painting: satisfying a demand for erotic paintings by "amateurs" offered under the pretext of the cultural prestige of their subject).[47] Similarly, Javier Portús affirms about Titian's *Poesías* that "el marco interpretativo en el que hay que situar la serie es el que se deriva de su concepción como obras destinadas al disfrute privado, dotadas de altas cualidades sensuales y eróticas, dominadas por el desnudo" (the interpretive framework in which the series must be situated is derived from its conception as works destined for private enjoyment, endowed with high sensual and erotic qualities, dominated by the nude).[48] Titian wrote to the king:

Figure 10.4. Lorenzo Lotto, *Portrait of a Woman Inspired by Lucretia*, c. 1537. National Gallery, London.

"[Y] porque la Dánae, que ya mandé a V.M., se veía toda por la parte de delante, he querido en esta otra poesía variar y hacerle mostrar la contraria parte, para que resulte el camerino donde había de estar, más agradable a la vista" (And because the Danae, which I already sent to Your Majesty, shows her fully from the front, I wanted in this other *poesía* to vary and have her shown from the opposite side so that the chamber where she is to appear will be more pleasing to the eye).[49]

An example that illustrates the ability of art to make itself known is the ekphrasis that Juan de Piña inserts into his novel *Casos prodigiosos y cueva encantada* (1628) of a version of Titian's Lucretia (see figure 10.5). In the fictional text, the painting is placed in the collection of a rich and refined gentleman, and it is pointed out that the room where the protagonist is housed is "adornada de pinturas del Ticiano y de los más excelentes pinceles" (adorned with paintings by Titian and the

Figure 10.5. Titian, *Tarquin and Lucretia*, 1571. Fitzwilliam Museum, Cambridge.

most excellent brushes).[50] For five whole pages the narrator dwells on a detailed description of "the rape of Lucretia," an account that clearly highlights the eroticism of this encounter. Everything is sensual and exciting for the gazing reader: the texture of the sheets, the fallen bedspread, Lucretia's nudity, the whiteness of her breasts, the beauty of her feet, the shape of her thighs, her shapely waist, the beauty of her face bathed in tears, the pearls of the necklace that adorns her neck. The ravishing beauty of a frightened and naked Lucretia justifies the rape. The narrator goes so far as to say that the sight of the lady's bare breasts was reason enough to believe that Tarquin would have deserved his ruin much more if he had respected her: "[Q]ue el rey, cuando no tuviera amor, tuviera disculpa y debiera perder la vida y el reino romano, más por no lograr tan rara hermosura, que por la injuria que la hizo" (That the king, when he had no love, had an excuse and should lose his life and the Roman kingdom, more for not possessing such rare beauty than for the injury he inflicted on her).[51] The text insists on how the lady's horror intensifies her beauty: "La vergüenza salió tan encendida a la bellísima cara ... sangrientas de encendidas [sus mejillas]" (The shame showed so ardently on her beautiful face ... [with her cheeks] inflamed with blood).[52]

The description is intensely erotic, and the violence of the scene is interspersed with allusions to nudity: "Defendíase Lucrecia, el rey le tenía con la mano izquierda la derecha, que como en alto, la no apretada camisa, dejándole caer, descubrió la mayor belleza de la no imitada hermosura" (Lucretia defended herself, the king held her right hand with his left; when she raised her arm, the loose tunic slowly fell, revealing the greatest allure of natural beauty).[53] I emphasize this ekphrasis of Lucretia's rape for two reasons, first because it captures the male gaze and the practice of collecting erotic paintings for the private enjoyment of men. In this case, the protagonist is lodged in the very room where the paintings hang. Second, there is somehow a connection between the motif of the rape of Lucretia and that of her suicide: Lucretia stabbing herself with a dagger will always lead the male viewer to imagine the act of sexual violence that so riveted collectors of the early modern era. After the five pages describing Titian's painting, the narrator adds: "Seguíase en otro cuadro la bellísima Lucrecia con el puñal a los pechos, difunta, en quien sola pareció hermosa la muerte ... que sangrienta parecía deidad bellísima de nieve y rosa" (In the next painting the most beautiful Lucretia appeared with the dagger at her breasts, lifeless, in whom death seemed beautiful ... bathed in blood she seemed a stunning deity of snow and rose).[54]

Lucretia becomes an ambivalent and controversial figure and, while she is still considered the epitome of conjugal chastity, she is transformed into an object of erotic contemplation. I believe that the cause of this merciless eroticization lies in the fact that rape somehow constitutes an insurmountable event in Christian culture. For the early modern society of *honra*, rape can never be a stimulus for heroism but an act that forever changes the semantics of feminine worth. A dishonoured body is an irreversible, useless, and abject one. The erotic involves the inscription of that body into the sphere to which it corresponds: that of desire offered outside the limits of marriage. Thus, a woman in the act of taking her own life is paying a moral debt while still offering herself symbolically to the viewer's gaze, as if a transgression were repeated *ad infinitum* that has nothing to do with her will but with an irremissible guilt inscribed on her body.

Unequivocally, Camila also becomes an object of visual enjoyment for Anselmo, who is led to imagine a painting in which Lucrecia is superimposed onto Camila. As we have seen, since Augustine a tradition of thought considers Lucrecia not to be a victim of rape but an adulteress. In this *tableau vivant*, the figure of Camila, in addition to showing herself as an aggrieved wife, acquires the connotation of an adulteress, which is implicit in the ambivalence with which Lucretia is represented in art. A raped wife or an adulteress in a sense shares the same devaluation of women in the eyes of society. Whereas Rome could extol Lucretia, Christianity, deep down, needs to have the imaginary option of "forgiving" the woman whose body has been irrevocably defiled. Furthermore, such incomplete forgiveness never comes without cost and requires immeasurable sacrifice on the woman's part. Camila, however, wants neither forgiveness nor approval. Her use of the image of Lucretia incorporates into the *Curioso impertinente* an ambiguous tradition about feminine worth, a tradition that she dramatizes and interprets, but whose sense of submission she subverts. Camila resembles the Roman Lucretia more than might be initially apparent because, by insincerely representing all the themes about honour that her own epoch anachronistically attaches to Lucretia, she approaches the awareness of the Roman heroine's own worth as a lady whose suicide demands the death of a prince. This can be seen in her stark independence from Anselmo's notions of feminine value. Her appeal to visual memory is an exercise in irreverence because, like other female characters in Cervantes, she has the enormous merit of not internalizing the guilt-laden discourse of dishonour.

Through this *tableau vivant* it would be expected that the theme of Lucretia's possible guilt would be transferred to Camila. However, the novel places the weight of the moral dilemma not on her but on Anselmo. As he would do later in the interlude *El retablo de las maravillas*, Cervantes subverts theatrical logic by making the spectator – in this case Anselmo – the main show. Indeed, Anselmo's hidden gaze, as he who watches but does not see, is the focus of attention for the other characters as well as for the novel's readers. Anselmo's voyeuristic character is already announced in a previous scene when he spies on Lotario and Camila without their knowledge:

> [H]abiendo dejado Anselmo solos a Lotario y a Camila, como otras veces solía, él se encerró en un aposento y por los agujeros de la cerradura estuvo mirando y escuchando lo que los dos trataban, y vio que en más de media hora Lotario no habló palabra a Camila, ni se la hablara si allí estuviera un siglo, y cayó en la cuenta de que cuanto su amigo le había dicho de las respuestas de Camila todo era ficción y mentira.

> (Anselmo, having left Lotario and Camila alone as he had done so many other times before, hid in a small antechamber and watched and listened to them through the keyhole, and he saw that in over half an hour Lotario did not speak a word to Camila and would not have spoken to her if he had been there for a century, and Anselmo realized that everything his friend had told him about Camila's responses was a fiction and a lie.)[55]

The next time, the hidden Anselmo will be spied upon while he watches without knowing that he is the sole intended audience of the play that Camila is performing.

Steven Hutchinson recalls the oldest source of *El curioso imperti-nente*, an extreme case of vicarious voyeurism: "La anécdota contada por Herodoto en la que el rey Candaules de Lidia alaba la hermosura de su mujer a su favorito Gyges y asimismo le obliga, muy contra su voluntad, a esconderse en el dormitorio real para admirar la extraor-dinaria belleza de la reina desnuda" (The anecdote told by Herodotus in which King Candaules of Lydia praises the beauty of his wife to his favourite Gyges and also obliges him, much against his will, to hide in the royal bedroom to admire the extraordinary beauty of the naked queen).[56] What is most interesting, according to Hutchinson, is the spectacle that Anselmo's scopophilic obsession offers: "A partir de cierto momento, el voyeurismo parece apoderarse de Anselmo y poseerlo, desplazando todas las demás motivaciones del personaje. Si no fuera así, ¿cómo explicar su *no* intervención en momentos críticos de la espléndida escena teatral montada por Camila, en la que ella sorprende a todos, Lotario y el narrador incluidos, con su vehemencia y su aparente intención de matar a Lotario y a sí misma?" (At a certain moment, voyeurism seems to take hold of Anselmo and possess him, displacing all the other motivations of the character. If it were not so, how would we account for his *non*-intervention in critical moments of the splendid theatrical scene staged by Camila, in which she surprises everyone, Lotario and the narrator included, with her vehemence and her apparent intention to kill Lotario and herself as well?)[57] As Frederick de Armas points out, *El curioso impertinente* is a work in which art invades everything and relates the visual richness of the interpolated novella to pictorial allusions to Lucrecia: "Lo visual se esconde tras alusiones fugaces a pinturas y estatuas, pero está siempre presente en las miradas, en cómo cada uno de los tres personajes observa a los otros" (The visual hides behind fleeting allusions to paintings and statues, but is always present in the gazes, in how each of the three characters observes the others).[58]

I would like to conclude with the image of Anselmo in his antechamber hidden behind the tapestries, whose figures also represent silent stories that are not revealed to us. This is a clear allusion to that private space of male contemplation in which art shapes the history of Anselmo's fantasies transposed into his marriage. *El curioso impertinente* is, in fact, an imaginary museum that actively conjures up artistic representations that act as visual quotes, thus creating a dialogic relationship with the novel's plot. Those tapestries, whose themes are unknown to us, remind us of the tapestry described by Zabaleta at the beginning of this chapter, and which he described as a theatre for the eyes. Camila's staging of Lucretia's suicide is the moment in which the pictorial imagination that runs through the entire text reaches its climax. At that instant the image of the wife plunging a dagger into her breast blends with the tapestries that adorn the antechamber. The superimposition of this *tableau vivant* with its own story is one of the keys to understanding the meaning of this Cervantine novella.

By analysing Lucrecia's suicide in *El curioso impertinente*, I have endeavoured to show how Cervantes utilizes the theatrical technique of dramatized paintings – *tableaux vivants* – filtered through the powerful pictorial culture of early modern Spain in order to actualize mythological, historical, or biblical themes in his narrative. The evocation of images that synthesize stories belonging to the common cultural heritage that is partly transmitted by painting is materialized through these visual quotes that converge with the main plot, adding connotations that both enrich it and make it more complex.

Meanwhile, the other two examples mentioned – the pictorial motif of "Venus and Mars" in Porras's version of *El celoso extremeño*, and "Susanna and the elders" in *Don Quixote* when Dorotea is startled while washing her feet in the river – illustrate the multiple narrative possibilities of the recreation of *tableaux vivants* in Cervantes's works. Ultimately, this literary device exemplifies the intertwined relationship between literary and artistic sources in the Golden Age, when the pictorial imagination played an essential role in the creation of a shared knowledge base and enhanced Cervantes's oeuvre with visual quotes that appealed to a common culture.

NOTES

1 Zabaleta, *El día de fiesta*, 350. All translations are my own unless otherwise noted.

2 See Ferré, "L'art des tableaux vivants."

3 See Ferré.

4 For example, Visentin ("La pratique des tableaux vivants") studies the practice of *tableaux vivants* at the French court, Stijn Bussels ("Powerful Performances") documents this practice upon Juana de Castilla's entry into the Netherlands, and Pouy ("Des feintes images") looks into the use of the *tableau vivant* as early as the seventeenth century, in Marie de Medici's visit to Amsterdam in 1638.

5 See Alcalá Galán, "Retórica visual"; De Armas, *Ekphrasis*; and Laguna, *Cervantes and the Pictorial Imagination*.

6 See Ripa, *Iconología*.

7 Morán Turina, "Velázquez," 49.

8 Morán Turina, 47.

9 Alcalá Yáñez, *El donado hablador*, 290.

10 For example, in Lope de Vega's play *La viuda valenciana*, an *estampa* appears that reproduces Titian's "Venus and Adonis" (430).

11 On the specific presence of the portrait in Golden Age theatre, see Bass, *Drama of the Portrait*.

12 Morán Turina, "Velázquez," 58–9.

13 Orozco Díaz, *El teatro*, 224 (my emphasis).

14 Maravall, *La cultura del Barroco*, 184.

15 Mitchell, "Showing Seeing," 244.

16 For Orozco Díaz, introducing painting into the development of a play "supone una compleja duplicidad de perspectiva de ficción y realidad – aunque la realidad del cuadro sea una ficción– que potencializa la realidad dramática de la escena" (involves a complex duplicity of perspective with regard to fiction and reality – even if the reality of the painting is a fiction – that reinforces the dramatic reality of the scene; *El teatro*, 223). For him, the painting is a real object (although in itself it is a representation) that, when staged, creates a dramatic intensity for the audience.

17 Bajtín [Bakhtin], *Estética de la creación*, 156.

18 Vološinov, *Marxism*, 116.

19 Foucault, "Las Meninas," 1226–7.

20 See Canavaggio, "Del *Celoso extremeño* al *Viejo celoso*" for a textual history of *El celoso extremeño*.

21 Cervantes, *El celoso extremeño*, 708.

22 Cervantes, 708; emphasis mine.

23 Martínez López briefly refers to a "tapestry" evoked by Lorenza ("Erotismo y ejemplaridad," 350), an image that Mattza in turn takes up ("Écfrasis discursiva").

24 Alcalá Galán, "Deceived Gaze," 71–2.

25 See Sánchez Jiménez, "Casta Susana" for a study of the visual aspects of the motif of "Casta Susana" in Lope's poem.

26 Bryson, "Two Narratives of Rape," 163.

27 Martín Puente, "La historia de Lucrecia," 1361–2.

28 Cervantes, *Don Quijote*, 1.34, 397; *Don Quixote*, 290.

29 Cervantes, *Don Quijote*, 1.34, 404; *Don Quixote*, 296.

30 Cervantes, *Don Quijote*, 1.34, 404; *Don Quixote*, 296.

31 Cervantes, *Don Quijote*, 1.34, 406; *Don Quixote*, 298.

32 Alcalá Galán, "Deceived Gaze," 55–6.

33 Cervantes, *Don Quijote*, 1.34, 407; *Don Quixote*, 299.

34 Cervantes, *Don Quijote*, 1.34, 408; *Don Quixote*, 300.

35 Cervantes, *Don Quijote*, 1.34, 409; *Don Quixote*, 300.

36 Cervantes, *Don Quijote*, 1.34, 409; *Don Quixote*, 301.

37 Cervantes, *Don Quijote*, 1.34, 412; *Don Quixote*, 303.

38 Cervantes, *Don Quijote*, 1.34, 412; *Don Quijote*, 303.

39 Cervantes, *Don Quijote*, 1.34, 414; *Don Quixote*, 304.

40 Augustine of Hippo, *De civitate dei*, 2.19.

41 Catty, *Writing Rape*, 30.

42 Jed, *Chaste Thinking*, 151

43 Jed, 151.

44 Alcalá Galán, "Ideología y violencia sexual," 3–8.

45 Herrschaft and Heydenreich, "Una Lucrecia de Lucas Cranach el Viejo," 90.

46 See Valtierra Lacalle, "Iconografía de Lucrecia," 247–50.

47 Valtierra Lacalle, 246.

48 Portús, *La sala reservada*, 76.

49 Portús, 74.

50 Piña, *Casos prodigiosos*, 45.

51 Piña, 49.

52 Piña, 50.

53 Piña, 50.

54 Piña, 51.

55 Cervantes, *Don Quijote*, 1.33, 392; *Don Quixote*, 285.

56 Hutchinson, "Anselmo y sus adicciones," 133.

57 Hutchinson, 134; original emphasis.
58 De Armas, "El mito de Dánae," 151. See also De Armas, "Pinturas de
    Lucrecia," about Lucrecia in *Don Quixote* in relation to Lope, Titian, and
    Raphael.

REFERENCES

Alcalá Galán, Mercedes. "The Deceived Gaze: Visual Fantasy, Art, and Feminine
    Adultery in Cervantes's Reading of Ariosto." In *Goodbye Eros: Recasting Forms
    and Norms of Love in the Age of Cervantes*, edited by Ana Laguna and John
    Beusterien, 53–79. Toronto: University of Toronto Press, 2020.
Alcalá Galán, Mercedes. "Ideología y violencia sexual: el cuerpo femenino
    subyugado según Rubens y Cervantes." *eHumanista/Cervantes*, no. 1 (2012):
    1–40.
Alcalá Galán, Mercedes. "Retórica visual: ékfrasis y teoría de la ilustración
    gráfica en el *Quijote*." In *Autour de "Don Quichotte" de Miguel de Cervantès*,
    edited by Philippe Rabaté and Hélène Tropé, 175–81. Paris: Presses
    Sorbonne Nouvelle, 2015.
Alcalá Yáñez, Jerónimo de. *El donado hablador: Alonso, mozo de muchos amos.*
    Edited by Enrique Suárez Figaredo. 2007. https://users.pfw.edu/jehle
    /cervante/othertxts/Suarez_Figaredo_ElDonadoHablador.pdf.
Augustine of Hippo. *De civitate dei.* Accessed 1 April 2022. https://www
    .thelatinlibrary.com/augustine/civ1.shtml.
Bajtín, M.M. [Mikhail Bakhtin]. *Estética de la creación verbal.* Translated by
    Tatiana Bubnova. Mexico: Siglo XXI, 1982.
Bass, Laura R. *The Drama of the Portrait: Theater and Visual Culture in Early
    Modern Spain.* University Park: Penn State University Press, 2009.
Bryson, Norman. "Two Narratives of Rape in the Visual Arts: Lucretia
    and the Sabine Women." In *Rape: An Historical and Cultural Enquiry*,
    edited by Sylvana Tomaselli and Roy Porter, 152–73. New York: Basil
    Blackwell, 1986.
Bussels, Stijn. "Powerful Performances. *Tableaux vivants* in Early Modern Joyous
    Entries in the Netherlands." In Ramos and Pouy, *Le tableau vivant*, 70–92.
Canavaggio, Jean. "Del *Celoso extremeño* al *Viejo celoso*: Aproximación a una
    reescritura." *Bulletin of Hispanic Studies* 82, no. 5 (2005): 587–98. https://doi
    .org/10.3828/bhs.82.5.3.
Catty, Jocelyn. *Writing Rape, Writing Women in Early Modern England: Unbridled
    Speech.* New York: Palgrave Macmillan, 1999.
Cervantes Saavedra, Miguel de. *El celoso extremeño* (Porras ms.). In *Novelas
    ejemplares*, edited by Jorge García López, 83–713. Barcelona: Galaxia
    Gutenberg, 2005.

Cervantes Saavedra, Miguel de. *Don Quijote de la Mancha*. Edited by Francisco Rico. 2nd ed. Barcelona: Crítica, 1998.

Cervantes Saavedra, Miguel de. *Don Quixote*. Translated by Edith Grossman. New York: HarperCollins, 2003.

Cervantes Saavedra, Miguel de. *Entremeses*. Edited by Eugenio Asensio. Madrid: Castalia, 1970.

Cervantes Saavedra, Miguel de. *Novelas ejemplares*. Edited by Harry Sieber. 2 vols. Madrid: Cátedra, 1980.

De Armas, Frederick A., ed. *Ekphrasis in the Age of Cervantes*. Lewisburg, PA: Bucknell University Press, 2005.

De Armas, Frederick A. "El mito de Dánae en *El curioso impertinente*: Terencio, Tiziano y Cervantes." *Anales Cervantinos*, no. 42 (2010): 147–62. https://doi.org/10.3989/anacervantinos.2010.008.

De Armas, Frederick A. "Pinturas de Lucrecia en el *Quijote*. Tiziano, Rafael y Lope de Vega." *Anuario de Estudios Cervantinos*, no. 1 (2004): 109–19.

de la Flor, Fernando R. *Imago: La cultura visual y figurativa del Barroco*. Madrid: Abada, 2009.

Ferré, Rose Marie. "L'art des tableaux vivants au Moyen Âge. Rappel de la question et enjeux." In Ramos and Pouy, *Le tableau vivant*, 34–51.

Foucault, Michel. "Las Meninas." Translated by Alan Sheridan. In *The Critical Tradition: Classic Texts and Contemporary Trends*, 2nd ed., edited by David H. Richter, 1222–31. Boston, MA: Bedford Books, 1998.

Herrschaft, Jana, and Gunnar Heydenreich. "Una Lucrecia de Lucas Cranach el Viejo en el Museo de Bellas Artes de Bilbao." *Boletín del Museo de Bellas Artes de Bilbao*, no. 8 (2014): 85–119.

Hutchinson, Steven. "Anselmo y sus adicciones." In *El "Quijote" desde América*, edited by Gustavo Illades and James Iffland, 119–38. Puebla: Benemérita Universidad Autónoma de Puebla and Colegio de México, 2006.

Jed, Stephanie H. *Chaste Thinking: The Rape of Lucretia and the Birth of Humanism*. Bloomington: Indiana University Press, 1989.

Laguna, Ana María G. *Cervantes and the Pictorial Imagination: A Study on the Power of Images and Images of Power in Works by Cervantes*. Lewisburg, PA: Bucknell University Press, 2009.

Maravall, José Antonio. *La cultura del Barroco: Análisis de una estructura histórica*. Barcelona: Ariel, 1983.

Martín Llanos, Pablo. "El adulterio de Marte y Venus en *Metamorfosis* de Ovidio: Relato, narradoras y auditorio internos." *Argos* 34, no. 2 (2011): 36–52.

Martín Puente, Cristina. "La historia de Lucrecia en prosa y en verso." In *DVLCES CAMENAE: Poética y Poesía Latinas*, edited by Jesús Luque, María Dolores Rincón, and Isabel Velázquez, 1359–70. Granada: Universidad de Granada, 2010.

Martínez López, Enrique. "Erotismo y ejemplaridad en *El viejo celoso* de Cervantes." In *Erotismo en las letras hispánicas: Aspectos, modos y fronteras*, edited by Luce López Baralt and Francisco Márquez Villanueva, 335–85. Mexico City: Colegio de México, 1995.

Mattza, Carmela. "Écfrasis discursiva y metateatro: Rodamonte en el entremés del Viejo celoso." In *Pictavia aurea: Actas del IX Congreso de la AISO*, edited by Alain Bègue and Emma Herrán Alonso, 973–80. Toulouse: Presses Universitaires du Mirail, 2013.

Mitchell, W.J.T. "Showing Seeing: A Critique of Visual Culture." In *Art History, Aesthetics, Visual Studies*, edited by Michael Ann Holly and Keith Moxey, 231–50. Williamstown, MA: Sterling and Francine Clark Art Institute, 2002.

Morán Turina, Miguel. "Velázquez, la pintura, y el teatro del Siglo de Oro." *Boletín del Museo del Prado*, no. 19 (2001): 47–71.

Morán Turina, Miguel, and Javier Portús. *El arte de mirar: La pintura y su público en la España de Velázquez*. Madrid: Istmo, 1997.

Orozco Díaz, Emilio. *El teatro y la teatralidad del Barroco*. Barcelona: Editorial Planeta, 1969.

Piña, Juan de. *Casos prodigiosos* y *Cueva encantada*. Madrid: Viuda de Rico, 1907.

Portús Pérez, Javier. *La sala reservada del Museo del Prado*. Madrid: Museo del Prado, 1998.

Pouy, Léonard. "'Des feintes images aux choses mêmes et à la vérité.' Rembrandt et l'entrée de Marie de Médicis à Amsterdam en 1638." In Ramos and Pouy, *Le tableau vivant*, 94–119.

Rabelais, François. *Quart livre*. In vol. 2 of *Oeuvres complètes*. Edited by Pierre Jourda. Paris: Garnier, 1962.

Ramos, Julie. "Affinités électives du tableau et du vivant. Une ouverture, dans les pas de Goethe." In Ramos and Pouy, *Le tableau vivant*, 13–33.

Ramos, Julie, and Léonard Pouy, eds. *Le tableau vivant, ou L'image performée*. Paris: Mare et Martin, 2014.

Ripa, Cesare. *Iconologia*. Vol. 1. Translated by Juan Barja, Yago Barja, Rosa María Mariño Sánchez-Elvira, and Fernando García Romero. Madrid: Akal, 2007.

Sánchez Jiménez, Antonio. "'Casta Susana': El baño de Susana, voyeurismo y écfrasis en un soneto de Lope de Vega." *Neophilologus*, no. 93 (2009): 69–80. https://doi.org/10.1007/s11061-008-9114-z.

Valtierra Lacalle, Ana. "Iconografía de Lucrecia: Repercusiones plásticas en la Península Ibérica." *Anas*, nos. 27–8 (2014–15): 241–61.

Vega, Lope de. *La viuda valenciana*. Edited by Teresa Ferrer. Madrid: Castalia, 2001.

Visentin, Hélène. "La pratique des tableaux vivants dans les entrées royales françaises." In Ramos and Pouy, *Le tableau vivant*, 52–68.
Vološinov, V.N. [and M.M. Bakhtin]. *Marxism and the Philosophy of Language*. Translated by Ladislav Matejka and I.R. Titunik. Cambridge, MA: Harvard University Press, 1986.
Zabaleta, Juan de. *El día de fiesta por la mañana y por la tarde*. Edited by Cristóbal Cuevas García. Madrid: Castalia, 1983.

11 "Muchas y muy verdaderas señales": The Theatrics of Truth and Sincerity of Fiction in *La Galatea*

PAUL MICHAEL JOHNSON

One of the most familiar tropes of early modern studies is that theatre, and theatricality in all its sundry guises, were pervasive fixtures of the Spanish Renaissance and Baroque.[1] So it is that critics, despite Cervantes's avowedly limited success in plying his trade for early modern playgoers, have analysed at some length the author's engagement with the dramatic arts in his writing. As this volume itself attests, Cervantes's plays and interludes have in recent years captured growing attention from scholars and been the object of valuable critical editions,[2] while his most prominent prose fiction – including *Don Quijote,* the *Novelas ejemplares*, and *Los trabajos de Persiles y Sigismunda* – has likewise inspired studies of the latent dramatic elements that dwell in Cervantine narrative.[3] With scarce exceptions, however, scholars have yet to apply similarly transgeneric tools to Cervantes's first effort at prose, *La Galatea*.[4] On the one hand, this is surprising because pastoralism has long been bound up with drama and theatricality. Decades before pastoral books like Jorge de Montemayor's *La Diana* enraptured early modern European readers, Juan del Encina and Lucas Fernández gave early sixteenth-century Spanish audiences a taste of the bucolic with eclogues in dramatic form. Even if it was expressed lyrically, the Renaissance eclogue had long been associated with drama, thanks especially to the dialogic nature of its amoebaean variant.[5] The polyvalent encounters that inhere in the pastoral between artificiality and authenticity and illusion and reality are another feature that makes the convention eminently theatrical. While many characters in pastoral romances, including *La Galatea,* are veiled references to real-life people,[6] in converse fashion it became a common diversion for early modern historical individuals to dress up as shepherds and shepherdesses at costume parties and social gatherings.[7] In the words of Mary

Gaylord, "The pastoral world, in short, is a world of representation and of self-representation."[8]

On the other hand, the critical inattention to dramatic features of *La Galatea* is somewhat predictable, not just because the 1585 work is the most understudied of the author's long narratives. Thematically, too, pastoral romance appears far removed from the theatre. With its *beatus ille* and *locus amoenus*, at an intradiegetic level the bucolic mode is defined by its purposeful isolation from the vices of urban life, by a herding community who has rejected the performative guile of the court for the simplicity and sincerity of the countryside.[9] Justifiably, it is not the genre of drama but that of poetry that has consumed the bulk of critical studies of *La Galatea*, a versiprose or prosimetrum work replete with not only the eclogue proper to pastoral but a vast diversity of metric styles. Other scholars have fixated on the "novelization" of the text, or the nascent features that may have augured the watershed appearance of *Don Quijote*, the next major work that Cervantes would publish after a two-decade drought in his literary output.[10]

Whatever the reasons for this critical neglect, a close reading of *La Galatea* reveals multiple incursions by drama into the pastoral domain. My intention in what follows is not merely to highlight the manifold presence of theatricality in the text but, more importantly, to show how it prompts us to revisit and revise some longstanding assumptions about the work and the pastoral mode at large.[11] Among enamoured yet discreet characters with a penchant for lyric poetry, what they readily desire is to hear and see others without pretence, to know another's candid feelings without the possibility that they are feigned or repressed. That is why eavesdropping is such a routine pastime, even an obsession, for what Cesáreo Bandera long ago called the text's curious "mirones" – the presumption being that, while alone, an individual's laments must be genuine, not curated for an audience.[12] Furtively gazing upon a fellow shepherd or shepherdess from afar, with the natural cover afforded by the wooded rural environment, becomes in *La Galatea* a principal means of ensuring that the spectator be in receipt of unaffected sincerity, a solution for the challenge encapsulated in the Renaissance proverb, rescued from antiquity by Alberti and others, that lamented the lack of a window on the chest that would allow one to know another's true feelings.[13] But what is one to do when face to face with the sentimental outpourings of another character, particularly one with a command of oratory, a mellifluous eloquence? How to interpret the word of someone whose previous vocation as a courtier, as is the case with many characters in Renaissance pastoral romance, allowed him to master the art of dissimulation and *sprezzatura*?[14] The answer in *La Galatea*, in short, is that one must carefully observe external cues, affects, bodily gestures, and other proto-linguistic signifiers.[15] If such non-verbal cues had long been regarded historically as a more reliable litmus test than words for appraising whether or not another's love was genuine,[16] then by the late sixteenth and early seventeenth centuries, emotional gestures were rather ironically becoming the touchstone of accomplished actors in the burgeoning sphere of the theatre. This historical ambivalence reminds us that gesture can materialize as something either purely involuntary (and therefore sincere) or histrionic (consciously feigned).

Nevertheless, my purpose here will be in part to suggest that *La Galatea* collapses, synthesizes, or otherwise troubles these distinctions. By studying the theatrical elements of *actio*, I contend that Cervantes's *libro de pastores* is infused with a tension between sincerity and performativity, and therefore represents a critical juncture in both the evolution of the pastoral convention and the development of the author's constitutive brand of fiction. Recognizing this tension is also valuable because it enables us to modulate a polarization between pretence and authenticity that has tended to prevail in critical studies of the work. On the one hand, scholars have stressed the presence of untruth and concealment in the text. Cleaving to the mimetic limitations of language, Gaylord has asserted, for instance, that in *La Galatea* "language cannot tell the truth; it fails absolutely as a mimetic mirror in the domain of feeling," and that "we cannot know with certainty" the emotional reality of another's interiority.[17] On the other hand, critics have underscored the centrality of sincerity in Cervantes's first narrative, affirming that the poetic laments of enamoured characters cannot but proceed from an authentic inner disposition that corresponds with their words or, in Lionel Trilling's formulation of sincerity, from "a congruence between avowal and actual feeling."[18] Along these lines, Felipe Valencia has insightfully argued in two recent essays that "Early modern pastoral runs on the assumption of sincerity" and that the "convention does not work if the feelings shared are not sincere, or if the participants express themselves insincerely."[19] Sincerity, indeed, has long been regarded as a hallmark of Renaissance pastoral romance – in Jacopo Sannazaro's late fifteenth-century *Arcadia*, the archetype of the genre, the first-person narrator's name is none other than Sincero. For critics like Valencia, the transmission of true utterances is thus a necessary precondition for the bucolic *modus vivendi*, a kind of shibboleth for communal life in the bower.[20]

By the time Cervantes took up his pen, theatre, in contrast, had long been derided for what some perceived as its precarious affiliation with truth, accusations whose intensity would ebb and flow throughout the author's lifetime and the later seventeenth century. Distrust of the theatre on the part of moralists and other heirs of Plato was largely rooted in its visual component, which granted the performative medium an innate verisimilitude that was lacking in other arts like poetry. Along with its intrinsic reliance on the body and wide popular appeal among audiences, this proximity to reality scandalized many early modern commentators, whose anxieties only intensified with the advent of the *comedia nueva* and innovative techniques popularly known as "true" acting. This blurring of the boundaries around fiction in the popular imaginary was symptomatic of historical misgivings about "the treacherous relationship between appearance and reality,"[21] and was also part and parcel of the *theatrum mundi* topos that became a critical trademark of the Baroque. Placing gesture in *La Galatea* centre stage, as it were, opens a hitherto neglected vantage point on these debates, allowing us to see that for Cervantes's *pastores* truth and sincerity are neither chimeras nor foregone conclusions. A thoroughgoing exploration of the gestural performatives these characters enact allows us to attain a more nuanced understanding of authenticity and artifice, to grasp that the clash of these two concepts is not a zero-sum game. By attending to the frequently overlooked history of the early performance tradition, we find that they can in fact be mutually enabling.

Readers familiar with Cervantes's *libro de pastores* will recall the eclogue and contest between Orompo, Marsilio, Crisio, and Orfenio as by far the most overtly theatrical episode of *La Galatea*, which I will study below. But upon closer examination and comparison with other pastoral romances, multiple features of the text reveal a dormant resemblance, even indebtedness, to drama. The sheer fact that Cervantes envisaged the possibility that the work might be read aloud, supported by narratorial references to aurality, already approximates it to live theatrical performance.[22] Pervasive action (*drao*), in the form of both dialogue and kinetic motion, betokens further affinities with the dramatic arts.[23] According to Elizabeth Rhodes, "Whereas traditional pastoral 'tells,' Cervantes' pastoral 'shows.'" Viewed from above, this dynamism can be seen to resemble the movements of actors who continually step onto and exit the stage of a play. The relative dearth of in-depth stories in *La Galatea* allows for more characters to transit in and out of the primary narrative plane, a mobility that likewise means they are incessantly walking from one place to another, "as if all time not reserved for sleeping were destined for physical activity."[24] Characters constantly cross paths with one another, which not only breeds more dialogue but sometimes generates a labyrinthine confusion reminiscent of a *comedia de enredo*. Such seemingly chance encounters make *La Galatea*'s setting in the Tagus River valley feel notably more congested than that of other pastoral books, whose rustic inhabitants are more likely to exploit the idyllic solitude of the sylvan environment for contemplation or soliloquy. Of course, when Cervantes's *pastores* think they are alone, more often than not they are actually being surveilled by the prying eyes and ears of fellow members of the herding community. Arboreal features of the omnipresent natural landscape, such as trees, briar, and shrubbery, thus become devices akin to stage curtains that conceal a character and set up a dramatic revelation.[25] What Rhodes calls "the characters' obsession with themselves as visual objects" suggests yet another analogy with play going, in which readers too become covert yet eager spectators.[26]

Theatricality can be perceived in several discrete episodes of *La Galatea* as well. The encounter with the character of Lisandro, the first of several embedded narratives, sets the stage for the importance of dramatic elements throughout the pastoral romance. The scene begins when Elicio and Erastro become casual witnesses to a murder – a sudden event that interrupts the shepherds' songs of love and disturbs the tranquillity of the Arcadian setting. Indeed, since violent death on the first narrative plane is alien to the plots of other practitioners of the pastoral mode,[27] the vengeful killing would immediately appear to be more proper to the *comedia* and may thus be regarded as a dramatic element in its own right. Perturbed by the homicide and eager to learn the motives behind it, when night falls, Elicio wanders into a dense forest only to overhear the woeful, poetic lamentations of the assassin. After cutting through the thick bramble that threatens to hamper his pursuit of the voice's origin, the shepherd steps out into a small, round glade "a manera de teatr[o]" (in the form of a theatre).[28] Cervantes's word choice here surely dashes any lingering ambiguity about the theatricality of the episode, which we can observe in several additional details. Of particular interest for our purposes, once again, is how the thicket, the botanical threshold between the forest and the field, serves to heighten the dramatic suspense: the "espesísimas e intricadas matas" (intricate and extremely thick shrubs) surrounding the open meadow function like a stage curtain that is slowly drawn to reveal a new scene or character.[29]

In this case, the revelation is of the forlorn assassin Lisandro, whom Elicio finds posed in the most theatrical of ways: "[C]on extremado brío, estaba con el pie derecho delante y el izquierdo atrás, y el diestro brazo levantado" (With extreme exuberance, he was standing with the right foot forwards and the left one behind, and with his right arm raised).[30] Though it is adopted in self-defence, Lisandro's posture recalls the actorly technique of body torque onstage, as he turns towards the unexpected arrival of his spectator. Elicio quickly assures Lisandro of his benevolent intentions and implores him to divulge the circumstances that led to the homicidal act, which the perpetrator consents to do by narrating the story of his life. Crucially, however, his acquiescence depends on non-verbal cues to determine Elicio's motives, to know that he is a "true" friend whose overtures are sincere: "[D]ando señales Elicio de ser verdadero amigo del pastor del bosque y conociendo él que no eran fingidos ofrecimientos, vino a conceder lo que Elicio rogaba" (Elicio giving signs of being a true friend of the shepherd of the forest, and he, learning that they were not feigned offers, came to grant that which Elicio was requesting of him).[31]

Lisandro proceeds to recount the vertiginous trajectory of his life and his precipitous downfall, ending as a tragedy in the classical sense. In brief, the son of a noble Andalusian family falls in love with Leonida, the daughter of a clan with equal standing yet on the opposing side of a bitter political feud. To surmount the challenge of courting an enemy of the family, Lisandro resorts to befriending Silvia, Leonida's confidante and erstwhile object of affection of Crisalvo, Leonida's choleric brother. Silvia's interventions on Lisandro's behalf eventually win over Leonida and persuade her to partake in a clandestine rendezvous. Unbeknownst to them, however, a jealous and duplicitous relative of Silvia named Carino, whom Lisandro believed to have their best interests at heart, had secretly been plotting to exact revenge on Silvia and not only convinces Crisalvo that she has betrayed him but arranges for him and his accomplices to ambush her. In a tragic case of mistaken identity, however, the person they hastily attack and stab to death is not Silvia but Crisalvo's own sister, Leonida. Lisandro arrives in time to hear her dying words and, devastated by the loss, pursues Crisalvo for six months before intercepting him in the forest and mortally avenging his beloved, the event to which Erastro and Elicio bore unforeseen witness.

Yet bodily gestures continue to perform a central role in the exchange. The narrator remarks that Lisandro shows "muestras de un interno dolor" (signs of an internal pain), even after the distraught shepherd himself confesses that "es muy poco el sentimiento que muestro a la causa que tengo de mostrarlo" (the feelings I am showing pale in comparison to the reason I have to show them).[32] There are several insights to be gleaned from these passages and the text's more general emphasis on expressive signs ("muestras"). First, and most obviously, such a visual idiom is the marrow of the dramatic arts. Seldom does the text exhibit the need to designate what specific facial, corporeal, gestural, or affective signs a given character produces because it is easy enough for readers, albeit unconsciously, to imagine them. One need not be a playgoer per se to intuit, with the aid of various contextual clues, the kinds of feelings that Lisandro's body betrays, even before he narrates in detail his past and his motives. What interests me nonetheless about his emotional self-characterization is the breach that emerges between outward expression and psychological stimulus, the incommensurability of the affects he displays relative to their underlying causes. The notion that, to do justice to his feelings, he would have to emote to a greater extreme suggests, on the one hand, a self-composure and discretion accordant with the implicit social etiquette and decorum of pastoral characters who tend to channel their lovelorn despair into more sophisticated forms of poetic and musical expression.[33] The *locus amoenus* of *La Galatea*, or at least the behaviour of the noble herders who inhabit it, is largely incompatible with, say, the conduct of a Cardenio, whose psychological torment in *Don Quijote* drives him to carnal fits of madness (and who is then emulated by that novel's titular character, throwing all propriety to the wind).

On the other hand, given the foregoing theatricality of the episode of Lisandro, it is tempting to read his emotional self-restraint ("the feelings I am showing pale in comparison to the reason I have to show them") as a tacit acknowledgment of the authorial limitations of the printed medium. We should recall that Cervantes's most prominent writings before *La Galatea* were dramatic – including at least the two plays that have survived from this period and whose authorship is not disputed, *Numancia* and *El trato de Argel* – as well as the ample testaments to the fact that the author was throughout his life an inveterate man of the theatre.[34] It is therefore not unreasonable to surmise that drama exerted a potent effect on his non-dramatic fiction, as critics have extensively argued with respect to his later narrative works.[35] In his first foray into prose, it is almost as though he felt the need to remind his readers of the importance of the body, as though the text were exposing a latent self-consciousness of the compromises required by the permutation from stage to page. In any event, the external cues that precede and accompany Lisandro's self-narration serve to reinforce its legitimacy, to corroborate that the story of his life is true, and to prove that, his homicidal tendencies notwithstanding, his motives are beyond reproach. The presence and mutual intelligibility of a gestural idiom, however subdued, likewise secures the sympathy and support of his audience, Elicio. This legitimizing power of emotional body language is particularly significant because Lisandro is dealt his fate by the deceit of someone in whom he had placed his trust.

Indeed, if we review the finer details of Lisandro's story, we find that outward emotional signs augment the trustworthiness of upstanding characters and, conversely, tend to be absent in dissembling characters. When Lisandro attempts to convince Silvia to intercede on his behalf before Leonida, his eloquence is not as persuasive as the facial cues that accompany his plea: "[E]l amor me ministró tales palabras que le dijese, que ella, vencida de ellas, y más por la pena que ella, como discreta, por las señales de mi rostro conoció que en mi alma moraba, se determinó de tomar a su cargo mi remedio" (Love delivered me such words to tell her that she [was] vanquished by them, and even more by the sorrow that dwelled in my soul, as she perceptively learned from the signs of my face).[36] Among such cues Lisandro goes on to note that "las lágrimas que yo derramaba" (the tears I was shedding) left her "[m]ovida ... y enternecida" (moved to compassion).[37] Tears and similar affects become meaningful, capacious signifiers, manifesting the feelings of his soul and endorsing the candour of his words. We find a similarly worthwhile yet contrasting example later in Lisandro's narration, when he describes the strategy behind Carino's betrayal. Attempting to convince Crisalvo that the reason his love for Silvia remained unrequited was that she harboured feelings for Lisandro instead, Carino claimed that "si él no hubiera estado ciego de la pasión amorosa, en mil señales lo hubiera ya conocido; y que para certificarse más de la verdad que le decía, que de allí adelante mirase en ello, porque vería claramente cómo, sin empacho alguno, Silvia me daba extraordinarios favores" (if [Crisalvo] had not been blinded by amorous passion, in a thousand signs he would have already recognized it, and that to further verify the truth of what he was telling him, from then on he should look closely, because he would clearly see how, without any modesty, Silvia was showing me extraordinary favour).[38] Prima facie, this citation may seem to contradict previous examples in which physical or physiognomic cues certify the truth, since in this case Carino is weaving a complete fabrication. It should also be noted that Crisalvo goes on to take Carino's advice, spying on Lisandro and Silvia in an effort to corroborate the pretence that they are in love. And, in effect, their close interactions – which in reality are the fruit of nothing more than a collaborative endeavour to set Lisandro up with Leonida – appear to Crisalvo to support this very notion.

However, we should not overlook the detail that observing them from afar prevents him from hearing the content of their conversations and, presumably, from scrutinizing the more minute facial cues that might signal that their relationship is purely platonic. Nor should we neglect the power of suggestion or, in the terminology of modern psychology, of confirmation bias: it is conceivable that Crisalvo and his spies only glean signs that appear to prove the existence of mutual romantic affection, while potentially ignoring others that would undermine Carino's initial allegation. The text's emphasis on Crisalvo's impulsive, irascible nature – he tries on more than one occasion to kill Lisandro after observing him with Silvia – reinforces this possibility. In other words, this example amounts to a misinterpretation of signs, not a realization that they are inherently ineffective or specious. While Carino's ploy shows that outward cues can be misleading without context, in Lisandro's telling of the ordeal they are still held up as the ultimate arbiters of truth. In fact, Lisandro reproaches himself for taking Carino's words at face value while failing to observe the potential omens of his treachery, even if he excuses the oversight by pointing out that the conspirator had seemingly little to lose in maintaining his loyalty: "¡Ay, mal aconsejado Lisandro! ¿Cómo, y no sabías tu [*sic*] las condiciones dobladas de Carino? Mas ¿quién no se fiara de sus palabras, aventurando él tan poco en hacerlas verdaderas con las obras?" (Oh, ill-advised Lisandro! How could you not see Carino's double-dealing? But who wouldn't have believed his words, since he would have ventured so little in making them true with his deeds?)[39] From his self-recrimination, we can infer that a greater attention to Carino's actions and non-linguistic cues might well have exposed him as a traitor and thus spared Leonida her fateful demise.

Myriad examples throughout *La Galatea* bolster the correspondence between gesture and truth, particularly as it relates to love. In the very first few pages of the text, non-linguistic signs confirm for Erastro that Elicio, too, is enamoured with the eponymous shepherdess: "Erastro, por muchas y descubiertas señales, conocía claramente que Elicio a Galatea amaba" (Erastro, by way of many noticeable signs, knew clearly that Elicio loved Galatea).[40] In his dispute with the loveless Lenio in book 4, Tirsi defends amatory devotion while conceding that an attention to affective semiotics is vital for assuring lovers that another's feelings are true:

> [E]s imposible que el amante esté contento hasta que a la clara conozca que verdaderamente es amado, certificándole de esto las amorosas señales que ellos saben. Y así estiman en tanto un regalado volver de ojos y [u]na prenda, cualquiera que sea, de su amada, un no sé qué de risa, de habla, de burlas, que ellos de veras toman como indicios que le[s] van asegurando la paga que desean; y así todas las veces que ven señales en contrario de estas, esle fuerza al amante lamentarse y afligirse.[41]

(It is impossible that the lover is content until he knows with clarity that he is truly loved, certifying this through the signs of love that they know. And thus they so value a gratuitous glance and a token, whatever it may be, from their beloved, an indescribable gesture of laughter, of banter, of joking, that they in truth take as indications that continually assure them of the pay-off they desire; and so every time they see signs contrary to these, the lover perforce engages in lamentations and suffering.)

While Tirsi's commentary partially aligns with the many Neoplatonic writings on love in the Renaissance, in particular Pietro Bembo's *Gli Asolani*, the nuanced attention to the finer external signs of affection is as much a product of Cervantes's own discerning skill in observing human interpersonal behaviour.[42]

Such signs are put to the test in the episode of Rosaura and Grisaldo, in which the dejected young woman attempts to commit suicide in front of the man she loves, an act whose theatrical overtones have recently been observed by critics.[43] It is only through the swift intervention of Grisaldo, and that of her travel companion, that Rosaura fails to stab herself in the heart, and only through his promise to marry her that she finally desists. Later, she recounts to Galatea and Florisa the various tribulations and vicissitudes that led to her despair. The key detail for our purposes is that she reports having felt "satisfecha que la voluntad de Grisaldo de la mía un punto no discrepaba, según él me lo dio a entender con muchas y muy verdaderas señales" (satisfied that Grisaldo's wishes did not differ from mine in the least, as he gave me to understand with many very true signs).[44] Rosaura's choice of words offers a telling window into the complexities of her psychological state. Her stress on the truth of Grisaldo's cues and on her own certainty in interpreting them betrays, *malgré elle*, the subtlest of doubts. For the perceptive listener or reader of her story, the indefinite adjective "muchas" (many), the intensifier "muy" (very), and the prepositive adjective "verdaderas" (true) actually throw her certitude under greater scrutiny. It is almost as though such emphasis gives away an attempt, albeit unconscious, to overcompensate or atone for the circumstances that led to her near-suicide, whether in the mere interest of appearing more chaste before Galatea and Florisa (the most prestigious female characters in *La Galatea*), or to convince herself that her intuition did not in fact lead her astray. Rosaura's flair for the dramatic notwithstanding, her case exposes the reality that bonds of sincerity on occasion are woven with gossamer threads.

The most patently theatrical episode of *La Galatea* is the same one that most decisively lays bare the sometimes-tenuous threshold between truth and pretence. Midway through the text in book 3, members of the herding community from surrounding regions have gathered for the wedding of Daranio and Silveria, whose nuptial festivities include a sumptuous meal and melodies by the most accomplished musicians. The climax of the event, however, is a postprandial performance by Orompo, Marsilio, Crisio, and Orfenio, famous throughout the bower for their poetic competitions over who is the most forlorn among them. A rudimentary stage ("un tablado") is erected to form a humble theatre ("humilde teatro") so that the troupe, replete with elaborate costumes, can act out the verses "que ellos mesmos de la ocasión de sus mesmos dolores habían compuesto" (that from their own heartache they themselves had composed for the occasion).[45] In true theatrical fashion, each performer depicts an archetype of the trials of love: the sad ("triste") Orompo, the jealous ("celoso") Orfenio, the loveless ("desamado") Marsilio, and the lonesome ("ausente") Crisio, whose beloved is absent.[46] Taking the form of an amoebaean eclogue, the spectacle allows the shepherds to enact their respective passions, "procurando cada uno mostrar como mejor podía que su dolor a cualquier otro se aventabaja, tiniendo por suma gloria ser en la pena mejorado; y tenían todos tal ingenio (o, por mejor decir, tal dolor padecían) que, como quiera que le significasen, mostraban ser el mayor que imaginar se podría" (each one endeavouring to show as best he could that his pain exceeded anyone else's, regarding as the utmost glory being the most grief-stricken; and they all had such talent [or, rather, they suffered such pain] that, however they were able to represent it, they showed their grief to be the greatest that one could imagine).[47]

Though a handful of critics have remarked upon the theatricality of the scene, most have overlooked the importance of visual and corporeal signifiers therein.[48] Let us observe how Orompo opens the performance with a vehement apostrophe in the imperative form to his own words:

> Salid de lo hondo del pecho cuitado,
> palabras sangrientas, con muerte mezcladas;
> y si los sospiros os tienen atadas,
> abrid y romped el siniestro costado.
> El aire os impide, que está ya inflamado
> del fiero veneno de vuestros acentos;
> salid, y siquiera os lleven los vientos,
> que todo mi bien también me han llevado.
> …
> Pero aunque salgáis, palabras, temblando,
> ¿con cuáles podréis decir lo que siento

si es incapaz mi fiero tormento
de irse cual es, al vivo pintando?
Mas ya que me falta el cómo y el cuándo
de significar mi pena y mi mengua,
aquello que falta y no puede la lengua,
suplan mis ojos, contino llorando.[49]

(Break free from the depths of my stricken breast,
bloody words, mixed with death;
and if my sighs have you constrained,
open and tear through my sinistral side.
The air impedes you, which is already inflamed
with the fierce venom of your intonations;
break free, even if the winds carry you away,
since they have also carried away all my good fortune.
…
But even if you do break free, words, trembling,
with which ones will you be able to say what I am feeling
if my fierce torment is incapable
of issuing forth as it is, painting itself in the flesh?
But since I lack the how and the when
of signifying my sorrow and my distress,
may my eyes, continuously crying,
make up for what my tongue lacks and cannot say.)

Orompo's lament portrays the body as a hermetic realm, which to access (or egress from) necessarily implies resistance, force, and violence. Along with this emphasis on the corporeal, the pneumatic imagery of the first stanza – generated by the sighs, air, and wind – reinforces a stifling sensation of pressure, a pressure that his verbal expression cannot fully release. Confounded by the impotence of his "bloody" and "trembling" words, the doleful shepherd summons his tears to the mimetic enterprise of representing his emotional agony, with the eyes acting as a conduit to the otherwise impermeable domain of his interiority.[50] The ineffability of his feelings is such that spoken language fails to capture them "al vivo" (in the flesh), an expression that forms a subtle antithesis with the death that has commingled with his words in verse 2 and left them lifeless, bereft of meaning. The turn of phrase also recalls the actorly advice of Leone de' Sommi, the Jewish-Italian author of the most complete treatise on theatre in the Renaissance, when he urges players to perform their parts in a "lively" and "very vivacious way" ("vivezza"; "vivacissima maniera").[51] Gesture becomes for Orompo and his fellow performers the brush with which to "paint" their passions, a means of enlivening their affliction.

A similar emphasis on body language and kinetic movement emerges throughout the poetic dialogue. Note, for example, the remonstrance aired by Orompo, followed by Marsilio's riposte:

OROMPO

Un pastor que se atreve,
con razones fundadas
en la pura verdad de su tormento,
mostrar que el sentimiento
de su dolor crecido
al tuyo se aventaja,
por más que tú le estimes,
levantes y sublimes.

MARSILIO

Vencido quedarás en tal baraja,
Orompo, fiel amigo,
y tu mesmo serás de ello testigo.
Si de las ansias mías,
si de mi mal insano
la más mínima parte conocieras,
cesaran tus porfías,
Orompo, viendo llano
que tú penas de burla, y yo de veras.[52]

(OROMPO

A shepherd who dares,
with reasoning founded
in the pure truth of his torment,
to show that the sentiment
of his abundant pain
exceeds your own,
as much as you esteem,
elevate, and embellish it.

MARSILIO

Defeated you will be in this wager,
Orompo, my loyal friend,
as you yourself will witness.
If of my yearning,

> if of my unsound woe
> you knew the slightest part,
> your determination would cease,
> Orompo, seeing plainly
> that you suffer falsely, and I truly.)

Salient in the shepherd-actors' staged dispute is the fundamental importance of the visual and gestural, couched predominately in the verb *mostrar* (to show). In fact, within the eclogue itself the verb and its nominal form of *muestras* (signs) appear more than twenty times, while those of *ver* (to see) and *mirar* (to look) emerge with nearly the same frequency. The pervasiveness of such words stands as a subtle yet striking reminder that, despite the priority of aurality in prosody, outwardly visible cues will be of equal, if not greater, weight in Orompo and company's competition. The winner will be judged not only by the sublimity of his lyric, the rationale of his motives, or the coherence of his words, but by their delivery – the affects, mien, body language, vocal modulation, and facial expressions that make a given competitor's suffering appear to be at once the most severe and the most genuine. Indeed, the narrator reports that Orompo initiates his lines only "después que con triste semblante los llorosos ojos a una y a otra parte hubo tendido, con muestras de infinito dolor y amargura" (after he had looked all around with his crying eyes, and with a sad countenance and signs of infinite pain and sorrow).[53]

The other point to observe is the dichotomy of truth and fiction that animates the dialogue between the performers. In an effort to gain the upper hand, Orompo and Marsilio mutually impugn one another's feelings and cast aspersions on the authenticity of their opponent's affliction. Their exchange reveals the hyperbolic lengths to which they go in order to discredit the other's emotional anguish, with Orompo invoking the "pure truth of his torment" and Marsilio retorting by alleging his opponent's agony to be feigned, while brandishing his own as genuine. Several verses later, Orfenio will similarly appeal to the truth when proclaiming "que no está en la elegancia / y modo de decir el fundamento / y principal sustancia / del verdadero cuento, / que en la pura verdad tiene su asiento" (that the foundation and principal substance of a true story is not in the elegance or way of telling it, but that it has its basis in pure truth).[54] Critics have often seized on these words as emblematic of a broader Cervantine poetics that champions truth over rhetorical eloquence or affectation. Gaylord, for her part, asserts that these lines "voice an anxiety: 'truth' may give words a foundation; but only words, trembling in their incapacity, can provide evidence of that truth." While I agree that the competing characters' declarations "call into question the power of language to communicate truth about the self,"[55] their performance clearly proves that words are not the only medium available to the speaking subject for conveying candid feelings. As my analysis has substantiated, for Cervantes's *pastores*, bodily cues and non-linguistic signifiers like tears play an equal, if not superior, role in externalizing the desires, passions, and woes of the heart. It would therefore be erroneous to take Orfenio's dismissal of the supposedly spurious "way of telling it" as a broader, authorial indictment of demeanour, declamation, or non-verbal mannerisms, when in reality his assertion is itself nothing more than a rhetorical strategy to discount the authenticity of his competitors' feelings.

It also matters little that, due to what he judges as the implacable nature of jealousy, Damón proclaims Orfenio the ultimate winner of the competition. Of greater significance is the manner in which his and his fellow shepherd-actors' fixation on truth reveals the specular aspects of their performance and of the text as a whole. Not only does their choice of diction afford us a glimmer of the metaliterary irony with which Cervantes would so magisterially infuse later works like *Don Quijote* or *Pedro de Urdemalas*, but it also betrays a consciousness on the part of Orompo and company themselves of the underlying artifice of the script they are enacting. Unlike a true poetic competition, it is evident that they have scrupulously studied their lines and collectively prepared for a spectacle whose content is nonetheless intended to appear spontaneous. The irony of this awareness is further brought into relief by implicit stage directions in the dialogue, such as when they pretend to hide behind bushes to eavesdrop on another's laments and act startled when catching sight of the voyeur.[56] And we must not forget that their audience is comprised exclusively of herders like Erastro, Elicio, Galatea, Florisa, Damón, and Tirsi who not only engage in precisely the same practices but who, one imagines, thus reap a peculiar sort of pleasure or catharsis upon seeing their own obsessions dramatized in such sensational form. For readers familiar with later examples of Cervantine irony, it is difficult not to detect in these details a playful, tongue-in-cheek irreverence towards the otherwise earnest nature of pastoral tradition.

Other Spanish pastoral novels feature a similar scene in which characters act out an eclogue, namely Luis Gálvez de Montalvo's *El pastor de Fílida* (1582) and Lope de Vega's *Arcadia* (1598).[57] Besides Cervantes's version being more theatrical,[58] the principal difference is that Gálvez de Montalvo's and Lope's performers adopt the role and name of others, whereas Cervantes has his characters act out what are ostensibly their own feelings. Critics have adduced this anomaly to proclaim the existence of a paradox: "Does one judge the merits and miseries of a soul on the basis of rhetorical skill or on the basis of actual suffering?"[59] It is true that Cervantes's rendition of the eclogue harbours significant implications, as I will elucidate momentarily. However, we should neither accede to the temptation to erect too strong a binary between "rhetorical skill" and "actual suffering," as even scholars who have studied the *mise en scène* of the episode have done,[60] nor presume that Orompo and company's dramatization, because based on their own feelings, is necessarily sincerer. Turning to the oft-neglected performance tradition, we instead should heed the fact that, as early as Plato, actors have drawn upon their own emotions in order to make a production appear more realistic. Though Socrates ascribes Ion's captivating recitation of Homer to divine inspiration, the rhapsode himself attributes his success to *feeling* the poetry: "Listen, when *I* tell a sad story, my eyes are full of tears; and when I tell a story that's frightening or awful, my hair stands on end with fear and my heart jumps."[61] In the *Ars poetica*, Horace will advance much the same notion by formulating the dictum "[S]i vis me flere, dolendum est primum ipsi tibi" (If you would have me weep, you must first feel grief yourself).[62] That one's genuine emotions can enable an actor to more convincingly portray artificial ones onstage does not enfeeble the overall performative thrust of a given representation.

The narrator's ambivalence in his description of Orompo and company's performance, cited above, is symptomatic of this concept: "[T]enían todos tal ingenio (o, por mejor decir, tal dolor padecían)" (They all had such talent [or, rather, they suffered such pain]).[63] The equivocation between whether the high quality of their acting is due to performative skill or real feelings recalls Lope's *Lo fingido verdadero*, likely written around the year 1608.[64] Based on the classical legend of Genesius of Rome, the play troubles the distinction between reality and illusion through the character of Ginés, whose sublime acting talents foil attempts by the audience of a play-within-the-play to discern whether his religious conversion onstage is bona fide or feigned. Ginés, much like Plato's Ion and the performers of Cervantes's eclogue, draws on his authentic feelings to enable the realism of the ones he portrays onstage. Lope's metatheatrical drama reminds us not only of the Baroque fixation on the slippages between truth and fiction, but also that the late sixteenth and early seventeenth centuries were a pivotal moment for the professionalization of actors. Players of the newly forming theatre companies that interpreted the expanding trove of *comedias* endeavoured to surpass the limitations of *imitatio, actio naturalis*, and the more general bellwether of Aristotelian verisimilitude by transforming themselves into their characters and embodying their emotions with an increasing degree of realism.[65] Such techniques required what in *Pedro de Urdemalas* Cervantes calls a "cuidadoso descuido" (careful carelessness), a nonchalance that one fastidiously rehearsed in order for it to appear effortlessly natural.[66] It is not without sufficient irony that these practices came to be known by early modern thinkers like El Pinciano as "de veras," or true acting.[67]

Such vacillation suggests that the question we should ask is not whether the pain that the shepherds enact in the eclogue fully corresponds with that which they genuinely feel. The fact that, due to the standards of early modern performance, such a correspondence is nearly impossible to prove one way or the other should induce us to ask, rather, what implications such ambiguity holds for the rest of the work and the pastoral mode at large. The episode makes clear that Cervantes's herders possess actorly talents, that they are not only well versed in the rhetorical art of *elocutio* but that they have honed a more complete mastery of delivery through *actio*. Even if the rustic spectators that witness the staged competition are not actors *stricto sensu*, their capability to judge the performance means that they at least carry an appreciation of emotional theatrics and a consciousness of its artifice. They are also deeply invested in their self-(re)presentation. According to Rosilie Hernández-Pecoraro, "The lover's misery is, not without irony, a profitable endeavor. The greater the lover's distress, the more he confirms his perfect nature. The shepherd is most coherent, most 'whole' when he is able to project successfully his ideal self as an absolutely happy – because tormented – lover." Moreover, his "worth, his 'sincerity' and virtue, are thus determined by the aesthetic value of his words" and, I would add, by the non-linguistic qualities of his performance of misery.[68] All of this suggests not necessarily that members of the herding community are insincere, but merely that their laments are refined, carefully wrought, and potentially exaggerated when they are conscious of having an audience. Their incessant habit of eavesdropping on one another thus seeks to verify whether their torments are truly as bad as they seem (even if, were a shepherd to desire to appear sincerely miserable, he could probably just cry out alone and assume that, eventually, another would eavesdrop on him, pervasive as that situation is in the text).

These slippages between truth and fiction subtly prefigure the trajectory that pastoral would follow in the late sixteenth and early seventeenth centuries, when it increasingly becomes a metaliterary reflection of itself, holding a critical and even parodic mirror up to its own Edenic artifice. In Tirso de Molina's *La fingida Arcadia* (1622) and Gabriel de

Corral's *La Cintia de Aranjuez* (1629), for example, a group of courtiers dons the pastoral guise to live out a "feigned Arcadia," which calls attention both to the artificiality of the plots themselves and to the utopian idealism of preceding exemplars of bucolic literature. In his later fiction Cervantes too will playfully assail the fanciful detachment from reality that underpins Renaissance pastoral, with the episode of the "fingida Arcadia" in *Don Quijote* and with Don Quijote's own pretension, albeit unrealized, of adopting a pastoral lifestyle that would allow him to exchange knight-errantry for another literary contrivance of apparently equal delusion.[69] Despite Cervantes's ongoing intention to write the sequel to *La Galatea*, as early as his *Novelas ejemplares* of 1613 the author will deride the charade-like fictionality of pastoral through the talking dog Berganza in *El coloquio de los perros*: "[T]odos aquellos libros son cosas soñadas y bien escritas para entretenimiento de los ociosos, y no verdad alguna" (All those books are dreamed-up and well-written things for the entertainment of idle people, and of no truth whatsoever).[70] Though Spanish pastoral literature had its roots in drama with early sixteenth-century eclogues, by the time the bucolic returns to the stage a century later, it is largely as a simulacrum. In the words of Manuel Piqueras Flores, "en el interior del propio texto literario se descosen las costuras de una ficción que resulta, en la nueva realidad histórica, insostenible" (in the interior of the literary text itself come unstitched the seams of a fiction that turns out, in the new historical reality, to be unsustainable).[71] Pastoral's migration from romance to drama becomes symptomatic of its exhaustion, of the fact that in the Baroque the convention has become, so to speak, played out.[72]

La Galatea can be regarded in this sense as a suggestive turning point for pastoral, evincing a tentative consciousness of its own performative artifice long before other works began to critique the convention in less reserved fashion. The text's kinetic dynamism, penchant for dialogue, emphasis on dramatic visualization and gesture, and other mimetic tendencies suggest a cross-pollination with a theatrical tradition that had awakened Cervantes's literary ambitions and was progressively enthralling spectators in Spanish courts and *corrales*. Yet if by the turn of the seventeenth century the notion of sincerity in pastoral literature appears quaint, so as not to say untenable, then in Cervantes's *libro de pastores* we still find it largely intact. Such is definitively not the case with Cervantes's last work, *Los trabajos de Persiles y Sigismunda*. As I have demonstrated elsewhere, for the characters of this novel "outward emotional cues can prove deceptive" and "facial legibility is precarious," and that is why they struggle at nearly every turn to determine the authenticity of others' feelings.[73] Founded on the secret identity of the eponymous protagonists, the plot is largely driven by duplicity, suspicion, and betrayal that would be anathema to the credo of trust and communal bonds that tacitly governs the bower. While both *La Galatea* and *Persiles y Sigismunda* traffic in the uncertainties of love, in the former they are typically allayed by gestural expressions, whereas in the latter they are often aggravated by them. These differences may have as much to do with genre (pastoral romance vs. Byzantine romance) as with the historical ideologies that prevailed at the time of their composition (Renaissance humanism vs. Baroque scepticism). But if we are to perceive an ongoing theatrical influence on Cervantes's prose, then I would suggest that historical developments in acting techniques may also have had a hand in the waning reliability of gesture in his later fiction. If so-called "true" acting increasingly allowed *farsantes* to embody their roles with greater realism in the theatre, then so too may they have eroded the credibility of gesture and body language in kindred fictional ambits like prose. Though such a correspondence would be difficult to prove without more intergeneric studies of the early modern Spanish performance tradition, what remains clear is that the "true signs" so prevalent in *La Galatea* would become, some thirty years later, a shell of their former veracity.

None of this means, once again, that we must forfeit the claim to sincerity in Cervantes's pastoral romance. A world away from the perfidious lovers populating much of the author's later fiction, more often than not the shepherds and shepherdesses of *La Galatea* are indeed sincere. Conscious of the artfulness of their poetic laments though they may be, it is not that everyone becomes an actor performing a role – a commonplace of Baroque cultural studies – or that their histrionics enact or conceal emotions at odds with what they profess through words. Gesture in the Cervantine idyll is not inherently deceptive, but rather a vehicle for ensuring precisely that a given character is not. By confirming, in Trilling's words, "a congruence between avowal and actual feeling," body language serves most frequently to certify a herder's natural sincerity, even as the text brooks the possibility that love may be feigned and shows on multiple occasions that pastoral is not altogether immune to the vice of mendacity.[74] A priori presumptions of sincerity typically prove insufficient for Cervantes's shepherds and shepherdesses, who seek material, empirical, or otherwise a posteriori verification of another's authenticity after the enunciation of personal feelings.[75] Such wariness towards the prospect of fabrication is of a piece with the path-breaking realism that other critics have perennially ascribed to Cervantes's pastoral, which not only includes mundane elements wholly foreign to the tradition such as naval skirmishes, duels, brigands, violent death, and political intrigue, but also eschews the mythical interventions and *dei ex machinis* that provided tidy denouements to his generic forebears.[76] Of course, not all gestures are theatrical per se, nor must one be a trained actor to produce them. Many are the same semiotic resources we employ and observe in everyday lived experience, albeit unconsciously. It is usually only when we harbour innate suspicion that someone is lying that we knowingly fixate on such outward cues as eye contact, bodily postures and movements, faltering, or faint indications of nervousness. What I wish to underscore is that the characters' constant scrutiny of external signs, along with the narrator's persistent reference to them, likewise alludes to the *possibility* of deceit and incredulity.

More importantly, I would argue that this possibility constitutes a fundamental tenet of Cervantes's fiction, an incipient awareness that compelling literature requires the potential, however fleeting or slight, of untruth. By displacing assuredness from oath to gesture, the author situates truth at one remove from its initial affirmation, deferring momentarily the fulfilment of desire for narrative closure. It is here that we can glimpse the author's investment in a readerly suspense that only uncertainty can supply, his conviction that, unlike previous avatars of pastoral, newly innovative forms of prose fiction necessitate an awareness of their own capacity for concealment. Just as death sullies the utopian *locus amoenus*, as foretold by the Virgilian locution *et in arcadia ego*, so too must the spectre of falsehood, however minute, enjoy free rein among upright standard-bearers of the bower. If for characters an attention to gesture permits access to the otherwise veiled truths of emotional interiority, then for critics it allows us to pull the curtain back on a number of correspondingly obscure questions, disclosing at once the vestigial theatricality of the text and its fledgling aspirations for metafiction, its finer shades of sincerity and artifice, and the dramatic realism, with all its innate contradictions, that Cervantes carried to prose from the proscenium.

NOTES

1 I gratefully acknowledge Marsha Collins and Felipe Valencia, who
   provided insightful feedback on an earlier version of this essay.
2 Cervantes, *Comedias y tragedias*, *Entremeses*.
3 The lion's share of such studies naturally belongs to *Don Quijote*; relatively
   recent examples include Ife, "From Stage to Page"; Maestro, "Cervantes
   y el teatro del *Quijote*"; Ricapito, "La teatralidad en la prosa"; and
   Syverson-Stork, *Theatrical Aspects of the Novel*. For the *Novelas ejemplares*,

see Casalduero, *Sentido y forma*, 110–11; Lugo Herrera, "Teatralidad y picaresca"; Navarro Durán, "Gestos y escenas"; Olid Guerrero, *Del teatro a la novela*; Piqueras Flores, "La música"; Santos de la Morena and Piqueras Flores, "Cervantes y el teatro breve"; and Ynduráin, "De entremés a novela." And for *Persiles y Sigismunda*, see Adde, "Teatro y novela cervantina"; and Márquez-Montes, "Las artes de la escena."

4 Exceptions include Egido, "Espacio y tiempo," 51–2; Nelson, "Bucolic Suicide"; and Santa A., "Paradojas de la puesta en escena."

5 On the diversity and generic complexities of the eclogue, its status among sixteenth-century debates over poetics, and its affinity with drama, see Fosalba, "Égloga mixta," "Teoría y praxis."

6 López Estrada and López García-Berdoy, "Introduction," 69.

7 López Estrada and López García-Berdoy, 20.

8 Gaylord Randel, "Language of Limits," 254.

9 Gaspar Gil Polo in *Diana enamorada* (1564) says that in cities "es el hablar contrario y diferente / de lo que el corazón y el alma siente" (speaking is different and contrary to what the heart and soul feel; quoted in Valencia, "Sincerity, Fiction, and the Space of Lyric," 122). Unless otherwise noted, all translations, including those of *La Galatea*, are my own.

10 To cite merely a couple of examples, Murillo, "Time and Narrative Structure," esp. 306, 314–15; and López Estrada and López García-Berdoy, "Introduction," esp. 31.

11 On the pastoral "mode" and its relationship to "genre," consult Alpers, *What Is Pastoral?*, 44–78.

12 Bandera, *Mímesis conflictiva*, 124.

13 See Martin, *Renaissance Individualism*, 29–30.

14 Cervantes's characters "operate on the tacit premise that subtlety of feeling can best be communicated by the subtle refinement of language called 'poetry.' Cervantes plays with that assumption by permitting several characters to champion less polished speech as proof of sincerity" (Gaylord Randel, "Language of Limits," 259).

15 Cammarata and Damiani, "Actio" underscores the pictorial qualities of these elements and their relationship to the visual arts. For an extensive study of gesture in *Don Quijote*, see Torres, *Cuerpo y gesto*.

16 Luhmann, *Love as Passion*, 70.

17 Gaylord Randel, "Language of Limits," 261. See also Rivers, who states that "the artifice of sincerity is very artful indeed" and thereby allows for a dialectic that is at least partially compatible with my analysis below ("Pastoral Paradox," 133).

18 Trilling, *Sincerity and Authenticity*, 2.

19 Valencia, "Sincerity, Fiction, and the Space of Lyric," 121; "Poetic Persona," 99. In part, the contested status of sincerity derives from longstanding

debates over lyric poetry that originated in antiquity and intensified in the latter half of the sixteenth century. The polemic centred on the question of whether lyric poetry was mimetic – the poet's words representing a fictional experience that could therefore appeal to multiple readers or listeners – or, rather, an authentic expression of the poetic self, by which the verse faithfully enacted the specific feelings of individual poets themselves. The juxtaposition of lyric poetry and drama provides a useful contrast between the relationship that each genre has maintained to truth in literary history. In some ways, lyric poetry and theatre lie on opposite ends of a mimetic spectrum that we might imagine spans the conceptual interval between, on one end, the highly abstract yet true (lyric) and, on the other end, the verisimilar yet wholly feigned (drama). For more on the historical debate over mimesis and sincerity in lyric poetry, and its relationship to the Silerio episode in *La Galatea*, see Valencia, "Sincerity, Fiction, and the Space of Lyric," esp. 124–8.

20 "The shepherds of Renaissance pastoral drama, poetry, and prose pity the love laments of others and dedicate considerable time and resources to provide help and consolation on the assumption that said feelings and words are sincere. In the ethical sense, Renaissance pastoral posited a community that finds its strongest cohesion and properly pastoral character not in the allegiance to a sovereign who holds the monopoly of legitimate violence, but rather in the solidarity that shepherds feel for the plight of one another upon hearing of such plight in sincere laments" (Valencia, "Sincerity, Fiction, and the Space of Lyric," 121–2).

21 García-Arenal, "Facing Uncertainty," 11–12. For more approaches to the historical problem of unbelief, see Fuchs and García-Arenal, *Quest for Certainty*.

22 Cervantes, *Galatea*, 6.477, 477n. Citations of *La Galatea* refer to the edition by Francisco López Estrada and María Teresa López García-Berdoy. I have also consulted the more recent edition by Juan Montero.

23 Francisco Ynduráin considered Cervantes's prose dramatic that which had "algún carácter marcado de acción (*drao*) particularmente los diálogos en estilo directo" (some marked character of action [*drao*], particularly the dialogues in direct speech; "La ironía dramática," 689). López Estrada and López García-Berdoy also note that the proximity of characters to one another and the prevalence of dialogue lends the text a "cierto corte teatral" (certain theatrical style; "Introduction," 21).

24 Rhodes, "Sixteenth-Century Pastoral Books," 358, 357.

25 On the natural environment, I recommend Ken Hiltner's *What Else Is Pastoral?*, which leverages gesture not in the bodily sense but as an ecocritical means of showing that, even if it lacks thick description of the

ecological landscape, Renaissance pastoral gestures meaningfully towards urgent issues like pollution, urban sprawl, and sustainability.
26 Rhodes, "Sixteenth-Century Pastoral Books," 358.
27 Damiani, "Death in Cervantes' *Galatea*."
28 Cervantes, *Galatea*, 1.187. López Estrada and López García-Berdoy note that the source manuscript uses the spelling *theatro*, which they surmise derives from Cervantes's experience in Italy (187n).
29 Cervantes, 1.187.
30 Cervantes, 1.187.
31 Cervantes, 1.188. Shannon Polchow accurately notes the "inestimable number of references to the adjectival form '*verdadero*'" in the text, and thus that "the imparting of truth" is a "prevalent concern in the *Galatea*" ("Embryonic Manifestation," 174).
32 Cervantes, *Galatea*, 1.188.
33 "Todo en *La Galatea* rezuma discreción. Discretos son los personajes, la cartas [*sic*], los discursos, las canciones. Discretos son los pastores y las pastoras ... y hasta el mismo amor.... No en vano Cervantes desarrolla en esta obra toda una práctica del disimulo amoroso que era fundamental en las fórmulas de comportamiento" (Everything in *La Galatea* exudes discretion. Discreet are the characters, the letters, the speeches, the songs. Discreet are the shepherds and shepherdesses ... and even love itself.... Not in vain does Cervantes develop in this work an entire practice of amorous dissimulation that was fundamental in prescriptions of behaviour; Egido, *El discreto encanto*, 23–4). For a noteworthy example, see Cervantes, *Galatea*, 6.556.
34 According to Antonio Rey Hazas, "La teatralidad es uno de los rasgos que mejor define el conjunto de la obra literaria cervantina" (Theatricality is one of the traits that best define the Cervantine literary oeuvre as a whole) and "la figura de nuestro más destacado novelista es también la de un auténtico hombre de teatro que estuvo metido de lleno en la vida teatral de su tiempo" (the figure of our most renowned novelist is also that of an authentic man of the theatre who was fully involved in the theatrical life of his time; "Cervantes y el teatro," 76, 56).
35 "In prose fiction, he found a way of bypassing and overcoming the limitations of theatrical performance and the personal frustrations he experienced as a dramatist. In short, he found a way of giving the novel many, if not all, of the qualities of live performance" (Ife, "From Stage to Page," 94).
36 Cervantes, *Galatea*, 1.191.
37 Cervantes, 1.191.
38 Cervantes, 1.195–6.

39 Cervantes, 1.198.

40 Cervantes, 1.173.

41 Cervantes, 4.444.

42 Cervantes, 4.444n.

43 Hernández-Pecoraro calls Rosaura's suicide attempt "a simultaneously sincere and manipulative act of desperation" and "a masterfully theatrical performance" (*Bucolic Metaphors*, 178). Nelson, for his part, studies the "emotional theatric" of Rosaura, asserting that "in Cervantes's bucolic community, the herders who attempt suicide only do so with spectators present. With an audience, they transform themselves into actors who threaten their lives while their loved ones watch. Thus, due to the presence of others, one has to question the verisimilitude of their *performance* and their intention of carrying it through" ("Bucolic Suicide," 6, 3; emphasis in original).

44 Cervantes, *Galatea*, 4.394.

45 Cervantes, 3.344–5.

46 Cervantes, 3.337.

47 Cervantes, 3.338. According to Collins, all of this insistent bewailing endows the eclogue with "a peculiar tone of ironic, comic performance," "creating a destabilizing, almost darkly humorous theatrical nucleus for wedding festivities" (*Imagining Arcadia*, 154). For the tradition of the *cuestión de amor* from which the content of the competition draws, see Lowe, "*Cuestión de amor.*"

48 I must differ with the assessment in Montero's edition of the text that, due partly to a perceived shortage of dialogic exchange, the eclogue "apenas esboza una acción dramática digna de tal nombre" (scarcely suggests dramatic action worthy of such a name; Cervantes, *Galatea*, 3.176n). The pervasiveness of gestural, non-verbal language, as I illustrate in what follows, refutes such a notion.

49 Cervantes, 3.346, vv. 1–8, 17–24.

50 Santa ("Paradojas de la puesta en escena," 268) interprets Orompo's tears as proof that, at least in part, his pain is sincere, neglecting the classical phenomenon of crocodile tears and the abundant anecdotes of early modern individuals, actors and otherwise, who were capable of crying at will. See Johnson, "Feeling Certainty," esp. 68–9.

51 Sommi, *Quattro dialoghi*, 46.

52 Cervantes, *Galatea*, 3.351–2, vv. 170–86.

53 Cervantes, 3.345.

54 Cervantes, 3.358, vv. 357–61.

55 Gaylord Randel, "Language of Limits," 259, 258. Other examples of the debility of words in Cervantes, *Galatea*, 5.507, 510.

56 "Mas, ¿quién es el que mueve / las ramas intricadas / de este acopado mirto y verde asiento?" (But, who is it that moves the tangled branches

of this rotund myrtle and green seat?; Cervantes, 3.351, vv. 167–9); similar
examples in vv. 83–4, 194–5, 296–8. Santa also recognizes the implicit stage
directions in the eclogue, and astutely observes that the wedding décor
partakes of a similar theatricality ("Paradojas de la puesta en escena," 276).

57 Gálvez de Montalvo, *El pastor de Fílida*, 182–212; and Lope de Vega, *La
Arcadia*, 271–89.

58 Santa, "Paradojas de la puesta en escena," 271n. Nevertheless, it should
be noted that Belisa, Sasio, and Arsiano – the characters in *El pastor de
Fílida* who respectively perform the roles of Liria, Delio, and Fanio in
the eclogue – also impress the audience with their acting talents, as the
narrator remarks: "Con tales afetos representaron los discretos Pastores,
que a los oyentes no les parecia Representacion, sino propio caso" (With
such affects did the discreet Shepherds and Shepherdesses perform, that
to the listeners it did not seem like a Performance, but their own feelings;
Gálvez de Montalvo, *El pastor de Fílida*, 212). That their acting appears as a
"propio caso" recalls El Pinciano's directive that "el actor mire la persona
que va a imitar y de tal manera se transforme en ella, que a todos parezca
no imitación, sino propiedad" (the actor look at the person he is going
to imitate and thus be transformed into that person, so that it appears to
everyone that he no longer imitates, but makes it his own; López Pinciano,
Philosophia antigua poética, 282).

59 Gaylord Randel, "Language of Limits," 258.

60 Santa, "Paradojas de la puesta en escena," 273.

61 Plato, *Complete Works*, 943; emphasis in original.

62 Horace, *Satires, Epistles, and Ars Poetica*, 458–9.

63 Cervantes, *Galatea*, 3.338.

64 Translations of the work's title have ranged from *Acting Is Believing* and
The Great Pretenders to *True Pretence* and *What You Pretend Has Become
Real*. More literally, it juxtaposes the feigned ("lo fingido") with the true
("verdadero").

65 López Pinciano, *Philosophia antigua poética*, 282.

66 Cervantes, *Comedias y tragedias*, 897, v. 2911.

67 López Pinciano, *Philosophia antigua poética*, 284. See also Rodríguez
Cuadros, *La técnica del actor español*, 396.

68 Hernández-Pecoraro, *Bucolic Metaphors*, 97, 83.

69 Cervantes, *Don Quijote*, 2.58, 1201–8; 2.67, 1283–7; 2.73, 1325–8.

70 Cervantes, *Novelas ejemplares*, 662.

71 Piqueras Flores, "De la literatura a la metaliteratura," 201.

72 Piqueras Flores, 200.

73 Johnson, *Affective Geographies*, 185.

74 Cervantes, *Galatea*, 3.331, 5.525, 6.599. On lies in pastoral fiction, including
La Galatea, see Albuixech, "Deceptive Behavior," esp. 197–8.

75 This assertion is at odds with Avalle-Arce, *Nuevos deslindes*, 28, who instead defends the posture that Cervantes, like early modern sceptics, was suspicious of the epistemological reliability of the senses. On this point, see also Cull, "El engaño de las apariencias."

76 Collins, for instance, observes that "the borders of Cervantes' Arcadia" are "remarkably porous," and that, particularly with the protagonists of *La Galatea*'s interpolated stories, "the baggage, the details and contingencies, of sociohistorical context ... lend the tale the aura of verisimilitude, the illusion of the reality effect, and render their world imaginatively closer, if not coterminous, with that of the reading public" (*Imagining Arcadia*, 178, 149).

REFERENCES

Adde, Amélie. "Teatro y novela cervantina: Interferencias de los géneros en *Los trabajos de Persiles y Sigismunda*." In *Cervantes y el mundo del teatro*, edited by Héctor Brioso Santos, 119–36. Kassel: Reichenberger, 2007.

Albuixech, Lourdes. "Deceptive Behavior in Sixteenth-Century Spanish Pastoral Romance." *eHumanista*, no. 11 (2008): 186–207.

Alpers, Paul. *What Is Pastoral?* Chicago: University of Chicago Press, 1996.

Avalle-Arce, Juan Bautista. *Nuevos deslindes cervantinos*. Barcelona: Ariel, 1975.

Bandera, Cesáreo. *Mímesis conflictiva: Ficción literaria y violencia en Cervantes y Calderón*. Madrid: Gredos, 1975.

Cammarata, Joan, and Bruno M. Damiani. "'Actio' in Cervantes' *Galatea* and the Visual Arts." *Arcadia: Zeitschrift für Vergleichen de Literaturwissenschaft* 21, nos. 1–3 (1986): 78–83. https://doi.org/10.1515/arca.1986.21.1-3.78.

Casalduero, Joaquín. *Sentido y forma de las "Novelas ejemplares."* 2nd ed. Madrid: Gredos, 1969.

Cervantes, Miguel de. *Comedias y tragedias*. Edited by Luis Gómez Canseco. 2 vols. Madrid: Real Academia Española, 2015.

Cervantes, Miguel de. *Entremeses*. Edited by Alfredo Baras Escolá. Madrid: Real Academia Española, 2012.

Cervantes, Miguel de. *La Galatea*. Edited by Francisco López Estrada and María Teresa López García-Berdoy. 3rd ed. Madrid: Cátedra, 2006.

Cervantes, Miguel de. *La Galatea*. Edited by Juan Montero. Madrid: Real Academia Española, 2014.

Cervantes, Miguel de. *Novelas ejemplares*. Edited by Jorge García López. 2nd ed. Barcelona: Crítica, 2010.

Cervantes, Miguel de. *Los trabajos de Persiles y Sigismunda*. Edited by Carlos Romero Muñoz. 5th ed. Madrid: Cátedra, 2004.

Collins, Marsha S. *Imagining Arcadia in Renaissance Romance*. London: Routledge, 2016.

Cull, John T. "Cervantes y el engaño de las apariencias." *Anales Cervantinos*, no. 19 (1981): 69–92.

Damiani, Bruno M. "Death in Cervantes' *Galatea*." *Cervantes* 4, no. 1 (1984): 53–78.

Egido, Aurora. *El discreto encanto de Cervantes y el crisol de la prudencia*. Vigo: Editorial Academia del Hispanismo, 2011.

Egido, Aurora. "*La Galatea*: Espacio y tiempo." In *Cervantes y las puertas del sueño: Estudios sobre* La Galatea, El Quijote, *y* El Persiles, 33–90. Barcelona: PPU, 1994.

Fosalba, Eugenia. "Égloga mixta y égloga dramática en la creación de la novela pastoril." In *La poesía del Siglo de Oro: Géneros y modelos*, edited by Begoña López Bueno, 121–82. Seville: Universidad de Sevilla, 2008.

Fosalba, Eugenia. "Teoría y praxis de la égloga en el siglo XVI." In *Idea de la lírica en el Renacimiento (Entre Italia y España)*, edited by María José Vega and Cesc Esteve, 261–96. Vilagarcía de Arousa: Mirabel, 2004.

Fuchs, Barbara, and Mercedes García-Arenal, eds. *The Quest for Certainty in Early Modern Europe: From Inquisition to Inquiry, 1550–1700*. Toronto: University of Toronto Press, 2020.

Gálvez de Montalvo, Luis. *El pastor de Fílida*. 6th ed. Valencia: Oficina de Salvador Faulí, 1792.

García-Arenal, Mercedes. "Introduction: Facing Uncertainty in Early Modern Iberia." In Fuchs and García-Arenal, *Quest for Certainty*, 3–24.

Gaylord Randel, Mary. "The Language of Limits and the Limits of Language: The Crisis of Poetry in *La Galatea*." *MLN* 97, no. 2 (1982): 254–71. https://doi .org/10.2307/2906103.

Hernández-Pecoraro, Rosilie. *Bucolic Metaphors: History, Subjectivity, and Gender in the Early Modern Spanish Pastoral*. Chapel Hill: University of North Carolina Press, 2006.

Hiltner, Ken. *What Else Is Pastoral? Renaissance Literature and the Environment*. Ithaca, NY: Cornell University Press, 2011.

Horace. *Satires, Epistles, and Ars Poetica*. Translated by H. Rushton Fairclough. Cambridge, MA: Harvard University Press, 2005.

Ife, B.W. "From Stage to Page: *Don Quixote* as Performance." In *The Art of Cervantes in* Don Quixote: *Critical Essays*, edited by Stephen Boyd, Trudi Darby, and Terence O'Reilly, 93–118. Cambridge: Legenda, 2019.

Johnson, Paul Michael. *Affective Geographies: Cervantes, Emotion, and the Literary Mediterranean*. Toronto: University of Toronto Press, 2020.

Johnson, Paul Michael. "Feeling Certainty, Performing Sincerity: The Emotional Hermeneutics of Truth in Inquisitorial and Theatrical Practice." In Fuchs and García-Arenal, *Quest for Certainty*, 50–79.

Lope de Vega. *La Arcadia*. Edited by Edwin S. Morby. Madrid: Castalia, 1975.

Lope de Vega. *Lo fingido verdadero: Obras escogidas*, vol. 3, *Teatro*. Edited by Federico Carlos Sainz de Robles. Madrid: Aguilar, 1967.

López Estrada, Francisco, and María Teresa López García-Berdoy. "Introduction." In Cervantes, *La Galatea*, edited by Estrada and García-Berdoy, 11–108.

López Pinciano, Alonso. *Philosophia antigua poética*. Edited by Alfredo Carballo Picazo. Vol. 3. Madrid: CSIC, 1973.

Lowe, Jennifer. "The *Cuestión de amor* and the Structure of Cervantes' *Galatea*." *Bulletin of Hispanic Studies* 43, no. 2 (1966): 98–108. https://doi.org/10.1080/14753826620003430 98.

Lugo Herrera, Lilianne. "Teatralidad y picaresca en Rinconete y Cortadillo de Miguel de Cervantes." In Maestro, *Cervantes en escena*, 203–18.

Luhmann, Niklas. *Love as Passion: The Codification of Intimacy*. Translated by Jeremy Gaines and Doris L. Jones. Stanford: Stanford University Press, 2008.

Maestro, Jesús G., ed. *Cervantes en escena: Nuevas interpretaciones del teatro cervantino*. Vigo: Editorial Academia del Hispanismo, 2017.

Maestro, Jesús G. "Cervantes y el teatro del *Quijote*." *Hispania* 88, no. 1 (2005): 41–52. https://doi.org/10.2307/20063074.

Márquez-Montes, Carmen. "Las artes de la escena en *Los trabajos de Persiles y Sigismunda*." In *Cervantes y los mares: En los 400 años del "Persiles*," edited by Maria Fernanda de Abreu, 359–78. Berlin: Peter Lang, 2019.

Martin, John Jeffries. *Myths of Renaissance Individualism*. Basingstoke: Palgrave Macmillan, 2004.

Murillo, Luis Andrés. "Time and Narrative Structure in *La Galatea*." In *Hispanic Studies in Honor of Joseph Silverman*, edited by Joseph V. Ricapito, 305–17. Newark, DE: Juan de la Cuesta, 1988.

Navarro Durán, Rosa. "Gestos y escenas en las *Novelas ejemplares*." *Anuari de Filologia*, no. 5 (1994): 101–14.

Nelson, Benjamin J. "Bucolic Suicide: Suicidal Shepherds and Shepherdesses in Miguel de Cervantes's *La Galatea* and Gonzalo de Saavedra's *Los pastores del Betis*." *L'érudit Franco-Espagnol*, no. 4 (2013): 2–12.

Olid Guerrero, Eduardo. *Del teatro a la novela: El ritual del disfraz en las* Novelas ejemplares *de Cervantes*. Alcalá de Henares: Universidad de Alcalá, 2015.

Piqueras Flores, Manuel. "De la literatura a la metaliteratura: Una aproximación al espacio pastoril en los Siglos de Oro." In *Dimensiones: El espacio y sus significados en la literatura hispánica*, edited by Raquel Crespo-Vila and Sheila Pastor, 195–203. Madrid: Biblioteca Nueva, 2017.

Piqueras Flores, Manuel. "La música como elemento constituyente de estructura dramática en las *Novelas ejemplares*." In "Actas del Congreso Internacional en honor de Aldo Ruffinatto, Turín, 5–7 de marzo de 2013," edited by Guillermo Carrascón. Supplement, *Artifara*, no. 13 (2013): 195–205. https://doi.org/10.13135/1594-378X/431.

Plato. *Complete Works*. Edited by John M. Cooper. Indianapolis: Hackett, 1997.

Polchow, Shannon M. "*La Galatea*: The Embryonic Manifestation of Cervantes's Narrative Genius." *Hispania* 93, no. 2 (2010): 165–76.

Rey Hazas, Antonio. "Cervantes y el teatro." *Cuadernos de Teatro Clásico*, no. 20 (2005): 21–98.

Rhodes, Elizabeth. "Sixteenth-Century Pastoral Books, Narrative Structure, and *La Galatea* of Cervantes." *Bulletin of Hispanic Studies* 66, no. 4 (1989): 351–60. https://doi.org/10.1080/1475382892000366351.

Ricapito, Joseph V. "La teatralidad en la prosa del *Quijote*." In "El teatro de Miguel de Cervantes ante el IV Centenario," edited by Jesús G. Maestro. Special issue, *Theatralia*, no. 5 (2003): 315–30.

Rivers, Elias L. "The Pastoral Paradox of Natural Art." *MLN* 77, no. 2 (1962): 130–44. https://doi.org/10.2307/3042857.

Rodríguez Cuadros, Evangelina. *La técnica del actor español, en el Barroco: Hipótesis y documentos*. Madrid: Castalia, 1998.

Santa A., Sara. "'En el humilde teatro …': Paradojas de la puesta de escena de la égloga de los cuatro discretos y lastimados pastores en *La Galatea*." In Maestro, *Cervantes en escena*, 265–78.

Santos de la Morena, Blanca, and Manuel Piqueras Flores. "Cervantes y el teatro breve más allá de la representación: Un entremés intranovelesco en *La ilustre fregona*." *Anagnórisis: Revista de Investigación Teatral*, no. 7 (2013): 6–17.

Sommi, Leone de'. *Quattro dialoghi in materia di rappresentazioni sceniche*. Edited by Ferruccio Marotti. Milan: Il Polifilo, 1968.

Syverson-Stork, Jill. *Theatrical Aspects of the Novel: A Study of* Don Quixote. Valencia: Albatros Hispanófila, 1986.

Torres, Bénédicte. *Cuerpo y gesto en "El Quijote" de Cervantes*. Alcalá de Henares: Centro de Estudios Cervantinos, 2002.

Trilling, Lionel. *Sincerity and Authenticity*. Cambridge, MA: Harvard University Press, 1972.

Valencia, Felipe. "'No se puede reducir a continuado término': Cervantes and the Poetic Persona." *Calíope* 21, no. 1 (2016): 89–106. https://doi.org/10.5325/caliope.21.1.0089.

Valencia, Felipe. "Sincerity, Fiction, and the Space of Lyric in the Silerio Episode of *La Galatea* (1585) by Miguel de Cervantes." *Hispanic Review* 88, no. 2 (2020): 111–32. https://doi.org/10.1353/hir.2020.0013.

Ynduráin, Domingo. "La ironía dramática en Cervantes." In *Homenaje a José Manuel Blecua: Ofrecido por sus discípulos, colegas y amigos*, 689–708. Madrid: Gredos, 1983.

Ynduráin, Domingo. "*Rinconete y Cortadillo*: De entremés a novela." *Boletín de la Real Academia Española*, no. 46 (1966): 321–33.

12   Eavesdropping or Spying? Secret Places and Spaces in *Don Quixote*

EDUARDO OLID GUERRERO

– Jocasta: But that is slavery, not to speak one's thought
Euripides, The Phoenician Women

In *Eavesdropping in the Novel from Austen to Proust*, Ann Gaylin notes "novelistic eavesdropping is as much about creating spaces for individual experience as it is about policing them."[1] Eavesdropping is also a basic technique in spy manuals, although "escuchar a escondidas" does not necessarily denote spying and its consequences can be multiple, depending on how much the eavesdropper is personally invested in the information intercepted. Mimicking life, in literature the agent is often portrayed as acquiring and reporting data that can be analysed to create intelligence, but if they cannot process or transmit the information noted, the reader-spectator joins the character in a voyeuristic experience with dramatic consequences. This chapter analyses the leitmotif of eavesdropping in *Don Quixote de la Mancha*, where in part 1 (1605) Cervantes models theatrical scenes of overhearing private conversations in domestic spaces, and in part 2 (1615) implicitly references the political intrigues that took place at court and in the private domains of the wealthy and powerful during the period.

As a spying technique, eavesdropping implies acquiring privileged information containing political or military secrets, but in fiction the eavesdropper is often personally involved. As Karen Stollznov states: "Typically, eavesdropping has the connotation that we are listening in secret, without permission or knowledge of the speakers, that we

This research forms part of a larger ongoing monograph project titled "Secret Diplomacy and Espionage in Early Modern Spanish Writers."

know the speakers and are invested personally in what they have to say, which is possibly about us. And that we are probably not expecting to hear praise or compliments. As the adage goes, eavesdroppers seldom hear anything good about themselves."[2] The term *eavesdropper* comes from the Old English *yfesdrype*, meaning "place around the house where the rainwater drips off the roof."[3] Stollznov notes that "the word appears around the 1500s as a name for people who lurked under the eaves of a house to overhear what was going on inside."[4] Known as "eavesdroppers," the permanent residents of the Great Hall at Hampton Court Palace (built between 1515 and 1540) are "carved wooden figures tucked into the 'eaves,' the overhanging edges of the beams in the ceiling."[5] In the English Court it was assumed that eavesdroppers were present and aware that their existence was known.[6] The presence of these decorative figures in a political environment would not simply deter those sharing secret information, but also remind those professional spies of the risk they were taking.

Philip II was known as the "Rey de espías" (King of Spies) for expanding the Spanish espionage network and establishing the official repository for government documents, the Archivo General de Simancas, in Valladolid (c. 1588). The king's sombre public image was of a conservative and mysterious monarch who knew secrets; and secrets mean power.[7] The architecture of English and Spanish courthouses reveals this dynamic of private conversations taking place in a setting marked by suspicion and control. If Hampton Court had its eavesdroppers, Philip II's isolated Royal Site of San Lorenzo de El Escorial (built between 1563 and 1585) had its room of secrets: a dank, unadorned chamber located in the building's west wing. Legend has it that the architect Juan de Herrera took Felipe II to this room, whose acoustics allow two people placed at opposite angles to communicate without those in the middle being able to hear a word. Incognito as The Guardian Angel of the Workers, and in front of a group of oblivious courtiers, Herrera discreetly informed the monarch that the workers were desperate to receive their unpaid wages. The trick worked, and the king immediately liquidated all pending payments. Was the King of Spies scared by the possibility of a supernatural force present in his palace? Probably, especially since El Escorial hosted the most important private library at the time, which many believed contained a hidden collection of prohibited books of astrology, alchemy, and magic. Some of these vox populi rumours most likely reached Cervantes's ears, and he will criticize the belief in magic and the occult in his masterpiece.

Taking examples from classical Greek literature and the early modern English and French traditions, Freddie Rokem concludes that eavesdropping scenes usually include a male spectator hiding behind a curtain, or something similar, becoming radically affected or changed by what he has "noted," and frequently paying with his life for this subversive act.[8] Rokem notes the paucity of classical Greek plays with eavesdropping scenes; two are Euripides's tragedy *The Bacchae* (first performed c. 405 BC) and Aristophanes's comedy *Thesmophoriazusae* (Women at the Thesmophoria or The Poet and the Women, first performed c. 411 BC).[9] In both pieces, male characters eavesdrop on a group of women who are performing a ritual that excludes them. Once the women are discovered, the diverse outcomes lead Rokem to conclude that there are "crucial differences between eavesdropping in tragedies and comedies:" In the former, the eavesdropper is severely punished, even by death, while in the latter this indiscreet action leads to an elaborate negotiation.[10] These pieces by Euripides and Aristophanes had an indirect influence on early modern writers, via the oral tradition and written commentaries about them by authors like Plato, Horace, Aristotle, and especially by Erasmus of Rotterdam in his *Ratione Studii* (1511). In this last influential handbook, Erasmus provides a list of recommended authors for young pupils that includes Lucian, Demosthenes, and Aristophanes.[11] Cervantes was such a pupil, and he became very familiar with these writers.

The tragicomic nature of early modern theatre presents a much more complex picture, with three types of participants: one who hides, one who knows about the "set-up," and one who is unaware of the eavesdropping. Finally, the audience is also invited to join the eavesdropper and reflect metafictionally upon their own role as observers. Rokem takes on Shakespeare's *Hamlet* (1609), with Polonius hiding behind tapestries in Gertrude's closet, and Molière's *Tartuffe* (1664), with Orgon hidden under a table, to show how victims and victimizers quickly exchange roles in this kind of climactic theatrical scene.[12] Eavesdropping evolved in transit from the dramatic text to the stage, to then become a tool in the creation of the new novelistic genre, exemplifying Cervantes's singular experience as a playwright spectator cum novelist.

I have argued elsewhere that Cervantes was not only a consummate reader but a perceptive spectator, and that he recycled theatrical and performative techniques to renovate the Spanish short story genre and create the modern novel.[13] He frequently uses a pivotal eavesdropping scene in his theatre and prose. In *Don Quixote* he recreates the same tragicomic theatrical dynamic but expands the dramatic irony by including both male and female eavesdroppers, and by inviting the rare early modern Spanish silent reader, together with the *more* common indirect reader who listens to his book being read, to spy and eavesdrop as well.

Furthermore, Cervantes explores the uncanny aspect of eavesdropping by taking his readers backstage to reveal the trick behind the ghost.

Examples of eavesdropping in *Don Quixote* are numerous: the priest, barber, and Cardenio observing Dorotea; the innkeeper and niece spying on Don Quixote at the knight's home; during several scenes at the inns, and on multiple other occasions during the first and second parts, especially in private spaces like the ducal palace. In *Don Quixote*, 2.33, Cide Hamete describes Sancho "levantando los doseles" ("lifting up the hangings") to check that "no nos escucha nadie de solapa" ("there is no one except the bystanders listening to us on the sly"), right before sitting next to one of the novel's most skilful eavesdroppers, the Duchess.[14] The irony of Sancho's concern to avoid unexpected listeners/readers underlines Cervantes's direct audiovisual experience as a spectator of the *comedia nueva* (new comedy). He is a playwright recycling his and other techniques to create a new genre. In what follows, I explore the most significant eavesdropping scenes in Cervantes's novel.

Cardenio

As we know, the character of Cardenio is the only direct connection between Shakespeare and Cervantes. This hypothetical unidirectional relationship suggests that the Bard could have read or known directly or indirectly Thomas Shelton's 1612 English translation of *Don Quixote*. Among all the speculation regarding Shakespeare's interest in this quixotic character, it seems to me that Cardenio's eavesdropping scene could be one of the reasons to argue for this connection.[15] After receiving a secret letter from Luscinda warning him about don Fernando's betrayal, Cardenio enters his lover's home on the day of her clandestine wedding to don Fernando. He knows this house very well and quickly finds a recess in a hall window covered by two tapestries: "[S]in ser visto tuve lugar de ponerme en el hueco que hacía una ventana de la mesma sala, que con las puntas y remates de dos tapices se cubría, por entre las cuales podía yo ver, sin ser visto, todo cuanto en la sala se hacía" (*Don Quixote*, 1.27; "Without being seen, I found an opportunity of placing myself in the recess formed by a window of the hall itself, and concealed by the ends and borders of two tapestries, from between which I could, without being seen, see all that took place in the room"). From this hidden space, he witnesses a disturbing ceremony in which Luscinda faints while holding a knife (like Camila and Hamlet), while don Fernando finds, reads, and meditates over a note accusing him. Cervantes's public and private readers join Cardenio in this secluded theatrical niche, where he struggles (they all struggle?) to make sense of the moment. Whereas time seems to stand still in the scene, at least in his retrospective narrative, Cardenio blames Luscinda for her inaction, but not his own inability to defend his and their rights. He eavesdrops but does not spy, since he is unable to create reliable intelligence. He is one of those impetuous tragicomic male eavesdroppers who are incapable of considering an alternative to the narrative they construct. Luckily for Cardenio, Dorotea's resolution will help him find the strength to act. Later, in another eavesdropping scene behind a door at the inn, he listens again to don Fernando and Luscinda, but now he controls his emotions and ultimately confronts his unfaithful friend.

The Tale of Ill-Advised Curiosity

In the interpolated story of *El curioso impertinente*, read aloud at the inn by the priest for all the characters except Don Quixote, Anselmo asks his good friend Lotario to test his wife Camila's fidelity. Cervantes punishes his impertinent curiosity with the most humiliating eavesdropping experience: "[C]ubierto detrás de unos tapices donde se había escondido" (*Don Quixote*, 1.34; "Hidden behind some tapestries where he had concealed himself"), Anselmo watches how his friend tries and apparently fails to seduce his wife. The dramatic irony, of course, is that Anselmo is unaware that they know he is listening to their interaction during a spectacularly dramatic love scene that includes Camila's suicide threat and another knife. Camila and Lotario are performing for Anselmo to cover up their adultery, and thus the eavesdropper, once a conniving victimizer, becomes a victim. There are three levels of eavesdropping here: Anselmo listening to Camila and Lotario, the characters of the novel sitting at the inn listening to the priest read the interpolated story, and finally the readers or collective listeners of *Don Quixote*. The story will end tragically for all three characters, with Anselmo recognizing that he deserves his fate for trying to test his wife. The inverse pedagogical lesson for the audience at the inn, and for Cervantes's readers, speaks to the consequences of domestic coercion.[16]

In the ten intervening years that separate both parts of his masterpiece, Cervantes digested the success of the first book and developed a more sophisticated sequel that would allow him to incorporate sociopolitical references by expanding old and creating new narrative techniques. In part 2 he adopts a more cynical perspective on Spain's national and international geopolitical conflicts.[17] Consequently, eavesdropping scenes take on a different focus, escaping the sentimental context of the love story to enter a more complex territory that includes economic and political interests, power dynamics, obsession with immortality, fake news about fake books, and espionage.

For R.M. Sheldon the process to produce intelligence using secret information is the same no matter the kind of government:

> One targets the geographic area on which one needs the intelligence; one collects the information as best as one can; one processes the raw data into a coherent picture, and then one disseminates the finished product to the consumer or decision maker who will act on it. All of this must be done in a timely manner that will make the intelligence useful. It would not be unusual in an ancient world much simpler than ours for one person to accomplish all these steps by him [or her] self.[18]

Most of these steps are present in the following characters, locations, and scenes in the second part of the novel.

Maese Pedro

From a diplomatic reading perspective, Maese Pedro fits the profile of a possible agent, albeit an unconventional one. This trickster does not have the social web a professional diplomatic agent would need to survive in a national and/or international context, but he uses similar skills to create and benefit from local and regional connections in his nomadic life.[19] Cervantes's fugitive criminal "pícaro" transforms himself into a master puppeteer who employs for his own benefit and self-preservation techniques used by those at the lower level of an espionage network.[20] His tricks work, his disguise works; even his improvisation in chaotic circumstances works. The metafictional element of Master Pedro's puppet show reflects and exemplifies the same experience of listening to *Don Quixote* being read, including Cervantes's interest in revealing what happens backstage for the reader-spectator.

These chapters have been amply studied as a metadramatic commentary on the author-reader relationship, but a diplomatic reading centred on the practice of eavesdropping may offer a new insight.[21] Maese Pedro's ape is the first contact with an uncanny eavesdropping experience that Cervantes offers to his readers. He is relentless in providing an exposé, revealing scammers, and not allowing readers to contemplate the possibility that magic and the supernatural could be real and not just a skilful and well-rehearsed trick. Chapter 2.27's long title starts with this sentence: "Donde se da cuenta de quiénes eran maese Pedro y su mono" ("Wherein it is shown who Master Pedro and his ape were").[22] Dramatic irony has been suspended for the previous two chapters, but the first two pages of chapter 27 quickly reveal the hoax and the real identity of this trickster in the character of Ginés de Pasamonte, the dangerous criminal Don Quijote saved from justice in the first part of the novel. This first encounter with the uncanny aspect of eavesdropping in *Don Quixote* part 2 reveals a very old roguish system to spy and benefit from others' secrets:

> Por la respuesta de cada pregunta pedía dos reales, y de algunas hacía barato, según tomaba el pulso a los preguntantes; y como tal vez llegaba a las casas de quien él sabía los sucesos de los que en ella moraban, aunque no le preguntasen nada por no pagarle, él hacía la seña al mono, y luego decía que le había dicho tal y tal cosa, que venía de molde con lo sucedido.

> (For each question answered he asked two reals, and for some he made a reduction, just as he happened to feel the pulse of the questioners; and when now and then he came to houses where things that he knew of had happened to the people living there, even if they did not ask him a question, not caring to pay for it, he would make the sign to the ape and then declare that it had said so and so, which fitted the case exactly.)[23]

Hence, Maese Pedro makes money by asking questions around town about people, learning as much as he can about them, and then pretending to have his ape tell him that information: "Con esto cobraba crédito inefable, y andábanse todos tras él. Otras veces, como era tan discreto, respondía de manera que las respuestas venían bien con las preguntas; y, como nadie le apuraba ni apretaba a que dijese cómo adevinaba su mono, a todos hacía monas, y llenaba sus esqueros" ("In this way he acquired a prodigious name and all ran after him; on other occasions, being very crafty, he would answer in such a way that the answers suited the questions; and as no one cross-questioned him or pressed him to tell how his ape divined, he made fools of them all and filled his pouch").[24] Like the protagonists Chirinos and Chanfalla in the interlude *El retablo de las maravillas* (1615), Ginés/Maese Pedro continues on to the next village to deceive its residents with his divining ape and to entertain them with his travelling puppet show. But *Don Quixote*'s readers and spectators have been made aware of the kind of ingenious scam they may fall victim to in the future, and from this perspective, fiction has revealed a true deception and a hidden secret.

The Duchess

Mercedes Alcalá-Galán has shown how behind the secret of the suppurating sores on the Duchess's legs lies the key to her infertility and lack of intimate support.[25] The spouse as shareholder of private information also reflects the reality of female roles in early modern secret diplomacy.[26] The Duchess is an excellent reader of *Don Quixote* part 1, perhaps only matched by Sansón Carrasco and don Antonio Moreno. As a result, she is very adept when it comes to obtaining information about her famous guests. First, she performs a perfect scene of a noblewoman who casually crosses the knight and squire's path while hunting. Then, she performs all the introductory ceremonials to welcome Don Quixote and Sancho to the most desired palace she knows both have been seeking throughout the first part of the novel. Once the humiliating ceremony of Sancho's beard washing concludes, and he is separated from Don Quixote for the first time, the Duchess takes the opportunity to question the knight. In order to relax the interviewee, she starts by asking about Dulcinea's beauty; then the Duke takes over after she is humiliated for her (feigned?) ignorance of classical Greek orators.[27] It is then that the Duke who, performing as Don Quixote's admirer, obtains the main piece of information both noble readers were seeking: Dulcinea has been enchanted and transformed from a princess into a peasant. Once these data are recorded, the rest of the interrogation is just an attempt to humiliate Don Quixote by questioning him about Dulcinea's identity, her existence, and her lineage.

The Duke and Duchess now know that they must cross-examine the squire to confirm the knight's version, and then they will have the information necessary to create intelligence and design their own spectacle within the story. But for the reader, the most relevant part is Don Quixote's spontaneous love and support for his squire: "[Y]o no le trocaría con otro escudero, aunque me diesen de añadidura una ciudad, y, así, estoy en duda si será bien enviarle al gobierno de quien vuestra grandeza le ha hecho merced, aunque veo en él una cierta aptitud para esto de gobernar" ("I would not exchange him for another squire, though I were given a city to boot, and therefore I am in doubt whether it will be well to send him to the government your highness has bestowed upon him; though I perceive in him a certain aptitude for the work of governing").[28] This is also proof of the strength of Don Quixote and Sancho's friendship. It must, however, be confirmed by the squire, and Cervantes dedicates the next chapter to the Duchess's scrutiny of Sancho: "*Ahora que estamos solos y que aquí no nos oye nadie*, querría yo que el señor gobernador me asolviese ciertas dudas que tengo, nacidas de la historia que del gran don Quijote anda ya impresa" ("*Now that we are alone, and that there is nobody here to overhear us*, I should be glad if the señor governor would relieve me of certain doubts I have, rising out of the history of the great Don Quixote that is now in print").[29] They are, of course, not alone: "[T]odas las doncellas y dueñas de la duquesa le rodearon atentas, con grandísimo silencio, a escuchar lo que diría" ("All the duchess's damsels and duennas gathered round him, waiting in profound silence to hear what he would say"). And the readers are there too, as per the explicit title of this chapter 33: "De la sabrosa plática que la duquesa y sus doncellas pasaron con Sancho Panza, digna de que se lea y de que se note" ("Of the delectable discourse which the duchess and her damsels held with Sancho Panza, well worth reading and noting"). The Duchess conducts the questioning alone, now very skilfully spying on Sancho:

A estas razones, sin responder con alguna, se levantó Sancho de la silla, y con pasos quedos, el cuerpo agobiado y el dedo puesto sobre los labios, anduvo por toda la sala levantando los doseles; y luego esto hecho, se volvió a sentar y dijo: «Ahora, señora mía, que he visto que no nos escucha nadie de solapa, fuera de los circunstantes, sin temor ni sobresalto responderé a lo que se me ha preguntado y a todo aquello que se me preguntare. Y lo primero que digo es que yo tengo a mi señor don Quijote por loco rematado.»

(At these words, Sancho, without uttering one in reply, got up from his chair, and with noiseless steps, with his body bent and his finger on his lips, went all round the room lifting up the hangings; and this done, he came back to his seat and said, "Now, señora, that I have seen that there is no one except the bystanders listening to us on the sly, I will answer what you have asked me, and all you may ask me, without fear or dread. And the first thing I have got to say is, that for my own part I hold my master Don Quixote to be stark mad.")[30]

Sancho then goes on to disclose the main piece of information the Duchess was pursuing: he confesses that he can manipulate the knight, and that he indeed has made him believe that Dulcinea is enchanted. But the Duchess presses on in her cross-examination of the squire's degree of fidelity towards Don Quixote: "Pues don Quijote de la Mancha es loco, menguado y mentecato, y Sancho Panza su escudero lo conoce, y, con todo eso, le sirve y le sigue y va atenido a las vanas promesas suyas, sin duda alguna debe de ser él más loco y tonto que su amo"

("If Don Quixote be mad, crazy, and cracked, and Sancho Panza his squire knows it, and, notwithstanding, serves and follows him, and goes trusting to his empty promises, there can be no doubt he must be still madder and sillier than his master").[31] The squire offers a compelling answer to the Duchess's challenge by admitting she is right, and like the knight before him, corroborates the same apparently foolish but true friendship that unites them:

> … que yo conozco que dice verdad, que si yo fuera discreto, días ha que había de haber dejado a mi amo. Pero esta fue mi suerte y esta mi malandanza: no puedo más, seguirle tengo; somos de un mismo lugar, he comido su pan, quiérole bien, es agradecido, diome sus pollinos, y, sobre todo, yo soy fiel, y, así, es imposible que nos pueda apartar otro suceso que el de la pala y azadón.

> (I know what you say is true, and if I were wise I should have left my master long ago; but this was my fate, this was my bad luck; I can't help it, I must follow him; we're from the same village, I've eaten his bread, I'm fond of him, I'm grateful, he gave me his ass-colts, and above all I'm faithful; so it's quite impossible for anything to separate us, except the pickaxe and shovel.)

This answer has a profound effect on Cervantes's readers because it is one of those moments when fiction transcends its own deceptive discourse by speaking sincerely. Sancho did not need to delve into his private feelings for Don Quixote, especially when his new governorship is at stake. Don Quixote and Sancho could have just defined each other in negative terms, or played politics and lied to the Duke and Duchess, but instead they chose to speak their truth, to own their opinion about recent events, and to fearlessly relate their personal experience. As a result, it is the first lesson they inflict on their noble hosts: knight and squire risk speaking their truth frankly, even if it may cost them. Nonetheless, the Duchess is rather successful in her manipulation, and she now has all the information necessary to analyse with her husband and close circle of servants, so that they can elaborate the script, and design a complex series of theatrical productions for their guests.

It seems that the only occasion when the Duchess loses control of the situation is precisely in another eavesdropping scene in which she and Altisidora "escuchan a escondidas" the conversation between doña Rodríguez and Don Quijote. After hearing how this senior lady-in-waiting declassifies very personal information regarding the two ladies' bodies and accuses the Duchess of being indirectly responsible for her husband's death, the noblewoman and her servant storm onto the scene. The naive knight believes that enchanters are to be blamed for the sudden and violent interruption, but doña Rodríguez knows that there are not (and never are) supernatural forces within those Cervantine walls. She dares to speak frankly and ask for help, but she has been exposed, and together with her daughter will now be marginalized and targeted within the palace. Thus, this highly comical scene will end in tragedy once the information is later processed by the Duke and Duchess.

In general, the Duchess shows impressive control when it comes to acquiring private information as part of the espionage strategy designed with her husband to discover exactly what has happened to the knight and squire since they left their village. As proficient readers, the couple has an irresistible desire for immortality, for playing their upper-class role by humiliating this laughable pair of friends. This obsession leads them to spend energy, time, money, human resources, and gifts to spy on, manipulate, and find out all the secrets about their guests. They want to have a major role in the second part and become famous once it is published, and they succeed, though anonymously.

Avellaneda

The Avellaneda episode immediately follows the knight and squire's first sojourn at the anonymous ducal palace. Chapter 2.59 opens with both friends travelling the road to Zaragoza and arriving at an inn where by chance Don Quixote and Sancho are soon eating and eavesdropping in their chamber, listening as Avellaneda's Second Part is read in an adjoining room:

> Parece ser que en otro aposento que junto al de don Quijote estaba, que no le dividía más que un sutil tabique, oyó decir don Quijote: «Por vida de vuestra merced, señor don Jerónimo, que en tanto que trae la cena leamos otro capítulo de la segunda parte de Don Quijote de la Mancha.» Apenas oyó su nombre don Quijote, cuando se puso en pie, y con oído alerto escuchó lo que dél trataban.

> (It seems that in another room, which was next to Don Quixote's, with nothing but a thin partition to separate it, he overheard these words, "As you live, Señor Don Jeronimo, while they are bringing supper, let us read another chapter of the Second Part of *Don Quixote of La Mancha*." The instant Don Quixote heard his own name he started to his feet and listened with open ears to catch what they said about him.)[32]

Having discovered the existence of Avellaneda's apocryphal *Don Qui-jote*, Cervantes decided to employ a casual eavesdropping scene to bring this most personal issue of authorship and intellectual property to light. He also makes Cide Hamete treat this very personal matter as if it were fake news about fake books. As an eavesdropper, the knight is neither spy nor agent, so he reveals his presence on the other side of the wall as soon as he hears the right input: "Oyendo lo cual don Quijote, lleno de ira y de despecho, alzó la voz y dijo: 'Quienquiera que dijere que don Quijote de la Mancha ha olvidado ni puede olvidar a Dulcinea del Toboso, yo le haré entender con armas iguales que va muy lejos de la verdad'" ("On hearing this Don Quixote, full of wrath and indignation, lifted up his voice and said, 'Whoever he may be who says that Don Quixote of La Mancha has forgotten or can forget Dulcinea del Toboso, I will teach him with equal arms that what he says is very far from the truth'").[33] Cervantes then uses his protagonists to make those explicit readers confess that they are reading an apocryphal book. This scene becomes the first attack on fake news that the writer develops to expose the fake author Avellaneda, sending the message that there is fiction that tells lies, and fiction that tells the truth, or at least the possibility of an alternative and plausible truth. Like Don Quixote and Sancho, Cervantes decides to speak up and not remain silent about this spurious second part of his masterpiece. He could have ignored it or pretended it did not exist, averting free publicity for this anonymous sequel, while avoiding displaying his resentment publicly. By telling his reader that his version is the true text, he risked much more than deceitful Avellaneda, but he also took the opportunity to stand his intellectual ground, and in the process find new and original ways to defend his creation.

Don Antonio Moreno and the Enchanted Head

After abandoning the ducal palace for the freedom of the road, Don Quixote and Sancho run into and spend some time with outlaws in the Catalonian mountains. With safe conduct to cross the sierra, they enter Barcelona and are welcomed by don Antonio Moreno, who has been contacted and is aware of the protagonists' whereabouts. As Christina Lee points out, don Antonio is "discreto" (discreet) like the Duke and Duchess or Maese Pedro, in the sense that he is an influential, well-positioned citizen who shows cold reasoning skills and the ability to quickly adapt to circumstances.[34] Lee also notes how don Antonio reveals almost nothing about his life, while he finds out everything about the knight, the squire, Sansón Carrasco, Ricote, Ana Félix, and don Gregorio.[35] We do know that he is married and wealthy, but we do not know his profession, only that he is very well connected in the city, for he is called "el avisado de Roque" ("he to whom Roque had sent word"), the outcast bandit, and he is also a confidant of his royal counterpart, the viceroy of Cataluña. If Maese Pedro would have been at the bottom of the espionage network, don Antonio Moreno can then be read as a professional agent, with a well-established social network ranging from the outcast to the upper echelons of the monarchy. Don Antonio also offers his diplomatic services at the court to Ricote to solve his irregular situation, but the returned Morisco declines the offer.[36] The intimidation tactics used by the Duke, Duchess, and don Antonio Moreno are subtle but evident, if we read closely.

Like the Duchess, don Antonio seems to lose control of the situation only once, and Cervantes precisely chose this lapse to highlight his social position in the episode of the enchanted head, when we enter a secluded, private, and wealthy home where the supernatural occurs in one of the rooms. In *Don Quixote*, 2.62, Cervantes uses don Antonio to introduce once again the uncanny aspect of eavesdropping:

> Levantados los manteles y tomando don Antonio por la mano a don Quijote, se entró con él en un apartado aposento, en el cual no había otra cosa de adorno que una mesa, al parecer de jaspe, que sobre un pie de lo mesmo se sostenía, sobre la cual estaba puesta, al modo de las cabezas de los emperadores romanos, de los pechos arriba, una que semejaba ser de bronce.

> (On the cloth being removed Don Antonio, taking Don Quixote by the hand, passed with him into a distant room in which there was nothing in the way of furniture except a table, apparently of jasper, resting on a pedestal of the same, upon which was set up, after the fashion of the busts of the Roman emperors, a head which seemed to be of bronze.)

As an introduction to his show, don Antonio pretends and performs the same search for eavesdroppers that Sancho innocently did in front of the Duchess:

> Paseóse don Antonio con don Quijote por todo el aposento, rodeando muchas veces la mesa, después de lo cual dijo: «Agora, señor don Quijote, *que estoy enterado que no nos oye y escucha alguno* y está cerrada la puerta, quiero contar a vuestra merced una de las más raras aventuras, o, por mejor decir, novedades, que imaginarse pueden, con condición que lo que a vuestra merced dijere lo ha de depositar en los últimos retretes del secreto.»

(Don Antonio traversed the whole apartment with Don Quixote and walked round the table several times, and then said, "Now, Senor Don Quixote, that I am satisfied that no one is listening to us, and that the door is shut, I will tell you of one of the rarest adventures, or more properly speaking strange things, that can be imagined, on condition that you will keep what I say to you in the remotest recesses of secrecy.")[37]

Don Antonio histrionically describes his mysterious object, which has similar properties to Maese Pedro's ape, based on being accurate when answering the questioner:

En esto, tomándole la mano don Antonio, se la paseó por la cabeza de bronce y por toda la mesa y por el pie de jaspe sobre que se sostenía, y luego dijo: «Esta cabeza, señor don Quijote, ha sido hecha y fabricada por uno de los mayores encantadores y hechiceros que ha tenido el mundo, que creo era polaco de nación y dicípulo del famoso Escotillo, de quien tantas maravillas se cuentan; el cual estuvo aquí en mi casa, y por precio de mil escudos que le di labró esta cabeza, que tiene propiedad y virtud de responder a cuantas cosas al oído le preguntaren. Guardó rumbos, pintó carácteres, observó astros, miró puntos y, finalmente, la sacó con la perfeción que veremos mañana, porque los viernes está muda, y hoy, que lo es, nos ha de hacer esperar hasta mañana. En este tiempo podrá vuestra merced prevenirse de lo que querrá preguntar, que por esperiencia sé que dice verdad en cuanto responde.»[38]

(Don Antonio taking his hand passed it over the bronze head and the whole table and the pedestal of jasper on which it stood, and then said, "This head, Senor Don Quixote, has been made and fabricated by one of the greatest magicians and wizards the world ever saw, a Pole, I believe, by birth, and a pupil of the famous Escotillo of whom such marvellous stories are told. He was here in my house, and for a consideration of a thousand crowns that I gave him he constructed this head, which has the property and virtue of answering whatever questions are put to its ear. He observed the points of the compass, he traced figures, he studied the stars, he watched favourable moments, and at length brought it to the perfection we shall see to-morrow, for on Fridays it is mute, and this being Friday we must wait till the next day. In the interval your worship may consider what you would like to ask it; and I know by experience that in all its answers it tells the truth.")[39]

Don Antonio finishes this spectacular introduction by emphasizing the head's fact-telling powers, which until then were unproved: "Contóles la propiedad que tenía, encargóles el secreto y díjoles que aquel era el primero día donde se había de probar la virtud de la tal cabeza encantada. Y si no eran los dos amigos de don Antonio, ninguna otra persona sabía el busilis del encanto" ("He explained to them the property it possessed and entrusted the secret to them, telling them that now for the first time he was going to try the virtue of the enchanted head; but except Don Antonio's two friends no one else was privy to the mystery of the enchantment").[40] Hence, it seems that Benengeli is suggesting that don Antonio is either lying, which is quite likely, and that other previous guests know about this wonder and are necessarily keeping the secret, or don Antonio is telling the truth, which means that this bust has never spoken before.

This magic head seemingly belongs to, or anticipates, a series of bizarre mechanical wonders from the Baroque tradition that were constructed by specialists within the Jesuit order for use in stage performances; they were deliberately designed to captivate, as well as convert, their audiences. But this is not *Hamlet*'s ghost, nor the *deus ex machina* of Tirso de Molina's *El burlador de Sevilla y convidado de piedra* (1616). While on the stage technology was used to conceal the modus operandi of these wonders, Cervantes once again reveals the trick behind the curtain: "El cual quiso Cide Hamete Benengeli declarar luego, por no tener suspenso al mundo creyendo que algún hechicero y extraordinario misterio en la tal cabeza se encerraba, y, así, dice que don Antonio Moreno, a imitación de otra cabeza que vio en Madrid fabricada por un estampero, hizo esta en su casa para entretenerse y suspender a los ignorantes" ("This [wonder] Cide Hamete Benengeli thought fit to reveal at once, not to keep the world in suspense, fancying that the head had some strange magical mystery in it. He says, therefore, that on the model of another head, the work of an image maker, which he had seen at Madrid, Don Antonio made this one at home for his own amusement and to astonish ignorant people").[41] Don Quixote and Sancho continue their journey believing in the extraordinary properties of the enchanted head, but not the reader. Cide Hamete explains that the bust, pedestal, and slab were hollow and led down into the room below, where don Antonio's clever nephew responded to the questions.

An illustration of a similar eavesdropping device, Athanasius Kircher's Panoucosticon – an invention to conduct and amplify sound – can be found in his 1650s *Musurgia universalis*, and at the entrance gallery of the Kircherianum Museum located in the Jesuit Collegium Romanum.[42] Caroline Wilkins notes that "visually inanimate, the stone bust becomes sonically animated by means of an intentional acousmatization or 'ventriloquism.'… Its inanimate, seeming non-presence is uncanny and suggests a double role – that of both hearer and teller, a vehicle of transmission."[43] Even though Kircher's Panousticon is post-Cervantes, the trick is not. From this point of view, don Antonio's talking head serves as entertainment for his guests but, as Cide Hamete promptly disclosed, it is a deliberately constructed surveillance system, and it could have been used to spy on them. After the episode with Don Quixote and Sancho, this nobleman quickly realizes his private toy is not solely for his elitist audience anymore, but vox populi, so he reports it to the Inquisition to avoid speculation about possible demonic influences. Benengeli narrates the adventure's possible Inquisitorial implications, explaining that don Antonio received a request to destroy the artefact without the accustomed investigation. This tells us first that don Antonio's social connections grant him certain privileges and leads us to wonder whether he has indeed followed through, or whether he kept the bust to continue exploiting its qualities. If we accept the non-textual possibility that the bronze bust has been functioning as an eavesdropper for don Antonio to spy on his guests, he has now exposed himself to all those who were once in that room, so they know that he knows their secrets.

As Joseph R. Jones notes, "Golden Age writers were aware of oracular statues among the ancients."[44] As a probable source for Cervantes, Antonio Vives Coll points to the puppet snake of the Greek cult of Glykon in the second century, which led to the publication in the year 180 of *Alexander, or The False Prophet* by Lucian of Samosata, translated into Latin by no other than Erasmus of Rotterdam, with several editions in the sixteenth century.[45] Many believed that the oracle of the serpent created by Alexander of Abonoteico was infallible; otherwise the pilgrim was to blame for not understanding it correctly. Thus, in addition to charging him extra for contemplating the snake and receiving an "autophone oracle," he could also acquire an "explanation du texte" of the prediction.[46] This was too much for Lucian, who risked his life denouncing Alexander's cult in a very similar style to the one Cide Hamete uses to expose Ginés/Maese Pedro's monkey and don Antonio's gadget. Steven Hutchinson reminds us that Cervantes and Lucian were obsessed with separating truth from lies, and truth tellers from liars within a credible fiction.[47] In the prologue to *A True Story*, Lucian uses the "liar's paradox" to declare: "I now make the only true statement you are to expect – that I am a liar" (13). In *Don Quixote*, 2.51 Sancho faces "la paradoja del puente" (the bridge paradox), an amusing logic problem based on the doctrine of fallacy but a public officer's waste of time. Solving the dilemma, Sancho exposes the real paradox of an illiterate governor using common sense to succeed where he was supposed to fail.[48] For Lucian and Cervantes, a hypocritical wise man is also a deceitful trickster.[49] They both understood the irony of factual fiction, but they also dared and valued telling the truth, even when you lie.

So, what is the possible Cervantine answer to the consequences of coercion caused by eavesdroppers, spies, and "magic" animals or echo chambers? It seems to me that the only ability left to our protagonists, emissaries in the middle of this deceitful fictional environment that forms the second part of the novel, is to speak candidly. And this is what they do when they interact with the rest of the characters in the second book. If we view these two friends as diplomatic ambassadors of their own fiction, we expect – along with most early modern theorists – that they will speak with measure and great care, and on occasions Don Quixote tries to do so, without much success.[50] As a soft power technique used in diplomatic circles, such prudence was also associated with a form of servility, and ultimately with a performance based on lies and dissimulation.[51] Instead, the knight and his squire mostly exercise a diplomatic tactic via a classical rhetorical figure of speech that is also a stoic and naive virtue, that of Parrhesia or to speak freely, emphasizing here its anti-tyrannical meaning.[52] As Michel Foucault notes: "The one who uses parrhesia, the parrhesiastes, is someone who says everything he has in mind: he does not hide anything, but opens his heart and mind completely to other people through his discourse."[53] In the dialogue "The Dead Come to Life, or The Fisherman," Lucian calls himself "Parrhesiades," and faces a list of dead philosophers who accuse him of depicting them comically.[54] In *The Phoenician Women* (first performed c. 412–408 BC), Euripides's Jocasta declares: "But that is slavery, not to speak one's thought." Her grandson Polyneices agrees, because if you do not dare to speak your mind: "One must endure the unwisdom of one's masters"; and Jocasta accedes: "This is also painful, to join with fools in folly."[55] Like Lucian and Erasmus showed before him, Cervantes finds a way to make this a less painful journey. In the fascinating self-reflective learning process Sancho experiences while he interacts with Don Quixote, the squire also assumes the importance of speaking frankly, and both friends make clear that, as Erasmus would say, we should praise the fools, especially those who speak truth to power. Freedom of speech implies a risk, but as Foucault clarifies, it is "not about dealing with the problem of truth, but with the problem of the truth-teller or truth-telling as an activity."[56] During the second part of the story, whether together or separate, Don Quixote and Sancho are ambassadors of their own fiction, for they have the courage to exercise parrhesia by openly speaking their version of the truth already written and read, to defend their name, legacy, friendship, and identity, even at personal risk.[57]

Cervantes's Cide Hamete Benengeli assumes that his story is being read and heard in an oral reading of the text. During chapter 2.66, "Que trata de lo que verá el que lo leyere o lo oirá el que lo escuchare leer" ("Which treats of what he who reads will see, or what he who has it read to him will hear"), the solitary reader and the collective audience share with the narrator the experience of returning home from Barcelona after the knight's defeat. It is not the same to read as to hear a reading, but ultimately the Cervantine lesson to observe, listen, read critically, and eventually speak freely can be achieved by all. Caught in the complex meta-discourse of a self-reflective book, the eavesdropping audience and readers are subject not only to the confessions of its individual protagonists, but also to their secrets. Cervantes makes his reading audience eavesdroppers for they become witnesses, gathering information and processing intelligence and thus holding power over the protagonists. And with this power comes responsibility. Like Parrehsiastes, Don Quixote and Sancho dare to speak the truth to everybody, and if they can do it, everybody can. Meanwhile, Cervantes, via Cide Hamete, uncovers the secret tragicomic space of the eavesdropper, unmasks the Spanish nobility's obsession with immortality, reveals cheating tricks and mechanisms to spy on others, and even denounces the author of an unsolicited and fake second part of his book. In the end, the ultimate eavesdropper, the perfect spy and whistle-blower, the trickster pretending to be a ghost, could be Cervantes himself, perhaps still hiding behind the hangings Sancho is lifting.

NOTES

1 Gaylin, *Eavesdropping in the Novel*, 184n35.

2 Stollznov, "Eavesdropping."

3 Online Etymology Dictionary, s.v. "eavesdropper": mid fifteenth century, with agent-noun ending + Middle English *eavesdrop*, from Old English *yfesdrype* ("place around a house where the rainwater drips off the roof") from *eave* (q.v.) + *drip* (v.). Technically, "One who stands at walls or windows to overhear what's going on inside."

4 Stollznov, "Eavesdropping."

5 Stollznov. As Stollznov reminds us, "More of a warning than decoration, eavesdroppers were gossip stoppers that smiled down on guests … a grim reminder that you were always being watched and heard by courtiers and servants."

6 Since the fourteenth century, eavesdropping was a minor public offence. According to Blackstone, "Eavesdroppers, or such as listen under walls or windows, or the eaves of a house, to hearken after discourse, and thereupon to frame slanderous and mischievous tales, are a common nuisance and presentable at the court-leet" (*Commentaries*, book 4, chap. 13, 169).

7 In many of Felipe II's portraits his black garb suggests sobriety, austerity, and Counter- Reformation conservatism. See Colomer, "Black and the Royal Image."

8 Rokem, "Processes of Eavesdropping," 112.

9 Rokem, 112. Caroline Wilkins adds that "Phaedra in *Hippolytus* by Euripides (428 BC) also eavesdrops, but from a visible position onstage that is witnessed by the audience, whilst her unseen 'victims' reveal their verbal secrets from behind a closed door" ("Panacousticon," 11).

10 Rokem, "Processes of Eavesdropping," 112.

11 On Euripides and his influence, see Harsh, *Handbook of Classical Drama*, 237. Aristophanes's Latin translations of the plays by Andreas Divus (Venice, 1528) circulated widely throughout Europe in the Renaissance, and these were soon followed by translations and adaptations in modern languages; see Peterson, *Laughter on the Fringes*, 185. Curiously, Demosthenes is mentioned by the knight in chapter 32 of part 2: "Retórica demostina – respondió don Quijote – es lo mismo que decir retórica de Demóstenes" (Demosthenian eloquence, said Don Quixote, means the eloquence of Demosthenes). This interaction shows the Duchess's pretended ignorance about classical Greek orators. All quotations from *Don Quijote* include the volume and chapter number and are from the 1998 Rico edition. All English translations are by Ormsby.

12 Rokem, "Processes of Eavesdropping," 113.

13 See Olid Guerrero, *Del teatro a la novela*.

14 Clemencín's 1833–9 edition of *Don Quijote* notes: "Solapa (de). 'He visto que no nos escucha nadie de solapa.' Esto es, encubierto ó escondido de propósito, para escuchar" (On the sly: "There is no one except the bystanders listening to us on the sly." Meaning, uncover or hidden on purpose, to listen; in Bradford, *Índice*, 496).

15 On Cardenio and Shakespeare, see Carnegie and Taylor, *Quest for Cardenio*; and Chartier, *Cardenio*.

16 Carrizales experiences a very similar dramatic situation in Cervantes's short novel *El celoso extremeño* (1613).

17 In the first decade of the seventeenth century, Cervantes witnessed how the Treaty of London (1604) ended sixteen years of Anglo-Spanish war. He also saw how Francisco Gómes de Sandoval y Rojas, first duke of Lerma, went from advisor to *privado* (minister), assuming most of the royal powers, because Philip III could not carry on his father's (Philip II) royal

duties. The tensions between court, nobility, and clergy produced a lack of clear leadership from Madrid, and as a result viceroys and ambassadors in Europe advanced diplomacy in terms of Spanish power but also as it suited their own interests. On the questionable role of the duke of Lerma as true advisor to King Philip III, see Feros, *Kingship and Favoritism*.

18 Sheldon, *Espionage*, 8.

19 Given his already established itinerant life, Maese Pedro fits the profile of a "captado" (hooked), those nonprofessional agents that under coercion or seduced by the promise of quick money could be hired to obtain privileged information. See Carnicer García and Marcos Rivas, *Sebastián de Arbizu*, 82–4.

20 Navarro Bonilla (*Los archivos del espionaje*, 67) synthetizes Carnicer García and Marcos Rivas's detailed description of the structure of the Spanish monarchy's intelligence apparatus, using a pyramid illustration divided into three levels: the first, the directional level, consisting of the "Rey, Secretario de Estado, Secretarios personales" (the king, the secretary of state, and personal secretaries); the coordination level, comprising the "Superintendente general de las inteligencias secretas - Espía mayor de la corte, and Delegados territoriales - Virreyes, embajadas, ..." (the General Supervisor of Secret Intelligence, the court's major spy; and territorial delegates – viceroys, embassies, and so on); and the collection level, consisting of "Espías principales, agentes ocasionales" (main spies and occasional agents).

21 On Maese Pedro's theatrical element, see Díez Borque, "Teatro"; on the use of the trick, see Rodríguez and García Sprackling, "Presencia." Regarding the language and technique of metadrama Cervantes uses with Maese Pedro's puppet show, see Olid Guerrero, "Donde lo verá."

22 The complete title of chapter 2.27 is "Donde se da cuenta de quiénes eran maese Pedro y su mono, con el mal suceso que don Quijote tuvo en la aventura del rebuzno, que no la acabó como él quisiera y como lo tenía pensado" (Wherein it is shown who Master Pedro and his ape were, together with the mishap Don Quixote had in the braying adventure, which he did not conclude as he would have liked or as he had expected).

23 Cervantes, *Don Quijote*, 2.27; *Don Quixote*, 2.27.

24 Cervantes, *Don Quijote*, 2.27; *Don Quixote*, 2.27.

25 Alcalá Galán, "Las piernas."

26 On the figure of the ambassadress, see Allen, "Rise of the Ambassadress"; and Oliván Santaliestra, "Amazonas.".

27 See previous note on Demosthenes.

28 Cervantes, *Don Quijote*, 2.32; *Don Quixote*, 2.32.

29 Cervantes, *Don Quijote*, 2.33 (emphasis mine); *Don Quixote*, 2.33.

30 Cervantes, *Don Quijote*, 2.33; *Don Quixote*, 2.33.

31 Cervantes, *Don Quijote*, 2.33; *Don Quixote*, 2.33.

32 Cervantes, *Don Quijote*, 2.59; *Don Quixote*, 2.59.

33 Cervantes, *Don Quijote*, 2.59; *Don Quixote*, 2.59.

34 Lee, "Don Antonio Moreno," 34. A previous analysis of the mysterious Don Antonio Moreno can be found in Joly, "Las burlas de don Antonio."

35 Lee, "Don Antonio Moreno," 36.

36 Teresa Panza has a similar distrusting reaction to the bachelor Sansón Carrasco when he offers to transcribe her letters to the Duchess and to her governor husband in chapter 2.50: "El bachiller se ofreció de escribir las cartas a Teresa de la respuesta, pero ella no quiso que el bachiller se metiese en sus cosas, que le tenía por algo burlón" (The bachelor offered to write the letters in reply for Teresa; but she did not care to let him mix himself up in her affairs, for she thought him somewhat given to joking). Regarding the letters between Teresa Panza and Sancho, see Martín, "Public Indiscretion."

37 Cervantes, *Don Quijote*, 2.62 (my emphasis); *Don Quixote*, 2.62.

38 In *El retablo de las maravillas* (1613), Chanfalla offers a very similar presentation of his show's magical origin.

39 Cervantes, *Don Quijote*, 2.62; *Don Quixote*, 2.62.

40 Cervantes, *Don Quijote*, 2.62; *Don Quixote*, 2.62.

41 Cervantes, *Don Quijote*, 2.62; *Don Quixote*, 2.62.

42 The Panacousticon is illustrated in Kircher, *Phonurgia*, 162.

43 Wilkins, "Panacousticon," 11.

44 Jones, "Historical Materials," 90. Jones believes that "the source of most of the Western European tales is what must have been a lost romance about Pope Sylvester II (999–1003). In Vincent of Beauvais's thirteenth-century *Speculum Historiale* (first printed in 1473), Sylvester appears as a necromancer and idolater who, after studying the black arts in Spain, cast a metal head under proper astrological conditions. His familiar spirit spoke from the head and eventually deceived the pope, who confessed his crimes before dying" (Jones, 91).

45 Vives Coll, *Luciano de Samosata en España*, 122–8. C.R. Thompson notes that "Erasmus's translations of Lucian were printed more than forty times between 1506 and 1550" (Thompson, "Translations of Lucian," 881).

46 Lucian's short frame story dialogue "The Lover of Lies" (c. AD 150) also satirizes belief in the paranormal.

47 Hutchinson, "Luciano, precursor de Cervantes," 252–3.

48 Regarding the origin and sources of this paradox, see Jones, "Liar Paradox." For an excellent analysis of the arrogant ignorance of the well educated, see Márquez Villanueva, *Personajes y temas*, 208–12.

49 Reed reads the adventure of the enchanted head as a *lusus scientiae*, or joke of knowledge ("Ludic Revelations").

50 A good example is the donkey braying dispute (*Don Quijote*, 2.27). For a diplomatic approach to this chapter, see Olid Guerrero, "En servicio de su rey."

51 On ambassadorial dissimulation, see Woodhouse, "Honourable Dissimulation."

52 Foucault also provides the etymology of *Parrhesia*: "The term parrhesia first appears in Greek literature in Euripides and can be found in ancient Greek texts throughout the end of the fourth century and during [the] fifth century B.C. The term is borrowed from the Greek παρρησία parrhēsía (πᾶν 'all' and ῥῆσις 'utterance, speech') meaning literally 'to speak everything' and by extension 'to speak freely,' 'to speak boldly,' or 'boldness.' It implies not only freedom of speech, but the obligation to speak the truth for the common good, even at personal risk" (Foucault, "Discourse and Truth," 2).

53 Foucault, 2.

54 See Montserrat Jufresa's recent study of Lucian's influence in *Don Quixote*. Jufresa also sees freedom of speech or parrhesia, a characteristic feature of the Lucian's hero, in the socially equal friendship between Don Quixote and Sancho. As in *Don Quijote*, 2.2 (*Don Quixote*, 2.2), when the knight notes to his squire: "[S]i a los oídos de los príncipes llegase la verdad desnuda, sin los vestidos de la lisonja, otros siglos correrían" ("… that if the naked truth, undisguised by flattery, came to the ears of princes, times would be different"); and when Sancho expresses fear to speak freely, Don Quixote insists: "'En ninguna manera me enojaré,' respondió don Quijote. 'Bien puedes Sancho, hablar libremente y sin rodeo alguno" ("'I will not be vexed at all,' returned Don Quixote; 'thou mayest speak freely, Sancho, and without any beating about the bush'"). Jufresa sees the same freedom of speech Sancho enjoys with Don Quixote in Lucian's dialogue *The Assembly of Gods* when Momus argues with Zeus ("Ecos lucianescos en el *Quijote*").

55 Euripides, *Phoenician Women*, 473, l. 392. I use the translation by Elizabeth Wyckoff.

56 Foucault, "Discourse and Truth," 65.

57 Bejan summarizes the history of parrhesia as follows: "As Greek democratic institutions were crushed by the Macedonian empire, then the Roman, parrhesia persisted as a rhetorical trope. A thousand years after the fall of Rome, Renaissance humanists would revive parrhesia as the distinctive virtue of the counselor speaking to a powerful prince in need of frank advice. While often couched in apologetics, this parrhesia retained its capacity to shock. The hard truths presented by Machiavelli and Hobbes to their would-be sovereigns would inspire generations of 'libertine' thinkers to come" ("Two Clashing Meanings").

REFERENCES

Alcalá Galán, Mercedes. "Las piernas de la duquesa: Praxis médica y claves hermenéuticas en el *Quijote* de 1615." *Cervantes* 33, no. 1 (2013): 11–47. https://doi.org/10.1353/cer.2013.0012.

Allen, Gemma. "The Rise of the Ambassadress: English Ambassadorial Wives and Early Modern Diplomatic Culture." *Historical Journal* 62, no. 3 (2019): 617–38. https://doi.org/10.1017/S0018246X1800016X.

Bejan, Teresa M. "The Two Clashing Meanings of 'Free Speech.'" *The Atlantic*, 2 December 2017. https://www.theatlantic.com/politics/archive/2017/12 /two-concepts-of-freedom-of-speech/546791/.

Blackstone, William. *Commentaries on the Laws of England in Four Books.* Oxford: Clarendon Press, 1765–9.

Bradford, Charles Frederick. *Índice de las notas de D. Diego Clemencín en su edición de* El ingenioso hidalgo Don Quijote de la Mancha (*Madrid, 1833–39, 6 vols., 4.°) con muchas referencias á pasajes obscuros y dificultosos del texto y á la historia de la literatura española de Mr. Ticknor (ed. de 1863, 3 vols.).* Madrid: Manuel Tello, 1885.

Carnegie, David, and Gary Taylor, eds. *The Quest for Cardenio: Shakespeare, Fletcher, Cervantes, and the Lost Play.* Oxford: Oxford University Press, 2012.

Carnicer García, Carlos J., and Javier Marcos Rivas. *Sebastián de Arbizu: Espía de Felipe II.* Madrid: Nerea, 1998.

Cervantes, Miguel de. *Don Quijote de la Mancha.* Edited by Francisco Rico. Madrid: Instituto Cervantes, 1998.

Cervantes, Miguel de. *Entremeses.* Edited by Adrián J Sáez. Madrid: Cátedra, 2020.

Cervantes, Miguel de. *The Ingenious Gentleman Don Quixote of La Mancha.* Translated by John Ormsby. New York: Thomas Y. Crowell, 1885. https:// www.gutenberg.org/ebooks/996.

Chartier, Roger. *Cardenio between Cervantes and Shakespeare: The Story of a Lost Play.* Translated by Janet Lloyd. Malden, MA: Polity Press, 2013.

Colomer, José Luis. "Black and the Royal Image." In *Spanish Fashion at the Courts of Early Modern Europe,* edited by José Luis Colomer and Amalia Descalzo, 1:77–112. Madrid: Centro de Estudios Europa Hipánica, 2014.

Diccionario de autoridades. Madrid: Gredos, 1726–39. https://apps2.rae.es /DA.html.

Díez Borque, José María. "Teatro dentro del teatro, novela dentro de la novela en Miguel de Cervantes." *Anales Cervantinos,* no. 11 (1972): 113–28.

Euripides. *The Phoenician Women.* Translated by Elizabeth Wyckoff. In *The Complete Greek Tragedies,* vol. 5, *Electra, The Phoenician Women, The Bacchae,* edited by David Grene and Richmond Lattimore. Chicago: University of Chicago Press, 1959.

Feros, Antonio. *Kingship and Favoritism in the Spain of Philip III, 1598–1621*. New York: Cambridge University Press, 2000.

Foucault, Michel. "Discourse and Truth: The Problematization of Parrhesia (Six Lectures Given by Michel Foucault at Berkeley, Oct–Nov. 1983)." 1983. https://foucault.info/parrhesia/.

Gaylin, Ann. *Eavesdropping in the Novel from Austen to Proust*. Cambridge: Cambridge University Press, 2003.

Harsh, Philip Whaley. *A Handbook of Classical Drama*. Stanford, CA: Stanford University Press, 1944.

Hutchinson, Steven. "Luciano, precursor de Cervantes." In *Cervantes y su mundo*, vol. 3, edited by A. Robert Lauer and Kurt Reichenberger, 241–62. Kassel: Reichenberger, 2005.

Joly, Monique. "Las burlas de don Antonio: En torno a la estancia de don Quijote en Barcelona." In *Actas del Segundo Coloquio Internacional de la Asociación de Cervantistas*, 71–81. Barcelona: Anthropos, 1991.

Jones, Joseph R. "Historical Materials for the Study of the *Cabeza Encantada* Episode in *Don Quijote* II.62." *Hispanic Review* 47, no. 1 (1979): 87–103. https://doi.org/10.2307/472926.

Jones, Joseph R. "The Liar Paradox in Don Quixote II, 51." *Hispanic Review* 54, no. 2 (1986): 183–93. https://doi.org/10.2307/473901.

Jufresa, Montserrat. "Ecos lucianescos en el *Quijote*: Una perspectiva helenista." *Atalaya*, no. 19 (2019): 4305. https://doi.org/10.4000/atalaya .4305.

Kircher, Athanasius. *Phonurgia nova sive conjugium mechanico-physicum artis & naturae paranymta phonosophia concinnatum*. Kempten: Rudolph Dreherr, 1673.

Lee, Christina. "Don Antonio Moreno y el 'discreto' negocio de los moriscos Ricote y Ana Félix." *Hispania* 88, no. 1 (2005): 32–40. https://doi .org/10.2307/20063073.

Lucian (of Samosata). *The Works of Lucian of Samosata: Complete with Exceptions Specified in the Preface*. Translated by H.W. Fowler and F.G. Fowler. Oxford: Clarendon Press, 1905.

Márquez Villanueva, Francisco. *Personajes y temas del* Quijote. Madrid: Taurus, 1975.

Martín, Adrienne L. "Public Indiscretion and Courtly Diversion: The Burlesque Letters in *Don Quijote* II." *Cervantes* 11, no. 2 (1991): 87–101.

Navarro Bonilla, Diego. *Los archivos del espionaje: Información, Razón de estado y servicios de inteligencia en la monarquía hispánica*. Salamanca: Caja Duero, 2004.

Olid Guerrero, Eduardo. *Del teatro a la novela: El ritual del disfraz en las* Novelas ejemplares *de Cervantes*. Alcalá de Henares: Instituto Universitario de Investigación Miguel de Cervantes, 2016.

Olid Guerrero, Eduardo. "Donde lo verá el que lo leyere y lo oirá el que lo escuchara leer: Sobre el lenguaje metadramático de los títeres de maese Pedro." *Anales Cervantinos*, no. 41 (2009): 63–81. https://doi.org/10.3989/anacervantinos.2009.003.

Olid Guerrero, Eduardo. "'En servicio de su rey en la guerra justa': La segunda parte del *Quijote* leída a través de las ideas de Nicolás Maquiavelo y Francisco Vitoria." In "¿Promete el autor segunda parte? Cuatrocientos años de una promesa cervantina," edited by Antonio Cortijo Ocaña and Francisco Layna Ranz. Special issue, *eHumanista/Cervantes*, no. 4 (2015): 356–87.

Oliván Santaliestra, Laura. "Amazonas del secreto en la embajada madrileña del Graf von Pötting (1663–1674)." *Memoria y Civilización*, no. 19 (2016): 221–54. https://doi.org/10.15581/001.19.221-254.

Online Etymology Dictionary. Accessed 2 April 2022. https://www.etymonline.com/.

Peterson, Anne. *Laughter on the Fringes: The Reception of Old Comedy in the Imperial Greek World*. Oxford: Oxford University Press, 2019.

Reed, Cory. "Ludic Revelations in the Enchanted Head Episode in *Don Quijote* (II, 62)." *Cervantes* 24, no.1 (2004): 189–216.

Rodríguez, Alfred, and Soledad García Sprackling. "Presencia y función del truco en la segunda parte del Quijote." *Anales Cervantinos*, nos. 25–6 (1987–8): 359–63.

Rokem, Freddie. "The Processes of Eavesdropping: Where Tragedy, Comedy and Philosophy Converge." *Performance Philosophy*, no. 1 (2015): 109–18. https://doi.org/10.21476/PP.2015.1120.

Sheldon, R.M. *Espionage in the Ancient World: An Annotated Bibliography of Books and Articles in Western Languages*. Jefferson, NC: McFarland, 2008.

Stollznov, Karen. "Eavesdropping: Etymology, Meaning, and Some Creepy Little Statues." *Karen Stollznov* (blog), 7 August 2014. https://web.archive.org/web/20210312081941/http://karenstollznow.com/eavesdropping/.

Thompson, C.R. "The Translations of Lucian by Erasmus and S. Thomas More." *Revue belge de philologie et d'histoire* 18, no. 4 (1939): 855–81. https://doi.org/10.3406/rbph.1939.1316.

Vives Coll, Antonio. *Luciano de Samosata en España*. Valladolid-La Laguna: Sever Cuesta, 1959.

Wilkins, Caroline. "The Panacousticon: By Way of Echo to Freddie Rokem." *Performance Philosophy* 2, no. 1 (2016): 5–22. https://doi.org/10.21476/PP.2016.2179.

Woodhouse, J.R. "Honourable Dissimulation: Some Italian Advice for the Renaissance Diplomat." *Proceedings of the British Academy*, no. 84 (1994): 25–50.

13 *Don Quixote* and the Performance of Aging Masculinities in Early Modern Spain

JOSÉ R. CARTAGENA CALDERÓN

In the fall of 1614, an unknown writer published under the assumed name of Alonso Fernández de Avellaneda a spurious continuation of Cervantes's *Don Quixote*. The pseudonymous author, whose identity still eludes us, was capitalizing on the extraordinary popular success that Cervantes's novel enjoyed since its publication almost a decade earlier in 1605. In his preface to his apocryphal sequel, Avellaneda fashioned himself as Cervantes's literary foe, equating his authority to write a continuation of *Don Quixote* to that of its originator. Avellaneda also took it upon himself to defend Lope de Vega, the most prolific and popular playwright of the period, from the thinly veiled satirical references that appeared in *Don Quixote*, attributing them to Cervantes's envy of Lope's success as a playwright.[1] Doubling down on his insults, Avellaneda loaded his prologue with more ad hominem attacks. He mocked Cervantes's old age and physical disability, branding him as an old soldier with a crippled hand. Not amused with the book's unauthorized nature and the personal attacks that Avellaneda hurled at him in his infamous preface, Cervantes, who was already at work on his own second part of *Don Quixote*, published it the following year, in late 1615. In his much-anticipated prologue, Cervantes pretended to take the high road. He declined to take on his literary nemesis with cheap shots and instead resorted to more ingenious ways to discredit him, such as weaving his criticism of Avellaneda into the fabric of the novel itself. Understandably, however, while writing his prologue, Cervantes did not resist the temptation to confront Avellaneda directly, not so much for the usurpation of his literary character, but for taking jabs at his old age and maimed hand: "Lo que no he podido dejar de sentir es que me note de viejo y de manco, como si hubiera sido en mi mano haber detenido el tiempo que no pasase por mí, o si mi manquedad hubiera nacido en alguna taberna, sino en la más alta ocasión que vieron los siglos pasados, los presentes, ni esperan ver los venideros" ("What I do mind, however, is that he accuses me of being old and one-handed, as if it had been in my power to stop time and halt its passage, or as if I had been wounded in some tavern and not at the greatest event ever seen in past or present times, or that the future times can ever hope to see").[2]

With these words, Cervantes, who was at the time sixty-eight years old and died a few months later at the age of sixty-nine in April of 1616, takes issue at being faulted for his advanced age, highlighting an inescapable reality: that he does not have any control over the passage of time and its ravages upon his body. He also proudly reminds his adversary and his readers, as he had done before in the prologue to his *Novelas ejemplares* in 1613, where he described himself as an aging author, that he lost the use of his left hand from an injury he sustained while fighting heroically in the naval battle of Lepanto, when he was a young, brave soldier. In fact, Cervantes, the wounded veteran, unfailingly wore his physical impairment as a badge of honour, a disability that gained him the moniker "El manco de Lepanto" (the One-Handed Soldier of Lepanto), thus making his crippled left hand an important component of his authorial self-fashioning.

But if Cervantes adopted a persona that called attention to his physical disability as a wounded and victorious soldier, presenting himself at times in a flattering light as a man of arms and letters (a positive masculine virtue in the early modern period), how did he regard and represent old age in relation to his male characters, to himself, and to early modern thinking about senescence? The discussion that follows will focus on the performance of aging masculinities in the context of this question, paying particular attention to two aged male characters in Cervantes's *Don Quixote*: Alonso Quijano / Don Quixote and his counterpart, don Diego de Miranda. As we shall see, an examination of the intertwining of masculinity and old age in *Don Quixote* against the backdrop of other social, cultural, and medical discourses on aging in early modern Spain teases out elements of Cervantes's novel that have been overlooked by studying each cultural construct separately.[3]

When considering *Don Quixote*, a sort of coming of "old age" novel, in a volume about Cervantes's theatre and theatrical acts, I follow the lead of other critics and artists who have long recognized the theatrical qualities of Cervantes's masterpiece. Indeed, Cervantes's dramatic corpus is finally receiving the attention it deserves in studies that move beyond the prevalent view of this literary giant as a failed or frustrated playwright whose genius was better manifested in imaginative prose.[4] Moreover, there is already a growing body of scholarship that explores how Cervantes's literary career as a playwright informed the writing of his works of prose fiction, including *Don Quixote*, a novel in which we find many references to the Spanish stage and an abundance of techniques borrowed from the realm of theatre.[5]

Although scholarly attention to the theatricality of *Don Quixote* has gained momentum in recent years, it was never at the margins of critical and aesthetic concerns, given the multiform and ubiquitous presence of Cervantes's theatrical prose in his novel. For instance, back in 1935 Spanish critic, novelist, and dramatist Azorín had already described *Don Quixote* as "[una] novela de un hombre de teatro" (a novel by a theatre man) in an essay suggestively entitled "El secreto de Miguel" (Miguel's Secret).[6] Azorín was more interested in uncovering other "secrets," such as Cervantes's engagement with Erasmian thought, but surely the author of *Don Quixote* has much more to reveal to us through his literary and dramatic craftsmanship, provoking the consideration of cultural issues that we are just beginning to shed light on. The question of how old age shapes masculinity is one of those cultural concerns that Cervantes's works bring to the forefront in meaningful but underappreciated ways.[7] Not insignificantly, Cervantes did so in the autumn and winter of his life, when he himself was facing old age and was reflecting on the impending end of his life. As he movingly wrote just days before his death in the prologue of his posthumous novel *Los trabajos de Persiles y Sigismunda* (1617): "Adiós, gracias, adiós, donaires; adiós, regocijados amigos, que yo me voy muriendo y deseando veros presto contentos en la otra vida" (Goodbye, humour, goodbye, wit, goodbye merry friends; for I am dying and hope to see you soon, happy in the life to come!).[8]

A fundamental tenet of the burgeoning field of age studies is that old age is a cultural construct that can be subjected to the same interdisciplinary critical inquiry that other categories of difference, such as gender, race, and sexuality have received. While aging itself is a biological process, what it means to be "young" or "old" is shaped by culture. One discernible implication of this idea is that we are aged by culture as much as by nature.[9] Additionally, given that cultural imperatives and assumptions about old age are historically situated, there has been much discussion about when early modern people were considered old by their contemporaries. Since definitions of old age were just as varied and contested then as they are today, attempting to unequivocally determine when a person was deemed old in the early modern period is a challenging endeavour. There are, however, ample examples throughout history of attempts to place chronological boundaries around old age from the earliest onset at thirty-five years old to the latest at past sixty. Jim Casey succinctly notes:

> Within a literary context, classical, medieval, and early modern authors all differ as to exactly when old age begins. [The sixteenth-century French surgeon] Ambroise Paré, basing his estimation on the work of Galen, suggests that aging begins just past thirty-five; [the thirteenth-century Franciscan monk] Bartholomaeus Anglicus, following Aristotle, argues that "senecta" begins around forty-five or fifty; [the famous ancient Roman orator and statesman] Cicero delineates forty-six as the beginning of old age; Erasmus, [one of the leading activists and thinkers of the European Renaissance] envisions elderliness and death coming by fifty years of age or earlier; [the Spanish Catholic bishop and scholar] Isidore of Seville [writing in the seventh century] sees fifty as the point of irreversible decline; and [in the fifth century] Augustine believes senescence does not begin until a man passes sixty.[10]

Furthermore, after examining numerous medical texts written by licensed practitioners across Europe between 1500 and 1800, historian Daniel Schäfer ably concludes that "despite different traditions and the lack of benchmarks for a social definition of old age (such as a fixed retirement age), fifty was the age most often named."[11]

The common association of the age of fifty with the onset of old age in the early modern period manifests itself in Alonso Quijano and, in what Rogelio Miñana has aptly called, recognizing the theatricality of Cervantes's text as well as the idea of a changeable and performative self, "the evolving product of his performance, Don Quixote."[12] We quickly learn in the opening chapter of the novel that the dyad character Quijano/Quixote is a rural *hidalgo* (the lowest rank of the Spanish nobility) whose physical appearance does not belie his age: "Frisaba la edad de nuestro hidalgo con los cincuenta años. Era de complexión recia, seco de carnes, enjuto de rostro" ("Our gentleman was approximately fifty years old; his complexion was weathered, his flesh scrawny, his face gaunt").[13] We also learn that despite his age, he is unmarried and childless and that he lives a sedentary life with his housekeeper who is past forty, a young nice who is not yet twenty and an errand boy of whom we never hear again after the first chapter. Thus, from the very beginning of the novel Cervantes's hero stands out as an aging minor nobleman of La Mancha whose prolonged bachelorhood calls into question his masculinity in a time and place where very strong gender expectations and obligations guided behaviour both in public and at home. Lisa Vollendorf makes this point when she asserts in a gendered reading of the novel that "normative masculinity for a hidalgo dictates that Don Quixote have an estate and a family to attend to."[14] We are reminded of this prescribed masculine gender role of heading a patriarchal household with a wife and children when in the second part of the novel the in-residence priest of the Duke and Duchess dramatically admonishes Don Quixote with the following imperative: "Andad enhorabuena, y en tal se os diga: volveos a vuestra casa, y criad vuestros hijos, si los tenéis, y curad de vuestra hacienda, y dejad de andar vagando por el mundo, papando viento y dando que reír a cuantos os conocen y no conocen" ("Go now in peace, and in peace I shall say to you: return to your home; and rear your children, if you have any, and tend to your estate, and stop wandering the world and wasting your time and being a laughingstock to all who know you and all who do not").[15]

That Don Quixote fails to fulfil and perform this mandate of proper manhood for someone of his age and social class is made clear again when he encounters his counterpart, the well-dressed and well-off don Diego de Miranda, also called El Caballero del Verde Gabán (the Knight of the Green Coat), who hosts the self-made and self-named knight errant and his squire, Sancho Panza, at his home for four days in chapters 16–18 of the second part of the novel. There are commonalities between Don Quixote (or his former self as Alonso Quijano) and don Diego de Miranda, but also fundamental differences. Both characters are about fifty years old, both are country *hidalgos* from La Mancha, although don Diego de Miranda appears to be somewhat wealthier, and both participate in the leisure activity of hunting, to name a few of their shared features. Yet, unlike Don Quixote / Alonso Quijano, don Diego de Miranda is married and has an eighteen-year-old son, an aspiring poet and student at the University of Salamanca whose literary inclinations are a source of concern for his father who would rather see him pursuing a more practical and remunerative career like law or theology.

Despite this tension between father and son, at first glance don Diego seems to be the embodiment of the perfect Christian gentlemen. As Charles D. Presberg's remarks, evoking Fray Luis de León's 1538 widely read manual of female behaviour *La perfecta casada* (The Perfect Married Woman), don Diego de Miranda appears to be the quintessential model of "'el perfecto casado,' a character who seems to emerge directly from either the philosophy of Christian Epicureanism, as described by Erasmus and his followers, or even from the Catechism of the Council of Trent."[16] But as Presberg and many other critics have compellingly argued, don Diego de Miranda is very far from perfect, a characterization that is not at all surprising given Cervantes's extraordinary skill at creating complex portraits of his characters that oftentimes contradict first and even second impressions. Certainly, a different image of don Diego de Miranda as "an archetype of both marital fidelity and parental love," in Presberg's words,[17] is subtly revealed through the detailed description of the character's attire, a narrative technique that has a close affinity with the early modern stage in which the visual imagery of clothing plays an important symbolic role beyond gendering (and oftentimes regendering) the characters as men or women or establishing other markers of social identity, such as class, race/ethnicity, age, profession, nationality, and so forth.

In a study that explores the significance of the appearance of the Knight of the Green Cloak vis-à-vis prior uses of the figure of the green knight in medieval chivalric romances, Darío Fernández-Morera has called attention to the fact that don Diego de Miranda is different in that "rather than [masculine] wildness, the clothes suggest a foppish concern with sartorial detail," and adds that the handsomely dressed man is so "meticulously attentive to the perfect matching of his attire" that "even the spurs are green."[18] The minutely detailed description of the flashy green outfit that the narrator offers allows for a more nuanced moral profile of the Cervantine character as an exemplary Christian gentleman in that it denotes, in Presberg's formulation, "at least a trace of vanity, which is one of the vices he claims to scorn as unchristian."[19]

In effect, although don Diego de Miranda is a country *hidalgo* who occupies a space different from a courtly one, supposedly devoid of any pretence of elegance and sophistication, the eye-catching stylish attire he dons brings to mind the courtiers' fashionable clothes. In his highly influential manual of masculine conduct *The Book of the Courtier* (1528), which was translated into Spanish in 1534 by the poet and courtier Juan Boscán, Baldassare Castiglione defined an idealized form of masculinity that considered youth and good looks an indispensable requirement for the perfect courtier.[20] Due to this emphasis on physical appearance and youthfulness, the courtiers' urban masculinity became associated throughout the early modern period with an aggregate of vices, such as ostentatious foppery, self-absorption, effeminacy, and vanity in sharp contrast with the chivalric masculinity of the medieval knights that Don Quixote, as a self-created knight errant and nonconforming character who defies age expectations, vainly tries to perform, despite his best efforts.

The sartorial habits of the courtiers, which were meant to display their social standing, reputation, and social worth as the court became more and more important to the political and economic livelihood of the nobility in the late medieval and early modern period, led to numerous condemnations targeting the perceived emasculation and the threat of effeminacy of elite men, from noble-born courtiers to striving social climbers.[21] One meaningful example is the oft-quoted sermon delivered in 1635 by Fray Francisco de León, in which he scathingly shames urban gentlemen like the courtiers when he refers to them as "men converted into women, from soldiers into effeminates, covered with hair cascading over their ears, trailing locks in back, and frizzed up in front, and who knows if they aren't made up and dressed up in things resembling what women wear."[22] Although with less vehemence, Don Quixote himself voices his own invectives against the courtiers' lack of masculinity, such as when he addresses the issue of the current status of Spain's nobility whose males have swapped the masculine armour that their predecessors wore on the battlefield for swanky clothes at court: "Los más de los caballeros que agora se usan, antes les crujen los damascos, los brocados y otras ricas telas de que se visten que la malla con que se arman" ("Most knights today would rather rustle in damasks, brocades, and the other rich fabrics of their clothes than creak in chain mail").[23]

Returning to don Diego de Miranda, in a study on the subject of the Spanish courtly gentleman of the sixteenth and seventeenth centuries, Francesco Raimondo notes that despite their lack of any direct interaction with the world of the court some of the male characters in *Don Quixote*, including don Diego de Miranda, "assume courtly postures or display behavioral patterns descriptive of the stereotyped *caballero cortesano*."[24] In Raimondo's view, contrary to representing don Diego de Miranda as "an ideal of human perfection,"[25] Cervantes assigns him "characteristics of a decadent modern knight" in that he "is interested in the amenities and comforts of life rather than becoming involved in real knightly pursuits and activities."[26] Likewise, Carroll Johnson asserts that don Diego de Miranda "is a decadent and idle seventeenth-century version of that class [*hidalgos*], which in the sixteenth century had conquered America and assured Spanish hegemony in Europe by force of arms."[27]

This interpretation is reinforced in the manicured appearance of don Diego de Miranda, whose flashy, green garb has prompted some critics to claim that his attire is incongruous with the country *hidalgo*'s old age.[28] For instance, Francisco Márquez Villanueva remarks that don Diego de Miranda's "gusto por tan vivo color no ... parece propio de la cincuentena" (taste for such vivid colour does not ... seem appropriate for a man in his fifties).[29] In a parallel observation, Alberto Sánchez claims that don Diego de Miranda is unsuitably dressed for his age since "el color verde más bien era de jóvenes o de justadores en fiestas cortesanas" (the colour green was more fitting for male youths or jousters participating in a courtly festival).[30] Thus it should come as no surprise, as Márquez Villanueva perceptively observes, that when Don Quixote first addresses the green knight he uses the epithet "señor galán como si se tratara de algún jovenzuelo" (Mr. Gallant, as if he were some youngster).[31] Indeed, Don Quixote utters the same appellative a few chapters later when he and Sancho come across a "mancebito" (young man) who is on his way to enlist in the royal army after having served unsuccessfully as a page at court. Mirroring the previous encounter with don Diego de Miranda, it is the lad's odd appearance that draws Don Quixote's attention, particularly his attire in the style of the court and the fact that he is not wearing breeches or trousers. Determined to get the young man's attention, the Manchegan knight exclaims: "Muy a la ligera camina vuesa merced, señor galán" ("Your grace travels very lightly, gallant Señor") and asks him where he is headed.[32] The young man replies that he is going off to war and explains that he travels lightly because of two harsh realities: the hot weather and because he is poor. Reminiscent of a picaresque character, the young page describes, albeit very briefly, his unhappy first-hand experience with court life and attributes his poverty to the stinginess and venality of his courtier masters who did not even allow him to keep the clothes in which they dressed him once their business was done.

Don Quixote seizes the opportunity provided by his encounter with the soldier-page to pronounce judgment, as he has done before, on the courtiers' masculinity by denouncing their idleness and effeminate refinement (in this case the use of perfumes) while vehemently endorsing the page's choice of arms over a career at court. He does so by telling the page that a soldier should smell like he has been on a battlefield or at war and not like "algalia," a musky secretion of civets (a cat-like mammal) used in perfumery because of its sweet scent, which the knight errant associates with the world of women as well as with the vain and emasculated courtiers: "Y advertid, hijo, que al soldado mejor le está oler a pólvora que a algalia" ("And remember, son, that the soldier prefers to smell of gunpowder to the scent of musk").[33] Equally relevant is the fact that Don Quixote concludes his remarks by taking up the issue of the fate of elderly soldiers whose lives, after their enactment of a martial masculinity of courage, honour, and sacrifice on the battlefields, are forgotten and abandoned to poverty:

> [Y] si la vejez os coge en este honroso ejercicio, aunque sea lleno de heridas y estropeado o cojo, a lo menos, no os podrá coger sin honra, y tal, que no os la podrá menoscabar la pobreza. Cuanto más que ya se va dando orden

como se entretengan y remedien los soldados viejos y estropeados, porque no es bien que se haga con ellos lo que suelen hacer los que ahorran y dan libertad a los negros cuando ya son viejos y no pueden servir, y echándolos de casa con título de libres, los hacen esclavos ahora de la hambre, de quien no piensan ahorrarse sino con la muerte.

(And if old age overtakes you in this honourable profession, even if you are full of wounds, and maimed or crippled, at least when it overtakes you, you will not be without honour, an honour that not even poverty can diminish; furthermore, laws are now being enacted that will protect and assist old and crippled soldiers, because it is not right they be treated the way blacks are treated who are emancipated and freed when they are old and can no longer serve, and are thrown out of the house and called free men, making them slaves to hunger from which only death can liberate them.)[34]

According to this episode and Don Quixote's impassioned speech, poverty leads young men (like the page) to military service only to find themselves later in life broken by old wounds and economic hardship, a fate that the knight errant bitterly compares to that of freed slaves. The passage mounts a critique of the conditions of military service in Cervantes's Spain as one can hear the old and maimed veteran of Lepanto advocating for himself and his fellow soldiers unfairly forgotten by the state in old age. Acting like an *arbitrista*, or an advocate of reforming projects, Don Quixote espouses the idea that the state has a moral obligation to the many old soldiers who suffered in its service.[35] Indeed, there are tinges of the autobiographical underlying this episode. Cervantes, who returned to Spain beset by financial troubles after valiantly serving as a young soldier in Philip II's forces in the Mediterranean, as well as being a prisoner of war for five years in North Africa, writes in his old age with a keen understanding of the challenges faced by forgotten disabled and elderly veterans of war in seventeenth-century Spain. Interestingly, he does so through the voice of Don Quixote, a character with no direct military experience, despite his self-fashioning project of reviving the old world of chivalry by acting out an outworn form of martial masculinity whose script he found in the pages of late fifteenth- and sixteenth-century *libros de caballerías* (romances of chivalry).

Here it is helpful to turn once more to the episode of the Knight of the Green Cloak, specifically to Don Quixote's use of the word *galán* in order to explore another aspect of the masculinity of both aged *hidalgos* that is subtly revealed through their highly dramatic encounter in which the two fifty-something knights cannot take their eyes off each other: "[Y] si mucho miraba el de lo verde a don Quijote, mucho más miraba don Quijote al de lo verde" ("And if the man in green looked at Don Quixote a great deal, Don Quixote looked even more at the man in green").[36] Cervantes's contemporary Sebastián de Covarrubias defined *galán* as "el que anda vestido de gala y se precia de gentil hombre, y porque los enamorados de ordinario andan muy apuestos para aficionar a sus damas, ellas los llaman sus galanes" ("an elegantly dressed man who appears to be a gentleman, and because men in love usually appear very smartly dressed in order to capture a woman's interest, the women call them their *galanes*").[37] Given that *galán* means gallant or elegant, but also lover or suitor, one might wonder if there is another underlying meaning in Don Quixote's use of the word when he first addresses don Diego de Miranda, particularly if we consider his subsequent self-identification with a paragon of virtues, most notably for this discussion, when he boasts about being a devoted husband and father: "[P]aso la vida con mi mujer y con mis hijos" ("I spend my time with my wife and my children").[38] One possible clue may be found in don Diego de Miranda's mention of *hijos* in plural (he subsequently acknowledges that he only has one child), which may well be a form of parapraxis that tacitly discloses the idea that the discreet Christian gentleman in green, whom Sancho half-jokingly equates with a saint, may after all be a *viejo verde* (an old letch).[39]

Not insignificantly, several decades ago Vernon A. Chamberlin and Jack Weiner pointed out with compelling literary sources that the colour green was known during Cervantes's time for its erotic overtones, while intriguingly positing that the character of don Diego de Miranda was likely based on a real-life adulterer of that name with whom Cervantes was acquainted. According to both critics the historical Diego de Miranda, who was a married man, "had been tried, reprimanded and punished for illegal cohabitation" when in 1605 he was accused of having an affair with a thirty-year-old widow who was living with other "ladies of easy virtue" on the top floor of the building where Cervantes lived in Valladolid.[40] Weiner and Chamberlin infer that Cervantes "wanted at least certain initiated readers (members of his family, close friends, and possibly Miranda himself) to recognize the character and understand the color symbolism intended."[41] Similarly, after considering the not-too-concealed implications of the colour green, as well as other details of the knight's outfit, Helena Percas de Ponseti notes that the Príncipe de los Ingenios (Prince of Wits) renders his fictional don Diego de Miranda as a man on a sexual hunt: "Since the gentleman in green is not out hunting – his partridge and ferret are not with him – the green of his hooded cloak with its connotations of desire, lust, sex, if we apply the literary color code, together with the feline texture of the velvet cap and stripes lashed across the cloak, and the questionable hunting methods implied by the decoy partridge and the sly ferret, suggest that his game is women."[42]

Presberg cautiously notes that there is "no textual evidence of Don Diego's alleged sexual dalliance," while asserting that "the reader remains tantalizingly uninformed about Don Diego's recent whereabouts."[43] Yet, it is precisely because of this deliberate ambiguity that we should also be mindful that Cervantes was a master at crafting implicit allusions, double entendres, and innuendos, particularly when it comes to eroticism and sexuality, as Adrienne L. Martín has shown in her incisive study on "erotic philology" in early modern Spain.[44] For instance, from the very beginning of this episode it seems less questionable, although it is expressed surreptitiously in a true Cervantine fashion, that the old gentleman in green has, indeed, sex on his mind. When Don Quixote and Sancho first come across don Diego de Miranda on the road, the narrator describes how the knight in green "los saludó cortésmente, y picando a la yegua, se pasaba de largo" ("greeted them courteously and spurred his mare in order to pass by").[45] Once Don Quixote initiates a conversation with him, the well-dressed knight immediately gives a peculiar explanation for his previous behaviour: "'En verdad,' respondió el de la yegua, 'que no me pasara tan de largo, si no fuera por temor que con la compañía de mi yegua no se alborotara ese caballo'" ("'The truth is,' responded the man on the mare, 'that I would not ride by so quickly if it were not for my fear that the presence of my mare might disturb your horse'").[46] Thus, as Weiner and Chamberlin have perceptively observed: "The very first words spoken by Diego are sexually centered."[47] Perhaps predictably, as a farmer well versed in animal behaviour, Sancho wastes no time to intervene in this exchange and offer a few words in defence of Rocinante's almost unsullied reputation in matters of sexual restraint. Trying to soothe don Diego de Miranda's fear, Sancho comically downplays Rocinante's past sexual exploits, describing Don Quixote's beloved companion as the "most chaste" old nag in full control of his sexual urges.[48] Barely hidden in his words is an ironic allusion to Don Quixote's unwavering sexual chastity, a comment that insinuates a troubled relationship with sexuality that has received considerable critical attention in recent years. For instance, Sherry Velasco underscores the idea that the chaste Don Quixote is the product of a new identity forged and assumed by Alonso Quijano, an elderly "lascivious country gentleman fantasizing about a lusty peasant from the countryside," and that Don Quixote is also "a fifty-something-year-old male virgin who fantasizes about sexual encounters yet insists on remaining celibate."[49] Moreover, we should bear in mind, as Howard Mancing observes, that Rocinante is in a sense Don Quixote's pitiable "double" in that "both are skinny, awkward, and no longer young."[50] In effect, similar to the wilful knight errant who is utterly unsuited for his role, the past-his-prime horse is made to undertake a task that exceeds his physical capabilities.[51]

It is relevant to restate at this juncture a fairly discernible but significant point about Cervantes's magnum opus: that the hero's adventures in knight-errantry are markedly at odds with his age. Anne Cruz highlights this incongruity in an illuminating study on fathers and sons in Cervantes's novel and the romances of chivalry whose young heroes Don Quixote sets out to imitate:

> Certainly, Don Quixote is an unusual, if not bizarre hero for a tale of adventure: at 50 years of age, physically gaunt and increasingly melancholy, he is the exact opposite of the vigorous alpha males who appear in the novels that he so loves to read, and whose sons are destined to carry on the literary tradition in inexhaustible sequels that constantly reiterate the fathers' own youthful feats. By contrast, Don Quixote had never left his village; without a wife or children, he lived solely in the company of a housekeeper and young niece who cared for his necessities while he sold off parcels of land to satisfy his obsession for chivalric romances.[52]

Cruz adds that Don Quixote's decision to sell arable land in order to buy books of chivalry in spite of his minimal means "resulted not only in the shrinkage of his property, but in the drying up of his brain, causing the old man to foolishly emulate the deeds of much younger knights."[53] Indeed, Don Quixote's numerous blunders when trying to perform a chivalric masculinity typically reserved in the medieval romances to younger heroes is one of the many unvarnished sources of humour in the novel. Furthermore, Don Quixote's melancholy and dried up brain are of interest here since they can provide additional insight on early modern understanding of old age, particularly through the prism of medical modes of thought that inform Cervantes's novel.

We learn when Don Quixote is first introduced that his brain dried up from too much reading and sleep deprivation: "[D]el poco dormir y del mucho leer, se le secó el celebro de manera que vino a perder el juicio" ("With too little sleep and too much reading his brains dried up, causing him to lose his mind").[54] We also learn that Don Quixote's dryness is not limited to his brain, as his facial skin is similarly dried up: "[S]u seco y polvoroso rostro" ("His dry, dusty face").[55] Early modern medical writers and practitioners made reference to the prevailing humoral model when explaining the physical changes of old age, particularly its drying effects on the body. This medical theory, which was based on the ancient traditions of Hippocratic and Galenic medicine, as well as on medieval Islamic medicine, viewed a person's good health as dependent on the balance of the four principal humours in the body: blood, phlegm, black bile, and yellow bile. These bodily substances were in turn linked with four elements and their qualities: yellow bile (warm-dry), phlegm (cold-moist), black bile (cold-dry), and blood (warm-moist). It was believed that the interaction of the four humours in the human body accounted for differences of gender (including inter-gender distinctions), emotions, disposition, age, and so forth. Accordingly, following Galen's humoral theory, in the early modern period it was thought that a man progressed gradually from a phase of abundant heat and wetness in childhood to one of an increased coldness and dryness in old age. Additionally, as Susan Mattern points out: "No stage of male development is cold and wet, but women are cold and wet. Men in the prime of life represent the most balanced opposition to women; this was in a sense the most masculine stage of life."[56] This was definitely the case in chivalric fiction, whose heroes, in contrast to Don Quixote, were typically knighted in Cruz's words, at "the vague age of 'mancebía,' a stage past adolescence but not quite reaching adulthood."[57]

Drawing heavily on the ancient humoral model of the attributes of aging, in his *Examen de los ingenios para las ciencias* (Examination of Men's Wits) the sixteenth-century physician Juan Huarte de San Juan describes the last stage of life in a way that resonates with the image that Cervantes rendered of Don Quixote's old age, particularly when he recovers his sanity at the end of his life and renounces his knightly identity: "La última edad del hombre es la vejez; en la cual está el cuerpo frío y seco, y con mil enfermedades y flaco; todas las potencias perdidas, sin poder hacer lo que antes solían" (The last of man's ages is old age, when the body is cold and dry, with thousands of illnesses and thin; with all abilities lost, without being able to do what was normal before).[58] Since the beginning of the last century critics have identified Huarte de San Juan's footprints in Cervantes's novel, especially with regards to Don Quixote's cognitive abilities, including not only his madness, but also his melancholy, a state of irreparable sadness prevalent in old age to which our hero surrenders as he lies on his deathbed. As Cide Hamete narrates at the close of the novel: "[F]ue el parecer del médico que melancolías y desabrimientos le acababan" ("It was the physician's opinion that melancholy and low spirits were bringing his life to an end").[59]

The early modern correlation between senescence and melancholy lies in the belief that men became increasingly colder and drier as their bodies aged and that melancholy as a temperament was cold and dry in nature. Though a more in-depth examination of this important topic exceeds the bounds of this essay, it is worth highlighting here, albeit briefly, that during Cervantes's time (and in his work) we can find an assortment of conditions included under the banner of "melancholy" that are not solely associated with the elderly. As Mario Pérez Álvarez states with respect to Cervantes's novel:

> Melancholy seems to be in everyone and everything.... Thus, "sad and melancholy" went a poor galley slave in chains (I, 22), "melancholy" was the princess Micomicona (I, 29), Rocinante himself appeared "melancholy and dejected" (I, 43), "melancholy" are some governments (II, 13), the Guadiana "wherever it goes, shows its sadness and melancholy" (II, 23), the sound of music is sometimes "extremely sad and melancholy" (II, 36), while omens pour forth "melancholy from the heart" (II, 58). As far as Don Quixote is concerned, we should not forget that he is the Knight of the Sad Countenance, as dubbed by Sancho (I, 19).[60]

In fact, we could add to this list Don Quixote's mimetic melancholy when, after arriving with Sancho in Sierra Morena in order to get away from the law, he decides to do penance for his imaginary ladylove, Dulcinea del Toboso, by imitating the young knights who suffered from love's torments in his favourite chivalric tales. This is a revealing instance of Don Quixote's awareness of his own theatricality in that he displays a sense of self based on the performance of a series of acts of masculinity that he found scripted in other works of fiction. Interestingly, Don Quixote was inspired to do so after witnessing the erratic behaviour of Cardenio, a much younger madman who, barefoot and wearing the tatters of his once refined clothes, is doing some sort of penance due to his lost love Luscinda, alternating between choleric outbursts and subdued melancholy. Significantly, the performances of masculinity intentionally carried out by both the elderly pseudo-knight and the unhinged young man take place in Sierra Morena, a special setting that emerges in the novel imbued with theatricality. As Stephen Gilman fittingly observes, the Sierra Morena episodes are replete with dramatic and "unlikely encounters, with every kind of disguise, and with incessant role-playing by all the actors except Sancho and the shepherds."[61] Gilman also notes with respect to the episodes in Sierra Morena that both characters and readers "make up the amused and bemused audience of a wilderness masque" or "an improvised and self-conscious comedia," while maintaining that "when Shakespeare selected this portion of the Skelton translation (1610) for his lost Cardenio play, he understood perfectly what his contemporary had up his sleeve."[62]

It is in this highly theatrical segment of the novel that Don Quixote deliberates between two literary models of lovelorn heroes for his eccentric role-playing enactment: "[I]mitar a Roldán en las locuras desaforadas que hizo, o Amadís en las melancólicas" ("To imitate Roland in his excessive madness or Amadis in his melancholy").[63] After some deliberation, El Caballero de la Triste Figura (the Knight of the Sorrowful Face) decides to purposefully follow the example of Amadís and his melancholy. Tellingly, Amadís's reaction to Oriana's disdain was much more restrained and milder than the boisterous fury that the passionate Roldán exhibited in Ludovico Ariosto's epic poem *Orlando furioso* after he learned that his beloved Angelica had fallen in love with a Moorish youth of extraordinary beauty. According to Don Quixote, the deranged Roldán "arrancó los árboles, enturbió las aguas de las claras fuentes, mató pastores, destruyó ganados, abrasó chozas, derribó casas, arrastró yeguas, e hizo otras cien mil indolencias" ("uprooted trees, befouled the waters of clear fountains, killed shepherds, destroyed livestock, burned huts, demolished houses, pulled down mares, and did a hundred thousand other unheard-of things").[64] Beyond the moral implications of killing innocent shepherds and defenceless animals, which Don Quixote acknowledges, calling these doings "locuras de daño" ("harmful mad acts"), imitating the exaggerated insanity of Ariosto's character to the letter or partially would have required at the very least a more strenuous performance from the elderly Manchegan knight.[65] Huarte de San Juan would have said that Don Quixote's choice to perform Amadís's pensive and grief-stricken masculinity wrapped up in sorrowful thoughts is more fitting for the self-proclaimed knight errant's aging body and melancholic mind than Roldán's choleric temperament, which is more characteristic, although not always exclusive, of younger men.

One final point remains to be made. Despite all the virtues of old age that Cicero defended in *De senectute* (BC 45 or 44), where the inexorable deterioration of the body is compensated by the attainment of prudence and wisdom, for the most part early modern thinkers did not follow the lead of the famous Roman orator, with some marshalling a negative view of old age while others adopted an ambivalent vision of later life: "So nobly tragic and derisorily comic, so mean in all its faults and so sublime in its qualities," as Georges Minois eloquently notes.[66] For instance, in *Praise of Folly* Erasmus refers to this stage of life with blunt words that still echo through history: "Old age is a burden, and death, a harsh necessity."[67] In keeping with this antipathy towards old age and following Aristotle, who identified six vices elderly men display due to their coldness, Huarte de San Juan flatly declares that the old tend to be cowardly, miserly, jealous, hopeless, unabashed, and incredulous.[68] In the same vein, renowned early modern Spanish writers and playwrights such as Lope de Vega, Mateo Alemán, Quiñones de Benavente, Tirso de Molina, and Francisco de Quevedo incorporated most of these unfavourable traits in their comic plots and satirical writings about aged and aging males, especially those with unbridled erotic desires.[69] Although this topic merits further and closer investigation, especially through the critical lenses of masculinity and old age studies, as I conclude this assessment of the performance of aging masculinities in *Don Quixote* it is worth briefly underlining that one salient feature that the works of these authors reveal is a gerontophobic attitude towards sex in old age in line with a *senex amans* tradition in which elderly men in love or lust who are thought to be impotent and sexually feeble to the detriment of their much younger sexual partners, are represented as risible victims of self-deception.[70] Cervantes himself gave life to comic elders who often, but not always, fit the stereotypical mould of the *senex amans* and figure in some of his humorous works, like El vejete (the Old Man) in the dramatic interlude *El juez de los divorcios* (The Divorce Judge) and Cañizares in his other short farce *El viejo celoso* (The Jealous Old Man), as well as his counterpart Carrizales in the exemplary tale *El celoso extremeño* (The Jealous Old Extremaduran). These aged characters fall short, in one way or another, of idealized forms of manhood.

What is of interest here is that the mockery of the *senex amans* in Cervantes's comic interludes corresponds to the conventions of the genre, in contrast to his narrative prose, where we find a much more nuanced and intricate representation of the amorous old man, such as in *El celoso extremeño* with the character of Carrizales, in the *Persiles*, with the figure of King Policarpo, and, as suggested in the previous pages, in *Don Quixote* with both its main protagonist and don Diego de Miranda. As Idoya Puig remarks, "Cervantes reworks some of the prevalent stereotypes providing a more human, sensitive and complex presentation of some older characters."[71] Furthermore, it is important to point out that, while Cervantes stages, for example, in *El viejo celoso* a mismatched and unhappy marriage between an old man and a young woman whose sexual yearnings the *senex* cannot satisfy, prompting her to commit adultery with a young man almost right in front of his eyes, the short play conveys, as Mercedes Alcalá Galán convincingly contends, a serious critique of unexamined and unquestioned cultural beliefs that condone male jealousy and condemn female adultery.[72] Ultimately, Cervantes's interlude connotes and calls into question a gender ideology that disallows full emotional and sexual experience to women.

The drama of aging masculinities comically depicted in several of Cervantes's dramatic and fictional texts in the form of sexual jealousy, marital impotence, and fear of cuckoldry reveals, as José I. Badenes argues, "early modern Spanish male anxieties around sexual virility," which in turn expose "a patriarchal understanding of aging masculine gender and sexual performance that is constricting rather than liberating" for both men and women.[73] This comment serves to illustrate the centrality of old age to understandings of early modern constructions of masculinities, an intersection whose examination currently stands as a fresh, vibrant, and vigorous line of inquiry in early modern literary scholarship (pun intended). In sum, as we have seen in this chapter's examination of various matters related to the performance of aged and aging masculinities in *Don Quixote*, Cervantes's distinctly theatrical novel reveals itself as an untapped treasure trove for further exploration of this timely and compelling topic in all its complexities.

NOTES

1 Martín reminds us that "Cervantes had praised Lope in both the *Galatea* and the encomiastic sonnet … 'En honor de Lope de Vega,'" adding that "by the time Cervantes was creating the *Quixote* preliminary and closing verses – probably the last part of the book to be written – their relationship was such that he filled them with sharply ironic allusions to his rival," which were not rare as "Lope found himself the constant butt of jokes and satirical pieces" from other contemporary writers, mainly due to his tremendous popularity with seventeenth-century audiences (*Cervantes and the Burlesque Sonnet*, 157).

2 Cervantes, *Don Quijote*, 433; *Don Quixote*, 455. All quotations in Spanish are from Tom Lathrop's *Don Quijote* (2005), with English translations from Edith Grossman's *Don Quixote* (2005).

3 On the handful of studies on masculinity in *Don Quixote*, see Cartagena Calderón, *Masculinidades en obras*; and Martínez-Góngora, *El hombre atemperado*. On the subject of old age in *Don Quixote*, see in particular the essays in Alonso, *El envejecimiento*.

4 For a fuller reflection on this, see Henry, *Signifying Self*, in particular the introduction, entitled "Cervantes: Writing Drama on the Margins," 1–14.

5 For a discussion of the theatrical characteristics of *Don Quixote*, see, for example, Syverson-Stork, *Theatrical Aspects of the Novel*; and Maestro, "Cervantes y el teatro del *Quijote*." For an enlightening study on the

manifold and multilayered meanings of theatricality in Cervantes's *Novelas ejemplares*, see Olid Guerrero, *Del teatro a la novela*.

6 Azorín, *El oasis de los clásicos*, 105.

7 For an in-depth appraisal of the female experience and representation of aging in early modern Spain, which had its own set of issues, see Juárez-Almendros, *Disabled Bodies*.

8 Cervantes, *Los trabajos de Persiles y Sigismunda*, 123; *The Trials of Persiles and Sigismunda*, 20.

9 This topic is developed with particular depth by Gullette in *Aged by Culture*.

10 Casey, "Shaken Manhood," 13.

11 Schäfer, *Old Age and Disease*, 8.

12 Miñana, *Living Quixote*, 50.

13 Cervantes, *Don Quijote*, 21; *Don Quixote*, 19.

14 Vollendorf, "Reading Gender," 73.

15 Cervantes, *Don Quijote*, 629; *Don Quixote*, 665.

16 Presberg, "Yo sé quién soy," 48.

17 Presberg, 47.

18 Fernández-Morera, "Chivalry, Symbolism, and Psychology," 532.

19 Presberg, "Yo sé quién soy," 55.

20 Taking into consideration Castiglione's manual of masculine conduct, Skenazi points out that "a handsome appearance was *de rigueur* for the social entertainments of a court life," adding that "for the perfect courtier to be old was hardly conceivable, since physical decline made it difficult to fulfill the demands of his station" (*Aging Gracefully*, 80).

21 For a more developed discussion of the courtiers' masculinity, see Cartagena Calderón, *Masculinidades en obras*, 254–324.

22 Cited in Maravall, *Culture of the Baroque*, 37.

23 Cervantes, *Don Quijote*, 444–5; *Don Quixote*, 465.

24 Raimondo, *Ideal of the Courtly Gentleman*, 204.

25 Raimondo, 204.

26 Raimondo, 208.

27 Johnson, *Quest for Modern Fiction*, 64.

28 As continually happens with the many differing and often mutually exclusive readings of *Don Quixote* in general, and this episode in particular, by way of contrast Gingras maintains that don Diego de Miranda's outfit "is entirely appropriate to his status as a wealthy and discreet country hidalgo" ("Don Diego de Miranda," 130).

29 Márquez Villanueva, *Personajes y temas*, 150.

30 Sánchez, "El Caballero del Verde Gabán," 181.

31 Márquez Villanueva, *Personajes y temas*, 151.

32 Cervantes, *Don Quijote*, 588; *Don Quixote*, 617.

33 Cervantes, *Don Quijote*, 589; *Don Quixote*, 619.

34 Cervantes, *Don Quijote*, 589; *Don Quixote*, 619.

35 Unfortunately, as Watts notes in his 1895 English translation of *Don Quixote*, "No such pension for the maintenance and relief of old soldiers was ever in use in Spain, until at least a century and a half after Cervantes' death" (Cervantes, *Ingenious Gentleman*, 267–8n3). For a more elaborated discussion on the old, disabled, and pensionless soldiers in early modern Spain and the efforts of Philip II's court physician, Cristóbal Pérez de Herrera, on their behalf, see Martínez, "Pérez de Herrera."

36 Cervantes, *Don Quijote*, 528–9; *Don Quixote*, 552.

37 Covarrubias Orozco, *Tesoro de la lengua*, 620; English translation from Sánchez Ortega, "Sorcery and Eroticism," 90n38.

38 Cervantes, *Don Quijote*, 530; *Don Quixote*, 554.

39 In developing this interpretation I take my cue from Presberg, who, when going over conflictive readings of the encounter between Don Quixote and don Diego de Miranda, suggests that the use of *hijos* might be interpreted as a "Freudian slip" that might contribute to the association of the knight in green with the figure of the *viejo verde* ("Yo sé quién soy," 54).

40 Chamberlin and Weiner, "Color Symbolism," 344.

41 Chamberlin and Weiner, 345.

42 Percas de Ponseti, *Cervantes the Writer*, 39.

43 Presberg, "Yo sé quién soy," 54.

44 See Martín, *Erotic Philology*.

45 Cervantes, *Don Quijote*, 528; *Don Quixote*, 552.

46 Cervantes, *Don Quijote*, 528; *Don Quixote*, 552.

47 Chamberlin and Weiner, "Color Symbolism," 346.

48 Cervantes, *Don Quijote*, 528; *Don Quixote*, 552.

49 Velasco, "Obscene Onomastics," 51, 55.

50 Mancing, *Cervantes Encyclopedia*, 618.

51 Laguna offers an insightful analysis of Rocinante "as the materialization of the erotic conflicts, expectations, and anxieties embodied not only in Don Quixote but in the ideal of masculinity that, as a knight, he attempts to fulfill" ("Eroticism in Unexpected Places," 113). On Cervantes and animal studies, including a thoughtful analysis of Rocinante, see, among other articles that the author has published on the subject, Martín, "Zoopoética quijotesca."

52 Cruz, "Fathers and Sons," 66.

53 Cruz, 66.

54 Cervantes, *Don Quijote*, 23; *Don Quixote*, 21.

55 Cervantes, *Don Quijote*, 29; *Don Quixote*, 26.

56 Mattern, *Galen and the Rhetoric of Healing*, 103.
57 Cruz, "Fathers and Sons," 66. One notable exception to the young knights normally depicted in chivalry fictions is the Caballero Anciano (Old Knight) in *Tristán de Leonís*, who is, like Don Quixote, a target of laughter, but occasionally an object of respect for his wisdom. On this, see Urbina, "El caballero anciano."
58 Huarte de San Juan, *Examen de ingenios*, 270; translation mine.
59 Cervantes, *Don Quijote*, 835; *Don Quixote*, 961.
60 Pérez Álvarez, "Psychology of Don Quixote," 19.
61 Gilman, *Novel*, 156.
62 Gilman, 156.
63 Cervantes, *Don Quijote*, 199; *Don Quixote*, 205.
64 Cervantes, *Don Quijote*, 188; *Don Quixote*, 193–4.
65 Cervantes, *Don Quijote*, 188; *Don Quixote*, 194.
66 Minois, *History of Old Age*, 112.
67 Erasmus, *Praise of Folly*, 45.
68 Huarte de San Juan, *Examen de ingenios*, 270.
69 For a helpful look at this subject, see Granjel, *Los ancianos*, 99–121.
70 For an extended treatment of this topic in England and Italy, see Ellis, *Old Age*, 38.
71 Puig, "Respect or Ridicule?," 208.
72 According to Alcalá Galán, in the interlude *El viejo celoso* Cervantes reworks "the theme of feminine adultery, exploring and questioning the misogynistic focus that indicts the woman as absolute culprit without taking into account her right to listen to her desires and to decide her actions" ("Deceived Gaze," 73).
73 Badenes, "Staging the *senex*," 344.

REFERENCES

Alcalá Galán, Mercedes. "The Deceived Gaze: Visual Fantasy, Art, and Feminine Adultery in Cervantes's Reading of Ariosto." In *Goodbye Eros: Recasting Forms and Norms of Love in the Age of Cervantes*, edited by Ana Laguna and John Beusterien, 53–79. Toronto: University of Toronto Press, 2020.

Alonso, Ismael, ed. *El envejecimiento en y desde El Quijote*. Madrid: Grupo Ars XXI de Comunicación, 2006.

Azorín. *El oasis de los clásicos*. Edited by José Martínez Ruiz. Madrid: Biblioteca Nueva, 1952.

Badenes, José I. "Staging the *senex*: Aging Masculinities in the Theater of Miguel de Cervantes and Federico García Lorca." *Romance Notes* 54, no. 3 (2014): 335–46. https://doi.org/10.1353/rmc.2014.0079.

Cartagena Calderón, José R. *Masculinidades en obras: El drama de la hombría en la España imperial*. Newark, DE: Juan de la Cuesta, 2008.

Casey, Jim. "Shaken Manhood: Age, Power, and Masculinity in Shakespeare." *Hungarian Journal of English and American Studies* 20, no. 2 (2014): 11–31.

Cervantes, Miguel de. *Don Quijote*. Edited by Tom Lathrop. Newark, DE: Juan de la Cuesta, 2005.

Cervantes, Miguel de. *Don Quixote*. Translated by Edith Grossman. New York: Harper, 2005.

Cervantes, Miguel de. *The Ingenious Gentleman Don Quixote de la Mancha*. Translated by Henry Edward Watts. Vol. 3. London: Adam and Charles Black, 1895.

Cervantes, Miguel de. *Los trabajos de Persiles y Sigismunda*. Edited by Carlos Romero Muñoz. Madrid: Cátedra, 2019.

Cervantes, Miguel de. *The Trials of Persiles and Sigismunda*. Edited by Celia Elaine Richmond Weller and Clark A. Colahan. Indianapolis: Hakett, 1989.

Chamberlin, Vernon A., and Jack Weiner. "Color Symbolism: A Key to a Possible New Interpretation of Cervantes' 'Caballero del Verde Gabán.'" *Romance Notes* 10, no. 2 (1969): 342–7.

Covarrubias Orozco, Sebastián de. *Tesoro de la lengua castellana o española*. Edited by Martín de Riquer. Barcelona: Alta Fulla, 2003.

Cruz, Anne J. "Fathers and Sons in *Don Quixote*." In *The Formation of the Child in Early Modern Spain*, edited by Grace E. Coolidge, 65–92. New York: Routledge, 2016.

Ellis, Anthony. *Old Age, Masculinity, and Early Modern Drama: Comic Elders on the Italian and Shakespearean Stage*. Farnham: Ashgate, 2009.

Erasmus, Desiderius. *Praise of Folly*. Translated by Betty Radice. London: Penguin, 1993.

Fernández-Morera, Darío. "Chivalry, Symbolism, and Psychology in Cervantes' Knight of the Green Cloak." *Hispanic Review* 61, no. 4 (1993): 531–46. https://doi.org/10.2307/474264.

Gilman, Stephen. *The Novel According to Cervantes*. Berkeley: University of California Press, 1989.

Gingras, Gerald L. "Don Diego de Miranda, 'Bufón' or Spanish Gentleman? The Social Background of His Attire." *Cervantes* 5, no. 2 (1985): 129–40.

Granjel, Luis S. *Los ancianos en la España de los Austria*. Salamanca: Universidad Pontificia, 1996.

Gullette, Margaret Morganroth. *Aged by Culture*. Chicago: University of Chicago Press, 2005.

Henry, Melanie. *The Signifying Self: Cervantine Drama as Counter-Perspective Aesthetic*. London: Modern Humanities Research Association, 2013.

Huarte de San Juan, Juan. *Examen de ingenios para las ciencias*. Madrid: Cátedra, 1989.

Johnson, Carroll B. *Don Quixote: The Quest for Modern Fiction*. Prospect Heights, IL: Waveland Press, 2000.

Juárez-Almendros, Encarnación. *Disabled Bodies in Early Modern Spanish Literature: Prostitutes, Aging Women and Saints*. Liverpool: Liverpool University Press, 2017.

Laguna, Ana. "Eroticism in Unexpected Places: Equine Love in *Don Quixote*." In *Sexo y género en Cervantes / Sex and Gender in Cervantes: Essays in Honor of Adrienne Laskier Martín*, edited by Esther Fernández and Mercedes Alcalá Galán, 113–32. Kassel: Reichenberger, 2019.

Maestro, Jesús G. "Cervantes y el teatro del *Quijote*." *Hispania* 88, no. 1 (2005): 41–52. https://doi.org/10.2307/20063074.

Mancing, Howard. *The Cervantes Encyclopedia*, vol. 2, *L–Z*. Westport, CT: Greenwood Press, 2004.

Maravall, José Antonio. *Culture of the Baroque: Analysis of a Historical Structure*. Manchester: Manchester University Press, 1986.

Márquez Villanueva, Francisco. *Personajes y temas del* Quijote. Madrid: Taurus, 1975.

Martín, Adrienne Laskier. *Cervantes and the Burlesque Sonnet*. Berkeley: University of California Press, 1991.

Martín, Adrienne Laskier. *An Erotic Philology of Golden Age Spain*. Nashville: Vanderbilt University Press, 2008.

Martín, Adrienne Laskier. "Zoopoética quijotesca: Cervantes y los Estudios de Animales." *eHumanista/Cervantes*, no. 1 (2012): 448–64.

Martínez, Marie-Véronique. "Pérez de Herrera y el estatus del soldado viejo en la España de Felipe II." In *De la caduca edad cansada: Discursos y representaciones de la vejez en la España de los siglos XVI y XVII*, edited by Nathalie Dartai, Cécile Iglesias-Slicaru, and Cécile Hue, 215–23. Saint-Etienne: Publications de l'Université de Saint-Etienne, 2011.

Martínez-Góngora, Mar. *El hombre atemperado: Autocontrol, disciplina y masculinidad en textos españoles de la temprana modernidad*. New York: Peter Lang, 2005.

Mattern, Susan P. *Galen and the Rhetoric of Healing*. Baltimore: Johns Hopkins University Press, 2008.

Miñana, Rogelio. *Living Quixote: Performative Activism in Contemporary Brazil and the Americas*. Nashville: Vanderbilt University Press, 2020.

Minois, Georges. *History of Old Age: From Antiquity to the Renaissance*. Translated by Sarah Hanbury-Tenison. Chicago: University of Chicago Press, 1989.

Olid Guerrero, Eduardo. *Del teatro a la novela: El ritual del disfraz en las* Novelas ejemplares *de Cervantes*. Alcalá de Henares: Universidad de Alcalá, 2015.

Percas de Ponseti, Helena. *Cervantes the Writer and Painter of Don Quijote*. Columbia: University of Missouri Press, 1988.

Pérez Álvarez, Marino. "The Psychology of Don Quixote." *Psychology in Spain* 10, no. 1 (2006): 17–27.

Presberg, Charles D. "'Yo sé quién soy': 'Don Quixote,' Don Diego de Miranda and the Paradox of Self-Knowledge." *Cervantes* 14, no. 2 (1994): 41–69.

Puig, Idoya. "Respect or Ridicule? The Representation of Old Age in Cervantes's Works." In *As Time Goes By: Portraits of Age*, edited by Joy Charnley and Caroline Verdier, 193–208. Newcastle upon Tyne: Cambridge Scholars, 2013.

Raimondo, Francesco. *Ideal of the Courtly Gentleman in Spanish Literature: Its Ascent and Decline*. Bloomington, IN: Trafford, 2014.

Sánchez, Alberto. "El Caballero del Verde Gabán." *Anales Cervantinos*, no. 9 (1961): 169–201.

Sánchez Ortega, María Helena. "Sorcery and Eroticism in Love Magic." In *Cultural Encounters: The Impact of the Inquisition in Spain and the New World*, edited by Mary Elizabeth Perry and Anne J. Cruz, 58–92. Berkeley: University of California Press, 1991.

Schäfer, Daniel. *Old Age and Disease in Early Modern Medicine*. London: Pickering & Chatto, 2011.

Skenazi, Cynthia. *Aging Gracefully in the Renaissance: Stories of Later Life from Petrarch to Montaigne*. Leiden: Brill, 2013.

Syverson-Stork, Jill. *Theatrical Aspects of the Novel: A Study of* Don Quixote. Valencia: Albatros Hispanófila, 1986.

Urbina, Eduardo. "El caballero anciano en *Tristán de Leonís* y Don Quijote, caballero cincuentón." *Nueva Revista de Filología Hispánica* 29, no. 1 (1980): 164–72. https://doi.org/10.24201/nrfh.v29i1.2714.

Velasco, Sherry. "Obscene Onomastics and the Sheep-Army Episode of Don Quixote." In *Millennial Cervantes: New Currents in Cervantes Studies*, edited by Bruce R. Burningham, 51–77. Lincoln: University of Nebraska Press, 2020.

Vollendorf, Lisa. "Reading Gender in *Don Quixote*." In *Approaches to Teaching Cervantes's* Don Quixote, 2nd ed., edited by James A. Parr and Lisa Vollendorf, 71–7. New York: Modern Language Association of America, 2015.

Contributors

Bruce R. Burningham is professor of Hispanic studies and theatre at Illinois State University.

José R. Cartagena Calderón is associate professor of Romance languages and literatures at Pomona College.

Julia Domínguez is professor of Spanish at the University of Delaware.

Esther Fernández is associate professor of Spanish at Rice University.

Mercedes Alcalá Galán is professor of Spanish at the University of Wisconsin–Madison.

Eduardo Olid Guerrero is associate professor of Spanish at Muhlenberg College.

B.W. Ife is Cervantes Professor Emeritus at King's College London and research professor at the Guildhall School of Music & Drama.

Catherine Infante is associate professor of Spanish at Amherst College.

Paul Michael Johnson is associate professor of Hispanic studies at DePauw University.

Ana Laguna is professor of early modern Spanish literature at Rutgers University–Camden.

Adrienne L. Martín is professor emerita of Spanish at the University of California, Davis.

John Slater is associate professor of Spanish at Colorado State University.

Sherry Velasco is professor of Latin American and Iberian cultures and gender and sexuality studies at the University of Southern California.

Sonia Velázquez is assistant professor of comparative literature and religious studies at Indiana University Bloomington.

Index

Note: Page numbers in *italics* indicate a figure.

abduction: in *La española inglesa* (Cervantes), 202, 207–12; in *La gitanilla* (Cervantes), 202, 212–14
actors: cross-dressing and, 43–4, 48, 49–56, 58–9, 60–1; professionalization of, 292–3
adultery: in *El celoso extremeño* (Cervantes), 182, 183, 189, 191–2; in *La cueva de Salamanca* (Cervantes), 183–4; in *El curioso impertinente* (Cervantes), 191–2, 257–62; in *El viejo celoso* (Cervantes), 181–3, 188–91. *See also* Venus and Mars caught by Vulcan (story)
Aeneid (Virgil), 116n9
Aguilera, Juan de, 113, 114
ahistoricism, 43
Alberti, Leon Battista, 162–3, 278
Alcalá Galán, Mercedes, 313, 346, 350n72
Alcalá Yáñez, Jerónimo de, 246–7
Alemán, Mateo, 346
Alexander, or The False Prophet (Lucian of Samosata), 321
Alexander of Abonoteico, 321
Algiers: Cervantes as captive in, 100–1, 104–12, 202, 222, 226, 233–5, 339; Christian captives in, 99–100, 139–42; collective memory and, 99–100. See also *Los baños de Argel*

(Cervantes); captivity; *El trato de Argel* (Cervantes)
Alicax, 111
allegory: in *Numancia* (Cervantes), 22; in *El rufián dichoso* (Cervantes), 42, 45–8, 50–2; in *El trato de Argel* (Cervantes), 100, 106–7
amante liberal, El (Cervantes), 217–18n2
Amelang, David, 26–7
anagnorisis, 4, 211, 213–14
Anderson, Ellen M., 64n32
Angulo, Juan Bautista de, 144–5n40
animals, 28–30
antonomasia, 44
Aranda, Miguel de, 111–14
Arcadia (Lope de Vega), 291–2
Arcadia (Sannazaro), 279
Archivo General de Simancas (Valladolid), 307
Ariosto, Ludovico, 345
Aristophanes, 308
Aristotle: on *anagnorisis*, 211, 213; on eavesdropping, 308; on memory, 101, 105, 110, 114, 119n53; on music, 127, 128; on old age, 346
Ars amatoria (Ovid), 252–3
Ars memorativa (Aguilera), 113, 114
ars memorativa (*ars memoriae*), 102–15
ars oblivionalis, 110
Art of Memory, The (Yates), 102
arte di ricordare, L' (Della Porta), 103

arte di scordare, L' (Gesualdo), 110–11
Arte nuevo de hacer comedias (Lope de Vega), 192, 231
artificial memory. See *ars memorativa (ars memoriae)*
Asensio, Eugenio, 179
Ass and the Lyre, The (Phaedrus), 116n9
Astrana Marín, Luis, 110, 134
audience: *Los baños de Argel* (Cervantes) and, 127, 132–4, 142; in *Don Quixote* (Cervantes), 224–8, 230–3; early modern theatre and, 248–50; eavesdropping and, 308; *gracioso* and, 74; *La gran sultana* (Cervantes) and, 151–2; illusory backstage and, 188–9; Lope de Vega and, 47; music and, 135–7; *El rufián dichoso* (Cervantes) and, 47–8, 50–6, 60–1, 77–8, 85; simple stage and, 179–81; theatricality and, 223–35; *El trato de Argel* (Cervantes) and, 105–6, 108–9, 111–15. See also *coup de théâtre*; metatheatricality; revelation and disclosure
Augustine of Hippo, 136–7, 142, 257, 261–2
autos sacramentales (liturgical drama), 22
Avalle-Arce, Juan Bautista, 302n75
Avellaneda, Alonso Fernández de, 4, 316–17, 331–2
Azevedo, Ángela de, 73–6, 93n27

Bacchae, The (Euripides), 308
Badenes, José I., 347
Baena, Julio, 63n20
Baker, Christina, 145n42
Bakhtin, Mikhail, 251
Bandera, Cesáreo, 278
Banerjee, Pompa, 166–7n13
baños de Argel, Los (Cervantes): captivity in, 126–37, 221; Catalina (actress) and, 134–7; cross-dressing in, 133–4; *garzones* in, 126, 133–5, 137–8, 140–2; jongleuresque tradition and, 25; martyrdom in, 141–2; metatheatricality in, 138–9;

music in, 126–37, 140–2; stage directions (*acotaciones*) in, 25, 134; staging of, 235–6n4; truth in, 137–42
bare stage, 3, 179–80, 184
Bazzi, Giovanni Antonio (il Sodoma), 255
Bejan, Teresa M., 326n57
Belmonte Bermúdez, Luis de, 25
Bennett, Susan, 223
Bermudo, Juan, 131–2
Beusterien, John, 29
black bile, 343
Blackstone, William, 324n6
blood, 343
bodily gestures, 278–9, 280, 281–90, 294–6
Bolzoni, Lina, 106, 110, 116n9
Book of the Courtier, The (Castiglione), 336
Boscán, Juan, 336
Botticelli, Sandro, 253, 255
Braga Riera, Jorge, 6
Braun, Georg, 99
bridge paradox (*paradoja del puente*), 321–2
Brioso Santos, Héctor, 6, 180, 185
Brook, Peter, 3, 179–80, 184
bucolics, 277–8
burlador de Sevilla y convidado de piedra, El (Tirso de Molina), 320
Burningham, Bruce, 18, 30, 31, 225, 236n14
Buscón (Quevedo), 47
Byron, 6th Baron of (George Gordon Byron), 29

Calderón de la Barca, Pedro, 25, 26, 83, 194–5n36
Caliari, Paolo (Veronese), 253, 255
cambalaches (swaps), 50, 54, 56–9, 61
Cambiaso, Luca, 255
Camillo, Giulio, 104
Campe, Rüdiger, 90n4, 92n26, 95n37, 95n48
Canavaggio, Jean, 5–6, 45, 67n82, 111–12, 129

Cancionero Musical de Medinaceli
(c. 1569), 129
Cántico espiritual (Juan de la Cruz), 103
captivity: in *Los baños de Argel*
(Cervantes), 126–37, 221; in *El
celoso extremeño* (Cervantes),
153–5, 163; Cervantes and, 100–1,
104–12, 202, 222, 226, 233–5, 339;
Christians in Muslim North Africa
and, 99–100, 139–42; in *Don Quixote*
(Cervantes), 221–2, 224–8, 230–3; in
La española inglesa (Cervantes), 202;
in *La fuerza de la sangre* (Cervantes),
202; fundraising processions
and, 222–3; in *El gallardo español*
(Cervantes), 221; in *La gitanilla*
(Cervantes), 202, 212–14; in *La gran
sultana* (Cervantes), 150–1, 152–3,
158–63, 164–5, 221; harem and,
150–1, 152–3; in *La ilustre fregona*
(Cervantes), 202, 214–15; marriage
as, 163–5 (*see also* domestic spaces);
masks and, 6–7; as metaphor
for love, 157–61; music and,
126–37; narratives of, 222–3, 233–5;
theatricality and, 221–3; in *Los
trabajos de Persiles y Sigismunda*
(Cervantes), 221, 223, 227, 228–30;
in *El trato de Argel* (Cervantes),
100–1, 104–12, 221, 229; in *El viejo
celoso* (Cervantes), 153
Carlson, Marvin, 227
Caro, Ana, 25
Carracci, Agostino, 253
Carruthers, Mary, 121n79
Caruth, Cathy, 101, 109
casa de los celos, La (Cervantes), 26, 27,
28, 29–30, 105
Casalduero, Joaquín, 5–6, 63n12
Cascardi, Anthony, 61
Casey, Jim, 334
casos de honra, 82
Casos prodigiosos y cueva encantada
(Piña), 264–7
Cassius Dio, 257
Castiglione, Baldassare, 336
Castro, Américo, 194n18

Castro, Guillén de, 25
Catalina (actress), 134–7
catharsis, 101
Catherine of Aragon, 169n55
cautivos de Argel, Los (Lope de Vega),
138–9, 143n3
Celestina, La (Rojas), 116n9
celoso extremeño, El (Cervantes):
adultery in, 182, 183, 189, 191–2;
captivity in, 153–5, 163; domestic
space in, 153–5, 163; *senex amans*
tradition and, 346; sexuality in,
153–5; *tableau vivant* in, 243–4, 245,
250–3, 270–1
Certeau, Michel de, 223
Cervantes, Miguel de: captivity and,
100–1, 222, 226, 233–5, 339; Lope
de Vega and, 17–18, 22, 203–4, 331;
old age and physical disability of,
331–2; passion for drama of, 202–4;
providentialist mindset of, 217; as
soldier, 339; theatrical success of,
3–4, 17–18. See also *specific works*;
theatricality in Cervantes's works
*Cervantes, Shakespeare y la Edad de Oro
de la Escena* (Braga Riera, González
Martínez, and Sanz Jiménez), 6
Cervantès dramaturge (Canavaggio),
5–6
Cervantes: Música y poesía (Pastor
Comín), 129
Cervantes y el mundo del teatro (Brioso
Santos), 6
Chamberlin, Vernon A., 340
Childers, William, 47, 62n8, 65n47
Christian Epicureanism, 335
Christiani matrimonii institutio
(Erasmus of Rotterdam), 169n55
Christianity: gambling and, 73,
79–81; memory and, 106–8; Pascal's
Wager and, 72, 84, 85–9, 92n26
Cicero, 11–12n7, 102, 114, 257, 345.
See also *Rhetorica ad Herennium*
[Cicero]
Cintia de Aranjuez, La (Corral), 293–4
circus, 29
Civitates orbis terrarum (Braun), 99

Claudian, 257
Clément, Catherine, 137, 142
Cleve, Joos van, 255
Close, Anthony, 45
collective memory, 99–100
Collins, Christopher, 19
Collins, Marsha S., 300n47, 302n76
coloquio de los perros, El (Cervantes), 17, 144–5n40, 206, 294
comedia nueva: Cervantes and, 44–5, 185, 191, 309; historical characters in, 49; jongleuresque tradition and, 18; reception of, 179–80; truth and, 280
comedias de cautivos: Cervantes and, 221 (see also *specific works*); Lope de Vega and, 138–9, 143n3. *See also* captivity
comedias de enredo, 280–1
comedias de santos (hagiographic plays): characteristics and reception of, 77; Lope de Vega and, 93n30; magic in, 184–5; *El rufián dichoso* (Cervantes) and, 42, 43, 45–6, 48, 77; stage machinery and, 77, 90n5
comedias villanescas (rural plays), 185
Comedy of Errors, The (Shakespeare), 210
commedia dell'arte, 21, 30–1, 33
Compañía Nacional de Teatro Clásico, 235–6n4
concubinage, 154–5
condenado por desconfiado, El (Tirso de Molina), 83
Congestorium artificiose memorie (Romberch), 107
Connor (Swietlicki), Catherine, 223
Corral, Gabriel de, 293–4
Cotarelo y Valledor, Armando, 110, 115
coup de théâtre: crime dramas and, 201; in *La española inglesa* (Cervantes), 201–2, 208–12; in *La fuerza de la sangre* (Cervantes), 201–2, 204–5, 214–16; in *La gitanilla* (Cervantes), 201–2, 213–14; in *La ilustre fregona* (Cervantes), 201–2, 214–15; Shakespeare and, 210
Covarrubias, Sebastián de, 93–4n32, 93n27, 234, 340
Cranach, Lucas the Elder, 255, 263, *264*
crime dramas and crime fiction, 201, 202
cross-dressing: in *Los baños de Argel* (Cervantes), 133–4; in *El rufián dichoso* (Cervantes), 43–4, 48, 49–56, 58–9, 60–1
Cruz, Anne, 342
cueva de Salamanca, La (Cervantes): adultery in, 183–4; domestic space in, 181; innovations in, 177–8; jongleuresque tradition and, 30–3; magic show in, 183–4, 185
cultural amnesia, 100
cultural studies, 11
curioso impertinente, El (Cervantes): adultery in, 191–2, 257–62; eavesdropping in, 310; metatheatricality in, 243–4; suicide in, 243–4, 260–2; *tableau vivant* in, 243–4, 245, 250–2, 255–62, 268–70; theatricality in, 258–62, 268–70; truth in, 258–62

Dante, 107
Danza de Don Gayferos y rescate de Melisendra (performance), 225
Dávila Padilla, Agustín, 89n3
De anima et vita (*The Passions of the Soul*) (Vives), 128, 130–1, 142
de Armas, Frederick A., 103, 169n55, 270
de Armas Wilson, Diana, 43, 44, 49, 50, 52, 162
De institutione feminae christianae (*Education of a Christian Woman*) (Vives), 155–6, 157–8, 159
De memoria et reminiscentia (Aristotle), 101, 114, 119n53
De oblivion (Fontana), 110

De oratore (Cicero), 114
De senectute (Cicero), 345
"Dead Come to Life, or The Fisherman, The" (Lucian of Samosata), 322
Declamatio Lucretiae (Salutati), 262
Declaración de instrumentos musicales (Bermudo), 131–2
Del teatro a la novela (Olid Guerrero), 6
Della Porta, Giambattista, 103–4, 110
Demosthenes, 308
D'Eshougues, Georges Robert, 235–6n4
Desire and Pleasure in Seventeenth-Century Music (McClary), 136
Devoción de la cruz (Calderón de la Barca), 83
día de fiesta por la mañana y por la noche, El (Zabaleta), 243
Diana, La (Montemayor), 277
Diana enamorada (Gil Polo), 297n9
dicha (blessedness, good fortune), 45. *See also* gambling
Dicha y desdicha del juego, y devoción de la Virgen (Azevedo), 73–6, 93n27
Dickens, Charles, 218n7
Diodorus Siculus, 257
Dionysius of Halicarnassus, 257
Discorso intorno alle imagini sacre e profane (Paleotti), 120n74
disfraz (disguise), 206–7
Divina commedia (Dante), 107
Divus, Andreas, 324n11
Dixon, Victor, 93n29, 144n37
domestic spaces: in *El celoso extremeño* (Cervantes), 153–5, 163; in *La cueva de Salamanca* (Cervantes), 181; in *La gran sultana* (Cervantes), 150–1; harem as, 150–1, 152–3; theatricality and, 180–6; in *El viejo celoso* (Cervantes), 153, 181–3
Don Quixote (Cervantes): on audience, 231; Avellaneda's apocryphal sequel of, 4, 316–17, 331–2; bridge paradox (*paradoja del puente*) in, 321–2; captivity in, 221–2, 224–8, 230–3; dramatizations of, 17; eavesdropping in, 306, 308–23; enchanted head in, 318–22; "fingida Arcadia" in, 294; *imagines agentes* in, 111; jongleuresque tradition in, 29; madness in, 283; Maese Pedro's puppet show in, 29, 222, 224–7, 233, 235, 311–12; masculinity in, 332, 334–47; memory in, 118–19n42; metaliterary irony in, 290; metaphorical spaces in, 105; on the novel, 206; as novel in dialogue, 206; old age in, 331–2, 334–5, 337–46; poetry in, 6; prologue to second part of, 331–2; publication of second part of, 177; reception of, 17; revelation and disclosure in, 5; Rodríguez de Montalvo and, 62n8; *El rufián dichoso* (Cervantes) and, 50, 58, 59; scholarship on theatricality of, 6; sexuality in, 255, 340–2; Shakespeare and, 309; sources of, 117n26; suicide in, 94n34; *tableau vivant* in, 243–4, 245, 250–2, 255, 270–1; on theatre, 11–12n7; theatre in, 104, 203; theatricality in, 6, 224–9, 230–3, 277, 308–23, 332–4, 344–5; translation in, 209; truth in, 224–8, 230–3, 315, 317, 321–3
donado hablador, El (Alcalá Yáñez), 246–7
dreams, 110
Dürer, Albrecht, 255

eavesdropping: audience and, 308; in classical Greek theatre, 307–8; in *Don Quixote* (Cervantes), 306, 308–23; in early modern theatre, 308; in fiction, 306–7; in *La Galatea* (Cervantes), 278, 290, 293; in *El retablo de las maravillas* (Cervantes), 268–9; as spying technique, 306–7

Eavesdropping in the Novel from Austen to Proust (Gaylin), 306
eclogues, 277–8, 291–2
Education of a Christian Woman (De institutione feminae christianae) (Vives), 155–6, 157–8, 159
EFE Tres Teatro, 31–3
Egginton, William, 192
Egido, Aurora, 103
elección de los alcaldes de Daganzo, La (Cervantes), 177–8, 186
Emporius, 257
Empty Space, The (Brook), 3
Encina, Juan del, 277
Engel, William E., 102–3
entremeses: Cervantes and, 30–3, 177–93 (see also *specific works*); characteristics of, 177–8; jongleuresque tradition and, 30–3
epiphany, 4
Erasmus of Rotterdam, 169n55, 308, 321, 322, 335, 345–6
escena imaginaria, La (Maestro), 20–1
Escorial, El (Royal Site of San Lorenzo de El Escorial), 307
española inglesa, La (Cervantes): captivity in, 202, 207–12; composition of, 207; *coup de théâtre* in, 201–2, 208–12
esperpento, 193n9
Euripides, 308, 322
Examen de los ingenios para las ciencias (Huarte de San Juan), 343, 346

Fabius Pictor, 257
Ferguson, Margaret, 170n73
Fernández, Lucas, 277
Fernández-Morera, Darío, 336
Ferrer, Juan, 135–6
Festejo de Los empeños de una casa (Juana Inés de la Cruz), 22–3
fingida Arcadia, La (Tirso de Molina), 293–4
fingido verdadero, Lo (Lope de Vega), 93n30, 292
Fischer, Susan L., 169n55
Fludd, Robert, 104

Fontana, Giovanni, 110
Fontana, Lavinia, 253
Forcione, Alban K., 224, 228
fortuna, 79–81. See also *dicha* (blessedness, good fortune); Wheel of Fortune
Fortunata y Jacinta (Galdós), 65–6n53
Foucault, Michel, 252, 322, 326n52
Fourth Book of Pantagruel, The (Rabelais), 250–1
Fox, Dian, 63n20
Fox, Harry, 166–7n13
Friedman, Edward H., 22, 45
Fuchs, Barbara, 43, 44, 47, 49, 52, 229
Fuenteovejuna (Lope de Vega), 27
fuerza de la sangre, La (Cervantes): captivity in, 202; composition of, 207; *coup de théâtre* in, 201–2, 204–5, 214–16; revelation and disclosure in, 5
funhouses, 181–3
Furey, Constance, 169n48
Fużūlī (Muhammad bin Suleiman), 156

Galán, Diego, 222
Galatea, La (Cervantes): bodily gestures in, 278–9, 280, 281–90, 294–6; eavesdropping in, 278, 290, 293; memory in, 118–19n42; metaphorical spaces in, 105; pastoral literature and, 277–9, 291–2, 294; revelation and disclosure in, 281–2; suicide in, 286; theatricality in, 277–9, 280–93, 295–6; truth and sincerity in, 278–9, 280–93, 294–6
Galdós, Benito Pérez, 65–6n53
Galenic medicine, 342–5
gallardo español, El (Cervantes): captivity in, 221; jongleuresque tradition and, 28, 29–30; staging of, 235–6n4
Gallego Zarzosa, Alicia, 58
Gálvez de Montalvo, Luis, 291–2
gambling: in *Dicha y desdicha del juego, y devoción de la Virgen* (Azevedo), 73–6; in early modern

Spain, 72–3; Pascal's Wager and, 72, 84, 85–9, 92n26; in *El rufián dichoso* (Cervantes), 72, 76–85, 87, 89
Garber, Daniel, 88, 89
Garcés, María Antonia, 107, 108, 109–10, 145n55, 162, 224, 226, 237–8n43
García Aguilar, Ignacio, 6
García Reidy, Alejandro, 193n3
García Santo-Tomás, Enrique, 72, 90n4, 187
garzones, 126, 133–5, 137–42
Gaylin, Ann, 306
Gaylord, Mary Malcolm, 55, 62n7, 277–8, 279, 297n14
Gazophylacium artis memoriae (Schenkel), 110
gender, 44–5. *See also* cross-dressing
Genesius of Rome, 292
Gentileschi, Artemisia, 255
Gerli, Michael, 185
Gesualdo, Filippo, 110–11
ghâzî fighters, 168n41
Gil, Juan, 233–4
Gil Polo, Gaspar, 297n9
Gilman, Stephen, 344–5
Giordano, Luca, 255
gitanilla, La (Cervantes): captivity in, 202, 212–14; composition of, 207; *coup de théâtre* in, 201–2, 213–14
Globe Theatre, 104
Glykon, 321
Goethe, Johann Wolfgang von, 244
Goffman, Erving, 222
Gómez Canseco, Luis, 6
González, Aurelio, 47, 180
González, Lola, 144–5n40
González Martínez, Javier J., 6
Goodwin, Robert, 234
gracioso: *comedias de santos* (hagiographic plays) and, 77, 79; in *Festejo de Los empeños de una casa* (Juana Inés de la Cruz), 22–3; in *El rufián dichoso* (Cervantes), 74, 93n27
gran sultana, La (Cervantes): captivity in, 158–63, 164–5, 221; domestic

space in, 150–1; elephant in, 30; harem in, 150–1, 152–3, 158–63, 164–5; jongleuresque tradition and, 30; martyrdom in, 161–2; Petrarchism and, 156–8; staging of, 235–6n4; suicide in, 161–2; theatricality in, 151–4
Granados, Antonio, 144–5n40
Guzmán, Pedro de, 73

Hacking, Ian, 95n37
Hafezism, 156
hagiographic plays. See *comedias de santos* (hagiographic plays)
hagiography, 49
Haley, George, 226
Hamlet (Shakespeare), 308, 320
harem, 150–1, 152–3, 158–63, 164–5
Harvey, Elizabeth, 52
Hazañas y la Rúa, Joaquín, 66–7n81
Henry, Melanie, 45
Henry VIII, 159
Heredia, Alonso de, 144–5n40
Heredia Mantis, María, 6
Hernández-Pecoraro, Rosilie, 293, 300n43
Hernández Verdeseca, Catalina, 134–6
Herrera, Juan de, 307
Herrschaft, Jana, 263
Heydenreich, Gunnar, 263
Hiltner, Ken, 298–9n25
Hippocratic medicine, 342–3
Historia de la fundación y discurso de la provincial de Santiago de México (Dávila Padilla), 89n3
Historia eclesiástica (Marieta), 45–6, 56, 57, 65n47, 76–7, 89n3
Hogenberg, Frans, 99
Homer, 252–3
homosocial spaces, 50
honra, 267–8
Horace, 308
Huarte de San Juan, Juan, 343, 346
humoral theory, 342–5
Huston, Hollis, 18–22, 25, 27, 30–4

Hutchinson, Steven, 162, 166n4, 167n25, 269, 321
Huyssen, Andreas, 99–100

Ife, B.W., 299n35
ilustre fregona, La (Cervantes): captivity in, 202, 214–15; composition of, 207; *coup de théâtre* in, 201–2, 214–15
imagines agentes, 101, 102–3, 111
industria, 81
Información de Argel (Cervantes), 222, 233–5
inocencia castigada, La (Zayas), 194–5n36
Irigoyen-García, Javier, 142n3
Islamic medicine, 342–3

Jakobson, Roman, 94n34
Johnson, Carroll B., 217
Johnson, Paul Michael, 233
Jones, Joseph R., 321, 326n44
Jones, Nicholas R., 43
jongleuresque tradition: Cervantes and, 18, 21–34; *commedia dell'arte* and, 21, 30–1, 33; EFE Tres Teatro and, 31–3; Lope de Vega and, 18; simple stage and, 18–22, 25, 27, 30–4
Juan de la Cruz, 103
Juana Inés de la Cruz, 22–3, 25
juez de los divorcios, El (Cervantes), 163–5, 189, 346
Jufresa, Montserrat, 326n54

Kallendorf, Hilaire, 94n33
Kapıdağlı, Konstantin, 151, *152*
Kenworthy, Patricia, 186
Kimmel, Seth, 94n34
Kircher, Athanasius, 320–1
Kluge, Sofie, 169n56

Laguna, Ana, 349n51
Lathrop, Thomas A., 63n20
Leahy, Chad, 43
Lectura y representación (Sánchez), 6

León, Francisco de, 337
León, Luis de, 335
Lerma, Francisco Gómes de Sandoval y Rojas, duke of, 324–5n17
Lettres philosophiques (Voltaire), 85–6, 89
Levisi, Margarita, 236n6
Lewis, Justin Jaron, 166–7n13
Life of Gargantua and of Pantagruel, The (Rabelais), 250–1
linguistic transvestism, 43, 55, 58
Livy, 255, 257
local memory. See *ars memorativa* (*ars memoriae*)
London, Treaty of (1604), 324–5n17
Lope de Vega: audience and, 231; Avellaneda and, 331; *casos de honra* and, 82; Cervantes and, 17–18, 22, 203–4, 331; *comedia nueva* and, 18, 179–80; *comedias de cautivos* and, 138–9, 143n3; *comedias de santos* (hagiographic plays) and, 49, 93n30; *comedias villanescas* (rural plays) and, 185; metatheatricality and, 291–3; on old age, 346; pastoral literature and, 291–2; publication of plays and, 205; stage directions (*acotaciones*) and, 25, 26
López Estrada, Francisco, 298n23, 299n28
López García-Berdoy, María Teresa, 298n23, 299n28
López Pinciano, Alonso, 75–6, 91n11
Lotto, Lorenzo, 263
Loughnane, Rory, 102–3
Lucian of Samosata, 308, 321–2
Lucius Accius, 257
Lucretia, 243–4, 245, 250–2, 255–67
Lukens-Olson, Carolyn, 177

madness, 283
Maestro, Jesús, 20–1, 178
magic shows, 183–6
Mallet du Pan, Jacques, 165–6n1
Mancing, Howard, 342
Maravall, José Antonio, 248

Mariana, Juan de, 142
Marieta, Juan de, 45–6, 56, 57, 65n47, 76–7, 89n3
Márquez Villanueva, Francisco, 337–8
marriage: as captivity, 163–5; in early modern Europe, 154–7, 162–3, 191; in *El juez de los divorcios* (Cervantes), 163–5; as martyrdom, 163–4. *See also* adultery; domestic spaces
Martial, 257
Martín, Adrienne L., 29, 139, 341, 347n1
Martín Llanos, Pablo, 252–3
Martín Morán, José Manuel, 230
Martín Puente, Cristina, 257
Martínez, Miguel, 236n6
martyrdom: in *Los baños de Argel* (Cervantes), 141–2; in *La gran sultana* (Cervantes), 161–2; marriage as, 163–4; in *El trato de Argel* (Cervantes), 111–14
masculinity: in *Don Quixote* (Cervantes), 332, 334–47; early modern models of, 336–7; old age and, 332, 334–5, 337–47
Massys, Jan, 255
Master of the Parrot, 255
Mattern, Susan, 343
Mazeppa (Byron), 29
McClary, Susan, 136
McGovern, Jimmy, 201
McKendrick, Melveena, 42
médico de su honra, El (Calderón de la Barca), 194–5n36
Megías, José Manuel Lucía, 59
melancholy, 342–5
memory: Algiers and, 99–100; ancient and early modern theories of, 101–12, 114; Cervantes and, 103–12; in *Don Quixote* (Cervantes), 118–19n42; in *La Galatea* (Cervantes), 118–19n42; music and, 130–3, 142; in *El rufián viudo llamado Trampagos* (Cervantes), 118–19n42; theatricality of, 100–1, 115

Memory Arts in Renaissance England, The (Engel et al.), 102–3
Merolico, El (EFE Tres Teatro), 31–3
Metamorphoses (Ovid), 116n9, 252–3
metatheatricality: in *Los baños de Argel* (Cervantes), 138–9; in *El curioso impertinente* (Cervantes), 243–4; *gracioso* and, 74; Lope de Vega and, 292–3; in *El rufián dichoso* (Cervantes), 46, 52; in *El rufián viudo llamado Trampagos* (Cervantes), 187–8; theatricality in Cervantes's works and, 3–4
Mexico, 44, 47–8, 61
Meyer, Heinrich, 244
Miguel de Cervantes: De la vida al mito (1616–2016) (Madrid, 2016), 99
Miñana, Rogelio, 334
Minois, Georges, 345
Mitchell, W.J.T., 249
Molière, 308
Montemayor, Jorge de, 277
Morán Turina, Miguel, 245–6, 247–8
Moreto, Agustín, 25
Murad III, 151
music: ancient theories of, 127–8; audience and, 135–7; in *Los baños de Argel* (Cervantes), 126–37, 140–2; early modern theories of, 128, 130–2, 142; memory and, 130–3, 142; sexuality and, 139–42; soprano fetish and, 136–7
Musurgia universalis (Kircher), 320–1
Mutio, Michele Luigi, 30

National Classical Theatre Company (Compañía Nacional de Teatro Clásico; CNTC), 6
Navarro, Juan, 129
Navarro Bonilla, Diego, 325n20
Nieremberg, Juan Eusebio, 127
Nieva, Francisco, 235–6n4
nostalgia, 128, 130
Novelas ejemplares (Cervantes): captivity in, 202, 207–17; composition and publication of, 201–2, 207; *coup de*

Novelas ejemplares (Cervantes; *continued*) *théâtre* in, 201–2, 204–5, 208–17; pastoral literature and, 294; prologue to, 332; theatricality in, 206–7, 277. See also *specific novelas*

Numancia (Cervantes): allegory in, 22; *imagines agentes* in, 103; jongleuresque tradition and, 21–2, 23–4, 28; stage directions (*acotaciones*) in, 23–4

Núñez Rivera, Valentín, 45, 46

Ocho comedias y ocho entremeses nuevos, nunca representados (Cervantes): jongleuresque tradition and, 24–6; publication of, 177; reception of, 3–4, 202–4, 221; unrepresentability of, 3–4, 42–5, 59–61, 204–6. See also *specific works*

Ocho comedias y ocho entremeses nuevos, nunca representados (Cervantes)—prologue: on audience, 211; on bare theatre, 179–80; on commercial success, 3, 17, 42, 203–4, 221; on memory, 101, 117–18n26

Odyssey (Homer), 252–3

old age: Avellaneda and, 331–2; Cervantes and, 331–2; as cultural construct, 333–4; in *Don Quixote* (Cervantes), 331–2, 334–5, 337–46; early modern views of, 342–6; masculinity and, 332, 334–5, 337–47; memories and, 130; sexuality and, 188–9, 191–2, 346–7; veterans and, 338–9

Olid Guerrero, Eduardo, 6, 206–7

Orlando furioso (Ariosto), 345

Orozco Díaz, Emilio, 247–8, 271n16

Ottoman Sultan Selim III (Kapıdağlı), 151, *152*

Ovid, 116n9, 252–3, 255, 257

Padilla, José, 59

painting: in Golden Age culture, 246–8; suicide of Lucretia (story) and, 255, 262–8, *264*, *266*; Susanna and the elders (story) and, 256; Venus and Mars caught by Vulcan (story) and, 253, *254*. See also *tableaux vivants*

Palacios, Vicente, 27

Paleotti, Gabriele, 120n74

Panoucosticon, 320–1

paradoja del puente (bridge paradox), 321–2

Parker, Alexander A., 47, 93–4n32

Parr, Anthony, 218n18

parrhesia, 322–3

pasajero, El (Suárez de Figueroa), 90n5

Pascal, Blaise, 72, 84, 85–9, 92n26

Passions of the Soul, The (*De anima et vita*) (Vives), 128, 130–1, 142

Pastor Comín, Juan José, 129

pastor de Fílida, El (Gálvez de Montalvo), 291–2

pastoral literature: eclogues in, 291–2; *La Galatea* (Cervantes) and, 277–9, 291–2, 294; Lope de Vega and, 291–2; theatricality and, 277–8, 291–3; truth and sincerity in, 278–9, 293–4

Pedro de Urdemalas (Cervantes), 290, 292–3

Peirce, Leslie P., 166n11

Pensées (Pascal), 86–9

Pérez Álvarez, Mario, 344

Pérez de León, Vicente, 20

perfecta casada, La (León), 335

Peribáñez (Lope de Vega), 26

peripeteia, 211

Persiles (Cervantes). See *Los trabajos de Persiles y Sigismunda* (Cervantes)

Petersen, Elizabeth, 27

Peterson, Michael, 29

Petrarchism, 156–8

Phaedrus, 116n9

phantasms, 101, 109–10

Philip II of Spain, 103, 263–5, 307

Philip III of Spain, 324–5n17

Philosophia antigua poetica (López Pinciano), 91n11

phlegm, 343

Phoenician Women, The (Euripides), 322

Piero di Cosimo, 253
Piña, Juan de, 264–7
Piqueras Flores, Manuel, 294
Plato, 102, 127, 292, 308
Plutarch, 257
Poesie (Titian), 264–5
Poetics (Aristotle), 101, 211
Politics (Aristotle), 127
Pollmann, Judith, 119–20n62
Porres, Pedro Gaspar de, 134–5
Portús, Javier, 245–6, 264
Poska, Allyson, 154–5
post-traumatic stress disorder, 119–20n62
Praise of Folly (Erasmus of Rotterdam), 345–6
Presberg, Charles D., 335–6, 341, 349n39
presentation of self, 222
prevenido, engañado, El (Zayas), 171–2n92
Profeti, Maria Grazia, 47
Protestantism, 93–4n32
prudentia, 102
Pufendorf, Samuel von, 92n26
Puig, Idoya, 346

queerness: in *El rufián dichoso* (Cervantes), 43–5, 48, 49–56, 60–2. *See also* cross-dressing
Quevedo, Francisco de, 47, 187, 346
Quiñones de Benavente, Luis, 37n54, 346
Quintilian, 102

Rabelais, François, 250–1
Radical Theatricality (Burningham), 18, 30, 31, 225, 236n14
Raimondo, Francesco, 337
Rancière, Jacques, 223
rape: in early modern Europe, 267–8; in *La fuerza de la sangre* (Cervantes), 202, 214–16; in *La ilustre fregona* (Cervantes), 202, 214–15. *See also* suicide of Lucretia (story)
Raphael (Raffaello Sanzio), 255

Ratione Studii (Erasmus of Rotterdam), 308
redemption: Cervantes and, 202; in *La española inglesa* (Cervantes), 202; in *La fuerza de la sangre* (Cervantes), 202; in *La gitanilla* (Cervantes), 202; in *La ilustre fregona* (Cervantes), 202
Reed, Cory, 178
Rembrandt, 255
Reni, Guido, 255
repetition, 46–7, 62
retablo de las maravillas, El (Cervantes): eavesdropping in, 268–9; innovations in, 177–8; jongleuresque tradition and, 31–3; magic show in, 184–6, 312; theatricality in, 180, 184–6
revelation and disclosure: *anagnorisis* and, 4, 211, 213–14; in *Don Quixote* (Cervantes), 5; in early modern theatre, 4–5; in *La fuerza de la sangre* (Cervantes), 5; in *La Galatea* (Cervantes), 281–2; Shakespeare and, 210. See also *coup de théâtre*; eavesdropping; truth
Rey Hazas, Antonio, 104, 299n34
Rhetorica ad Herennium [Cicero], 102, 111, 112, 113
Rhodes, Elizabeth, 280–1
Ribera, Pedro de, 233–4
Riley, Edward, 111, 115
Rivers, Elias L., 297n17
Roach, Joseph, 223
Rodríguez Cuadros, Evangelina, 135
Rodríguez de la Flor, Fernando, 245
Rodríguez de Montalvo, Garci, 62n8
Rojas, Fernando de, 116n9
Rojas Zorrilla, Francisco de, 25
Rokem, Freddie, 307–8
Romano, Giulio, 255
Romberch, Johannes, 107
Rosa Rivero, Álvaro, 45, 64–5n39
Rosselli, Cosimo, 106–7, 110
Rouhi, Leyla, 159, 169n50
Roxelana, 161
Royal Site of San Lorenzo de El Escorial, 307

Rueda, Lope de, 30, 33
rufián dichoso, El (Cervantes):
allegory in, 42, 45–8, 50–2;
cambalaches (swaps) in, 50, 54,
56–9, 61; as *comedia de santos*
(hagiographic play), 42, 43, 45–6,
48, 77; composition of, 89n3; cross-
dressing in, 43–4, 48, 49–56, 58–9,
60–1; as dare or unworkable play,
42–5, 59–61; gambling in, 72,
76–85, 87, 89; *gracioso* in, 74, 93n27;
hagiographic sources of, 44, 45–6,
50–6, 57, 76–7, 89n3; jongleuresque
tradition and, 25; metatheatricality
in, 46, 52; Mexico in, 44, 47–8, 61;
queerness in, 43–5, 48, 49–56, 60–2;
same-sex relationships in, 44–5;
stage directions (*acotaciones*) in, 25,
42, 44, 46–7, 49, 50–3, 56, 59, 62;
theatricality in, 43, 52–4, 72, 77–85,
89; truth in, 50–6
rufián viudo llamado Trampagos,
El (Cervantes): innovations in,
177–8; memory in, 118–19n42;
metatheatricality in, 187–8;
revelation and disclosure in, 5;
street performances in, 186–8
Ruiz de Alarcón, Juan, 25
rural plays (*comedias villanescas*), 185
Rycaut, Paul, 150–1, 153

Sáez, Adrián J., 6
Salutati, Coluccio, 262
same-sex relationships, 44–5
San Isidro Labrador (Lope de Vega), 49
Sánchez, Alberto, 337–8
Sánchez, Francisco, 6
Sánchez de Vargas, Hernán, 144–5n40
Sannazaro, Jacopo, 279
Santa A., Sara, 300n50, 300–1n56
Santos, Enrique, 61
Sanz Jiménez, Miguel, 6
Saraceni, Carlo, 253
Schäfer, Daniel, 334
Schenkel, Lambert, 110
Schjeldahl, Peter, 47

Scorel, Jan van, 255
Sellaer, Vincent, 255
Sellier, Philippe, 95n35
semantic discrimination, 245–6
Seneca, 257
senex amans tradition, 346–7
Sentido y forma del teatro de Cervantes
(Casalduero), 5–6
seven (number), 107
Sevilla Arroyo, Florencio, 26
Seville, 153, 155
sexuality: in *El celoso extremeño*
(Cervantes), 153–5; in *Don Quixote*
(Cervantes), 255, 340–2; *garzones*
and, 126, 133–5, 137–42; harem
and, 150–1, 152–3, 161–2; music
and, 139–42; old age and, 188–9,
191–2, 346–7; suicide of Lucretia
(story) and, 262–8, *264, 266*; in *El*
viejo celoso (Cervantes), 188–91,
254–5. *See also* adultery; marriage;
Susanna and the elders (story)
Shakespeare, William: Cervantes
and, 309; eavesdropping and, 308;
Globe Theatre and, 104; prose
fiction by, 207; publication of plays
and, 205; revelation and, 210; stage
machinery and, 320
Sheldon, R.M., 311
Shelton, Thomas, 309
Simonedes of Ceos, 102
simple stage, 18–22, 25, 27, 30–4
sincerity: in *La Galatea* (Cervantes),
278–80, 285–93, 294–6; pastoral
literature and, 278–9, 293–4; in *Los*
trabajos de Persiles y Sigismunda
(Cervantes), 294–5
Skenazi, Cynthia, 348n20
slavery: in early modern Spain, 155.
See also captivity; *garzones*
Smart, Mary Ann, 137
Socrates, 292
soprano fetish, 136–7
Sosa, Antonio de, 100, 109, 111–12,
139–42, 233–4
Spadaccini, Nicholas, 47, 184–5, 186

spectacle: in *La fuerza de la sangre* (Cervantes), 5; funhouses and, 181–3; magic shows and, 183–6; stage conversions and, 82; street performances and, 186–8. *See also* revelation and disclosure

Speculum Historiale (Vincent of Beauvais), 326n44

Sperling, Jutta Gisela, 171n87

Stackhouse, Kenneth A., 235n1

stage directions (*acotaciones*): in *Los baños de Argel* (Cervantes), 25, 134; in early modern theatre, 25–6; Lope de Vega and, 25, 26; in *Numancia* (Cervantes), 23–4; paintings and, 247–8; in *El rufián dichoso* (Cervantes), 25, 42, 44, 46–7, 49, 50–3, 56, 59, 62; in *El viejo celoso* (Cervantes), 190

stage machinery: *comedias de santos* (hagiographic plays) and, 77, 90n5; in early modern theatre, 320–1; *entremeses* and, 177; spectacle and, 82

Stagg, Geoffrey, 116n6

Stallybrass, Peter, 166–7n13

Stollznov, Karen, 307

street performances, 186–8

Strozzi, Alessandra, 171n87

Suárez de Figueroa, Cristóbal, 90n5

suicide: in *El curioso impertinente* (Cervantes), 243–4, 260–2; in *Don Quixote* (Cervantes), 94n34; in *La Galatea* (Cervantes), 286; in *La gran sultana* (Cervantes), 161–2

Suicide of Lucretia, The (Cranach the Elder), 264

suicide of Lucretia (story), 243–4, 245, 250–2, 255–67

Suleiman I, 151, 161

Sullivan, Henry W., 93–4n32, 119n48

Susanna and the elders (story), 243–4, 245, 250–2, 255, 256, 270–1

Susanna and the Elders (Tintoretto), 256

Syverson-Stork, Jill, 18

tableaux vivants: audience and, 248–50; in *El celoso extremeño* (Cervantes), 243–4, 245, 250–3, 270–1; in *El curioso impertinente* (Cervantes), 243–4, 245, 250–2, 255–62, 268–70; in *Don Quixote* (Cervantes), 243–4, 245, 250–2, 255, 270–1; history of, 244–6

Talens, Jenaro, 47

tapestries, 243, 270

Tarquin and Lucretia (Titian), 263, 266

Tartuffe (Molière), 308

tauromaquia, 29

Taylor, Diana, 30–1

teatro de Cervantes, El (Zimic), 5–6

teatro de Miguel de Cervantes, El (García Aguilar, Gómez Canseco, and Sáez), 6

Tertullian, 257

Tesoro (Covarrubias), 93n27

Teulade, Anne, 77

Thacker, Jonathan: on Cervantes's plays, 17–18, 24–5; on *El rufián dichoso* (Cervantes), 42–3, 45, 47, 51, 52, 59, 64–5n39

theatricality: concept of, 77; audience and, 223–35; bare stage and, 3, 179–80, 184; captivity and, 221–3; memory and, 100–1, 115; mimetic understanding of, 94n34; Pascal's Wager and, 72, 85–9; pastoral literature and, 277–8, 292–3

theatricality in Cervantes's works: captivity and, 221–2, 223–35; in *El curioso impertinente* (Cervantes), 258–62, 268–70; domestic spaces and, 180–6; in *Don Quixote* (Cervantes), 6, 224–9, 230–3, 277, 306, 308–23; *Don Quixote* (Cervantes), 332–4, 344–5; *entremeses* and, 177–80, 192–3 (see also *specific works*); funhouses and, 181–3; in *La Galatea* (Cervantes), 277–9, 280–93, 295–6; in *La gran sultana* (Cervantes), 151–4; illusory backstage and, 188–92;

theatricality in Cervantes's works
(*continued*)
jongleuresque tradition and, 18,
21–34; magic shows and, 183–6;
masks and, 6–7; metatheatricality
and, 3–4; in *Novelas ejemplares*
(Cervantes), 206–7, 277; poetry
and, 6; in *El retablo de las maravillas*
(Cervantes), 184–6; revelation
and disclosure and, 4–5 (see
also *anagnorisis*); in *El rufián
dichoso* (Cervantes), 43, 52–4,
77–85; scholarship on, 5–6; street
performances and, 186–8; in *Los
trabajos de Persiles y Sigismunda*
(Cervantes), 277. *See also*
eavesdropping; *tableaux vivants*
theatrum mundi, 280
Thesaurus artificiosae memoriae
(Rosselli), 106–7, 110
Thesmophoriazusae (Aristophanes),
308
Thomas Aquinas, 57
Thompson, C.R., 326n45
Tigner, Amy, 20–1
Times (newspaper), 201
Tintoretto, Jacopo, 253, 255, *256*
Tirso de Molina, 83, 293–4, 320, 346
Titian, 253, *254*, 255, 263, 264–7, *266*
Topica (Aristotle), 105
topographia, 106
Topographia e historia general de Argel
(Sosa), 100, 109, 111–12, 139–42
topotesia, 106
Torres, Catalina Eugenia de,
144–5n40
Tott, Baron de, 165–6n1
trabajos de Persiles y Sigismunda, Los
(Cervantes): captivity in, 221,
223, 227, 228–30; prologue to, 333;
theatricality in, 277; truth and
sincerity in, 294–5
translation, 209
trato de Argel, El (Cervantes): allegory
in, 100, 106–7; *Los baños de Argel*
(Cervantes) and, 138; captivity in,

100–1, 104–12, 221, 229; Cervantes's
memories and, 100–1, 103–15;
jongleuresque tradition and,
21–2, 24–5; martyrdom in, 111–14;
reception of, 221; theatricality in,
109–10
trauma, 101, 105, 109, 128, 224
Trent, Council of, 93–4n32, 107–8, 155
Trilling, Lionel, 279
Tristán de Leonís (1501), 350n57
True Story, A (Lucian of Samosata),
321–2
truth: in *Los baños de Argel*
(Cervantes), 137–42; in *El curioso
impertinente* (Cervantes), 258–62;
in *Don Quixote* (Cervantes),
224–8, 230–3, 315, 317, 321–3;
early modern theatre and, 279–80,
292–3; *Lo fingido verdadero* (Lope
de Vega) and, 292–3; in *La Galatea*
(Cervantes), 278–9, 280–93, 294–6;
hagiography and, 49; in *Información
de Argel* (Cervantes), 234–5; in
pastoral literature, 278–9; pastoral
literature and, 278–9, 293–4; in *El
rufián dichoso* (Cervantes), 50–6; in
Los trabajos de Persiles y Sigismunda
(Cervantes), 227, 228–30, 294–5.
See also *anagnorisis*; *coup de théâtre*;
revelation and disclosure
Twilight Memories (Huyssen), 99–100

Valencia, Felipe, 279
Valerius Maximus, 257
Valle Inclán, Ramón del, 193n9
Valor, fortuna y lealtad
(Lope de Vega), 26
Valtierra Lacalle, Ana, 263–4
Varro, 257
Vasco, Eduardo, 6
Vázquez, Mateo, 108
Velasco, Sherry, 43, 44, 52, 64–5n39,
341–2
Velázquez, Sonia, 64n31
Vélez de Guevara, Luis, 25
Venus and Mars caught by Vulcan

(story), 243–4, 245, 250–4, *254*,
270–1
Venus and Mars (Titian), *254*
Veronese (Paolo Caliari), 253, 255
Viaje de Turquía (Anon.), 223
Viaje del Parnaso (Cervantes), 6
vida es sueño, La (Calderón de la
Barca), 26
Vida y escritura en el teatro de Cervantes
(Heredia Mantis and Gómez
Canseco), 6
Vieira, António, 66–7n81
viejo celoso, El (Cervantes): adultery
in, 181–3, 188–92; captivity in,
153; domestic space in, 153, 181–8;
EFE Tres Teatro and, 31–3; illusory
backstage in, 188–92; jongleuresque
tradition and, 30–1; *senex amans*
tradition and, 346; sexuality in,
254–5; stage directions (*acotaciones*)
in, 190
Villa, Fernando, 31–3
Vincent of Beauvais, 326n44
Virgil, 116n9
Vitkus, Daniel, 222
Vives, Juan Luis, 128, 130–1, 142,
155–6, 157–8, 159

Vives Coll, Antonio, 321
Vollendorf, Lisa, 334–5
Vološinov, V.N., 251
Voltaire, 85–6, 89
Vouet, Simon, 255

Watts, Henry Edward, 349n35
Weber, Samuel, 77
Weiner, Jack, 340
Weissberger, Barbara, 162
Wheel of Fortune, 79–80,
116–17n9
Wilkins, Caroline, 320–1, 324n9
Williams, Grant, 102–3
Williamsen, Vern, 59
Winter's Tale, The (Shakespeare), 210

Yates, Frances, 102
yellow bile, 343
Ynduráin, Francisco, 184, 298n23

Zabaleta, Juan de, 73, 243
Zamora Vicente, Alonso, 110
Zayas, María de, 25, 169–70n65,
171–2n92, 194–5n36
Zimic, Stanislav, 5–6, 45, 107, 192
Zugasti, Miguel, 45, 56, 57, 65n47

Toronto Iberic

1 Anthony J. Cascardi, *Cervantes, Literature, and the Discourse of Politics*
2 Jessica A. Boon, *The Mystical Science of the Soul: Medieval Cognition in Bernardino de Laredo's Recollection Method*
3 Susan Byrne, *Law and History in Cervantes'* Don Quixote
4 Mary E. Barnard and Frederick A. de Armas (eds.), *Objects of Culture in the Literature of Imperial Spain*
5 Nil Santiáñez, *Topographies of Fascism: Habitus, Space, and Writing in Twentieth-Century Spain*
6 Nelson Orringer, *Lorca in Tune with Falla: Literary and Musical Interludes*
7 Ana M. Gómez-Bravo, *Textual Agency: Writing Culture and Social Networks in Fifteenth-Century Spain*
8 Javier Irigoyen-García, *The Spanish Arcadia: Sheep Herding, Pastoral Discourse, and Ethnicity in Early Modern Spain*
9 Stephanie Sieburth, *Survival Songs: Conchita Piquer's* Coplas *and Franco's Regime of Terror*
10 Christine Arkinstall, *Spanish Female Writers and the Freethinking Press, 1879–1926*
11 Margaret E. Boyle, *Unruly Women: Performance, Penitence, and Punishment in Early Modern Spain*
12 Evelina Gužauskytė, *Christopher Columbus's Naming in the* diarios *of the Four Voyages (1492–1504): A Discourse of Negotiation*

13 Mary E. Barnard, *Garcilaso de la Vega and the Material Culture of Renaissance Europe*

14 William Viestenz, *By the Grace of God: Francoist Spain and the Sacred Roots of Political Imagination*

15 Michael Scham, *Lector Ludens: The Representation of Games and Play in Cervantes*

16 Stephen Rupp, *Heroic Forms: Cervantes and the Literature of War*

17 Enrique Fernandez, *Anxieties of Interiority and Dissection in Early Modern Spain*

18 Susan Byrne, *Ficino in Spain*

19 Patricia M. Keller, *Ghostly Landscapes: Film, Photography, and the Aesthetics of Haunting in Contemporary Spanish Culture*

20 Carolyn A. Nadeau, *Food Matters: Alonso Quijano's Diet and the Discourse of Food in Early Modern Spain*

21 Cristian Berco, *From Body to Community: Venereal Disease and Society in Baroque Spain*

22 Elizabeth R. Wright, *The Epic of Juan Latino: Dilemmas of Race and Religion in Renaissance Spain*

23 Ryan D. Giles, *Inscribed Power: Amulets and Magic in Early Spanish Literature*

24 Jorge Pérez, *Confessional Cinema: Religion, Film, and Modernity in Spain's Development Years, 1960–1975*

25 Joan Ramon Resina, *Josep Pla: Seeing the World in the Form of Articles*

26 Javier Irigoyen-García, *"Moors Dressed as Moors": Clothing, Social Distinction, and Ethnicity in Early Modern Iberia*

27 Jean Dangler, *Edging toward Iberia*

28 Ryan D. Giles and Steven Wagschal (eds.), *Beyond Sight: Engaging the Senses in Iberian Literatures and Cultures, 1200–1750*

29 Silvia Bermúdez, *Rocking the Boat: Migration and Race in Contemporary Spanish Music*

30 Hilaire Kallendorf, *Ambiguous Antidotes: Virtue as Vaccine for Vice in Early Modern Spain*

31 Leslie Harkema, *Spanish Modernism and the Poetics of Youth: From Miguel de Unamuno to La Joven Literatura*

32 Benjamin Fraser, *Cognitive Disability Aesthetics: Visual Culture, Disability Representations, and the (In)visibility of Cognitive Difference*

33 Robert Patrick Newcomb, *Iberianism and Crisis: Spain and Portugal at the Turn of the Twentieth Century*

34 Sara J. Brenneis, *Spaniards in Mauthausen: Representations of a Nazi Concentration Camp, 1940–2015*

35 Silvia Bermúdez and Roberta Johnson (eds.), *A New History of Iberian Feminisms*

36 Steven Wagschal, *Minding Animals in the Old and New Worlds: A Cognitive Historical Analysis*

37 Heather Bamford, *Cultures of the Fragment: Uses of the Iberian Manuscript, 1100–1600*

38 Enrique García Santo-Tomás (ed.), *Science on Stage in Early Modern Spain*

39 Marina Brownlee (ed.), *Cervantes'* Persiles *and the Travails of Romance*

40 Sarah Thomas, *Inhabiting the In-Between: Childhood and Cinema in Spain's Long Transition*

41 David A. Wacks, *Medieval Iberian Crusade Fiction and the Mediterranean World*

42 Rosilie Hernández, *Immaculate Conceptions: The Power of the Religious Imagination in Early Modern Spain*

43 Mary Coffey and Margot Versteeg (eds.), *Imagined Truths: Realism in Modern Spanish Literature and Culture*

44 Diana Aramburu, *Resisting Invisibility: Detecting the Female Body in Spanish Crime Fiction*

45 Samuel Amago and Matthew J. Marr (eds.), *Consequential Art: Comics Culture in Contemporary Spain*

46 Richard P. Kinkade, *Dawn of a Dynasty: The Life and Times of Infante Manuel of Castile*

47 Jill Robbins, *Poetry and Crisis: Cultural Politics and Citizenship in the Wake of the Madrid Bombings*

48 Ana María Laguna and John Beusterien (eds.), *Goodbye Eros: Recasting Forms and Norms of Love in the Age of Cervantes*

49 Sara J. Brenneis and Gina Herrmann (eds.), *Spain, World War II, and the Holocaust: History and Representation*

50 Francisco Fernández de Alba, *Sex, Drugs, and Fashion in 1970s Madrid*

51 Daniel Aguirre-Oteiza, *This Ghostly Poetry: Reading Spanish Republican Exiles between Literary History and Poetic Memory*

52 Lara Anderson, *Control and Resistance: Food Discourse in Franco Spain*

53 Faith Harden, *Arms and Letters: Military Life Writing in Early Modern Spain*

54 Erin Alice Cowling, Tania de Miguel Magro, Mina García Jordán, and Glenda Y. Nieto-Cuebas (eds.), *Social Justice in Spanish Golden Age Theatre*

55 Paul Michael Johnson, *Affective Geographies: Cervantes, Emotion, and the Literary Mediterranean*

56 Justin Crumbaugh and Nil Santiáñez (eds.), *Spanish Fascist Writing: An Anthology*

57 Margaret E. Boyle and Sarah E. Owens (eds.), *Health and Healing in the Early Modern Iberian World: A Gendered Perspective*

58 Leticia Álvarez-Recio (ed.), *Iberian Chivalric Romance: Translations and Cultural Transmission in Early Modern England*

59 Henry Berlin, *Alone Together: Poetics of the Passions in Late Medieval Iberia*

60 Adrian Shubert, *The Sword of Luchana: Baldomero Espartero and the Making of Modern Spain, 1793–1879*

61 Jorge Pérez, *Fashioning Spanish Cinema: Costume, Identity, and Stardom*

62 Enriqueta Zafra, *Lazarillo de Tormes: A Graphic Novel*

63 Erin Alice Cowling, *Chocolate: How a New World Commodity Conquered Spanish Literature*

64 Mary E. Barnard, *A Poetry of Things: The Material Lyric in Habsburg Spain*

65 Frederick A. de Armas and James Mandrell (eds.), *The Gastronomical Arts in Spain: Food and Etiquette*

66 Catherine Infante, *The Arts of Encounter: Christians, Muslims, and the Power of Images in Early Modern Spain*

67 Robert Richmond Ellis, *Bibliophiles, Murderous Bookmen, and Mad Librarians: The Story of Books in Modern Spain*

68 Beatriz de Alba-Koch (ed.), *The Ibero-American Baroque*

69 Deborah R. Forteza, *The English Reformation in the Spanish Imagination: Rewriting Nero, Jezebel, and the Dragon*

70 Olga Sendra Ferrer, *Barcelona, City of Margins*

71 Dale Shuger, *God Made Word: An Archaeology of Mystic Discourse in Early Modern Spain*

72 Xosé M. Núñez Seixas, *The Spanish Blue Division on the Eastern Front, 1941–45: War Experience, Occupation, Memory*

73 Julia Domínguez, *Quixotic Memories: Cervantes and Memory in Early Modern Spain*

74 Anna Casas Aguilar, *Bilingual Legacies: Father Figures in Self-Writing from Barcelona, 1975–2005*

75 Julia H. Chang, *Blood Novels: Gender, Caste, and Race in Spanish Realism*

76 Frederick A. de Armas, *Cervantes' Architectures: The Dangers Outside*

77 Michael Iarocci, *The Art of Witnessing: Francisco de Goya's* Disasters of War

78 Esther Fernández and Adrienne L. Martín (eds.), *Drawing the Curtain: Cervantes's Theatrical Revelations*